Designing Social Research

The Logic of Anticipation

Norman Blaikie

polity

First published in 2000 by Polity Press
in association with Blackwell Publishing Ltd.

Reprinted 2001, 2003

Editorial office:
Polity Press
65 Bridge Street
Cambridge CB2 1UR, UK

Marketing and production:
Blackwell Publishing Ltd
108 Cowley Road
Oxford OX4 1JF, UK

Published in the USA by
Blackwell Publishing Inc.
350 Main Street
Malden, MA 02148, USA

ISBN 0–7456–1766–2
ISBN 0–7456–1767–0 (pbk)

A catalogue record for this book is available from the British Library.

Library of Congress Cataloging-in-Publication Data

Blaikie, Norman W. H., 1933–
    Designing social research : the logic of anticipation / Norman Blaikie.
        p.   cm.
    Includes bibliographical references and index.
    ISBN 0–7456–1766–2 (alk. paper). – ISBN 0–7456–1767–0 (pbk. : alk. paper)
    1. Social sciences–Methodology.   I. Title.
H61.B47763   2000
300'.7'2–dc21   99–31730
                                                                                    CIP

Typeset in 10 on 12 pt Sabon
by Kolam Information Services Pvt Ltd, Pondicherry, India
Printed in Great Britain by MPG Books Ltd, Bodmin, Cornwall

This book is printed on acid-free paper.

For further information on Polity, please visit our website: http://www.polity.co.uk

Designing Social Research

To my children
Shayne, Virginia and Simon
and my children's children
Hannah, Luka, Benjamin and Saro

Contents

Detailed Chapter Contents

Figures

Tables

Acknowledgements

To the hundreds of postgraduate students who have taken some version of my Research Methods course over the past fifteen years, I offer my sincere thanks. Without them I would never have been faced with the challenge to write this book. Their struggles, uncertainties, excitement and feedback have helped me sharpen my own thinking and practices. My colleagues and friends, Erica Hallebone, Otome Hutheesing, Bill Foddy and Ray Pawson, and three anonymous reviewers, provided many valuable comments on various drafts. I am very much in their debt, in spite of the fact that they caused me weeks of extra work. Their suggestions, I am sure, have resulted in significant improvements. That I was unable (or unwilling) to accept all their ideas may be due to some stubbornness on my part, and certainly to the diversity in their comments. I am also indebted to my colleagues at RMIT for allowing me time to get started on the writing. If it were not for the regular care of Azid Omar's healing hands, to repair the damage caused by the rigours of long hours at the keyboard, I doubt that I would have survived the task. Gill Motley humanized our negotiations through her understanding, encouragement and patience as deadlines were not met, Lynn Dunlop and Ann Bone managed the pre-production and production processes with efficiency and skill, and Janet Moth sorted out my idiosyncratic style, habitual grammatical errors and typing mistakes. Finally, I am profoundly grateful to Catherine who has provided invaluable support and encouragement while also having to put up with the consequences of an author's isolated and distracted journey.

The author and publishers are grateful to the following for permission to use copyright material:

Allen & Unwin for table 6.1, from D. A. de Vaus, *Surveys in Social Research*, 4th edition, Sydney, 1995.

Allyn & Bacon for table 2.2, from W. L. Neuman, *Social Research Methods: Qualitative and Quantitative Approaches*, 3rd edition, © 1997 by Allyn & Bacon.

Sage Publications for figure 5.2, from M. Waters, *Modern Sociological Theory*, London, 1994.

Stanford University Press for figure 5.9, from J. H. Turner, 'Analytic Theorizing', in A. Giddens and J. H. Turner, eds, *Social Theory Today*, Stanford, 1987; © 1987 Polity Press, Cambridge, also by permission.

Wadsworth Publishing, a division of International Thomson Publishing, for figures 5.4, 5.5 and 5.8, from *Structure of Sociological Theory*, 5th edition, by J. Turner, © 1991.

Introduction

It is a nuisance, but God has chosen to give the easy problems to the physicists. (Lave and March 1975)

Purpose of the Book

Social research has three main phases: the planning, the execution and the reporting. In some kinds of research, these three phases are discrete and follow this sequence. In other research, the three phases may blend into each other. This book is about the first phase, the designing of social research, not about the details of how to do it. Of course, the planning has to anticipate how the research will be done, and detailed knowledge of research methods is necessary at the planning stage in order to make good decisions.

Planning is vital in any kind of social research. Failure to plan is to run the risk of losing control of the project and failing to complete it successfully. The fact that some kinds of research require some planning decisions to be made as the research proceeds is no excuse for avoiding careful planning at the outset. However, the planning process may require some preliminary or exploratory research to provide information needed to make research design decisions.

A discussion of the core elements of a research design, and the connections between them, may look very much like the steps involved in doing social research. However, it is important to recognize the difference between the planning process, the execution of the research and the reconstruction of this process at the reporting phase. Kaplan (1964) has referred to the difference between 'logic in use' and 'reconstructed logic', between how research is done and how it is made to appear to have been done. The latter frequently converts a somewhat messy process into an apparently ordered and controlled one. This is particularly true of field research or ethnography.

> In the research worker's mind little did happen the way it is put down on paper, in terms of substance and sequence. What was ultimately assembled and ascertained,

got caught in the familiar bouts of rationalizations that straighten out a zig-zag approach and turn the entire study into a well-organized logical design with a beginning and a rounded-off ending. (Hutheesing 1990: 10)

I wish to add the 'logic of anticipation' to Kaplan's two categories, i.e. the process of planning how the research will be conducted. Of course, it is always possible that the logic of anticipation cannot be followed in its entirety; changes may be required as unanticipated obstacles are encountered and the researcher's understanding of the phenomenon increases. I suspect that many researchers write up their projects to make them look as if they began with an anticipated logic when, perhaps, there was none, or it was poorly formulated.

From my observations of academics and postgraduate students over many years, a common approach to social research is to just muddle through. It is rare to encounter a fully developed research design that has been prepared before serious research begins. Novice researchers may be unaware of the dangers in not planning thoroughly, and, without appropriate guidance, may end up with very precarious, sometimes disastrous, outcomes. It is hard enough to do good social research without building in limitations due to poor planning. Hakim (1987: 1) has argued that while individual researchers may be able to muddle through, 'large-scale studies, contract research for central government and other organisations, studies involving multi-disciplinary teams, and research programmes that involve a range of studies concerned with a central topic or set of issues' require highly visible designs at the beginning. I can agree with the latter but not with the former. Individual researchers also need to plan their research carefully.

This book reviews the major elements of a research design and discusses the choices that need to be made with regard to each of these elements. While all or some of these elements may be discussed in general textbooks on social research methods, their treatment is usually rather superficial. The concern is to introduce undergraduate students to the techniques of collecting and analysing data. While knowledge of these techniques is necessary, choices from among them have to relate to more fundamental aspects of research, the research questions that are to be answered and the research strategies that will be used to answer them.

The Audiences

I have written the book primarily for postgraduate students in the social sciences who are setting out on an empirical research project for a thesis or dissertation. By 'an empirical research project' I mean research that attempts to produce answers to research questions by collecting and/or analysing empirical data related to some aspects of social life. The book is not intended for students who are undertaking purely theoretical theses, i.e. those that involve the review, critique or integration of existing theory, or projects that rely entirely on existing literature as a resource. However, parts of it may be useful to students who are undertaking historical studies, although this will depend on the particular style of historical research.

The target audience includes students in disciplines such as sociology, anthropology and political science, and interdisciplinary fields such as social work, social geography, communications, planning and development studies. While I hope that economics and psychology students will also find it useful, I am very aware that coming from my background in sociology, with its own peculiar range of approaches to social research, I may be meeting these latter two disciplines at a limited number of points. Nevertheless, my hope is that the book will help to broaden the view of research normally adopted in these disciplines.

The book is also intended for academics, particularly those who are new to the role of postgraduate research supervision. It is not intended as a guide to that role but as a framework for assisting students to prepare a research design and/or a research proposal. It will also be useful for academics who involve their undergraduate students in individual and group research projects.

What I have to offer is the result of my own peculiar experiences in teaching courses in research methodology to postgraduate students; in teaching research methods, statistics, and the philosophy of social science to undergraduate students; in supervising the research of many postgraduate students and groups of undergraduate students; and in undertaking my own research. These postgraduate students and I have had to struggle to formulate research designs and proposals with limited help from available textbooks.

The process of formulating a research design is probably the most difficult part of social research. Over the years, I have developed ways of helping students through this process. This book is an attempt to explicate these strategies and techniques.

There are no doubt many ways in which this task can be undertaken. Some versions will be related to the discipline-based views within which the research is occurring, while others will relate to a particular individual's preferences or views of research. It is not possible to write a book that will satisfy the preferences of all social researchers; the field is too diverse and many of the differences may be irreconcilable. While I have set out to challenge some of the positions that I regard to be unsatisfactory, I have also tried to be eclectic enough to satisfy a range of social research styles. However, my prejudices will no doubt show from time to time.

Writing the Book

Except for a brief period in the United Sates, my academic career has been pursued away from the main centres of social science activity. It began and, until recently, has been conducted on the furthermost fringes of the southern hemisphere, in the South Island of New Zealand and the southernmost tip of the Australian continent. There have been both advantages and disadvantages in occupying this marginal position. While work on the book began in this remote region of the world, the bulk of the writing has been done on a tropical island in South-East Asia. It was stimulated by problems encountered in teaching a compulsory postgraduate research methods/methodology course at the Royal Melbourne Institute of Technology. Students setting out on research for a master's or Ph.D. degree by social research, for either a major or minor thesis/dissertation, have been required to take this course. A few of these students came from social science disciplines such as sociology and political science. However, most came from disciplines and programmes such as psychology, social work, communications, history, planning, economics, accountancy and management, and even engineering, industrial design, information systems, computer science, and the fine arts. The only thing they shared in common was that their research topic required them to undertake some kind of social research. They were mostly older students who were returning to study on a part-time basis. Many had little idea, or had very confused views, about how social research is conducted, let alone how to design a research project. They also had little or no understanding of or exposure to social theory and issues in the philosophy of social science.

In the brief span of a semester, my task has been to prepare these students to undertake a social research project. This has involved:

- introducing them to the logic of social enquiry;
- providing them with some acquaintance with the role of social theory in research;
- providing them with a critical understanding of the range of major research methods; and
- helping them prepare a research design.

My *Approaches to Social Enquiry* (Blaikie 1993a) was written to satisfy the first two of these requirements, and there is no shortage of books that cover the third. This book is intended to cover the fourth requirement.

In the course of writing, I have had the opportunity to teach a similar course to master's by research students in the social sciences, and master's of public administration students, at the Universiti Sains Malaysia. I discovered that their needs and concerns are almost identical to those of the students in Melbourne. Again, their academic backgrounds have been diverse and many have been older students. Most have had no experience in doing social research and have had no idea of how to go about designing a research project. They have provided me with a number of opportunities to try out the following chapters in lecture format, and their responses and feedback have had a big impact on the book's content and structure. (Well over 500 students have passed through these courses in Melbourne and Penang in the last ten years.)

While the structure and content of the book have been influenced considerably by teaching these courses, it has also emerged from supervising postgraduate students over many years, from twice being a postgraduate research student myself and, subsequently, from my experience in conducting research. All this has produced some firm convictions, including:

- the need to design social research in detail;
- the fundamental importance of research questions to provide focus and direction;
- the need to be clear about the differences in the research strategies (logics of enquiry) available in the social sciences, and to know how and when to use them;

- being aware of different ontological and epistemological assumptions behind these research strategies and how these impinge on research practice and outcomes;
- being very clear on what is involved in sampling;
- avoiding the misuse of tests of significance;
- knowing how case studies can be used;
- understanding the relationship between quantitative and qualitative methods; and
- being aware of the legitimate ways in which research strategies and methods can be combined.

This is a somewhat idiosyncratic list, and my views on these points might also be regarded by some in the same way. I make no apology for this. I can only hope that the positions I have adopted will either ring bells with some readers, or stimulate others to re-evaluate their taken-for-granted positions.

Two underlying principles have been used in writing the book. The first is to introduce the reader to new ideas and activities in stages, with each successive encounter taking the idea further. The second principle is to revisit an idea or activity from different points of view, or from the points of view of different themes. The decision to adopt these principles was based on my experience in teaching this material. I also believe that it is good educational practice. Therefore, if you experience repetition as you work your way through the book, you will know that it is intentional. I shall have to leave you to judge whether or not the strategy has been helpful.

Structure of the Book

The book reviews and elaborates the main elements that need to be addressed in preparing a research design. It focuses on the critical decisions that need to be made about each element and the options that are available. The path covers both conventional and unconventional ground.

Chapter 1 sets out the requirements for both a research design and a research proposal. It distinguishes between these two documents in terms of their purposes and the audiences to whom they are directed. In brief, a research design is a working document used mainly by a researcher and close associates, while a research proposal is used to obtain academic approval for a research project or to apply for research funds. The remainder of the book goes through the details of what is involved in each element of a research design, the alternatives that are available and how choices can be made.

Chapter 2 begins with a review of conventional views on designing research in the social sciences, and the types of designs that are commonly discussed. An alternative view is then proposed in which the fundamental requirements and the eight core elements are elaborated. The implication of this view is that there is a wide variety of possible research designs rather than just a limited set. This variety is produced by the range of possible combinations of choices that can be made on each of the core elements. This is followed by a discussion of how to get started on a research design by formulating the topic and stating the research problem to be investigated. Some consideration is given to the possible influences on this process. The chapter concludes with a discussion of the differences between basic and applied research.

The major design elements are dealt with in chapters 3 to 7. Chapter 3 commences with a discussion of the nature, role and development of research questions. This is followed by an elaboration of research objectives, and the links between research questions and research objectives, hypotheses and the literature review. The rest of the book stands on the foundations laid in this chapter.

Chapter 4 outlines the four research strategies that are available to advance social scientific knowledge. Research strategies provide alternative procedures for answering research questions. Each one sets out a logic of enquiry and entails a particular combination of ontological and epistemological assumptions. They provide a view of social reality and a series of steps for establishing knowledge about some part of it. Researchers need to choose one or more research strategies to help them provide answers to their research questions. The choice of research strategy, or strategies, in conjunction with the research questions, will have a major influence on the decisions to be taken on the remaining design elements, and will largely determine the way the research proceeds.

Before the four research strategies are outlined and discussed, the first instalment of 'A Parable of Four Paradigms' is presented. This is a story about visits to Earth by a party of social scientists from outer space. Their attempt to conduct research in a completely unfamiliar environment is used to illustrate some of the choices that are available to social scientists on Earth, and to anticipate the more philosophical elaboration of the four research strategies that follows.

In chapter 5, four of the more complex and perplexing aspects of designing and undertaking research are explored: the role of concepts, theories, hypotheses and models. Different views of the role of concepts are discussed, followed by an examination of what constitutes 'theory' and a review of some classical and contemporary views on the relationship between theory and research. This leads to an examination of the major views on the use of models in social research. To conclude, the role of concepts, theories and models in the four research strategies is reviewed.

The next two chapters cover the more technical aspects of social research. Chapter 6 deals with the sources of and methods for selecting data: it examines the types and forms in which data are produced in the social sciences; it discusses the variety of contexts from which data can be obtained; it compares the techniques used to select data, particularly sampling methods; and it concludes with a critical review of the role of case studies.

Methods for collecting, reducing and analysing data are explored in chapter 7. This begins with a discussion of the important role that the timing of data collection has in determining the nature of a research design. Many discussions of research design focus almost exclusively on this element and its relationship to experimental procedures. In this book, timing is related particularly to data collection; decisions about it will follow from the form of particular research questions. The bulk of the chapter centres on the qualitative/quantitative distinction. It provides a critique of the use of these two concepts, arguing against their use in the context of paradigms or research approaches, and for restricting their use to contrasts in types of methods, researchers, research, and data. The chapter does not include a discussion of the actual techniques or methods used in social science research. Instead, attention is given to the links between research strategies and methods. The main argument is that while research strategies entail onto-logical assumptions, methods do not. In other words, at least some methods can be used in the service of different research strategies and, hence, different onto-logical assumptions. The second instalment of the Parable sets the scene for a critical review of the use of triangulation in social research and the legitimate and illegitimate combinations of research strategies and methods.

The final chapter presents four sample research designs on a set of related research topics. These designs are based on my own research programme, but modified to suit the present purposes. The intention of the designs is to illustrate how the individual choices about each of the core design elements can be brought together into a cohesive package. While these sample designs might be used as models, this is not their main purpose. Rather, they make it possible to review what has been covered in the book and illustrate some of the ways in which social research can be undertaken.

The Nature of Science in the Social Sciences

It is a common practice in introductory books on sociology and social research methods to include a brief discussion of 'the scientific method' (see e.g. Chadwick et al. 1984; Kidder and Judd 1986; Sedlack and Stanley 1992; Ellis 1994; Kumar 1996; Neuman 1997). This usually includes an outline of a set of criteria that must be satisfied if social research is to be regarded as scientific. Unfortunately, many of these discussions perpetuate outdated notions of both science and social research. What is required is a discussion of the different 'methods', or logics of enquiry, that are available in the natural and social sciences.

It is not possible here to engage in a discussion of the nature of science. There is now an extensive literature on this topic, as well as on whether and, if so, how social science can be a science. (See e.g. Chalmers 1982; O'Hear 1989; and Riggs 1992 on the natural sciences, and Giddens 1976; Hughes 1990; Blaikie 1993a; Williams and May 1996 and Smith 1998 on science in the social sciences.) However, the elaboration of the research strategies in chapter 4 will deal with some aspects of these issues.

This latter discussion is intended, among other things, to show that there are four possible views of science in the social sciences. Three of the 'methods' that have been used in the natural and physical sciences have been advocated, by different scientific communities, as also being appropriate for the social sciences. In addition, there is another method, with many versions, that has been presented as being exclusive to, and, according to some writers, the only one appropriate for, the social sciences.

For over 100 years, advocates of these four views of social science have engaged in heated debates about their relative merits. The debates continue to rage. For those readers unfamiliar with these views and debates, all that is necessary for the moment is to recognize that there is no such thing as *the* scientific method, that there is a variety of logics of enquiry available in the social sciences, and that, in order to conduct social research, it is necessary to choose from among them. These logics, and the considerations relevant to choosing between them, form an integral part of what follows.

Foundation Concepts

Four related concepts are used extensively in the book: ontology and epistemology, and methodology and methods. From a philosophical point of view, *ontology* is 'the science or study of being'. However, the concept is used here in a more specific sense to refer to the claims or assumptions that are made about the nature of social reality, claims about what exists, what it looks like, what units make it up and how these units interact with each other. In short, ontological assumptions are concerned with what we believe constitutes social reality. Again, the philosophical meaning of *epistemology* is 'the theory or science of the method or grounds of knowledge'. An epistemology consists of ideas about what can count as knowledge, what can be known, and what criteria such knowledge must satisfy in order to be called knowledge rather than beliefs. For the present purposes, epistemology will refer to the claims or assumptions made about possible ways of gaining knowledge of social reality, whatever it is understood to be. In short, claims about how what is assumed to exist can be known.

The concepts of *methodology* and *method* are frequently used interchangeably. This is unfortunate and undesirable. The practice is equivalent to the shift that has been made from 'technique' to 'technology'. What is now commonly referred to as technology is really only the techniques for doing things. For example, information technologies are techniques for storing, retrieving and manipulating information. Strictly speaking, information techn*ology* should be the study, analysis and critical evaluation of these techniques. There seems to be a need to add 'ology' to many words, perhaps to inflate the status of the related activities. I fear the battle over 'technology' has been lost with little resistance. However, I hope that the slide from *method* to *methodology* might still be reversed. In any case, in this book I shall refer to research *methods* as the techniques or procedures used to collect and analyse data. *Methodology*, on the other hand, refers to discussions of how research is done, or should be done, and to the critical analysis of methods of research. *Methodology* also deals with logics of enquiry, of how new knowledge is generated and justified. This includes a consideration of how theories are generated and tested – what kinds of logic should be used, what a theory looks like, what criteria a theory has to satisfy, how it relates to a particular research problem, and how it can be tested.

These definitions are consistent with those provided by C. Wright Mills many years ago.

Methods are the procedures used by men [*sic*] trying to understand or explain something. Methodology is a study of methods; it offers theories about what men are doing when they are at work at their studies. Since there are many methods, methodology tends necessarily to be rather general in character and, accordingly, does not usually – although of course it may – provide specific procedures for man at study. Epistemology is still more general than methodology, for its practitioners are occupied with the grounds and the limits, in brief, the character, of 'knowledge'. (Mills 1959: 57–8)

When writers use the concept of method in the context of 'the scientific method', they are usually referring to a logic of enquiry rather than to specific research techniques. To avoid this confusion, I use the concept of research strategy to refer to logic of enquiry, to the steps involved in answering research questions. These steps include the starting-point of enquiry, the end-point, and the stages needed to get from the beginning to the end.

Unfortunately, it is common practice to use the term *methodology* to refer to 'the entire research process from problem identification to data analysis' (Creswell 1994: xvii). Hence, in this view, to outline one's 'methodology' is to discuss the plan and execution of a research process, including all the choices and decisions that have been made. Instead, I will use the term *research design* for the planning aspect of a research project, *research strategy* for the logic of enquiry, and *methods* for the execution of the project. *Methodology*, on the other hand, includes a critical evaluation of alternative research strategies and methods.

A Manifesto for Social Research

The approach to social research taken in this book deviates in a number of ways from conventional wisdom and the views of social research expounded in many standard texts on the subject. Rather than leave the reader to discover these differences in the body of the text, I am setting them out here as assertions.

1 Social research is about answering research questions.
2 Three types of research questions can be asked: 'what', 'why' and 'how'.
3 All research questions can be reduced to these three types.
4 Social research will also address one or more of the following objectives: exploration, description, understanding, explanation, prediction, intervention (change), evaluation and impact assessment.
5 'Why' questions are concerned with understanding or explanation.
   'How' questions are concerned with intervention.
   All other objectives involve the use of 'what' questions.
6 Hypotheses are possible answers to 'why' and some 'how' questions. They are normally expressed as statements of relationships between two concepts. Hypotheses direct the researcher to collect particular data.
7 'What' questions do not require hypotheses. Nothing is gained from hazarding an answer to a question that simply requires research to produce a description.
8 Research questions are answered by the use of four research strategies: the *inductive*, *deductive*, *retroductive* and *abductive* (see Blaikie 1993a).

9 The major characteristics of the research strategies are as follows: the *inductive* strategy produces generalizations from data; the *deductive* strategy tests theories by testing hypotheses derived from them; the *retroductive* strategy proposes causal mechanisms or structures and tries to establish their existence; and the *abductive* strategy generates social scientific accounts from everyday accounts.

10 When a research project includes a variety of research questions, more than one research strategy may be required to answer them.

11 Because research strategies entail different ontological and epistemological assumptions, they may only be combined in sequence.

12 Hypotheses are used mainly in the *deductive* research strategy as part of the process of testing theory. While the testing of hypotheses commonly involves the use of quantitative methods, it need not do so. The *deductive* strategy can also use qualitative methods, in which case hypothesis testing is more in terms of a discursive argument from evidence.

13 The *abductive* research strategy may use hypotheses in the course of generating theory, but in a different way to the *deductive* strategy. These hypotheses are possible answers to questions that emerge as the research proceeds. They are used to direct subsequent stages of the research.

14 The hypothetical models of possible causal structures or mechanisms that are developed in the *retroductive* research strategy are not hypotheses. The researcher's task is to establish whether a postulated structure or mechanism exists and operates in the manner suggested.

15 Social science data normally start out in the qualitative form, in words rather than numbers. They may continue in this form throughout a research project or be transformed into numbers, at the outset, or during the course of the analysis. Ultimately, research reports have to be presented in words. When numbers are used, they need to be interpreted in words.

16 The use of tests of significance is only appropriate when data have been generated from a probability sample. These tests establish whether the characteristics or relationships in the sample could be expected in the population. Tests of significance are inappropriate when non-probability samples are used, and are irrelevant when data come from a population.

17 As methods of data collection and analysis can be used in the service of different ontological assumptions, there is no necessary connection between research strategies and methods.

18 Methods of data collection can be combined, in parallel or in sequence. However, it is only legitimate to combine methods in parallel when they are used with the same or similar ontological assumptions. That is, data generated in the service of different ontological assumptions cannot be combined, only compared. It *is* legitimate to combine methods in sequence, regardless of their ontological assumptions. In this case, it is necessary to be aware of the implications of switching between assumptions.

19 Case studies are neither research designs nor methods of data collection. They constitute a method of data selection and, as such, require particular procedures for generalizing from the results produced.

20 The results of all social research are limited in time and space. Hence, making generalizations beyond a particular time and place is a matter of judgement. While quantitative data from a probability sample can be statistically generalized to the population from which the sample was drawn, this type of research is in the same position as any other when it comes to moving beyond that population.

I trust that the arguments that follow in support of these assertions are sound and convincing.

1

Preparing Research Proposals and Research Designs

A research proposal is intended to convince the reader that the proposed work is significant, relevant, and interesting; that the design of the study is sound; and that the researcher is capable of successfully conducting the study. (Marshall and Rossman 1995)

Introduction

The ultimate purpose in exploring the issues and processes covered in the following chapters is to facilitate the preparation of a detailed research design. In order to understand these processes, I shall begin by setting out some guidelines for the structure and content of both a research proposal and a research design.

It is first necessary to distinguish between *research proposals* and *research designs*. While there is considerable overlap between their requirements, they are intended for different audiences. There is also likely to be a sequence to their development; the latter can provide a basis for the former.

The *research proposal* may be used for:

- making public presentations and receiving feedback;
- obtaining official approval from the appropriate university authorities for the project to proceed, including the endorsement of a human ethics committee; and
- applying for research grants.

The *research design* is a more technical document than the research proposal. The decisions that need to be made at the beginning of the research project, or soon after some exploratory work has been completed, are stated, justified, related and evaluated. The aim is to:

- make these decisions explicit;
- spell out why they have been made;
- ensure that they are consistent with each other; and
- allow for critical evaluation.

NB

In postgraduate research, a research design is a working document that may be the outcome of courses in research methodology and methods, and the dialogue between student and supervisor/adviser. It should be the constant point of reference and guide throughout the research. If it is necessary to make changes as the research proceeds, or if it is necessary to allow some elements of the research design to evolve in the course of the research, this will happen in the context of the initial set of research design decisions. Amendments will need to achieve the same consistency between the research design elements.

Before proceeding to outline the requirements for research proposals and research designs, I must point out that I am trying not to be prescriptive (although I certainly am with my own students!). Rather, I offer two frameworks that will no doubt need to be adapted to local requirements and practices. In some situations, maybe only one document is required; in other situations, the distinctions between them may be drawn differently. My purpose is to identify the many elements that should be considered, and about which decisions may need to be made, in planning social research.

Depending on its purpose, the *research proposal* can be prepared in a number of versions. It also differs from the research design in a number of respects: some information may be in a different form, and it may need some additional information. The research proposal may be less technical than the research design, in that it may not include all the details of the decisions and justifications related to each design element. When the research proposal is intended for public presentation, it may include more details on the background to the research problem, including how it arose and the current state of knowledge on it. Hence, it is likely to be a longer and a more discursive document than the research design. On the other hand, an application to a committee for approval of the project may be much briefer, and may emphasize the justification for the research and the more technical aspects of data sources, collection and analysis. An application for research funds may be similar to an approval version, but will usually require a detailed budget and justification for the various categories of expenditure.

Two important points need to be made at this stage. The first concerns the common view that social research consists of a set of linear stages. These stages commonly include the formulation of the problem, the statement of hypotheses, the development of measuring instruments (e.g. an attitude scale or a questionnaire), the selection of a sample, the collection of the data, the analysis of the data, and the preparation of the report (see e.g. Babbie 1992; Bailey 1994; Kumar 1996). I believe that such conceptions are not only much too simplistic, but are also inappropriate for certain kinds of research. In much the same way, the process of designing social research may also be represented as a linear sequence of decisions. While some of the diagrams used in this book could be interpreted in this way, I want to stress that, in practice, the preparation of a research design is likely to involve many iterations, and is a cyclical rather than a linear process. Because the elements of a design must be intimately related, the process of making decisions about any of them will have an impact on other decisions. For example, early decisions may need to be reviewed and changed in the light of problems encountered in making later decisions, and decisions may need to be changed when the design is reviewed for consistency. In short, a complex process is required to make the various decisions compatible.

The second point is concerned with the view that all research design decisions should be made before the research begins in earnest. I will argue that every effort should be made to do this. The discipline of having to confront the decisions will be beneficial in the long run. To avoid doing this could mean losing control of the research and, ultimately, failure to complete it satisfactorily. However, this ideal needs to be tempered with some practicalities. It is necessary to recognize that research designs differ in the extent to which it is possible to finalize all the design decisions before the major stages of a project commence. In some research projects, what is learnt in one stage of the research will help to determine what will be done in a later stage. Some research projects that use qualitative methods may have this character. In other research projects, some exploratory and developmental work may be required in order to be able to make important research design decisions. In fact, to fail to do this may jeopardize the project. This exploratory work will usually occur at the beginning, but may have to be undertaken later, particularly if unanticipated problems are encountered. Therefore, while it is important to strive for the ideal, the realities of a particular project must be taken into consideration.

It is in research projects that are concerned with theory generation rather than testing that flexibility in the research design is certainly necessary. In these cases, the design may need to evolve as the research proceeds. Nevertheless, this should not be used as an excuse for sloppy designing at the beginning, or for not dealing with design decisions rigorously, as they need to be made. I believe that in this developmental type of research, no harm is done by trying to think through the design decisions at the beginning, and then being prepared to amend them at the appropriate stage.

It is inevitable that research projects will differ in the time needed to prepare the research design; some research topics are just more complex than others, or may be venturing into relatively uncharted territory. Hence, the time and effort required to produce a research design is usually much greater when a researcher starts a project from scratch, rather than by joining a research team or by picking up a project to which someone else has already made a significant contribution. It seems to be a common feature of postgraduate research in the social sciences that students are expected to, or wish to, define and develop their own project. Consequently, the design stage of postgraduate social science research is more demanding and time-consuming than it appears to be in the natural and physical sciences. In the latter disciplines, students usually become part of a research team, or make a contribution to their supervisor's research programme.

Research Proposals

Given the two common functions of a research proposal, obtaining approval for the research to proceed, including obtaining clearance from a human ethics committee and applying for research funds, its preparation needs to be taken seriously.

The preparation of a proposal is not some arbitrary task imposed by authority; it is in a student's interest to be as clear as possible about what he or she is going to do. A proposal should be the result of careful thought, and several drafts should be prepared and discussed before the final product is submitted. (Preece 1994: 202)

The purpose of the proposal is to ensure that the research is well designed and meets the requirements of the discipline and/or the institution in which it will be undertaken. It should communicate clearly and concisely what is to be studied, why it is being studied, and how the research will be conducted. The details of the design of the research are likely to receive close scrutiny. It is also an opportunity for students to receive some feedback and advice from a wider audience than their supervisor(s)/adviser(s). While this feedback is not always sympathetic, and may produce confusing and conflicting recommendations, it is nevertheless very useful for a project to be subjected to such an examination before it proceeds.

The research funding proposal has a different purpose. It is designed to persuade a funding body that the project is worthy of financial support. Committees that are set up for such purposes will look closely at the aims and justification of the research, at whether the design is sensible and feasible, at the budget details and the justification for each item, and at whether the project can be completed with the available resources and in the time allocated.[1] In short, this is a rather different audience to the one involved in obtaining academic approval. Hence two versions of the research proposal may be required.

As the requirements for these and other versions of a research proposal vary considerably in terms of their purpose and local requirements, no attempt will be made here to provide models of each type. Rather, I shall set out a range of headings, a selection of which will be relevant to most types of research proposals.

I have chosen to discuss the requirements for the *research proposal* before those for the *research design*, as the former tends to be more comprehensive while the latter goes into greater detail on a more limited range of topics. Some sections are common to both, some are the same but are given a different emphasis, while others are specific to only one version.

All or most of the following sections are typical of *research proposals*.

Title

The title of a research project needs to be both concise and informative. It should capture the essence of what the project will be about and where and with whom it will be conducted. It is sometimes useful to divide the statement of the topic into two parts: the first part can refer to the issue under investigation; and the second part can locate the study. (See chapter 8 and the Appendix for examples of the wording of research topics.)

---

[1] What follows should not be read as advice on how to prepare applications for research grants. Numerous books have been written on this. Rather, the purpose is to improve the quality of research by improving the quality of design and planning.

Statement of the topic/problem

The topic or problem is the intellectual puzzle that the researcher wants to explore. The statement will normally consist of a few paragraphs that present a concise description of the nature of the problem to be investigated. This will usually require reference to some literature, such as reports of previous research in the field and related areas, both academic and non-academic, theoretical discussions, official statistics, and, perhaps, newspaper articles. It might be informed by the findings of exploratory research that has already been undertaken.

A research design may set out with more than one problem or a related set of puzzles. As the work on the design proceeds, the one to be investigated should become clear. To recapitulate, a research proposal is the product of a developmental process. It is likely to involve a number of iterations before all the choices are made and it becomes coherent. In many research projects, the problem is likely to be refined in the course of the research (see chapter 2, 'Getting Started').

Aims and significance

It is important to state what the research is designed to achieve; what it is intended to contribute to the state of knowledge in a discipline or disciplines, to some group, organization or community, or to the society as a whole. Most social research projects will contribute to one or more of the following:

- the development of a particular area of theory or methodology;
- the collection or accumulation of a new body of information or data;
- the development of research methods or techniques;
- knowledge about or understanding of an issue or problem; and/or
- policy and practice in a particular area.[2]

It is also useful to state such aims in a manner that will make it possible to assess whether, or to what extent, they have been achieved at the end of the research.

The statement of aims is normally accompanied by some justification for pursuing them, i.e. why the topic is worth studying. All social research requires the use of resources, even if it is just the researcher's own time. In the context of postgraduate research, students may need to pay fees, and the university will devote considerable resources to supporting such students. As research resources are scarce, their allocation needs to be husbanded. Funding bodies will certainly want to know what contributions a study is likely to make. This is not to suggest that all research must be able to make immediate contributions to areas of priority established by public and/or private interests. However, some good reasons for doing it should be articulated, even if it is just to satisfy the researcher's curiosity.

[2] This list comes from the British Economic and Social Research Council application form for research funds. Similar lists will be found in other such documents.

Background

Some versions of the research proposal will normally require a discussion of how the research problem has arisen, who views it as a problem, evidence for its existence, the context in which it occurs and who are the stakeholders. In more theoretical research, it may be necessary to specify where the gap in knowledge exists and why it needs to be bridged. In short, a concise review of some of the literature will connect the proposed project with the existing state of knowledge.

In my experience, there is a tendency among postgraduate students to devote most of their proposal to a review of the literature. This may include erudite discussions of the ideas of a favourite or fashionable theorist. However, the connection between such discussions and the research project are often not very clear. Therefore, this version of the literature review, unlike that in the thesis itself, should be very concise, although its length will no doubt depend on the type of research being planned and local requirements.

Research plan and methods

The main aim of this section is to communicate, both to experts in the field and to lay audiences, from where and how the data will be collected, and how it will be analysed. What is needed is an outline of the way in which the research will be conducted. The research design is invaluable for the preparation of this section of the proposal. It will have dealt in detail with all the research design decisions about the sources, types and forms of data needed to answer the research questions, the method of selecting the data (including sampling design), and the methods of collecting, reducing and analysing the data. If these research design decisions have been made carefully, then summarizing them for the research proposal should be straightforward. The components of this section of the research proposal will be dealt with in more detail in the discussion on the requirements of a research design.

The research questions that are to be investigated should also appear in this section. If appropriate, any related hypotheses should be stated and their sources indicated. In some types of research, it may be necessary to discuss how research instruments will be developed. For example, if an attitude scale is required, and if no existing scale is suitable, an explanation should be given as to how existing scales might be adapted and supplemented, or a new one constructed. In addition, there needs to be a discussion of how its relevance to this particular population or sample will be established, including pre-testing and/or post-testing for unidimensionality or multidimensionality. Similarly, proposed pilot studies should be outlined and their purposes clearly stated.

Budget

Regardless of whether the project is receiving support from a funding agency, a budget is normally required to indicate what funds are needed and how they will be spent. As even postgraduate research costs money, it may be useful to anticipate what the costs are expected to be and how they will be covered. In the case where an application for a research grant is to be made, a detailed budget is normally required. The following headings are standard:

- *personnel* (e.g. research assistance, interviewers, coders, data analysts, interview transcribers);
- *equipment* (major items such as computing, audio recording and transcribing equipment);
- *maintenance* (day-to-day running expenses such as stationery, telephone, photocopying, computer disks, audio cassettes, interlibrary loans and purchase of reports);
- *travel and subsistence* (to research sites, for interviewing, or to libraries); and
- *publication and presentation expenses* (preparation of the report, printing, graphics, etc.).

Justification of the budget

Applications for research grants normally require a justification for the need and the amount for each item in the budget. Some research funds require the budget items to be prioritized, thus forcing the researcher to be very clear about their relative importance for the successful completion of the project. Where equipment (e.g. computers, software and cassette recorders) and other resources (e.g. personnel for data entry) are already available, and can be used on the project, these should be noted. Bodies that fund academic research usually expect that some costs (e.g. office space and furniture, and some basic equipment) will be covered by the university or research centre in which the researcher is located.

Budget items need to match the details of the research design. For example, if 200 interviews are to be conducted in dispersed locations, then realistic costing of these is necessary, in terms of equipment and consumables, interviewers' time for the interviews and travel to the sites, as well as the cost of travelling. It is here that the flaws in the research design and planning can become evident.

Timetable

In order to ensure that a research project is manageable and doable, it is useful to plan the duration of each of the components and stages within the time-frame allocated to it. The major components commonly include the following: preparation of the research design; review of the literature; selection of data sources (including sampling); development of the research instruments; collection of the data; analysis of the data; and writing the thesis/report. However, the components will need to be modified, depending on the nature of the research. In the case of research grants, the literature review and research design stages are assumed to have been completed before the application is prepared. The same applies in those universities that require a detailed research proposal to be prepared before a candidate is accepted into the programme. Where the development of the research design follows acceptance for candidature, it is desirable to include all stages, even if retrospectively, as the clock will have been running since the time of acceptance.

These components can overlap in time (e.g. the research design and literature review, or data collection and analysis), and some may occur at more than one time (e.g. the literature review) or extend over much of the life of the project (e.g. writing drafts). While it is difficult to be precise about how long each component will take, a realistic estimate should be made. This will help to reveal whether the project as planned can be completed within the time limits, and whether the workload is manageable in each time period. It is useful to do this diagrammatically in terms of a time line for each component.

One component that is usually underestimated is the writing. A good thesis needs many drafts (at least three in my opinion). If insufficient time is allowed for redrafting at the end, a poor product is likely to be the result. Writing can easily take between a third and a half of the total time, and will certainly take at least a quarter.

Some research grant bodies require the specification of definite 'milestones' so that progress can be checked. In these cases, the anticipated completion date for the major research stages (e.g. data collection) would need to be stated. If a project runs over an extended period, for example, two or three years, progress reports may be required at regular intervals. The work actually completed by a particular date can then be compared with the anticipated date in the proposal. Discrepancies may need to be satisfactorily accounted for if funding is to continue. I believe the same practice is desirable in postgraduate research programmes.

Expected outcomes or benefits

It has become a common practice, particularly in publicly funded research, for the anticipated benefits to be stated.[3] Traditionally, academic research has been about the pursuit of knowledge, the real benefits of which are to be left to posterity to determine. However, in this age of economic rationalism, even academic research may be expected to make some reasonably direct and useful contribution to some field of high priority in the public or private sectors. In the case of applied and policy research, someone other than the researcher may determine the expected outcome. If research grant bodies have their agenda and priorities, an application would need to address these.

Ethical issues

Most social research involves intervention in some aspects of social life. There is always a risk that even asking someone quite innocent questions could be disturbing to that person. It has therefore become normal practice for the ethical implications of a social research project to be made explicit, together with the

---

[3] This may be included in the 'Aims and significance' section as it follows logically from its specifications.

procedures to be used to deal with them. For research conducted within universities and independent research organizations, it may be mandatory for every social research project to be considered and approved by a human ethics committee. Professional associations in the social sciences now usually have a code of ethics, and these can also be used to guide professional research and to judge unethical practices.

The major ethical issue in most social research is related to the treatment of human respondents or participants. Procedures need to be in place to provide them with adequate information about the nature of the project, what is expected of them, how the research procedures might affect them and how their anonymity will be assured, as well as assuring them that the information they provide will be treated in confidence, and that they have the right to withdraw from the process at any stage. Judgements have to be made about what is reasonable and appropriate, and informed consent should be obtained, preferably in writing if possible. For a great deal of social research, there are few, if any, ethical problems. However, this does not mean that consideration of ethical issues can be avoided. Most textbooks on social research methods now have chapters on research ethics (see e.g. de Vaus 1995 and Neuman 1997).

It is important to note that ethical issues are not the same as the practical problems that the researcher expects to encounter.[4] The latter are dealt with in the next section. However, finding appropriate ways of dealing with the ethical aspects of a project can create practical problems. For example, the need to inform potential interviewees about the nature of a project may increase the refusal rate and, hence, threaten the researcher's ability to produce useful results.

Problems and limitations

An important step in the preparation of a research proposal is to stand back and evaluate it. First, it is useful to state what problems are likely to be encountered and how they will be dealt with. These will include both practical and theoretical problems, such as getting the co-operation of respondents, or knowing what further case studies will be required after the first one. The problems listed here should only be those that cannot be resolved at the design stage. For example, getting permission to use a list of names and addresses, or getting access to the research site, are matters that cannot be left to chance after the research commences.

Secondly, it is a good idea for the researcher to make an explicit assessment of the particular strengths and weaknesses of the research design. All projects have their secure and predictable aspects as well as their less secure and uncertain parts. In addition, those parts of the design that require further development as the research proceeds can be identified. If this assessment is done conscientiously, the researcher should be in a position to anticipate possible problems before they arise, rather than inadvertently ending up down a blind alley or falling in a great hole.

---

[4] I mention this point out of exasperation at the number of occasions, in spite of clear instructions, in which this confusion occurs.

I have noticed that some students are reluctant to expose the weakness of their research design for fear that their work will be judged as being inadequate. The reverse is in fact the case. Lack of awareness of both the strengths and weaknesses of a research design can be interpreted as indicating a shallow understanding of research.

Communication of findings

It has been argued that one criterion that *scientific* research should satisfy is that it should be made public. It can be argued that researchers have a responsibility to communicate their findings to people who can benefit from them. How this is to be done should be considered as part of the research proposal. Research grant administrators may be keen to know how the researcher plans to do this, and they may be willing to cover or contribute to the costs. However, the onus is also on thesis writers to consider ways of making the results of their research known to a wider audience than just those who read theses in university libraries. Following the completion of a thesis, some universities have a requirement that students make a public presentation to the university community and, perhaps, selected outside guests. Of course, traditional methods include conference presentations, journal articles and books. Some research lends itself to reporting in the media, such as newspapers and magazines. There are now other possibilities in this electronic age.

Some kinds of research, such as applied, commissioned or sponsored research, may have more limited, in some cases even restricted, audiences. However, applied researchers might want to insist on retaining the right to publish at least some of the findings themselves before accepting such commissions.

Research Designs

Unlike a research proposal, a *research design* is usually not a public document and may be seen by only a few people close to the researcher. It is an integrated statement of and justification for the more technical decisions involved in planning a research project. Ideally, designing social research is the process of making all decisions related to the research project before they are carried out. This involves anticipating all aspects of the research, then planning for them to occur in an integrated manner. Designing a research project is the way in which control is achieved.

> To design is to plan; that is, design is the process of making decisions before the situation arises in which the decision has to be carried out. It is a process of deliberate anticipation directed toward bringing an expected situation under control.... If, before we conduct an inquiry, we anticipate each research problem and decide what to do before-hand, then we increase our chances for controlling the research procedure. (Ackoff 1953: 5)

This process is analogous to the activities of an architect in designing a building: it involves recording, relating and then evaluating the decisions that need to be made. Careful attention to detail, and a concern with the overall workability of the design, is required. Designing social research involves the same processes. In particular, it is necessary to make sure that individual design decisions are consistent and fit together. These decisions then need to be evaluated critically, and, to do this, the design decisions need to be made explicit. This book is about how to achieve this.

The components of a research design can be organized in many ways. The following framework is presented as an example of what the structure of a research design might look like. (Examples of four different research designs are presented in chapter 8.)

Title

The requirements are the same as for the research proposal.

While it is useful to have a clear statement of the topic at the beginning of the research design process, this is not always possible. Not only is the nature of the research likely to be clarified during the course of preparing the research design, but also the best title may not emerge until after the research is completed. Therefore, it is unwise to waste time at the beginning trying to get the wording of the topic perfect. As we shall see, it is better to concentrate on preparing the research questions and other elements of the design, and then come back to the wording of the title later.

Statement of the topic/problem

The requirements here are also the same as for the research proposal.

While it is important to try to get the ideas on the topic clear as soon as possible, as with the title, it is unlikely that a precise statement can be formulated at the beginning of the design process. It is more likely to evolve as the design develops and may only become clear towards the end of the process. In addition, it is often necessary to make changes to the topic as the research proceeds (see chapter 2, 'Getting Started').

Motives and goals

The research design is the place where a researcher's personal motives and goals for undertaking the research can be stated. Academic researchers, including postgraduate students, will have personal reasons both for doing research at all, and for choosing a particular topic. Making these motives and goals explicit is a useful exercise and is often quite revealing. Personal reasons might include satisfying curiosity, solving a personal problem, achieving a credential or pursuing career goals. In addition, a researcher may have other more public or altruistic reasons, such as making a contribution to knowledge in a discipline, solving some social problem, or contributing to some organization or sector of society.

Research questions and objectives

Research questions constitute the most important element of any research design. It is to the answering of them that the research activities are directed. Decisions about all other aspects of the research design are contingent on their contribution to answering the research questions. In many ways, *the formulation of research questions is the real starting-point in the preparation of a research design.*

Research questions are essential and need to be stated clearly and concisely. They can be reduced to three main types: 'what', 'why' and 'how' questions. It is important to distinguish between these types of questions as they are related to different research objectives. In general, 'what' questions seek descriptions, 'why' questions seek explanations or understanding and 'how' questions are concerned with interventions to bring about change.

It may be useful to separate major research questions from secondary or subsidiary questions. The latter are either related to the background and context of the research, or help to elaborate the major questions. Major research questions presuppose other questions; they can sometimes also be broken down into a series of questions.

It is not necessary to state aims in a research design. They were included in the guidelines for a research proposal as it is intended for public consumption; stating aims is a useful way of communicating what the research is about. Instead, in a research design, consideration might be given to listing research objectives. These are defined in a more technical way than research aims and specify what the research is intended to achieve: it may be to 'explore', 'describe', 'explain', 'understand', 'predict', 'change', 'evaluate' or 'assess the social impact of' some aspect(s) of the phenomenon under investigation. Such objectives help to define the scope of the study, and, together with the research questions, provide a clear direction.

I consider it to be acceptable to simply present the research questions and not to state research objectives. However, the reverse is not. In many ways, research questions state the ideas contained in the research objectives in a different way. While it is possible that research questions will emerge before the objectives, in my experience working with them together has many benefits. The interplay between the requirements of each helps to sharpen and clarify both.

It is important not to confuse research objectives with the activities that are required to undertake the research. I have frequently encountered statements which say that the research will: 'review the literature', 'obtain documents related to...', 'design a questionnaire', 'select a sample', or 'collect data related to...'. Such a list is unnecessary, as these details will be covered in other sections of the research design (see chapter 3).

Review the literature

A research design should include a brief literature review. Its major function is to link the proposed research with the current state of relevant knowledge. Many areas of literature may need to be examined, for example, to provide the background and justification for the research, and to select theory, research strategies and methods. However, this section of the research design will normally be confined to indicating clearly what is known with regard to each of the research questions, on the basis of previous research, or what could be anticipated in the light of existing social theory. In the case of research for a thesis, a longer version will need to be produced and will probably become a chapter. Work on this will usually continue throughout the duration of the research. However, only a summary is normally included here.

The research questions can provide the framework for both this brief review and the chapter in the thesis; they determine the boundaries of what is relevant. Literature that is unrelated to a research question need not be included. Using this device can save endless hours of directionless activity in libraries.

Of course, consulting previous research and relevant theory may have inspired the project in the first place, or it may need to be consulted to define the topic and develop the research questions. In addition, the language used to define and discuss the research problem, and the key concepts that are used, are likely to be drawn from some theoretical perspective, the work of a particular theorist or a research programme.

Another purpose of the literature review is to find possible answers to research questions, particularly 'why' questions. In other words, we may need to search for possible hypotheses. If hypotheses are considered to be necessary, ideally they should be derived from a theory, either an existing one that will be included in the literature review (and might later form the basis of a separate theory chapter), or one that the researcher has constructed for the research in hand. The latter will normally modify an existing theory, or integrate ideas from a number of them. There is always the remote possibility that the review of the literature will reveal that answers to all or some of the research questions are already available and that the research project is, therefore, unnecessary. Another topic will then have to be selected. For practical guides see Hart (1998) and Fink (1998), as well as books on writing theses/dissertations (see chapter 3, 'Research Questions and the Literature Review').

Research strategies

Research strategies provide a logic, or a set of procedures, for answering research questions, particularly 'what' and 'why' questions. However, there is not just one way to do this. As the social sciences have developed, a number of views have emerged on how this can be done.

In my view, the choice of research strategy, or a combination of them, constitutes the second most important research design decision. The reason for this is that I believe knowledge can only be advanced in the social sciences by using one or more of these research strategies (see Blaikie 1993a).

In brief, the four research strategies, the *inductive*, *deductive*, *retroductive* and *abductive*, provide distinctly different ways of answering research questions. They present alternative starting- and concluding-points, and different sets of steps between these points. The *inductive* research strategy starts with the collection of data and then proceeds to derive generalizations using so-called inductive logic. The aim is to determine the nature of the regularities, or networks of regularities, in social life. Once these are established, they can be used to explain the occurrence of specific events by locating them within the pattern of established regularities. This strategy is useful for answering 'what' questions but rather limited in its capacity to answer 'why' questions.

The *deductive* research strategy adopts a very different starting-point. It is particularly appropriate for the answering of 'why' questions. The strategy begins with some regularity that has been discovered and which begs an explanation. The researcher has to find or formulate a possible explanation, a theoretical argument for the existence of the behaviour or the social phenomenon under consideration. The task is then to test that theory by deducing one or more hypotheses from it, and then to collect appropriate data. Should the data match the theory, some support will be provided for its continuing use, particularly if further tests produce similar results. However, if the data do not match the theory, the theory must be either modified or rejected. Further testing of other candidate theories can then be undertaken. Therefore, according to this research strategy, knowledge of the social world is advanced by means of a trial and error process.

The *retroductive* research strategy also starts with an observed regularity but seeks a different type of explanation. In this strategy, *explanation* is achieved by locating the real underlying structure or mechanism that is responsible for producing the observed regularity. To discover a structure or mechanism that has been previously unknown, the researcher has to first construct a hypothetical model of it, and then proceed to establish its existence. This may need to be done by indirect methods, as the structure or mechanism may not be directly observable. The search is for evidence of the consequences of its existence; should it exist, certain events can be expected to occur. *Retroduction* uses creative imagination and analogy to work back from data to an explanation.

The *abductive* research strategy has a very different logic to the other three. It is sometimes described as involving induction, but this grossly underestimates the complexity of the task involved. The starting-point is the social world of the social actors being investigated: their construction of reality, their way of conceptualizing and giving meaning to their social world, their tacit knowledge. This can only be discovered from the accounts which social actors provide. Their reality, the way they have constructed and interpreted their activities together, is embedded in their language. Hence, the researcher has to enter their world in order to discover the motives and reasons that accompany social activities. The task is then to redescribe these motives and actions, and the situations in which they occur, in the technical language of social scientific discourse. Individual motives and actions have to be abstracted into typical motives for typical actions in typical situations. These social scientific typifications provide an *understanding* of the activities, and may then become the ingredients in more systematic explanatory accounts.

While the advocates of each strategy claim superiority for their own, each also has its critics. No strategy is without its faults or limitations. Because of their deficiencies, researchers need to adopt a pragmatic attitude towards them.

A research design should include a brief description of the research strategy or strategies that have been selected, and justification for the selection in terms of its/ their appropriateness for the task. It is desirable to make explicit the ontological and epistemological assumptions entailed in the choice of research strategy or strategies, as these have a bearing on how the use of the methods of data collection and analysis will be interpreted (see chapters 4 and 7).

Concepts, theories, hypotheses and models

Somewhere in a research design a discussion of concepts and theory is likely to be required. This may occur in a separate section (e.g. 'Conceptual Framework' or 'Theoretical Model'), or may be integrated in another section (e.g. 'Literature Review'). Just what will be required, and how it will be handled, will depend on a number of things, including, particularly, the research strategy or strategies that are to be used.

All social research uses technical concepts; they form the special language of every discipline. Technical concepts are required at the outset of the research design process to state the topic and research questions. However, after this, the way they enter into the research process differs, depending on the research strategy that is adopted. Some research will set out with some key concepts, perhaps even with a conceptual framework, and these concepts will become variables through the specification of procedures for measuring them. In other research, only sensitizing concepts will be used at the outset. Technical concepts will either emerge out of an intense examination of lay concepts, or will be created or borrowed to organize qualitative data.

The manner in which theory enters into research is a matter of great controversy and confusion, particularly for novice researchers. A common criticism of some research is that it is atheoretical, that it neither uses nor contributes to the development of social theory. On the other hand, some researchers may wish to argue that descriptive research does not need theory, that measuring variables and correlating them is a purely technical matter. However, I believe that it is impossible to avoid using theory in research. Even descriptive studies that may be concerned with just a few concepts cannot escape, as all concepts carry theoretical baggage with them.

Theory enters into social research in many ways. A social theory may be a source of a theoretical language or specific concepts, and of general theoretical ideas or specific hypotheses. The four research strategies entail different views of what constitutes theory and how it enters into the research process. Focusing on these four views will help to reduce some of the complexity. The four research strategies also differ in terms of whether they set out with a theory to be tested, or whether their aim is to produce a new theory, i.e. whether they are concerned with theory testing or theory generation. Research that is concerned with theory generation may require sensitizing concepts but no hypotheses. On the other hand, research that is concerned with theory testing will require the researcher to borrow or construct a theory before the research begins. In this case, it is desirable to at least do some work on this theory at the research design stage; it can then be stated, its origins and relevance explained and, if appropriate, hypotheses can be derived from it.

Hypotheses are tentative answers to research questions. They are frequently stated in the form of a particular kind of relationship between two concepts. Testing them involves seeing if the associated variables have the same relationship as that predicted in the hypothesis. However, not all research questions, or all research projects, require hypotheses. They are particularly relevant to 'why' questions, and perhaps to some 'how' questions, but they are not relevant to 'what' questions. In addition, hypotheses are only relevant when research is about theory testing, and they are not relevant when the concern is with theory development. The latter may use many tentative hypotheses in the trial and error process of developing theoretical ideas to account for the data at hand, but these cannot be formulated at the research design stage.

Unless a researcher is testing an existing hypothesis, the formulation of good hypotheses requires a great deal of theoretical work. The testing of personal hunches as hypotheses constitutes a much lower level of research activity and should, therefore, be avoided in good-quality research. Such hypotheses usually make very little contribution to the advancement of knowledge because they are not well connected to the current state of knowledge. But let me repeat, hypotheses are more appropriate to some research strategies than others.

As with theory, the role of models in social research is a complex issue on which there is a diversity of ideas and practices. 'Model' can refer to a conceptual framework, a hypothesized set of relationships between concepts, a hypothetical explanatory mechanism, or a method of organizing research results. It is not uncommon to use 'theory' and 'model' interchangeably, or even in combination, for example in the phrase 'theoretical model'. Add the notion of 'modelling', and we have another range of activities and products to confuse the new researcher.

Some research strategies, particularly the *deductive* and *retroductive*, may require models to be developed at the outset. These may be conceptual models, theoretical models, or hypothetical models of causal mechanisms. Other research strategies, particularly the *inductive*, can introduce models at the data analysis stage where they represent the patterns in the data in a simplified form. Familiarity with the research strategies will be required before this part of the research design can be dealt with.

This section of the research design is likely to be the most difficult to complete. A broad understanding of the role of concepts, theories, hypotheses and models is required, and, possibly, a detailed knowledge of a range of theories (see chapter 5).

Data sources, types and forms

It is necessary to give consideration to the context or setting from which data will be collected, and to recognize the differences between them in terms of the nature of the data that they can produce. Data can be collected from four main types of sources, as well as from or about individuals, small groups and larger groups of many kinds. First, people can be studied in the context in which the activities of interest to the researcher occur, where people are going about their everyday lives, in their natural social environment. For example, family interaction may be studied in a home, or religious rituals in a temple. The size of the social unit studied in this way can range from individuals and small groups, through organizations and communities, to multinational bodies. These are referred to as *natural* social settings.

Second, a great deal of research studies people in *semi-natural* settings, when they are not actually engaged in the activities of interest. For example, people may be interviewed individually, or participate in discussions in focus groups, *about* the activities in which they engage in their natural settings. Sometimes data are not particularly about a social setting at all, but may deal with the attitudes and values of individuals. The third context is *artificial* settings. The classical form is the experiment; focus groups, games and simulation research are similar.

Fourth, the wide range of data that do not come from people directly are usually referred to as *social artefacts*. They are the traces or products that individuals and groups leave behind them, directly or indirectly, as a result of activities in their natural settings. People in groups produce statistics and documents and keep records for a variety of purposes, and these may be of use to the researcher. They may come out of natural settings, or be about activities in these settings.

While a research project may draw on data from only one of these sources, the use of a combination of them is common. The choice of data source will normally be incidental to other research design decisions. It is included here to highlight the need to be aware of the consequences of this decision in terms of the number of steps that the researcher can be removed from where the relevant social activity occurs.

At a more concrete level, decisions about data sources are contingent on the researcher's ability to access them. It is vital at the design stage to obtain the approvals that are necessary from the relevant gatekeepers. This may involve getting written permission from some authority to enter a natural setting (e.g. school classrooms), to conduct interviews in a semi-natural setting (e.g. with members of a work organization) or to get access to some records (e.g. case files on welfare recipients). Of course, some forms of permission have to wait until the time of data collection (e.g. individual interviews with householders).

Before the decision is made about what methods to use to collect and analyse the data to be used to answer the research questions, it is useful to give consideration to the type of data needed and the form in which the data are required. This involves a number of related decisions, although these will not necessarily be made in the order in which they are discussed here.

Three main types of data can be used in social research: *primary*, *secondary* and *tertiary*. Primary data are collected by the researcher, secondary data have been collected by some other researcher and are used in their raw form, and tertiary data are secondary data that have also been analysed by someone else. Hence, researchers may generate their own data directly from the people being studied. Alternatively, it may be possible to use data produced by someone else, either in the form of official government statistics, privately compiled statistics, or data from a previous research project. Sometimes these data may be available in raw form, for example as a data matrix or as interview transcripts, or they may have already been analysed and only be available in tabular or summary form.

Depending on the nature of the research topic and the research questions, a researcher may have little or no choice about the type of data that can be used. However, the critical issue is the distance of the researcher from the source of data. Each type of data implies a different degree of control that a researcher has over the data to be used. The further the researcher is removed from the collection process, the more difficult it is to judge the quality of the data and to ensure that they are appropriate for the project. These matters need to be made explicit in the research design, and the problems associated with the particular decisions, and methods for dealing with them, discussed.

Consideration should also be given to the form or forms in which the data will be collected and analysed. The common distinction used for this is between *quantitative* and *qualitative* data, between data in numbers or in words. However, this is not a simple distinction. Data may remain in one of these forms throughout the research process, or they may be transformed from one to the other at later stages. Data may start out as words, be manipulated soon after into numbers, may be analysed numerically, be reported in numbers, but then be interpreted in words. Alternatively, data may start out as words, and then be recorded, analysed and reported as text. Research projects can use data in both forms and they can be combined in a variety of ways. In the case of quantitative data, the levels of measurement, nominal, ordinal, interval or ratio, should be specified for each of the variables to be used.

The reason why it is desirable to give consideration to this issue at the research design stage is to ensure that the methods for collecting and analysing data are selected appropriately, and that the technology, mainly computer hardware and software, is available (see chapter 6, 'Types of Data', 'Forms of Data' and 'Sources of Data').

Selection of data sources

A critical stage in any research is the process of selecting the people, events or items from which or about which the data will be collected. This involves the definition of the population of such people, events or items. Some research projects will collect data from the whole population; others will select only certain members or items for study.

Textbooks on social research methods usually discuss data selection in the form of a review of methods of sampling. While data selection is a much broader topic than sampling, one or more sampling methods are frequently used in social research. This is true whether the study uses quantitative or qualitative methods of data collection.

A series of research design decisions is involved in the selection of the data. The first is whether a whole population, however that is defined, will be studied or whether only a segment will be used. If a segment is to be used, the second decision is whether the selection process should allow results to be used to represent the population from which it was drawn, i.e. will the selection process use random (probability) or non-random (non-probability) methods? Probability sampling selects units or elements from a defined population such that each unit has a known and non-zero chance of being selected. In other words, every unit has a chance of being selected, and, if all units do not have the same chance of being selected, the differences in these chances are known. Non-probability sampling does not satisfy this criterion. A number of selection methods are available within each category, and these methods can also be used singly or in combination (see chapter 6, 'Populations and Samples').

Whether samples are intended to represent the population, and how this can be achieved, is a central design issue. However, a collection of people can be studied as the result of a selection process that is not concerned with representativeness. In other words, while random selection may be necessary for sample data to be used to generalize to a population, other criteria of selection can be used, particularly when the concern of the research is with theory generation.

Regardless of whether probability or non-probability sampling methods are to be used, the method should be elaborated in detail and the choice of method(s) justified. In addition, the source and size of the population or sample needs to be determined and justified. If some other method of selection is to be used, such as case studies, the procedures should be stated and also justified (see chapter 6, 'Selection of Data').

Data collection and timing

Collecting and analysing data are frequently regarded as the core activities in social research. Novice researchers have a tendency to want to launch into data collection as soon as a research topic has been selected, for example, to get on with constructing a questionnaire or start interviewing. If this book does nothing else, I hope it will temper this practice and show that decisions about data collection and analysis must await many other considerations.

A wide array of quantitative and qualitative methods is available in the social sciences, and there are countless books available on how to develop and use them. They discuss a variety of types of observational methods, ranging from highly structured to unstructured, and from a very detached position to a very involved position. Similarly, many types of interviewing are reviewed, ranging from highly structured to unstructured or in-depth methods, and including both individual and group interviews. A range of methods for the content analysis of secondary data is also likely to be included.

The research design needs to specify clearly the method or methods to be used to collect the data. It is extremely important in quantitative research to decide, before the research begins, how the data are to be collected and to do all that is necessary to prepare for this. This may seem obvious, but it is not always taken seriously. Just muddling through will not do. The same is true for many qualitative studies, although there will be exceptions where some of these decisions may have to be made as the research proceeds. However, as I have argued earlier, this should not be used as an excuse for avoiding careful planning.

If quantitative data are to be collected using an existing measuring instrument, its source should be stated and a copy should be attached. If a measuring instrument needs to be developed, such as an attitude scale or a questionnaire, the process by which this will occur, including any pre-testing and piloting of the instrument, needs to be outlined and justified. In the case of qualitative data, it is important to indicate what method or methods will be used to generate and record them and to state why these are considered to be the most appropriate.

The time(s) at which data are collected is a critical element in a research design. Data can be collected at one point in time or at a series of points over time. One of these points can be the present time, while others may have occurred in the past or be planned for some time in the future. Decisions about timing will determine whether the study is cross-sectional or longitudinal, retrospective or prospective or historical. Experimental research also involves the collection of data at different times. Hence, the role that the timing of data collection will play in the project needs to be stated.

Data reduction and analysis

The final core element of a research design is the specification and justification of the methods to be used to reduce and analyse the data. Methods of data reduction transform the raw data into a form in which they can be analysed. This may involve transforming qualitative data into quantitative data by some from of numerical coding, or re-coding existing numerical data into different categories. An example of the latter would be reducing the number of categories to be used, and/or reordering the categories. Coding may also be used to organize and simplify data that have been collected in the quantitative form, for example by the creation of indexes, scales, factors or clusters. Alternatively, when qualitative data are collected, the processes of reduction and analysis may be integrated with data collection into a continuous and evolving process of theory construction. This will involve establishing categories and doing various kinds of coding.

There is another important stage between data reduction and analysis. The data have to be organized in such a way that they can be transferred into an appropriate database for manipulation by computer. The relevant design decisions here are who will do this and how the cost will be covered. Significant time and expense can be involved in this process. With quantitative data, it is usually a case of keying in responses to a questionnaire or structured interview. With some kinds of qualitative data, it may be necessary to transcribe cassette recordings of in-depth interviews and then format these for entry into a database. It has been estimated that an experienced transcriber, with clear recordings, will take at least three hours to do one hour of recorded interview.

Finally, we come to the choice of methods for analysing the data. If all the other design decisions have been made carefully and consistently, the decisions about the method of analysis should be straightforward. A variety of methods may need to be used, depending on the type of research questions, objectives or hypotheses being explored.

The quantitative/qualitative distinction is most evident when techniques of data analysis are discussed. Quantitative methods can be used for producing descriptions, for establishing associations, and, possibly, causal relationships between variables. They can also be used for making inferences from the results produced from a probability sample to the population from which the sample was drawn. For each of these aspects of quantitative analysis, an array of statistical techniques is available. Just which one is appropriate will depend on the level of measurement that has been used to collect the data, and perhaps the size of the sample. Qualitative methods of analysis can also be used for description at various levels of abstraction (in words rather than numbers), and, more particularly, for theory generation. A number of techniques are now available for the latter analysis, although they are still evolving. When data are in the form of text, the methods generally deal with creating categories, indexing or coding documents, sorting data to locate patterns, describing the patterns, generating theories from the data, and validating these theories. For both qualitative and quantitative analysis, appropriate software packages, as well as suitable hardware, need to be identified and their availability confirmed.

I have observed a tendency in many research designs to discuss methods of data collection but to ignore both data reduction and data analysis techniques. At best, a computer program might be mentioned, but just how the data are to be prepared for entry into a database, and what manipulations will be undertaken to relate the data to the research questions, are often not mentioned.

Each method of data reduction and analysis selected should be identified, briefly described and its use justified. The important point is that the decision on methods of analysis needs to be made in conjunction with many other research design decisions, and before the research commences. It can be fatal to wait until after the data have been collected. Not only do the methods of analysis need to be appropriate for the research questions, and also hypotheses if they are being used, but they also need to match the methods of data collection. Hence, a critical issue in research design is to achieve consistency between the type and form of the data, the source of the data, its selection, and the methods of collection, reduction and analysis. The possible combination of choices here can be overwhelming and should be given very careful attention. Finally, the choice of all these methods must make it possible to answer the research questions (see chapter 7).

Problems and limitations

As for the research proposal.

Conclusion

Having proposed possible structures and content for both *research proposals* and *research designs*, the next task is to find out how to prepare them. For the remainder of the book, I shall concentrate exclusively on the preparation of a research design. This will be done by discussing the three main components: the

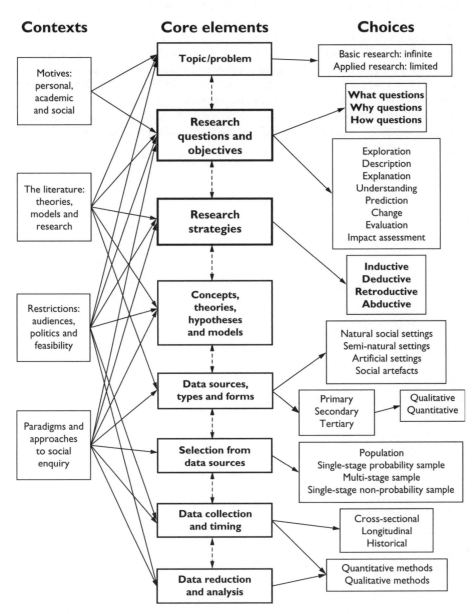

Figure 1.1 Elements of a social research design

core elements, which follow closely the headings just used to structure the research design; for each element, the range of alternatives from which *choices* are made; and the *context* in which these choices are made, i.e. the factors that can influence the choices.

To set the scene, figure 1.1 is presented as a representation of these three components. While many features of the core elements and the choices have already been introduced, the elaboration of the figure will now follow step by step.

It is important to note that the connections between the core components of a research design (the centre column in figure 1.1) are shown with double-headed arrows to indicate that the design process is not linear and is bound to involve movement in both directions. In fact, the figure could have included many more such arrows linking all the core components with each other. While this would have more faithfully represented the iterative nature of the processes of research design, it would have turned the figure into an unintelligible spaghetti of connecting lines.

2

Designing Social Research

A research design is an action plan for getting from here to there.
(Yin 1989)

Introduction

Social research is the use of controlled enquiry to find, describe, understand, explain, evaluate and change patterns or regularities in social life. This control is achieved through a series of decisions that are made before the research commences and other decisions that may need to be made in the course of the research. This is not to suggest that complete control of all aspects of the research process is always possible. All eventualities cannot be anticipated, and in some areas of research control may be very difficult to achieve. For example, some methods of data collection, such as participant observation, are very unpredictable in terms of how they will develop and where they will take the researcher. However, there are many aspects of research that can and should be planned in advance. The aim should be to achieve maximum control in all aspects, where possible.

The main purpose in designing research before it commences is to:

- make the research design decisions explicit;
- ensure that the decisions are consistent with each other and with the ontological assumptions adopted; and
- allow for critical evaluation of the individual design elements, and the overall research design, before significant research work commences.

Without such an overall plan, social enquiry cannot be controlled and the possibility of a successful outcome is severely jeopardized.

This chapter:

- sets the scene for what will follow in the later chapters;
- critically evaluates the common views and classifications of research design in the social sciences;

- presents an alternative view;
- discusses the fundamental requirements of a research design;
- provides an overview of the range of the core elements of a research design;
- outlines the choices available for each element; and
- discusses the first steps in preparing a research design.

The subsequent chapters deal with the major research design decisions in detail.

Common Views of Research Design

The concept of 'research design' has a range of meanings, from narrow to broad. At the narrow extreme is the experiment, the type of design against which most other designs are regarded as compromises; this design is supposed to be able to establish causation. Concern focuses on how to ensure that an experiment is capable of answering a particular 'why' research question, such that the effect of the independent variable, which is manipulated, can be assumed to be respons-ible for the observed changes in the dependent variable, the outcome. The design should rule out the possibility that some other features of the experimental situation can confound the independent variable. These design decisions are about the selection of experimental and control groups, the administration of the observations or measurements, and the type of statistical analysis to be used.

This view of research design is very common in psychology (see e.g. Labovitz and Hagedorn 1976; Keppel and Saufley 1980; Christensen 1988; Davis 1995).

> A *research design* designates the logical manner in which individuals or other units are compared and analysed; it is the basis for making interpretations from the data. The purpose of a design is to ensure a comparison that is not subject to alternative interpretations.... [However, i]t should be made clear that no design results in absolute certainty that only one interpretation is possible, although some designs have fewer alternative interpretations than others. (Labovitz and Hagedorn 1976: 55–6)

These authors go on to say that four criteria can be used to evaluate this type of research design: spatial control, temporal control, analysis of changes and repres-entativeness. Spatial and temporal control is achieved by the use of one or more control groups in at least one of which the individuals do not receive the experi-mental treatment. The experimental and control groups can be made roughly equal in composition either by matching individuals in terms of relevant charac-teristics, or by assigning individuals to the experimental and control group by a random procedure. Analysis of change is achieved by comparing the individual responses in the pre-test and post-test groups, rather than the overall or average change for the group. Representativeness refers to the need to allocate individuals randomly to the experimental group if it is intended that the results are to be generalized to a wider population (Labovitz and Hagedorn 1976: 56–60).

An example of a broader but very conventional view of research design can be found in Kerlinger and Pedhazur (1973).

Research design is the plan, structure, and strategy of investigation conceived so as to obtain answers to research questions and to control variance. The *plan* is the overall scheme or program of the research. It includes an outline of what the investigator will do from writing the hypotheses and their operational implications to the final analysis of the data. The *structure* of the research is more specific. It is the outline, the scheme, the paradigm of the operation of the variables. When we draw diagrams that outline the variables and their relation and juxtaposition, we build structural schemes for accomplishing operational research purposes. *Strategy*, as used here, is also more specific than plan. It includes the methods to be used to gather and analyse the data. In other words, strategy implies *how* the research objectives will be reached and *how* the problems encountered in the research will be tackled. (Kerlinger and Pedhazur 1973: 300)[1]

As Lincoln and Guba (1985) have pointed out, this view of research design requires the following to be spelt out before the research begins:

- the overall plan of the study;
- variables to be included;
- expected relationships between these variables (hypotheses);
- methods for data collection; and
- modes of data analysis.

They go on to suggest that this conventional view of research design is narrower than it needs to be. A more elaborate version is proposed.

- State the problem, including justification for researching it and the objectives to be achieved.
- Outline the theoretical perspective.
- Indicate the procedures to be employed: sampling; instrumentation (operational definitions of the variables); data-analytic procedures (statistical tests to be used to test the hypotheses or answer the research questions).
- Establish a time schedule and the establishment of 'milestones' to monitor progress.
- Designate agents who will undertake the various steps and tasks in the research.
- Provide a budget; give estimates of resources needed (time, people, funds).
- Indicate the expected end product(s): what the report will look like, including 'dummy tables'; and when the report will be available.

This set of research design requirements has served countless research projects very well as a disciplined starting-point. However, it has been argued that some styles of research cannot be planned as precisely as this at the outset. Much of the information that is needed to make these decisions will not be known until the research has been in progress for some time. In addition, some of these requirements may not be relevant to certain styles of social research (e.g. specifying variables and their measurement, and using statistical tests). In the context of

[1] 'Strategy' is given a somewhat different meaning in this book.

what they have called *naturalistic inquiry,* and what is more frequently referred to as qualitative research, Lincoln and Guba (1985: 224–5) have outlined why it may not be possible to meet these requirements.

- The focus of the study may change.
- Theory emerges in the course of the research rather than being stated at the beginning.
- Sampling serves different purposes; some samples need not be representative for the purposes of generalizing, but are concerned with the scope and range of information.
- Instrumentation is not about operational definitions but is a 'sensitive homing device that sorts out salient elements and targets in on them' (Lincoln and Guba 1985: 224).
- As the focus of the study changes, so do the procedures.
- Data analysis is open-ended and inductive rather than focused and deductive.[2]
- Statistical manipulations may have no relevance; the task is to 'make sense' of the data and to search for understanding.
- Timing cannot be predicted in advance because of the emergent nature of this kind of research.
- It is difficult to specify budgets precisely for the same reason.
- End products are difficult to specify, as the course of the research is unpredictable. All that can be said is that 'understanding will be increased'.

In short, 'the design of a naturalistic inquiry (whether research, evaluation, or policy analysis) *cannot* be given in advance; it must emerge, develop, unfold' (Lincoln and Guba 1985: 225).

Here, then, are three views of research design: the controlled experiment; the planned linear stages based on a very quantitative view of research; and the developmental process characteristic of much qualitative research. All three views are legitimate. However:

- few social scientists use experiments, mainly because they are either inappropriate or impossible to set up;
- many social scientists use the conventional linear approach to research design even when it is not appropriate; and
- some extreme types of naturalistic research may be as unpredictable as Lincoln and Guba have suggested.

The critical issue here is that the approach to research has to match the requirements of the research questions posed. Many design elements have to be considered in an attempt to answer these questions. As a wide variety of combinations of decisions on these elements are possible, there are many kinds of research designs.

While the flexibility of a developmental approach to research design may be attractive, most research, particularly that conducted by postgraduate students,

---

[2] This distinction between inductive and deductive forms of enquiry is elaborated in chapter 4. An alternative to 'inductive' is also proposed for the processes to which Lincoln and Guba refer.

has to meet deadlines and needs some assurance of a useful outcome. Therefore, it is necessary to plan as carefully as possible at the outset, and to review the plan from time to time, as changes are necessary.

My position has been expressed in a more general way by Yin (1989). *Research design* refers to the process that links research questions, empirical data, and research conclusions.

> Colloquially, a research design is an action plan for getting from here to there, where 'here' may be defined as the initial set of questions to be answered, and 'there' is some set of conclusions (answers) about these questions. Between 'here' and 'there' may be found a number of major steps, including the collection and analysis of relevant data. (Yin 1989: 28)

Classifications of Research Designs

Textbooks on social research methods have reduced research design to a few common types. Most books refer to *experiments*, *social surveys* and *field research* or ethnography. A somewhat accidental sample of major texts on social research methods or research design gives an indication of the range and frequency of the types of research designs identified. All these books usually classify research designs into a number of types and devote a chapter or significant section to each one (see table 2.1). However, other textbooks confine their attention to only one of these designs. For example: experiments (e.g. Campbell and Stanley 1963a, 1963b); social surveys (e.g. Aronson and Carlsmith 1968; Rosenberg 1968; Moser and Kalton 1971; Marsh 1982; Babbie 1990; Fowler 1993; de Vaus 1995); field research or ethnography (e.g. Burgess 1982a, 1984; Atkinson 1990; Hammersley and Atkinson 1995); action research (e.g. McNiff 1988; Winter 1989; Whyte 1991); evaluation research (Campbell and Stanley 1963a; Cronbach 1963, 1982; Weiss 1972, 1976; Cook and Campbell 1979; Weiss and Bucuvalas 1980; Rossi and Freeman 1985; Guba and Lincoln 1989; Pawson and Tilley 1997); impact assessment (e.g. Wathern 1988; Vanclay and Bronstein 1995; Becker 1997).

Some classifications make a division between experimental, quasi-experimental and non-experimental designs. The latter include social surveys, sometimes referred to as *correlational* designs because they, unlike experiments, cannot establish causation.[3] It has also become a common practice to group these different designs into two broad categories, quantitative and qualitative, with divisions within each category (see e.g. Creswell 1994; Neuman 1997). However, I shall question the usefulness of this latter classification in chapter 7.

In the context of applied social research, Hedrick et al. (1993) have discussed three types of design: *descriptive*, *experimental* and *quasi-experimental*. They regarded *descriptive* designs as essentially exploratory; one variable is described, variables are compared with some standard, or relationships between variables

---

[3] The question of whether causation can be established in such non-experimental designs has been a matter of considerable debate.

Table 2.1 Classification of research designs

Type of design	Sources
Experiment and survey	Denzin (1970); Krausz and Miller (1974); Labovitz and Hagedorn (1976); Open University (1979); Smith (1981); Chadwick et al. (1984); Kidder and Judd (1986); Hakim (1987); Yin (1989); McNeill (1990); Babbie (1992); Sedlak and Stanley (1992); Bell (1993); Bailey (1994); de Vaus (1995); Blaxter et al. (1996); Nachmias and Nachmias (1996); Neuman (1997); Sarantakos (1998)
Fieldwork/ethnography	Denzin (1970); Krausz and Miller (1974); Open University (1979); Smith (1981); Kidder and Judd (1986); McNeill (1990); Babbie (1992); Bell (1993); Neuman (1997); Sarantakos (1998)
Comparative/historical	Yin (1989); McNeill (1990); Neuman (1997)
Case study	Denzin (1970) (as part of Life History method); Labovitz and Hagedorn (1976); Hakim (1987); Yin (1989); Bell (1993); de Vaus (1995); Blaxter et al. (1996); Sarantakos (1998) (with Ethnography under Field Studies)
Content analysis	Chadwick et al. (1984); Sedlak and Stanley (1992); Bailey (1994); Neuman (1997); Sarantakos (1998)
Secondary analysis	Denzin (1970) (as part of Life History method); Krausz and Miller (1974); Chadwick et al. (1984); Hakim (1987); Yin (1989); McNeill (1990); Sedlak and Stanley (1992); Neuman (1997); Sarantakos (1998)
Observation	Smith (1981); Chadwick et al. (1984); McNeill (1990); Sedlak and Stanley (1992); Bailey (1994); Sarantakos (1998)
Simulation and gaming	Smith (1981); Bailey (1994)
Evaluation research	Smith (1981); Chadwick et al. (1984); Babbie (1992)
Social impact assessment	Chadwick et al. (1984)
Action research	Blaxter et al. (1996)

are summarized. *Experimental* designs test causal relationships by randomly assigning individuals or entities to experimental and control groups and then applying different procedures or treatments to these groups.[4] *Quasi-experimental* designs also test causal relationships by using some compromise on random assignment to the experimental and control groups. These designs try to approximate an experiment and are regarded as a fallback position when the ideal conditions cannot be met.

At best, the concept of research design used in these classifications is very limited and confusing. Of course social researchers can do surveys and conduct experiments, but surveys are about particular methods of data collection and analysis, and an experiment is about selecting groups and timing data collection. Similarly, secondary analysis is mainly about sources of data, observation is mainly about data collection, and content analysis is mainly about coding. In addition, ethnography, comparative research, case studies, evaluation research and action research are particular approaches to research that can combine a number of methods of data collection and analysis. Hence, the first problem with these classifications is that each type of research design deals with some elements but none of them deals with them all.

A rare attempt to recognize these difficulties can be found in Chadwick et al. (1984). They have classified research designs according to six criteria:

- method of data collection;
- primary objectives (e.g. description, hypothesis testing, evaluation, social impact assessment);
- time orientation (cross-sectional, longitudinal, retrospective);
- whether the data are to be collected to answer a specific research question (primary and secondary); and
- the degree to which the methods impinge on the respondents (obtrusive and unobtrusive).

The approach taken to research design in this book is essentially an elaboration of this classification.

The second problem is that the categories listed in table 2.1 are not mutually exclusive. For example, content analysis can be used on existing documents; surveys can be used in comparative studies, case studies and evaluation research; and experiments, comparative studies, case studies and evaluation research can use a number of methods of data collection and analysis. The third problem is that the categories are not exhaustive of the aspects of research that they do cover. For example, there are other ways of achieving control over variables, and there are many other sources of data and methods for producing and analysing data than those identified. These conventional categories tend to mask the many choices that need to be considered in preparing a research design.

---

[4] There is no shortage of textbooks on experimental designs, or chapters in standard textbooks on social research methods.

An Alternative View

A research design contains many elements (see figure 1.1) and each element involves a choice from among alternatives. Most elements require a choice from at least three alternatives and one has eight. While some combinations may be more common, and others may not be legitimate, there is potentially a wide variety of possibilities. Some research topics may require a very particular and unusual design. The resulting combinations of decisions produce a wide variety of actual designs that cannot easily be described by simple labels. For this reason, I will not follow the conventional classifications.

Adopting this approach avoids a ritualistic adherence to recipe book solutions. As a first step in this direction, I will examine in broad outline what any research design should achieve.

Fundamental Requirements

In general, a research design needs to answer three basic questions.

WHAT will be studied?
WHY will it be studied?
HOW will it be studied?

The last question can be broken down into four further questions.

WHAT research strategy will be used?
WHERE will the data come from?
HOW will the data be collected and analysed?
WHEN will each stage of the research be carried out?

If these questions are answered satisfactorily, a researcher should be clear about how the research is to proceed. If they are written down in the form of a research proposal, others will be in a position to provide feedback on whether the project is sensible and feasible. These others can include supervisors/advisers and academic research committees, in the case of postgraduate research, and academic research committees, funders, sponsors and potential consumers, in the case of other social research.

In practice, however, to answer these seven questions, a number of aspects of research have to be addressed and many decisions need to be made. Because of the variety of types of research undertaken in the social sciences, it is not possible to be dogmatic about all the details to be considered in a research design. Nevertheless, some components are relevant to most designs.

Core Elements

I wish to propose eight research design elements about which choices need to be made (see figure 2.1). Because the elements are connected in complex ways, a

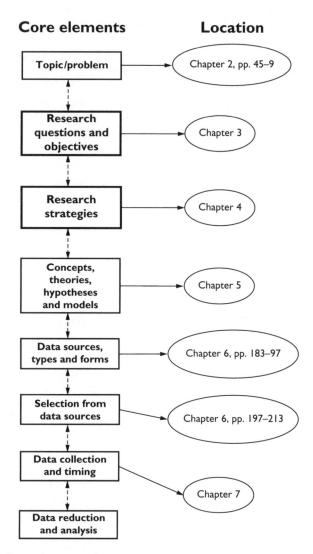

Figure 2.1 Core elements of a social research design

choice on one will have consequences for choices on other elements. The research design decisions that novice researchers usually give the most attention are 'data sources' and methods of 'data collection and analysis'. However, before these specific decisions can be made, several others must be considered.

The obvious starting-point in a research design is the statement of the 'research topic' or problem that is to be investigated. Following closely behind is the consideration of two closely related research design elements, the 'research object-ives' and the all-important 'research questions'. The latter provide the focus and direction for the study; they are what the study will attempt to answer. Then follows the selection of a 'research strategy' or strategies that will be used to answer these questions. The decisions that are made about the 'research questions' and research strategies' will have a big influence on the decisions about 'data sources', 'data selection' and methods of 'data collection' and 'data reduction and analysis'.

Associated with these last four design elements are three others, the most fundamental of which concerns the timing of data collection. The role of time in a research design is frequently seen as being its defining characteristic. The other two elements are concerned with the 'type of data' and the 'form of data' to be used. Choices related to the former are concerned with the proximity of the researcher to the phenomenon being studied, and choices in the latter have to do with whether the data will be in words or numbers.

The order in which these eight elements are discussed does not follow any particular logic. While the decisions made on the earlier ones may limit the decisions that can be made on the later ones, the process of designing research is spiral or cyclical in nature rather than being a set of linear steps. As the implications of the earlier decisions are explored, they may turn out to be impractical or unachievable. Therefore, the process is likely to require a number of iterations before a consistent and workable set of design decisions can be achieved.

The Ideal and the Practical

As I have argued earlier, all decisions that are concerned with the design of a research project should, ideally, be made before any substantial work has commenced. This is possible in studies that are conducted on topics which have already been well researched and for which there is adequate background information. Such studies may be the next step in a programme of research that has used well-tried methods and for which appropriate published reports are available. As already indicated, some studies may require preliminary or exploratory research to establish an adequate background against which choices can be made. This preliminary work may just involve the examination of statistical data, such as that produced in a census, but it may also require some field work, i.e. some contact with the site and the people who are to be involved in the research. In other studies, it may not be possible to make all the choices before the research commences, either because not enough is known about the field or the social context, or because the nature of the methods being used requires a developmental process to be adopted. The latter involves the making of choices at the end of each stage of the research, based on what was learned in the previous stage. The fact that some kinds of research need to be done in this developmental mode is no excuse for failing to make choices that should and can be made at the beginning, regardless of the category into which the project falls.

It is possible for researchers to avoid dealing with these choices if they operate within a research community that consistently adopts a particular research paradigm in a taken-for-granted manner. The need for choices will not be evident because those implicit in the paradigm will be adopted without discussion, or, perhaps, any awareness that choices have been made; the assumptions and methods to be used will be regarded as self-evident. Other researchers may avoid the need to examine critically the range of choices by simply adopting methods with which they are most familiar and comfortable, and designing the research project to use such methods.

Making the choices necessary to design a research project requires careful consideration of many factors, from fundamental philosophical and value positions to technical and practical matters. These choices are interdependent. The choice of research questions, and the way they are worded, places limitations on the choices of research strategy. The choice of a particular research strategy may limit the choice of research methods. The choice of a particular method of data gathering limits the choices of methods of data analysis, and so on. However, choices made in the early stages of the research design process may have to be revised in the light of circumstances that require a change in the sample or methods of data collection. Problems with access to people, organizations or other data sources may require compromises from the ideal design, and these compromises require a revision of other choices. For example, a chain of choices may lead to a decision to use a mail questionnaire to gather data. However, if it is discovered that access to the required names and addresses cannot be obtained in order to draw a random sample and contact respondents, then it may be necessary to use snowball sampling, and in-depth interviews. Therefore, it will be necessary to choose a different method of data analysis and, possibly, to reformulate the research questions and adopt a different research strategy. Hence, before settling on all the choices, it is usually necessary to go through the design decision sequence a few times in order to deal with the obstacles and limitations that are encountered.

Getting Started

Having now defined the fundamental requirements of a research design, and laid out the range of elements that need to be considered, we are now in a position to begin the task of preparing a research design. The formulation of a research topic, and an outline of the problem to be investigated, usually constitute the first or very early steps in setting out on a research project.

Research Topic and Problem

The statement of the research topic is both a signpost and a set of boundary markers: it sets the researcher on a specific path and defines the territory to be explored. However, while it is useful to try to define the project in this way at the outset, it is not uncommon for this initial definition to be rather vague and imprecise. The main reason is that, until the research design is completed, the researcher cannot be sure just what the project will be like. It may take much thought and reading, a number of trial runs, and even some exploratory research, before a clear and precise statement can be produced. The direction in which the signpost points, and the inscription on it, may change in the course of pre-paring the research design. In fact, the final version of the topic may not

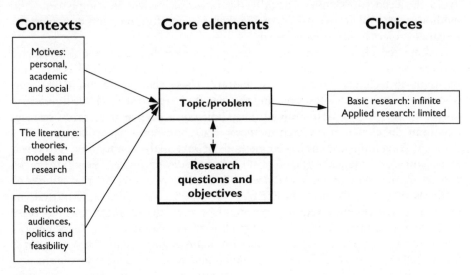

Figure 2.2   Research topic and problem

become clear until the time of writing the report or thesis. Therefore, novice researchers should not be concerned if difficulties are encountered in formulating the topic in the early stages (see figure 2.2).

Nevertheless, it is important to try to state the topic clearly and concisely, and in a way that communicates the general nature of the research. After all, someone is bound to ask what you are researching. A well-considered topic provides an easy answer. Here are some examples of how research topics might be stated. These topics will be used throughout the book and, particularly, in chapter 8 where a research design for each one will be outlined. They are part of a research programme on environmentalism that I have been conducting over the last ten years. (See the Appendix for examples of other topics.)

Environmental Worldviews and Behaviour among Students and Residents

Age and Environmentalism: A Test of Competing Hypotheses

Gender Differences in Environmentalism: Towards an Explanation

Motivation for Environmentally Responsible Behaviour: The Case of Environmental Activists

It is a common mistake to believe that, having defined the topic, the researcher is in a position to commence the project. Even if it is possible to begin with a well-formulated topic, the topic itself provides very little direction for the design of the project. Something more is required to give the research a clear focus and direction. I shall argue in chapter 3 that this is achieved mainly by clearly stating a set of research questions.

Research topics can also be stated in the form of a problem to be investigated. Problems can be either *social* or *sociological*. A *social* problem is a state of affairs that is judged by someone, for example a sociologist or a policy-maker, to be unsatisfactory and in need of some form of intervention. A *sociological* problem is a puzzle that a sociologist considers needs to be solved, i.e. explained or understood. Social research addresses both types of problems.[5]

Influences on the Choice of Topic

An important aspect of any research project is the reasons why it is to be undertaken. Some social research requires a considerable investment of resources, and even if this is mainly the researcher's time, justification for doing it is necessary. There are a number of dimensions on which this justification can be made, involving motives and goals of various kinds. Most projects will entail several of these. At the same time there are various factors that can place limitations on the choice of topic.

Motives

In an academic environment, lecturers/professors and students do social research for *personal*, *academic* and *social* reasons. *Personal* reasons include:

- satisfying curiosity;
- seeking credentials and/or pursuing career goals;
- trying to solve a personal problem; and
- pursuing personal interests and commitments.

Academic reasons for undertaking social research centre around making a *contribution to the discipline* or disciplines in which one works. These can include:

- contributing to knowledge in a particular field;
- seeking answers to current intellectual puzzles;
- participating in intellectual debates; and
- developing social theory.

Social researchers working in any context, be it in a university or in the public or private sectors, may wish to make a *contribution to the society*, or to some sector of the society, in which they are located. Their motives may include:

- contributing to the solution of a social problem;
- helping some group, community or organization achieve its goals;
- assisting in the development of social policy; and
- contributing to public or private sector decision-making.

[5] Just as differences between 'method' and 'methodology', and 'technique' and 'technology' (see the Introduction), have become blurred with inappropriate usage, so too has the distinction between 'social' and 'sociological'. 'Social' problems are frequently referred to incorrectly as 'sociological' problems. 'Social' has to do with social life; 'sociological' has to do with the discipline that studies social life.

An examination of the motives behind the four sample research topics discussed earlier will help to illustrate how *personal*, *academic* and *social* motives can be combined. The first of the research topics, 'Environmental Worldviews and Behaviour', was motivated by a personal curiosity about the kind and level of environmental attitudes and behaviour currently adopted by Australians. This arose from reading some of the American literature on environmental sociology. This curiosity was then translated into a desire to fill a gap in knowledge and, at the same time, to compare the Australian situation with that in the United States and other parts of the world. The main motive for the second topic, 'Age and Environmentalism', was an academic concern to advance our knowledge of why some people have more favourable environmental attitudes and engage in higher levels of environmentally responsible behaviour than others. Of course, this knowledge could also have some practical benefits for the design of environmental education programmes and for groups and organizations that are committed to improving the quality of the natural and built environments. Topic three, 'Gender Differences in Environmentalism', was motivated by an academic desire to make more sense of the rather confused findings in previous research on gender and environmentalism. Are women more environmentally conscious than men, and, if so, what are the nature and origins of these differences? Again, the results of research on this topic could also benefit environmental education programmes and, perhaps, make a contribution to the ultimate survival of the human race. Perhaps men need to adopt more feminine qualities if they are to act more responsibly towards the environment. The fourth topic, 'Motivation for Environmentally Responsible Behaviour', is essentially a theoretical puzzle: why do some people behave responsibly and others not? However, this puzzle is also related to specific social problems, for example, reducing litter and pollution, and saving energy. It may be necessary to understand the motivation for environmentally responsible behaviour in those who practise it in order to know what would be necessary to change the behaviour of others. Hence research that is primarily directed towards solving a *sociological* problem can also assist in the solution of *social* problems.

It is important for researchers to articulate their motives for undertaking a research project, as different motives may require different research design decisions. This articulation will also help to reveal conflicts or inconsistencies in an individual's motives, within a research team, or between the researcher(s) and other stakeholders. It is sensible to resolve these differences before the research commences.

Motives

Personal interests and goals

Discipline contribution

Social contribution

The literature

A major source of influence on the nature and choice of a research topic, particularly in basic or theory-oriented research, is the body of literature on theory and research related to the topic, in both the researcher's discipline and in related disciplines. A research project can be stimulated by the results of previous research and by problems posed by theorists. Even if the topic originates else-where, one or other of these bodies of literature is likely to help shape the way the topic and the problem are formulated. Of course, 'the literature' plays other roles in research, as we shall see in due course.

Restrictions

A number of factors can place restrictions on the choice of topic. These include the range of possible *audiences* the researcher has to, or wishes to, take into consideration, the *political* restrictions that may be imposed by authorities such as governments and universities, the types of research that *funding bodies* are willing to support, and practical factors such as the ability to get access to desired research sites.

Audiences include:

- clients on whose behalf the research is being conducted (whether or not they are paying for it);
- sponsors who are funding the research;
- colleagues;
- scientific communities (particularly the editors of journals);
- employers; and
- potential future sources of funding (Smaling 1994).

Of course, each audience may have different expectations of and different degrees of influence on the design and execution of a research project, let alone what it might find. This is particularly important in the case of applied research, as, in contrast to basic research, the researcher may have much less freedom in deter-mining the topic and other research design decisions. This can certainly occur if the sponsor(s), the main audience and the major benefactor(s) coincide.

Basic and Applied Research

Motives for undertaking research are associated with the type of research, i.e. whether it is basic or theory-oriented research, or whether it is applied or policy-oriented research.[6] The former is concerned with producing knowledge for under-standing and the latter with producing knowledge for action (Majchrzak 1984; Hakim 1987). Both types of social research deal with problems, basic research with theoretical problems, and applied research with social or practical problems. *Basic* research is concerned with advancing fundamental knowledge about the social world, in particular, with the development and testing of theories. *Applied* research is concerned with practical outcomes, with trying to solve some practical

---

[6] Refinements have been made to this dichotomy (e.g. pure basic, oriented basic, applied strategic and applied specific). However, this distinction is adequate for the present purposes.

problem, with helping practitioners accomplish tasks, and with the development and implementation of policy. Frequently, the results of applied research are required immediately, while basic research usually has a longer time-frame.

Basic and applied researchers have different orientations to their work. Basic researchers are more detached and academic in their approach, and tend to have their own motives. Applied researchers are more pragmatic and change-oriented, and generally have to pursue goals set by others. However, the issue of detachment is rather more complex than this simple comparison suggests. In some research traditions, detachment is considered to be necessary to achieve objectivity. In other traditions, it is claimed that detachment and, hence, objectivity, is impossible. It is also important to note that the theoretical and/or political commitments of some researchers, for example critical theorists and feminist researchers with emancipatory commitments, can produce basic research from which detachment is absent. We shall come back to these issues later. However, with these caveats in mind, it is possible to suggest an ideal typical contrast between these two types of research (see table 2.2).

For an example of basic research, I draw on a research project conducted in New Zealand in the 1960s (Blaikie 1968, 1969, 1972). I was curious as to

Table 2.2 Basic and applied social research

BASIC	APPLIED
1. Research is intrinsically satisfying and judgments are made by other sociologists.	1. Research is part of a job and is judged by sponsors outside the discipline of sociology.
2. Research problems and subjects are selected with a great deal of freedom.	2. Research problems are narrowly constrained to the demands of employers and sponsors.
3. Research is judged by absolute norms of scientific rigor, and the highest standards of scholarship are sought.	3. The rigor and standards of scholarship depend on the uses of results. Research can be 'quick and dirty' or may match high scientific standards.
4. The primary concern is with the internal logic and rigor of research design.	4. The primary concern is with the ability to generalize findings to areas of interest to sponsors.
5. The driving goal is to contribute to basic, theoretical knowledge.	5. The driving goal is to have practical payoffs or uses for results.
6. Success comes when results appear in a scholarly journal and have an impact on others in the scientific community.	6. Success comes when results are used by sponsors in decision making.

Source: Neuman 1997: 23, based on Freeman and Rossi 1984: 572–3.

whether the relationship between religion and occupation that Weber (1958) had found in Germany around the turn of the century, and that Lenski (1961) and others had found in the United States in the early 1960s, was also present in New Zealand. If this relationship did exist, I wanted to know whether it was the result of the survival of the Protestant work ethic in this largely European outpost. This research clearly had no immediate practical value; it was designed to satisfy academic curiosity and to continue a tradition of research in the United States that was largely inspired by Weber's thesis.

An example of applied research comes from a commissioned study I did with some colleagues in the late 1970s. A developer wished to build houses on a site close to the Melbourne airport. He engaged a firm of architects and planners to assist him. Planning restrictions determined how close houses could be built to the flight paths associated with the runways. This restriction was established in terms of maximum decibel readings, and was shown as a line on a map down each side of the flight path. The developer was concerned about his ability to sell houses if they were built close to the flight path. Would purchasers be willing to live right up to the legal planning limit? If not, how close would they be willing to live? The firm of architects and planners engaged us to answer these questions. The study was done by interviewing residents who were living at different intervals from the flight path in an adjoining location, including some whose houses were built under the flight path before the airport was established at this location, and before the planning restrictions came into force. The developer would have liked us to draw a line on the map for him, but since people's responses to living close to aircraft noise were very varied this was not possible. We found that people differed considerably in the extent to which they could tolerate aircraft noise and the possible dangers of living close to an airport. Some people appeared to be willing to put up with aircraft noise if the price of the house was attractive. In the end, the developer adopted a conservative position and left some open space adjoining the planning limit.

In the social sciences, research is often a mixture of basic and applied: some stages of a project may have a basic flavour, while other stages may be more applied. For example, a researcher may be commissioned to assist the managers of an organization in changing the organization's culture. After undertaking research to describe the existing culture of the organization, the researcher may then proceed to refine and test a particular theory of organizational change. Only when they are satisfied that this theory is relevant to this particular organization will the researcher proceed to engage in some form of action research which helps the members of the organization to bring about the changes desired by management.

Few if any social research projects are exclusively concerned with advancing knowledge for its own sake. While the basic researcher may not be interested in the practical benefits, basic research can eventually produce such outcomes. Implicitly or explicitly, most social researchers appear to have some social issue or problem in mind when they undertake research. The fundamental question is whether the researcher chooses to define the problem and the research project, or whether the problem has been defined by someone else, for example a sponsor who may also have a substantial say in how the project is to be conducted.

It is worth noting, however, that in basic research that is competitively funded there are usually some constraints on research design. Funding bodies not only have expectations about what kinds of research projects are legitimate or important, but they are also likely to have prejudices about what are regarded as appropriate methods for data collection and/or analysis. In order to obtain research funds, prudent researchers need to take these expectations into account in designing a project, or be well prepared to defend less popular methods.

Roles for Researchers

An important choice that all social researchers have to make is what stance to take towards the research process and participants. These positions range from complete detachment to committed involvement (see Blaikie 1993a). There are at least six possible positions.

Roles for Researchers

Detached observer

Empathetic observer

Faithful reporter

Mediator of languages

Reflective partner

Dialogic facilitator

The traditional 'scientific' stance is that of *detached observer*. The researcher is regarded as an uninvolved spectator, particularly during the process of data collection. It is argued that the researcher's values and preferences can threaten the objectivity of the research and, hence, the value of the results. Therefore, detachment is a requirement for producing reliable knowledge. This position is still widely advocated in spite of the many criticisms that have been raised against it.

The second position, the *empathetic observer*, still aims to achieve some kind of objectivity but insists that it is necessary for researchers to be able to place themselves in the social actors' position. Only by grasping the subjective meanings used by the social actors can their actions be understood. This is commonly referred to as *verstehen* (Weber 1964; Outhwaite 1975).

This second position has developed into a third, the *faithful reporter*, in which the researcher's role becomes much less detached. Its aim is to report a way of life by allowing the research participants to 'speak for themselves'. Thus, the researcher's task is to present the social actors' point of view. To do this, the researcher may have to become immersed in that way of life in order to grasp these meanings. This position is commonly referred to as 'naturalism' and was advocated by sociologists of everyday life (see e.g. Lofland 1967; Blumer 1969; Matza 1969; Denzin 1971; Douglas 1971; and Guba 1978). The researcher is required to study social phenomena in their 'natural' state, to be sensitive to the nature of the social setting, to describe what happens there and how the participants see their own actions and the actions of others. A related requirement is that the researcher 'retain the integrity of the phenomenon'. This means that the researcher is required to remain faithful to the phenomenon under investigation by only producing reports in which the social actors can recognize themselves and others. Schütz presented this idea in his *postulate of adequacy*, in which he argued that social scientific concepts must be derived from and remain consistent with lay concepts.

> Each term in a scientific model of human action must be constructed in such a way that a human act performed within the life-world by an individual actor in the way indicated by the typical construct would be understandable for the actor himself [*sic*] as well as for his fellow-men [*sic*] in terms of commonsense interpretation of every-day life. (Schütz 1963b: 343)

In other words, if social actors cannot recognize themselves and their colleagues in the accounts produced by the social scientist, then the latter must have produced a distortion of the social actors' world. This process of checking social scientific accounts with the social actors' accounts is sometimes referred to as 'member validation' or 'member checks' and is a major form of validity checking in qualitative research. However, this process is not without its difficulties.

A fourth position, which rejects the idea of detachment, is an extension of the third. In this case, the researcher becomes the *mediator of languages* (Giddens 1976; Gadamer 1989), between everyday, lay language and social scientific or technical language. Studying social life is akin to studying a text, and this involves interpretation on the part of the reader. The researcher actively constructs an account based on the accounts provided by the participants. This process of construction is not neutral; researchers have to invest something of themselves into their account. Social, geographical and historical locations, as well as the interests of the researcher, have a bearing on the nature of the account produced. Hence, detached objectivity is seen to be impossible, as the author's voice will always be present in the researcher's account (Geertz 1988).

A fifth position is associated with critical theory. The researcher is viewed as a *reflective partner* who is committed to the emancipation of the participants from whatever kind of oppression they are experiencing (Habermas 1970, 1972). Following Husserl, Habermas rejected the 'objectivist illusion' of Positivism, according to which the world is conceived as a universe of facts independent of the 'observer' whose task is to describe them. He accepted the same premise as Interpretivism, that social and cultural reality is already pre-interpreted by the participants as a cultural symbolic meaning system, and that these meanings can be changed over time. Therefore, the process of understanding this socially con-structed reality is 'dialogic'; it allows individuals to communicate their experi-ences within a shared framework of cultural meanings. In contrast, the process in the natural sciences is 'monologic'; it is the technical manipulation by the researcher of some aspect of nature. In the latter, the researcher is a 'disengaged observer' who stands in a subject-to-object relationship to the subject-matter while, in the former, the researcher is a 'reflective partner' whose relationship is that of subject to co-participant (Blaikie 1993a: 53).

Another version of this fifth position is associated with feminist research and involves *conscious partiality*. Again, the concern is with emancipation, in this case of women. Much more than empathy is involved here. The researcher not only participates in women's struggles but is also expected to be changed by them. This view of research involves the conscientization of both the researcher and the researched. By conscientization is meant learning to perceive social, political and economic contradictions and to take action against oppressive elements of reality (Freire 1970).

> *The research process must become a process of conscientization*, both for the so-called 'research subjects' (social scientists) and for the 'research objects' (women as target groups)...People who before were objects of research become subjects of their own research and action. (Mies 1983: 126)

The fourth and fifth positions have now culminated in a sixth, postmodern view of the role of the researcher. In this case, the researcher is regarded as another actor in the social context being investigated. Rather than being the 'expert', as in the *detached* position, an *empathetic observer*, or a *faithful reporter*, the postmodern researcher takes elements from the positions of *mediator of languages*, *reflective partner*, and *conscientizer*, and seeks to reduce the researcher's authorial influence on the products of the research by allowing a variety of 'voices' to be expressed. These researchers

> still rely on their understanding of the situation, but they attempt to minimize their authorial bias by letting the natives speak for themselves as much as possible. The aim is to produce a 'polyphony' of voices rather than a single voice, in order to reduce bias and distortion. (Fontana 1994: 214)

The emphasis is on the dialogue between the researcher and the researched. Hence, this position might be described as *dialogic facilitator*.

Clearly, there are incompatibilities between most of these positions, and there is an extensive literature that debates their relative merits. As we shall see in chapter 4, these positions are associated with the four dominant research strategies used in social research. However, before we leave this discussion here, there is a related concept that needs to be discussed, reflexivity.

The notion of *reflexivity* is integral to the ethnomethodologist's views on how social actors make their actions and their social world meaningful to themselves and others. Giddens has incorporated this idea into his structuration theory as the 'reflexive monitoring' that social actors need to engage in to maintain continuity in their social practices. For Giddens, *reflexivity* is more than self-consciousness; it involves the active monitoring of the ongoing flow of social life.

> The reflexive monitoring of activity is a chronic feature of everyday action and involves the conduct not just of the individual but also of others. That is to say, actors not only monitor continuously the flow of their activities and expect others to do the same for their own; they also routinely monitor aspects, social and physical, of the contexts in which they move. (Giddens 1984: 5)

There is a growing acceptance of the idea that if reflexivity is an integral part of everyday social practices, then it must also be involved in the 'everyday' activities of social researchers. If the construction and maintenance of social worlds by social actors involves, among other things, reflexive monitoring, then the social researcher's creation of new social scientific knowledge will entail the same processes. In other words, wherever new knowledge is generated through a process of interaction between the researcher and the researched, the social researcher will draw on the same skills that social actors use to make their activities intelligible (Giddens 1976: 157–61).

Recognition of the need for social researchers to be reflexive can be found in the writings of qualitative researchers in general, and ethnographers in particular, as well as among feminist researchers (see Stanley and Wise 1993; Maynard and Purvis 1994). For example, Hammersley and Atkinson have argued that reflexivity implies that

> the orientations of researchers will be shaped by their socio-historical locations, including the values and interests that these locations confer upon them. What this represents is a rejection of the idea that social research is, or can be, carried out in some autonomous realm that is insulated from the wider society and from the particular biography of the researcher, in such a way that its findings can be unaffected by social processes and personal characteristics. (Hammersley and Atkinson 1995: 16)

Similarly, Mason (1996) has regarded *active reflexivity* as one of the essential features of qualitative research; researchers need to be active and reflexive in the process of generating data rather then being neutral data collectors.

> Qualitative research should involve critical self-scrutiny by the researcher, or active *reflexivity*. This means that the researcher should constantly take stock of their actions and their role in the research process, and subject these to the same critical scrutiny as the rest of their 'data'. This is based on the belief that a researcher cannot be neutral, or objective, or detached, from the knowledge and evidence they are generating. Instead, they should seek to understand their role in that process. Indeed, the very act of posing difficult questions to oneself in the research process is part of the activity of reflexivity. (Mason 1996: 6)

Mason has also argued that 'we should be reflexive about every decision we take, and that we should not take any decisions without actively recognising that we are taking them' (1996: 165). Therefore, *reflexivity* applies to the process of designing social research as much as to the research process itself.

The difference between adopting a reflexive stance in research and other possible positions is illustrated in the distinction that Mason has made between the three choices that qualitative researchers have in the way they 'read' their data: literal, interpretive or reflexive.

> If you are intending to 'read' your data *literally*, you will be interested in their literal form, content, structure, style, layout, and so on.... An interpretive reading will involve you in constructing or documenting a version of what you think the data mean or represent, or what you think you can infer from them.... A reflexive reading will locate you as part of the data you have generated, and will seek to explore your role in the process of generation and interpretation of data. (Mason 1996: 109)

Recognition of the impossibility of detachment as well as the reflexive nature of social research poses some difficult philosophical problems with regard to the status of social scientific knowledge. Part of this dilemma centres on different ideas on whether objectivity is possible, and whether it is possible to produce 'true' knowledge. There seems to be a fear that giving up on the possibility of being an objective researcher means that all social research degenerates into the production of competing 'subjective' accounts, the relative merits of which can only be established by political processes. However, Hammersley and Atkinson have argued that a commitment to reflexivity does not imply 'that research is necessarily political, or that it should be political, in the sense of serving particular political causes or practical ends. For us, the primary goal of research is, and must remain, the production of knowledge' (1995: 17). On the other hand, critical theorists and feminist researchers see commitment to the cause of emancipation as an essential part of all social scientific activity. (See Blaikie 1993a for a brief review of these issues, and Hammersley 1992: ch. 2, Guba and Lincoln 1994 and Hammersley and Atkinson 1995: ch. 1 for discussions relevant to social research.)

I have not included the role of the researcher as a research design element as I suspect that adopting a particular role is something that occurs independently of the research design. Of course, it is possible that an ideological commitment to a particular role may have an influence on the research topics that are likely to be entertained, and on other design decisions. Having said this, in my view, reflexivity is not really a matter of choice. All social researchers should be reflexive, regardless of the role they adopt. It will, however, be easier for researchers who reject the detached stance to be reflexive.

Conclusion

There are various ideas in the literature about what constitutes a research design. Many of these are unhelpful because they produce categories that deal with limited aspects of a research design, they are not mutually exclusive or they are not comparable. In this chapter I have proposed that designing research involves giving consideration to a range of core elements, each with a number of choices. Combination of these decisions leads to a wide variety of possible research designs.

The basic aim in designing social research is to achieve maximum control over the research process. While a researcher's ability to achieve control will vary according to the nature of critical elements in the design, careful planning before the research commences makes it possible to evaluate the suitability and compatibility of the combination of decisions that need to be made. This will help to ensure a successful outcome.

The preparation of a research design can start with different elements and proceed in a variety of sequences. However, at some stage, and probably early in the process, a statement of the topic or problem needs to be produced. This will no doubt be reviewed and possibly modified as the research design evolves and the research itself proceeds.

An important issue for all researchers is how to regard their relationship with the research participants. At least six different positions have been identified, each with its particular ontological and epistemological baggage. It is essential to maintain consistency between the stance adopted and the assumptions entailed in the choices made about the research design elements, in particular, the research strategy and the methods of data collection.

We now turn to what I regard as one of the two critical core design elements, the formulation of research questions.

3

Research Questions and Objectives

The purpose of research is to discover answers to questions through the application of systematic procedures. (Berg 1995)

Introduction

The use of research questions is a neglected aspect in the design and conduct of social research. This is surprising given that the fundamental purpose of social research is to provide new knowledge about the social world, to answer puzzles about what the social world is like and how it works, and to find ways to solve problems and bring about change. In my view, formulating research questions is the most critical and, perhaps, the most difficult part of any research design. It is only through the use of such questions that choices about the focus and direction of research can be made, that its boundaries can be clearly delimited, that manageability can be achieved and that a successful outcome can be anticipated. Establishing research questions also makes it possible to select research strategies and methods with confidence. In other words, *a research project is built on the foundation of its research questions*. However, getting these questions clear and precise requires considerable thought and sometimes some preliminary investigation.

This chapter discusses:

- three main types of research questions;
- the functions of research questions;
- how to develop and refine research questions;
- the relationship between research questions and hypotheses, and the functions of the latter;
- how research questions can provide a guide and framework for the review of the literature;
- the nature and range of research objectives that can be pursued; and
- the relationship between research objectives and research questions.

The aim of the chapter is not only to argue that research questions are necessary, but also that good research needs high-quality questions. A rare attempt to deal with the issue of the quality of research questions has been undertaken by Campbell et al. (1982). They reviewed articles in five journals in psychology, organizational behaviour and management, taking a two-year period for each journal. A list of the research questions was compiled and then they surveyed researchers in the fields covered to see what questions they thought should be asked. Their aim was to find gaps in research and to establish priorities for future research. The important thing about their work is that they focused on research questions.

Research Questions

Conventional wisdom suggests that research should be guided by one or more hypotheses. In order to get started on a research project, this view advocates that the researcher should, first, select a research problem, second, state one or more hypotheses to be tested, and, third, measure and correlate the variables related to the concepts in the hypotheses. However, this procedure is only relevant to quantitative research conducted within the *deductive* research strategy. While there is a role for hypotheses in particular kinds of research, they neither provide the foundation for a research design nor are they very useful for defining the focus and direction of a research project. In fact, the ritual of formulating and testing hypotheses can lead to unnecessary and unhelpful rigidities in the way in which research is conducted. In some kinds of research, it is impossible or unnecessary to set out with hypotheses. A much more useful procedure is to establish one or more research questions.

Few textbooks on research methods give much attention to the formulation of research questions, and some ignore this vital part of the research process entirely. Exceptions can be found in some recent texts on research methods, for example Yin (1993), Hedrick et al. (1993), Miles and Huberman (1994), Creswell (1994, 1998), Marshall and Rossman (1995), Blaxter et al. (1996), Mason (1996), Neuman (1997) and Flick (1998). It is interesting to note that these books are concerned with qualitative research methods or include a significant discussion of them.

Neuman, for example, has regarded research questions as the bridge between the research topic and hypotheses; he has also discussed techniques for narrowing a topic into a research question. Yin has linked research questions to types of research designs (or what he has called strategies): experiment, survey, archival analysis, history and case study. Flick has argued for the importance of research questions in qualitative research.

> A central step, and one which essentially determines success in qualitative research, but tends to be ignored in most presentations of methods, is how to formulate the research question(s). The researcher is confronted with this problem not only at the beginning, when the study or the project is conceptualized, but in several phases of the process: in conceptualizing the research design, in entering the field, in selecting the cases and in collecting data. (Flick 1998: 47)

Creswell has offered advice on how to formulate research questions in quantitative and qualitative research (1994) and in five traditions of qualitative research (1998).

Mason set her discussion of research questions in the context of intellectual puzzles that seek some kind of explanation. These puzzles take a variety of forms, depending on the ontological and epistemological positions adopted by the theoretical and intellectual traditions from within which they emerge.

> Intellectual puzzles, then, will contain different sets of ontological and epistemological assumptions and prescriptions, and will suggest distinctive types of social explanation. In formulating your own intellectual puzzle, you must ensure that you have thought through what these are, and be confident that they are consistent – that is, that your puzzle is ontologically meaningful, and epistemologically explainable or workable. (Mason 1996: 15)

Intellectual puzzles then lead to research questions that she also regarded as forming the backbone of a research design and as having much greater significance than hypotheses or propositions, particularly in qualitative research. For her, research questions

> should be clearly formulated (whether or not you intend to modify them or add to them later), intellectually worthwhile, and researchable (both in terms of your epistemological position, and in practical terms), because it is through them that you will be connecting what it is that you wish to research with how you are going to go about researching it. They are the vehicles which you will rely upon to move you from your broad research interest to your specific research focus and project, and therefore their importance cannot be overstated.
>
>   Research questions, then, are those questions to which you as researcher really want to know the answers, and in that sense they are the formal expression of your intellectual puzzle. (Mason 1996: 15–16)

I hope these examples are sufficient to reinforce my argument about the pivotal role played by research questions in social research.

Types of Research Questions

Research questions can be grouped into three main types, 'what' questions, 'why' questions and 'how' questions. I have restricted the research questions to 'what', 'why' and 'how' to maintain simplicity and to achieve a correspondence with the three main categories of objective: description, explanation/understanding and change (see figure 3.1).

What questions require a descriptive answer; they are directed towards discovering and describing the characteristics of and patterns in some social phenomenon, for example categories of individuals, social groups of all sizes, and social processes. They include the following types of questions.

- What types of people are involved?
- What characteristic knowledge, beliefs, values and attitudes do they hold?

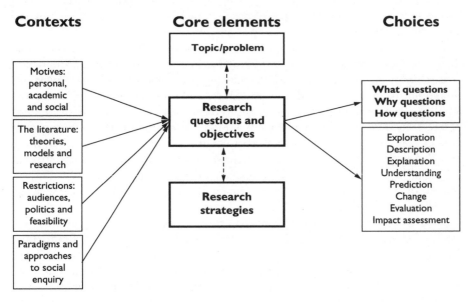

Contexts   **Core elements**   **Choices**

Figure 3.1   Research questions and objectives

- What is their characteristic behaviour?
- What social processes have brought this behaviour about?
- What are the patterns in the relationships between these characteristics?
- What are the consequences of these activities?

Why questions ask for either the causes of, or the reasons for, the existence of characteristics or regularities in a particular phenomenon. They are directed towards understanding or explaining the relationships between events, or within social activities and social processes. For example:

- Why do people think and act this way?
- Why did these patterns come to be this way?
- Why do the characteristics or social process change, or remain stable?
- Why does this activity have these particular consequences?

How questions are concerned with bringing about change, with practical outcomes and intervention. For example:

- How can these characteristics, social processes or patterns be changed?
- How can they be made to stop changing, or to slow down or speed up their rate of change?

These three types of research questions form a sequence: 'what' questions normally precede 'why' questions, and 'why' questions normally precede 'how' questions. We need to know what is going on before we can explain it, and we need to know why something behaves the way it does before we can be confident about introducing an intervention to change it. However, most research projects will include only one or two types of research questions, most commonly 'what' and 'why' questions.

Some research may not proceed beyond one or more 'what' questions. While there may be a strong desire to include 'why' and possibly 'how' questions in a research project, the significance of producing good answers to 'what' questions should not be underestimated. In some fields, and on some topics, little research may have been undertaken anywhere, or recently, or in the context of interest. Before 'why' questions can be tackled, a good description of what is going on is needed. This may be an opportunity to make an important contribution to knowledge. In addition, some social scientists have argued that good description is all that is needed for an adequate understanding of many topics. Certainly, in comparative studies, description is the fundamental task. In short, good description is a vital part of social research.

Some writers have proposed more than three types of research questions. Yin (1993), for example, has discussed seven types: 'who', 'what', 'where', 'how many', 'how much', 'how' and 'why'. However, he does acknowledge that 'who', 'where', 'how many' and 'how much' questions are different forms of a 'what' question. Blaxter et al. have suggested five types of questions: 'how', 'who', 'what', 'when' and 'why'. Similarly, the first four of their questions can all be transposed into 'what' questions: 'what individuals' in 'what places', at 'what time', in 'what numbers or quantities' and in 'what ways'.

A different approach to research questions can be found in Hedrick et al. (1993: 23–32). They have identified four types of research questions that are relevant to applied research: descriptive, normative, correlative and impact. Marshall and Rossman (1995) have classified research questions as theoretical, as focusing on particular populations and as being site-specific. These categories relate to the context in which they are examined.

> Questions may be theoretical ones, which can be researched in any one of a number of different sites or with different samples. Or they may be focussed on a particular population or class of individuals; these too can be studied in various places. Finally, the questions may be site-specific because of the uniqueness of a specific program or organization. (Marshall and Rossman 1995: 27)

Throughout the book, I shall discuss only the three types of research questions, 'what', 'why' and 'how'. The process of developing research questions will inevitably produce a range of question wording similar to that discussed by Yin (1993). However, I believe the discipline of reducing all questions to these three types helps to make the links between research questions and research objectives clear.

The Purpose of Research Questions

Research questions are needed to define the nature and scope of the research. By selecting questions, and paying attention to their wording, it is possible to determine what is to be studied, and, to some extent, how it will be studied. The way a particular research question is worded can have a significant influence on how much and what kind of research activity will be required.

Let us return to the four research topics discussed in chapter 2 and examine some possible research questions for each one.

Environmental Worldviews and Behaviour among Students and Residents
1 To what extent do students and residents hold different environmental worldviews?
2 To what extent is environmentally responsible behaviour practised?
3 What is the level and type of involvement in environmental movements?
4 To what extent, and in what ways, is environmental behaviour related to environmental worldviews?
5 In what ways and to what extent will environmental worldviews and behaviour change over the next five years?

As these are all 'what' questions, the study will have only *descriptive* objectives. It seeks to describe the distributions of environmental worldviews and behaviour in these populations, and the pattern of the relationship between these variables, now and in the future.

Age and Environmentalism: A Test of Competing Hypotheses
1 To what extent is age related to environmental worldviews and environmental behaviour?
2 If there are significant relationships, what are the forms of these relationships?
3 Why do these relationships exist?

These are straightforward research questions, two 'what' questions followed by a 'why' question. The study wishes to establish the nature of these relationships and to explain them.

Gender Differences in Environmentalism: Towards an Explanation
1 To what extent do women hold more favourable environmental attitudes than men?
2 To what extent are women more willing than men to engage in environmentally responsible behaviour?
3 Why do these gender differences in environmentalism exist?

Again, this is a combination of 'what' and 'why' questions seeking descriptions of relationships and explanations for them.

Motivation for Environmentally Responsible Behaviour: The Case of Environmental Activists
1 In what range and types of behaviour do environmentally responsible individuals engage?
2 Why do these people act responsibly towards the environment?
3 Why do some of these people manage to sustain this behaviour?
4 How can the incidence of this type of behaviour be increased?

Now we come to a combination of all three types of research questions. The study seeks to describe environmentally responsible behaviour, and then to explain why people engage in and manage to sustain that behaviour. Then comes the sting in the tail – how to get more people to engage in this behaviour. It will be unlikely that this study can do anything more than point in the direction of possible answers to this last question, using the answers to questions 2 and 3. But it could also suggest ideas for further research to pursue it. (See the Appendix for examples of different and more complex sets of research questions.)

It is important to recognize that while it is highly desirable to produce a well-formulated set of research questions as part of an integrated research proposal or design, this may not always be possible without some preliminary research being undertaken. In addition, what is discovered in the process of undertaking the research is likely to require a review of the research questions from time to time. No research design can completely anticipate how a research project will evolve. It may turn out that some research questions cannot be answered because it is not possible to obtain the necessary data. What the researcher assumed, or was led to believe, about the availability of or access to the necessary data may turn out to be wrong. Consequently, the design may require some revision, and part of this may involve a change to one or more research questions. Hence, while it is necessary to be as clear as possible about the scope and direction of the research at the beginning, what the researcher learns in the course of undertaking the research may necessitate some changes. This is simply the nature of research in any discipline.

Research projects differ in the extent to which it is possible to be able to produce precise research questions. This is certainly true of exploratory research, the aim of which can be to provide information to assist in the development of research questions. It might also be argued that some studies that use qualitative or ethnographic research methods involve the researcher in a learning process. In these cases, the research questions may evolve in the course of the research. However, even this kind of research requires careful consideration of scope and direction at the beginning in order to ensure that it will be manageable and will have a high probability of successful completion. The developmental nature of a research design should not be used as an excuse for avoiding the effort required to formulate appropriate research questions.

A common feature of the research process is for the researcher to be deflected or distracted from their original intentions. Many influences may be at work:

- encountering new ideas, for example in published research, in conference papers or presentations, in previously unfamiliar theory, or in the media;
- discussion with colleagues;
- changing academic fashions;
- changing political agendas; and, more particularly,
- learning that takes place during the course of the research, for example, from observations, from interviews and discussions, and from working with data.

It is very easy to lose one's way and to forget or neglect the original research questions. Changes to research questions should be made only after careful consideration and not by just drifting away from them. One way to counter this drift is to print the questions in large type and display them in prominent places, such as in your regular work space, or in the front page of your field book or journal. They should be read regularly to keep the focus of the research clear.

Developing and Refining Research Questions

The process of developing a set of research questions can be the most challenging part of any research project. This is particularly the case when the researcher initiates the project, as is the case in much academic and postgraduate research in the social sciences. However, the problem still exists in research that is commissioned by someone else for problem-solving or policy-related purposes. Organizations or groups that commission research are very often vague about what they want done, and usually need some assistance to clarify the research questions and objectives.

It is very rare for a researcher to commence a project with clearly formulated research questions already provided. This might occur where a researcher has joined a research programme in which the research questions have already been established, or if a researcher is taking up questions posed in previous research. However, it is much more common in the social sciences for researchers to approach a topic or field in which previous research is limited, or in which previous research has used an approach different from the one the researcher wants to use, or considers to be appropriate.

All researchers have to devise their own way of developing research questions. What I offer here is a process that I have used myself and found to work successfully with many postgraduate students. Research questions can be stimulated in many ways: from casual observation of possible regularities; from previous research; from theory; from reports in the media; or from discussions with colleagues. The source is not really important. What it is usually necessary is to bring some order into a range of loosely connected ideas about what should be researched. Neuman (1997: 122) has offered a similar set of techniques.

1 Write down every question you can think of Let both the results of your reading and imagination run riot for a reasonable period of time, and record every question that occurs to you. Brain-storming sessions, on your own or with others, may stimulate the process. Note down questions when they occur to you, wherever and for whatever reason. The list will include all kinds of questions; some will be seeking descriptions, some explanations, some will be concerned with action, and so on. There is no need to try to achieve any order or consistency in the list; simply record the questions as they arise. One question will usually stimulate other questions; they should all be recorded. This activity may produce a very long list, sometimes many scores of questions. The purpose in doing this is to try to expose all the ideas that you have on the topic, particularly those that may be taken for granted and which later you wish you had been fully aware of at the design stage. No question should be censored, even if it may seem to be marginal, outrageous or impractical.

2   Review the list of questions   Once you are satisfied that you have pretty well exhausted all the ideas you have on the topic, you should review your list. There are a number of strategies for doing this.

- Group the questions under similar themes or topics, if such exist in your list. This is likely to reveal overlaps between questions which will make it possible to eliminate some and to consolidate others. Part of this consolidation can be achieved by developing a single, general or abstract question that summarizes a group of more specific questions.
- Set aside questions that seem to be outside your main area(s) of interest, that *are* too outrageous, or that seem to take you in directions that may be too difficult or too demanding to deal with. You can always review these questions later if you decide to change the direction of the research.

3   Separate 'what', 'why' and 'how' questions   Within each group of questions, begin to identify those that appear to be 'what', 'why' and 'how' questions. Of course, some studies may be concerned ultimately with only one type of question, for example one or more 'what' questions, or just a 'why' question.

The wording of 'what', 'why' and 'how' questions requires very careful consideration, as the way a question is stated initially can be deceptive: 'what' and 'why' questions can begin with 'How', and 'how' questions can begin with 'What'. For example: 'How are environmental behaviour and environmental worldview related?' This needs be transposed into a descriptive question, as: 'What is the relationship between environmental behaviour and environmental worldview?' or 'To what extent, and in what ways, is environmental behaviour related to environmental worldview?' The question, 'How do some people manage to behave in an environmentally responsible way?' needs to be transposed into an explanatory question: 'Why do these people act responsibly towards the environment?' The question, 'What can be done to increase the incidence of environmentally responsible behaviour?' needs to be transposed into an intervention question: 'How can the incidence of environmentally responsible behaviour be increased?'

Make sure each question is worded as clearly and as simply as possible and that each one can be identified unambiguously as a 'what', 'why' or 'how' question. Complex questions may need to be broken down into a series of questions. For example, the question, 'What is the incidence of student plagiarism?' would be better broken down into at least two questions: 'What has been the extent of detected student plagiarism over the past five years?' and 'In what types of plagiarism have students engaged?' (see the Appendix).

4   Expose assumptions   Check each question to see what it assumes. Many questions, particularly 'why' questions, presuppose other questions. It is important to expose the 'what' question that must be answered before a 'why' question can be asked, or, perhaps, even formulated.

'How' questions may presuppose both 'what' and, particularly, 'why' questions. A research project may need to examine all three types of questions. Rather than reducing the number of questions on the list, this part of the process may add further questions.

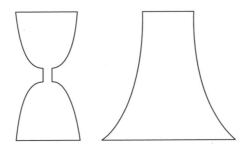

Figure 3.2   The hourglass analogy

5   Examine the scope of the questions   Now is the time to get practical and ask yourself how many groups of questions, and questions within groups, can be tackled in the project. A judgement has to be made about what is going to be manageable within the time and with the other resources available. There is an inevitable tendency to try to do too much; the questions for the topic on student plagiarism are a good example (see the Appendix). Therefore, it is advisable at this stage to reduce the project to what may appear to be an extremely limited or even trivial set of questions. Such innocent-looking questions usually have other questions lurking in their shadows.

A metaphor to illustrate the need to narrow the focus of the project at this stage can be taken from the shape of an hourglass, the ancient method of measuring time (see figure 3.2). At the beginning of the design of a project, our ideas are usually wide-ranging and scattered, as represented by the broad top of the hourglass. What we need to do is to narrow, consolidate and focus these ideas so that they can easily pass through the neck of the hourglass. Once we have achieved this, and the research commences, we are likely to find that the ideas and questions begin to expand, and by the end of the project they may have grown to the size of the base of the hourglass. What we must ensure is that the size of the project at the final stage is still manageable and that it can be successfully completed. If the narrowing process is avoided at the design stage, the inevitable expansion during the course of the research is likely to produce a project that becomes unmanageable or directionless.

6   Separate major and subsidiary questions   Once the list of questions has been reduced to what appears to be a manageable set, further work can be done on them. It may be useful to separate the questions into two broad categories, *major* questions and *subsidiary* questions.[1] Major research questions are those that will form the core of the research project, the key questions that are to be answered. They may also be stated more abstractly than some of the other questions. Research projects may have only one major research question, perhaps a 'what'

---

[1] Hedrick et al. (1993) have suggested a similar division between 'primary' and 'subordinate' research questions.

question. However, most are likely to have a combination of major questions: 'what' questions and a 'why' question, or a set of 'what', 'why' and 'how' questions. About five or six major research questions is probably more than enough for any project. Subsidiary questions will include those that deal with background information or issues that are presupposed by one or more major questions that, while being necessary, are not absolutely central to the project. Here is an example of a set of major and subsidiary questions.

Major research question
- To what extent is environmentally responsible behaviour practised?

Subsidiary research questions
- What proportion of residents regularly recycle household waste products?
- What proportion of residents avoid buying environmentally damaging products?
- What proportion of university students are actively involved in environmental groups?

In this example, the subsidiary questions can be used to specify categories of environmental behaviour and thus focus the study.

7   *Is each question necessary?*   As your set of questions begins to take shape, you need to subject them to critical scrutiny by asking of each question: 'Why am I asking this question?' 'Is it necessary?' 'Why do I want to know this?' 'What will I do with the results from it?' 'How does it relate to other questions?' 'Is it researchable?' 'Can I manage all these questions?' This process needs to be taken very seriously and not glossed over quickly. It is very easy to include questions because 'that would be interesting to explore', or 'I would really like to know about that'. This critical examination needs to be ruthless.

A common mistake in drafting research questions is to confuse them with questions used to elicit information from respondents or participants, for example interview questions, or questions that would go into a questionnaire. Research questions are what you want the research project to answer. Questions you ask respondents can provide the basis for answering research questions, but their style and scope are very different. A wide variety of data may contribute to the answering of any research question.

Many postgraduate students seem to have a desire to do the definitive piece of research on their topic. Even if the research is for a Ph.D., and even if the degree is based entirely or almost entirely on a thesis, the research must be limited and focused in order to be manageable. There is just so much that one person can do within the time limits prescribed, and this can only make a small contribution to knowledge. While some students may be quite pragmatic about doing just what is necessary to qualify for a higher degree, many appear to have a strong need to be seen to be making a major contribution to knowledge. This is not only an unrealistic expectation for a fully research-based Ph.D.; it is impossible in research for any other kind of postgraduate degree. The problem is most acute for students undertaking a coursework (taught) master's degree in which there is a minor thesis/dissertation/project component. Because of its limited duration, such a research project is very difficult to design.

In short, the number and nature of the questions selected has got to reflect the available resources. This is the stage at which the scope of the project is determined, and bad decisions can produce serious problems later.

Influences on the Choice of Research Questions

The choice of research questions and objectives can be subject to the same influences as those affecting the choice of the topic itself. Research questions may be developed to satisfy *personal* or *academic* curiosity as well as to address *social* problems. They may be inspired by the work of a particular social theorist or by the results of previous research. In addition, they may be influenced by a variety of audiences. The latter is particularly the case in applied research where someone other than the researcher sets the agenda. In the end, however, the task of formulating research questions, and ensuring that they form a consistent set, lies with the researcher (see 'Influences on the Choice of Topic' in chapter 2 above).

Research Questions and Hypotheses

It is a common view that social research should be directed by one or more hypotheses. However, in some types of research it is impossible or inappropriate to set out with hypotheses. In the types of research in which hypotheses are considered to be essential, it is not always clear what the role of these hypotheses is or where they are to come from. In some traditions of research, it is expected that hypotheses will be stated very precisely, in the null and directional forms, to facilitate statistical testing. In other traditions, hypotheses are stated much more loosely, and their acceptance or rejection is a matter of general evidence and rhetoric rather than tests of significance. In practice, hypotheses are drawn from a variety of sources, such as hunches or intuition, previous research, discursive argument and carefully formulated theories. While the latter is advocated in some traditions (see the discussion of the *deductive* research strategy in chapter 4), their source is frequently vague and their purpose unclear.

Lundberg's early (1942) textbook on social research provides a classical view of the role of hypotheses. He argued that there are four steps in 'the scientific method': the formulation of a working hypothesis, the observation and recording of data, the classification and organization of the data collected, and the production of generalizations that apply under given conditions. In this context, Lundberg defined a hypothesis as 'a tentative generalisation, the validity of which remains to be tested. In its most elementary stages, the hypothesis may be any hunch, guess, imaginative idea or intuition whatsoever which becomes the basis for action or investigation' (1942: 9). This view of a hypothesis simply requires the researcher to have a guess at what they think the data might reveal, and then proceed to see if it is the case. So conventional has this view become that the novice researcher feels compelled to make such guesses, even if it makes no sense to do so; one feels naked without a hypothesis for a fig leaf. The fear of not being able to 'prove' their hypothesis hangs like the sword of Damocles over the novice's head; guessing the wrong hypothesis, or the wrong version of it, can be regarded as a disaster. The stress in this tradition of research is on having a hypothesis, not always on where it comes from, what it might be connected to, and what purpose it serves. It is not uncommon to invent such hypotheses after the research has been completed.[2]

Some writers conflate hypotheses and research questions: 'We do research to get answers to questions. Therefore, to do research, we must start with a research question that can be answered. This question is usually stated as a **hypothesis** – an idea, a prediction, capable of being disproven' (Mitchell and Jolley 1992: 15). The confusion is further compounded in their view that hypotheses can be deduced from theories, and that theories can be expressed as a series of hypotheses. From this, it is difficult to know what a research question is and what role it is supposed to play.

It is my view that *hypotheses are tentative answers to 'why' and, sometimes, 'how' research questions*. They are our best guesses at the answers. But they are not appropriate for 'what' questions. There is little point in hazarding guesses at a possible state of affairs. Research will produce an answer to a 'what' question in due course, and no amount of guessing about what will be found is of any assistance; it might even prejudice the answer. Therefore, hypotheses should be reserved for the role of tentative answers to 'why' and 'how' questions, and particularly 'why' questions. While it may not always be possible to produce a hypothesis for such research questions, to do so is to give research a much clearer sense of direction; decisions about what data to gather, and how to analyse them, are easier to make. However, it is important to note that some traditions of research that are concerned with 'why' questions may not set out with hypotheses. In grounded theory, for example, hypotheses are proposed in response to the patterns in the accumulating data, and they will be tested in a continuing trial and error process, being refined and, perhaps, discarded along the way.

A central issue that researchers confront at the stage of formulating research questions and hypotheses (if required) is what concepts to use and how to define them. How this is handled will depend largely on the particular research strategy or strategies, and theories or theoretical perspectives, adopted. This issue will be introduced in the next section and will be discussed in more detail in the early part of chapter 5.

---

[2] I was a victim of this kind of thinking while undertaking research for my master's degree back in the 1960s. The thesis reported over thirty hypotheses, most of which were only very loosely connected to previous research or theory. The research was reported in such a way that it appeared that I had been guided by these hypotheses and had systematically tested them. The whole performance was nothing more than a ritual that I was required to perform by the conventions of the discipline at the time. What I really needed was a clear set of research questions, but none of the textbooks discussed the need for such questions; one had to have hypotheses for the research to be acceptable. Little seems to have changed since then!

Research Questions and the Literature Review

A literature review is a customary component of any research report or thesis. Its main purpose is to provide a background to and context for the research, and to establish a bridge between the project and the current state of knowledge on the topic. This review may include:

- background information that establishes the existence of the problem to be investigated;
- previous research on the topic, or related topics;
- theory of relevance to the 'why' question(s);
- theoretical perspective(s) as a source of concepts as well as ontological and epistemological assumptions;
- methodological considerations of relevance to the selection of a research strategy or strategies; and
- a review and/or elaboration of the methods to be used.

These components of the literature review may end up in various places in the thesis or research report. The first may be part of the introductory chapter; the last two may appear in a methodology and methods chapter; and the fourth may be part of a discussion on the choice of research strategy or strategies. It is the second and third, on previous research and theory, that are particularly relevant to the research questions.

A major dilemma in any research project is to establish what literature to review – what literature is relevant. This can be a daunting and confusing task, particularly for novice researchers. I have observed many students spending an excessive amount of time reading rather aimlessly. Some will not really be satisfied until they have read 'everything', but the problem is to know what to include in 'everything'.

One solution to this problem is to use the research questions to guide and structure the review of previous research and relevant theory. Each question can be used to put a boundary around a body of literature, be it theory, published research or reports. *The aim of the literature review is to indicate what the state of knowledge is with respect to each research question, or group of questions.*

If hypotheses are used, they should have some connection with this literature. In some cases it may be possible to derive such an answer from existing theory, or it may be necessary to construct a new theory for the purpose. As we shall see, within the *deductive* research strategy, the development of a theory from which a hypothesis or hypotheses can be deduced is an essential part of answering 'why' questions. In the *retroductive* research strategy, the literature review may provide some assistance in the construction of hypothetical explanatory models. When the *abductive* research strategy is used for theory generation, hypotheses are an integral part of the continuing process of data collection and analysis, of observation, reflection, hypothesizing and testing. However, advocates of this strategy usually argue that research should *not* begin with hypotheses.

Research Objectives

In contrast to the researcher's personal motives and goals for undertaking a particular research project, research objectives are concerned with the types of knowledge to be produced. Social research can have a number of objectives ranging from relatively simple to very complex, and encompassing both basic and applied research. Research objectives include *exploration, description, explanation, understanding, prediction, change, evaluation,* and *impact assessment* (see figure 3.1).

A research project can pursue just one of these objectives or, perhaps, a number of them in sequence. For example, a study may be purely *descriptive*, or it might begin with a *descriptive* stage and then proceed to *explanation* and then to *change*. Basic research focuses on the first five objectives, *exploration, description, explanation, understanding* and *prediction*, but particularly *description, explanation* and *understanding*. While applied research may include some of these 'basic' objectives, it is particularly concerned with *change, evaluation* and *impact assessment*.

Types of Objectives

Basic Research

To *explore* is to attempt to develop an initial, rough description or, possibly, an understanding of some social phenomenon.

To *describe* is to provide a detailed account or the precise measurement and reporting of the characteristics of some population, group or phenomenon, including establishing regularities.

To *explain* is to establish the elements, factors or mechanisms that are responsible for producing the state of or regularities in a social phenomenon.

To *understand* is to establish reasons for particular social action, the occurrence of an event or the course of a social episode, these reasons being derived from the ones given by social actors.

To *predict* is to use some established understanding or explanation of a phenomenon to postulate certain outcomes under particular conditions.

Applied Research

To *change* is to intervene in a social situation by manipulating some aspects of it, or to assist the participants in doing so, preferably on the basis of established understanding or explanation.

To *evaluate* is to monitor social intervention programmes to assess whether they have achieved their desired outcomes, and to assist with problem-solving and policy-making.

To *assess social impacts* is to identify the likely social and cultural consequences of planned projects, technological change or policy actions on social structures, social processes and/or people.

In case you might be wondering why *comparison* is not included as a research objective, I regard it either as a form of *description* or as a technique for arriving at *explanation* or *understanding*, i.e. for theory generation or testing. In fact, comparison is one of the best methods for generating theory, as is evident in grounded theory (Strauss and Corbin 1999). As such, it is not an objective but it can be a means for achieving such objectives. Therefore, a list of objectives should not include statements like 'To compare the environmental attitudes of university students and logging contractors'. A research project might set out to *describe* the attitudes of each group, and to try to *explain* why they hold particular attitudes, but a comparison of their attitudes can be part of either of these objectives.

Exploration Exploratory research is necessary when very little is known about the topic being investigated, or about the context in which the research is to be conducted. Perhaps the topic has never been investigated before, or never in that particular context. Basic demographic characteristics of a group of people, or some aspects of their behaviour or social relationships, may need to be known in order to design the study. The relevance of particular research questions, or the feasibility of using certain methods of data gathering, may also need to be explored. Essentially, exploratory research is used to get a better idea of what is going on and how it might be researched.

While exploratory research is usually conducted at the beginning of a research project, it may also be necessary at other stages to provide information for critical design decisions, to overcome an unexpected problem, to better understand an unanticipated finding, or to establish which avenues of explanation would be worthwhile pursuing.

The methods used to conduct exploratory research need to be flexible and do not need to be as rigorous as those used to pursue other objectives. The researcher may need to be creative and resourceful in gaining access to the information required. In terms of the pursuit of other objectives in later stages of the research, exploratory research is double-edged. On the one hand, it may help to establish rapport with individuals or groups being studied and thus smooth the way for later stages of the project; on the other hand, it has the potential danger of raising suspicion and developing resistance. Therefore the management of exploratory research cannot be taken lightly, as it may have long-term consequences for the project.

In the context of his advocacy of symbolic interactionism, Blumer (1969) gave exploratory research a more substantial role. He believed this was necessary to counter the common tendency to move straight into research without an adequate understanding of the sector of social life being investigated. He saw the exploratory phase as being necessary to sharpen the focus of the research; not as an optional extra, but as an essential part of any project.

> On the one hand, it is the way by which a research scholar can form a close and comprehensive acquaintance with a sphere of social life that is unfamiliar and hence unknown to him [*sic*]. On the other hand, it is a means of developing and sharpening

his inquiry so that his problem, his directions of inquiry, data, analytical relations, and interpretations arise out of, and remain grounded in, the empirical life under study. Exploration is by definition a flexible procedure in which the scholar shifts from one to another line of inquiry, adopts new points of observation as his study progresses, moves in new directions previously unthought of, and changes his recognition of what are relevant data as he acquires more information and better understanding. In these respects, exploratory study stands in contrast to the prescribed and circumscribed procedure demanded by current scientific protocol. The flexibility of exploratory procedure does not mean that there is no direction to the inquiry; it means that the focus is originally broad but becomes progressively sharpened as the inquiry proceeds. The purpose of exploratory investigation is to move toward a clearer understanding of how one's problem is to be posed, to learn what are the appropriate data, to develop ideas of what are significant lines of relation, and to evolve one's conceptual tools in the light of what one is learning about the area of life. (Blumer 1969: 40)

Exploratory research should provide as detailed and accurate a picture of the phenomenon as is necessary to enable the researcher to feel at home and to be able to speak about the research problem with some confidence.

> The picture provides the scholar with a secure bearing so that he knows that the questions he asks of the empirical area are meaningful and relevant to it, that the problem he poses is not artificial, that the kinds of data he seeks are significant in terms of the empirical world, and that the leads he follows are faithful to its nature. (Blumer 1969: 42)

Blumer has left us in no doubt about how essential exploratory research is to the development of a good research design.

Description   Descriptive research seeks to present an accurate account of some phenomenon, the distribution of characteristics in some population, the patterns of relationships in some social context, at a particular time, or the changes in those characteristics over time (Bulmer 1986: 66). These descriptive accounts can be expressed in words or numbers. They can include the characteristics of a social group or a demographic category, the stages or sequences in social processes, or patterns in social relationships. They may involve the development of sets of categories or types.

In practice, the boundary between exploratory and descriptive research is blurred. Descriptive research is more rigorous and is usually narrower in its focus; it should be directed by clearly stated research questions. However, both types of research require the use of concepts and they will be structured by at least some theoretical assumptions.

Explanation and understanding   Explanatory research seeks to account for patterns in observed social phenomena, attitudes, behaviour, social relationships, social processes or social structures (Bulmer 1986: 66–7). *Explanation* is making intelligible the events or regularities that have been observed and which cannot be accounted for by existing theories; explanation eliminates puzzles. To explain some phenomenon is to give an account of why it behaves in a particular way or why particular regularities occur.

Explanations provide intellectual satisfaction; they make the obscure plain to see. This is true of both semantic and scientific explanation. Semantic explanation is concerned with the meanings of words and phrases, while scientific explanation seeks the causes for the occurrence of a particular event or regularity. However, making something intelligible is not just a subjective matter.

> There is a difference between *having* an explanation and *seeing* it. In the case of semantic explanation, we do not have one unless and until we see it, but in the case of scientific explanation either the having or the seeing may occur without the other. That an explanation is often resisted when it is first offered is a commonplace of the history of science – men [*sic*] have it, but do not see it. The reverse is characteristic of the sort of explanations occurring in myths, paranoia, the occult 'sciences', and the like.... They provide a certain intellectual satisfaction, but it is one unwarranted by the actual state of affairs. Those who accept them only see an explanation, but do not have one. (Kaplan 1964: 330)

In everyday language, *explanation* refers to all attempts to achieve intelligibility. In short, explanations produce understanding. However, it could be argued that descriptions also provide understanding; they give us the details of what is going on. Detailed descriptions can begin to provide the beginnings of explanations. Nevertheless, I am going to use the distinction between *explanation* and *understanding* that has been discussed by writers such as Taylor (1964) and von Wright (1971) and, subsequently, by Giddens (1979: 258). The latter regarded them as different ways of answering queries in the social sciences.

The difference between *explanation* and *understanding* is a matter of how intelligibility is achieved; it is the difference between *causal* explanation and *reason* explanation. *Explanations* identify *causes* of events or regularities, the factors or mechanisms that produced them, and *understanding* is provided by the *reasons* or accounts social actors give for their actions. The latter is also associated with the *meaning* of an event or activity in a particular social context, either that given by social actors or the meaning that researchers derive from social actors' accounts. *Explanations* are produced by researchers who look at a phenomenon from the 'outside', while *understanding* is based on an 'inside' view in which researchers grasp the subjective consciousness, the interpretations, of social actors involved in the conduct (Giddens 1976: 55).

The distinction between *erklären* (to explain) and *verstehen* (to understand) has a long history in German scholarship. While some writers (e.g. Winch 1958) have argued that causal explanation is appropriate in the natural sciences and reason explanation is appropriate in the human or social sciences, other writers have argued either that both can be used in the social sciences (e.g. Habermas 1972), or that characterizing the two fields of science as being exclusively concerned with only one of these is inappropriate (e.g. Giddens 1976). The position adopted here is that both *explanation* and *understanding* are appropriate objectives in the social sciences, but that they produce rather different kinds of intelligibility.

Hence, various strategies to achieve *explanation* or *understanding*, based on different assumptions and the use of different logics of enquiry, have been advocated in both the natural and social sciences. These strategies look in different places and in terms of different factors or mechanisms for answers to their puzzles. In chapter 4, three of these explanatory strategies (the *inductive*, *deductive* and *retroductive*), and one that is used to achieve understanding (the *abductive*), will be outlined and compared in terms of their relevance to the design and conduct of social research. For the present, a brief introduction to them will have to suffice.

In the *inductive* research strategy, explanation is achieved by locating a particular pattern within a known and more general pattern or network of relationships (Kaplan 1964: 298, 333). The growth of knowledge is achieved by indefinitely filling in and extending the patterns. This form of explanation is also known as structural explanation, using network or functional theories. Network explanations have three main forms: they refer to broader patterns of which the case in point can be seen as a specific case; they identify developmental sequences in social relationships; or they specify certain patterns in the way interaction occurs. Functional explanations locate events or patterns of behaviour and relationships within a larger social system; the phenomenon being investigated is explained in terms of the functions it performs for the larger system (Neuman 1997: 53–5).

In the *deductive* research strategy, explanation is achieved by constructing a deductive argument to which the phenomenon to be explained is the conclusion. The premises of the argument will be either well-established abstract propositions, or hypothetical propositions that are to be tested. While each proposition in the argument may consist of nothing more than a statement of a relationship between two concepts, a set of such propositions provides the *explanation* by linking the lower-level concepts, associated with the described pattern, to more abstract theoretical concepts.

The *retroductive* research strategy seeks to explain a pattern by locating the causal mechanism that produces it. The pattern of association between two concepts is usually viewed as entailing a direction of influence, and the existence of a causal mechanism provides the *explanation* for the influence. For example, the explanation of the association between religion and occupation, which was of concern to Weber (1958) as part of his account of the rise of capitalism in Europe, can be explained by the mechanism of the meaning particular social actors gave to work.[3]

This type of causal explanation should not be confused with more common forms which, while not fitting neatly into any of these three research strategies, comes closest to the *deductive* strategy. The classical conception involves a cause and an effect, and is based on four principles:

- temporal order in which the cause must precede the effect;
- association which requires that the two events occur together;
- the elimination of alternatives in order to be able to claim that the effect was due to the specified cause and not something else; and

---

[3] While Weber did not frame his explanation in this way, it is possible to reconstruct his concern with the meaning of work as a causal mechanism. This example will be taken up again later.

- making sense of the causal relationship in terms of broader theoretical ideas or assumptions.

Another version involves not just one cause but a sequence or chain of events or variables which cumulatively produce the effect. While it is normally expressed in diagrammatic form and/or in statistical models rather than as a deductive argument, this view of causal explanation does much the same as a deductive argument: they both involve connected sequences of relationships between concepts, which together produce an *explanation*.

The fourth research strategy is different from the other three in that it is the only one that specifically addresses the objective of *understanding*. *Abduction* is the logic of enquiry in which the researcher, at least initially, takes on the role of learner and seeks to be educated by the people being studied. The initial task is to learn about their form of life and the way they conceptualize and make sense of it. With this knowledge as an ingredient, the researcher may then proceed to redescribe lay accounts of the social world in social scientific language. The objective is to both describe and understand the problem at hand.

Whereas *explanation* is concerned with abstract patterns of relationships in deductive arguments or causal sequences, *understanding* is concerned with the reasons social actors give for their actions. The focus is not so much on the explanations that the researcher constructs but on the explanations social actors can offer and which can be used by the social researcher to construct a social scientific account of their activity.

Prediction   The objective of *prediction* in research is to make claims about what *should* happen under certain conditions. *Prediction* needs to be distinguished from prophecy; the latter makes claims about what will happen in the future while the former makes claims about what will happen if certain laws or mechanisms operate under certain conditions (Popper 1961: 128). Prediction involves time only in the sense that, whenever particular laws or mechanisms operate under the specified conditions, the predicted outcome can be expected. Therefore, the possibility of prediction is dependent on the state of knowledge at a particular time.

Prediction can be achieved in two ways: in terms of well-established patterns of association between concepts (as in the *inductive* research strategy); or by shifting the emphasis in a theoretical argument (as in the *deductive* research strategy). In the case of established patterns, whenever one part of a relationship is present, it can be expected that the other part will also be present. For example, if it has been consistently established that juvenile delinquents come from broken homes, then locating particular juvenile delinquents can lead to the prediction that they will be found to have come from broken homes, or, alternatively, that children from broken homes are likely to become delinquents.

Some writers have argued that the logic involved in *explanation* and *prediction* is essentially the same; it is just a matter of where the emphasis is put and what can be taken as given (Popper 1959, 1961; Hempel 1966). This claim is based on the assumption that a set of propositions that has been used as an explanation of an observed pattern can also be used to predict another pattern. For example, if an explanation has been constructed to explain why the suicide rate is low in a country in which a particular religion is predominant, and if religion has been shown in the deductive argument to be related to suicide rates (as Durkheim claimed to have established), then it is possible to predict that other countries of a similar religious composition will have similar suicide rates (see the discussion of Homans's (1964) reconstruction of Durkheim's theory of suicide in chapter 4).

Writers who have advocated the *retroductive* research strategy (e.g. Bhaskar, 1979) have argued that *prediction* is only possible in closed systems, perhaps only under experimental conditions. As social scientists have to work in open systems, it follows that prediction is not possible in the social sciences. While *explanation* in terms of causal mechanisms is possible, there is no scope for *prediction* because the conditions under which a mechanism operates can never be fully established. As the natural sciences also operate in open systems, apart from artificially controlled experiments, the advocates of this position also claim that prediction is not possible in the natural sciences.

Change   Research that adopts the objective of *change* endeavours to intervene in the social world to bring about partial or major changes, either in conjunction with the research itself, or as a consequence of the research outcomes. Change can only be achieved with confidence if the actions taken are based on those that a well-established *explanation* or *understanding* would suggest. However, the process of intervention itself can be used as a learning process. Knowledge of a phenomenon can be developed in a trial and error process, as intervention is conducted in stages. What is learnt from one stage can be used to decide what action to take in the next stage. The outcome can be *understanding* and *explanation*, as well as *change*. In fact, some philosophers of science (e.g. Popper) have argued that this trial and error process is the only way scientific knowledge can be advanced; that all research involves the use of 'piecemeal technology' rather than gigantic leaps into unknown territory. Nevertheless, it is possible to distinguish between intervention that is used primarily for the purpose of advancing knowledge, and intervention that tries to change the world; between purely scientific concerns or essentially social or political concerns; between basic research and applied research.

The 'action research' tradition has the joint objectives of increasing knowledge and changing some aspect of the world at the same time. It differs from more conventional research in that the researcher may take the role of facilitator or resource person to help a group of people change their own situation from the inside, rather than the researcher adopting the role of outside expert who tries to bring about change by 'external' intervention (see e.g. Winter 1987, 1989; McNiff 1988; Oja and Smulyan 1989; Whyte 1991; Stringer 1996; Zuber-Skerrit 1996).

Some schools of social theory (e.g. critical theory and feminist theory) have argued that *change* is the fundamental objective of social science; all other objectives must serve that of the emancipation of oppressed groups. Therefore, while the objective of *change* may be regarded as an add-on stage in research, it has been regarded by some as being either the only way to generate scientific knowledge, or the only legitimate form of social science.

Hence, intervention research may adopt 'outside' or 'inside' methods; it may be done to a group or community at the researcher's initiative, or on behalf of someone else, or it may be done in conjunction with, or as a result of the initiative of, a group or community. In the latter case, it is directed towards the goals *they* have defined or have been helped to define. This type of research is usually referred to as 'participatory action research' (Whyte 1991).

Intervention research can also be done 'top down', thus serving the needs of the powerful, or 'bottom up' by serving the needs of the powerless. Hence, it may be viewed loosely as either 'radical' or 'conservative'. Radical interventionist research is emancipatory research that is designed to improve the conditions of less powerful sections of society and to replace oppressive regimes (Habermas 1971, 1987; Fay 1975, 1987; Bhaskar 1979, 1986). Some radical interventionist research is also 'bottom up' because it begins with the felt needs of oppressed people, it helps them to understand the causes of their oppression and then it tries to bring about change to overcome it. A major example of 'radical' intervention research is that based on critical theory (Fay 1987; Habermas 1987). Habermas has described this kind of researcher as being a 'reflective partner' who helps to raise consciousness and facilitate action.

More conservative versions of intervention research can be found in fields such as organizational change. While some organizational research may be concerned with producing a more humane working environment, and with the welfare of employees, generally the ultimate concern is to bring about changes that will achieve greater productivity and efficiency.

Evaluation   *Evaluation* research, as well as *impact assessment* of various kinds, is concerned with policy and programme development and implementation in particular, and with problem-solving and decision-making in general. Evaluative research seeks to examine the consequences of the adoption of particular courses of action. It sets out to determine whether a particular policy or programme has achieved what it set out to achieve, that is, the extent to which it has been effective in achieving certain policy or programme goals. Evaluation research compares 'what is' with 'what should be' (Weiss 1972: 6): 'The purpose of evaluation research is to measure the effects of a program against the goals it set out to accomplish as a means of contributing to subsequent decision making about the program and improving future programming' (Weiss 1972: 4).

Evaluation research has many uses:

- to continue or discontinue a programme;
- to improve a programme's practices and procedures;
- to add or drop specific programme strategies and techniques;
- to institute similar programmes elsewhere;
- to allocate resources amongst competing programmes; and
- to accept or reject a programme approach or theory (Weiss 1972: 16–17; Bulmer 1986: 156).

However, Weiss has argued that, in practice, 'evaluation is most often called on to help with decisions about improving programs. Go/no go, live or die decisions, are relatively rare' (1972: 17).

Evaluation research seeks answers to questions posed by decision-makers, not academics. However, as Levine (1987: 30–1) has pointed out, in providing decision-makers with analysed information, the evaluation researcher has to accept that these decisions are likely to be made according to poorly specified personal, political and national goals.

In arguing for 'responsive constructivist evaluation', Guba and Lincoln (1989) have shifted the focus from decision-makers to the claims, concerns and issues of stakeholders. The latter include any groups whose stake may be placed in jeopardy by the evaluation. Their concern is to adopt an approach that will make it possible to take the concerns of all stakeholders into account.

There are two types of evaluation research: *formative evaluation*, in which built-in monitoring or continuous feedback is used during the implementation of a policy as a basis for helping to improve it; and *summative evaluation*, which is conducted after a policy has been implemented to establish its overall effectiveness in achieving the original goals.

Pawson and Tilley (1997) have identified four main perspectives on evaluation research: the *experimental* (Campbell and Stanley 1963a; Cook and Campbell 1979); the *pragmatic* (Weiss 1972, 1976; Weiss and Bucuvalas 1980); the *naturalistic* (Guba and Lincoln 1989); and the *pluralist* (Cronbach 1963, 1982; Rossi and Freeman 1985). The first on the scene in the 1960s, the *experimental* perspective, used classical or quasi-experimental procedures to try to establish whether change is the result of the planned intervention. In the wake of disappointing results from this first phase, the *pragmatic* perspective became less ambitious and advocated the careful use of any kind of sound research. The *naturalistic* perspective took a different turn and saw evaluation as a matter of negotiation between stakeholders with different interpretations (constructions) of a programme. The *pluralists* called for greater depth and breadth in programme evaluation by examining the way programmes are conceptualized, dealing with both institutional and individual diagnoses of the problem and focusing on outcome effectiveness. Pawson and Tilley have added a fifth perspective, *realistic evaluation*, based on scientific realism (see chapter 4), for which they claim superiority over the other perspectives. They have provided eight rules for the conduct of evaluation research.

Commonly used tools in both *evaluation* research and *impact assessment* are *needs analysis* and *cost-benefit analysis*. However, it is because of the deficiencies in cost-benefit analysis, due to its narrow economic focus, that the development of both *social impact assessment* and *environmental impact assessment* has occurred.

Impact assessment   Impact assessment (IA) has been defined as '*the process of identifying the future consequences of a current or proposed action*' (Becker 1997: 2). In the case of social impact assessment (SIA), these consequences are related to '*individuals, organizations, institutions and society as a whole*' (Becker 1997: 123). Following the definition of SIA in the United States by the Inter-organizational Committee on Guidelines and Principles (1994), Burdge and Vanclay have included cultural as well as social impacts. They include

> all social and cultural consequences to human populations of any public and private
> actions that alter the way in which people live, work, play, relate to one another,

organise to meet their needs, and generally cope as members of society. Cultural impacts involve changes to norms, values, and beliefs of individuals that guide and rationalise their cognition of themselves and their society. (Burdge and Vanclay 1995: 32)

Becker limited his definition of SIA to future consequences of present or proposed actions. The assessment of the consequences of past actions is seen to be part of evaluation research. However, because of the particular concerns in the practice of SIA, it is possible to work with a broader definition. Hence SIA can be concerned with assessing or predicting the demographic, socio-economic, institutional, community and psychological impacts of resource development and large-scale construction projects, as well as social or economic policies and programmes. The tasks of SIAs are to:

- assess and predict potential impacts;
- mitigate and monitor these impacts; and
- audit and analyse the impacts of past actions.

Social impact assessment attempts to complement the study of natural, or biophysical, environmental impacts with information on the social and socio-economic impacts which may be associated with a new project, policy or programme. These impacts, or alterations in living conditions, include changes in psychological and physiological factors, community processes, and changes in the production, distribution and consumption of goods and services. (Bulmer 1986: 146)

For example, a major road construction scheme may lead to population movements, the fragmentation of social communities, psychological stress and changes in property values. Similarly, a new social welfare policy may lead to disadvantages among groups that it was supposed to benefit. SIA will endeavour to identify the range and extent of such impacts; it can be used to trade off the benefits of the project (e.g. reduced traffic congestion and accidents) against social costs. An important aspect of *social impact assessment* is the relative gains and losses that particular groups in a community or society are likely to experience as the result of a construction project. Some form of compensation for such losses might then be built into the costing of the project (see also Finsterbusch 1983, 1985).

In many ways, SIA has grown out of the related and increasingly significant field of *environmental impact assessment* (EIA). While the latter's primary concern is with the natural and biophysical impacts of major physical projects, it is now generally accepted that EIA and SIA are complementary and that the latter must accompany the former.

A narrow definition of EIA is the assessment of the impact of a planned activity on the environment. However, it can be conceived more widely as a process for identifying, predicting and evaluating the biogeographical, socio-economic and human health and welfare consequences of implementing particular activities (Wathern 1988). The ultimate purpose is to indicate to decision-makers the likely consequences of their action, and, therefore, to improve the quality of their decisions (Wathern 1988; Ortolano and Shepherd 1995).

The positive influences of EIA are:

- withdrawal of unsound projects;
- legitimation of sound projects;
- selection of improved locations;
- reformulation of plans, for example land use;
- redefinition of goals and responsibilities of project proponents (van de Gronden 1994: 12–18; Ortolano and Shepherd 1995: 8–9).

Relationships among Research Objectives

The four research objectives of *exploration, description, explanation* and *prediction* can occur as a sequence in terms of both the stages and the increasing complexity of research. *Exploration* usually precedes *description*, and *description* is necessary before *explanation* or *prediction* can be attempted. *Exploration* may be necessary to provide clues about the patterns that need to be described in a particular phenomenon. The sequence, beginning with the *description* of patterns, and followed by an *explanation* of why they occur, is central in any form of social research. Description of what is happening leads to questions or puzzles about why it is happening, and this calls for an explanation or some kind of understanding.

The importance of *description* is often underrated in research, with *explanation* being seen as the ultimate goal. However, without adequate description there may be nothing to explain; it is necessary to be sure what the patterns or regularities are before any attempt is made to explain them. In addition, some forms of *explanation* for example, pattern explanations, are nothing more than complex descriptions. It has been argued that explanation works 'not by involving something beyond what might be described, but by putting one fact or law in relation to others' (Kaplan 1964: 329). This is known as the 'pattern' model of explanation and is characteristic of the *inductive* research strategy (to be discussed in chapter 4).

There are a variety of views on the relationship between *explanation* and *prediction*. It is possible to make *predictions* without having an *explanation* of a phenomenon. This kind of *prediction* relies on well-established generalizations about patterns of relationships between concepts, sometimes referred to as statistical laws. It is a common belief that the natural sciences aim to establish *universal laws* about the regularities in the natural world, laws that are claimed to hold at all times and in all places. Whether it is possible to establish such laws in the social sciences is a matter of considerable dispute. What might be claimed is that the social sciences can establish patterns or regularities, but that these are limited in time and space. The concept of statistical law refers to such regularities.

While some philosophers have argued that these patterns provide a basis for *explanation*, others have argued that it is necessary to find the mechanism that produces such patterns before explanation can be achieved (see chapter 4). However, the *description* of patterns or relationships between concepts can be used for *prediction*.

The objectives of *evaluation* and *impact assessment* share much in common. They, together with *intervention*, constitute the main fields of applied research. As we have seen, a major distinguishing feature of applied research is that it has a sponsor and/or client. Its goals are either set by the sponsor, or are the outcome of negotiation between the sponsor and researcher, and its outcomes have to address the concerns of the client. While it may be possible to attempt *evaluation* and *impact assessment* from an atheoretical point of view, by building on only a descriptive research base and side-stepping the objectives of *explanation* or *under-standing*, sophisticated *evaluation* and *impact assessment* need to use existing theories. If relevant theories are not available, they will need to be developed. Because applied research is normally done within severe time and resource constraints, there is pressure to take short cuts to avoid these essential components. Good applied research has to draw on well-established theories, because, after all, there is nothing as practical as a good theory.

It is unlikely that the whole gambit of objectives can be or need to be tackled in most research projects, and certainly not within the limitations of post-graduate research. Previous research may have achieved some objectives that can be used as a background in a particular research project. For example, if good *descriptive* research has already been done in the field, it may be possible to begin with an *explanatory* objective, or if well-established and relevant theories are available, it may be possible to engage directly in the objectives of *change*, *evaluation* or *impact assessment*. But, to repeat an earlier comment, without an adequate descriptive base, it is not possible to begin to pursue the other research objectives.

Research Objectives and Questions

Each of the eight research objectives is related to a particular type of research question. If we take some imaginary social process as an example, the three types of research questions would be associated with the eight research objectives are as follows.

Exploration	**What** might be happening?
	What people are involved? In **what** way?
Description	**What** is happening?
	What people are involved? In **what** way?
Understanding	**Why** is it happening?
Explanation	**Why** is it happening?
Prediction	**What** is likely to happen?
Change	**How** can it be made to be different?
Evaluation	**What** has happened? **Why** did it happen?
Assessment	**What** have been, or are likely to be, its individual, social and environmental consequences? **Why** have these consequences occurred?

The objectives of *understanding* and *explanation*,[4] and, to a lesser extent, *evaluation* and *impact assessment*, are the only ones that require 'why'-type

---

[4] While *understanding* and *explanation* entail the same kind of research question, it is necessary to keep them separate as research objectives as they answer 'why' questions in different ways.

questions. *Change* is the only objective that requires 'how'-type questions. All the other objectives have questions beginning with 'what', or their questions can be transposed into this form. They are, therefore, either descriptive in nature, or involve comparisons between situations in the present, between a present and a past situation, or between a present situation and a desired future. To avoid the confusion that can result from other question wording, for example the pursuit of the objectives of *description* or *explanation* with questions that commence with 'how', this three-category classification of questions should be followed.

Conclusion

By way of summary, let me review the key points that emerge from this discussion of the role of research questions in social research.

- All research projects are built on the foundation of research questions.
- Research questions define the nature and scope of a research project.
- Research questions can be grouped into three main types, 'what', 'why' and 'how' questions.
- The three types of questions form a sequence for the research process; 'what' questions followed by 'why' questions followed by 'how' questions.
- Many research objectives require 'what' questions. It is only the aims of *understanding* and *explanation*, and possibly *evaluation* and *impact assessment*, that require 'why' questions, and the aim of *change* that requires 'how' questions.
- The importance of answering 'what' questions should not underestimated.
- The developmental nature of a research design should not be used as an excuse to avoid the effort required to formulate appropriate research questions.
- While the process of developing a set of research questions can be the most challenging part of any research project, techniques are available to assist the process.
- Research questions are what the research is designed to answer, not the questions asked of respondents or participants.
- The aim of the literature review is to indicate what the state of knowledge is with respect to each research question, or group of questions.
- Hypotheses are our best guesses at answering 'why' and, possibly, 'how' questions.
- If required, hypotheses should be derived from the literature review, particularly from theory or research results. On rare occasions, a theory may have to be generated.
- In some research, hypotheses may emerge, and be tested, in the course of the data collection and analysis.

As an aid to the conception, clarification and classification of research questions, it is useful to think about a research project in terms of its objectives. These objectives are not a list of the activities the researcher is going to carry out. Rather, they can be either the analytical or the practical aims of a project.

4

Strategies for Answering Research Questions

Every inquiry must start somewhere. (Kaplan 1964)

Introduction

Having established a set of research questions, the next task is to devise ways to answer them. The approach taken to answering research questions depends on the type of question. Answering a 'what' question is usually easier than answering a 'why' or 'how' question. 'What' questions can be dealt with by making appropriate observations or measurements, i.e. collecting appropriate data, and then producing descriptions based on them. However, this process is not as simple as it sounds; descriptions of what we believe we have observed may not be, perhaps cannot be, pure descriptions. The observer, as an active participant in the process, has to make many decisions before a description can be produced, and cannot avoid imposing concepts and categories.

Answers to 'how' questions require a different kind of description; a possible state of affairs has to be described and ideas about how to get there have to be provided. As we saw in chapter 3, 'how' questions usually require answers to related 'what' and 'why' questions, either in the research being undertaken, or in previous research. Unless a good understanding of the nature of the phenomenon being investigated has already been achieved, and why it behaves the way it does, it is difficult, undesirable and even dangerous to begin to propose any form of intervention. However, the monitoring of limited interventions in 'safe' situations (i.e. ones that will not have ethically undesirable or socially unacceptable consequences) is one way of discovering answers to 'why' and 'how' questions. Action research is such a learning process. I will come back to the ways of answering 'what' and 'how' questions later in the chapter. In the meantime, I want to concentrate on how to answer 'why' questions.

The main problem in answering 'why' questions is where to look for the answers. How we deal with this will determine where the research process begins and how it

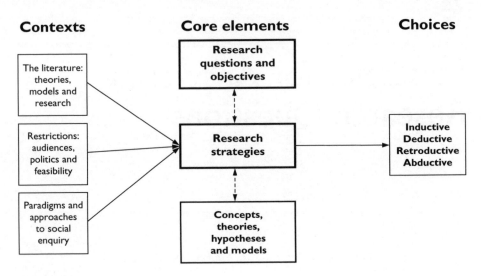

Figure 4.1   Research strategies

will proceed. Answering them involves dealing with theory in one form or another; *explanation* and *understanding* require either a theory or a very complex description. Hence 'why' questions present us with complex issues and choices.

There is a daunting array of possibilities. Are the answers to be found by collecting data and generalizing from them, by finding a suitable theory that will provide some hypotheses to test, by searching for underlying causal mechanisms, or by seeking social actors' meanings and interpretations? The choice made from alternatives such as these will depend on the research strategy that is adopted. A *research strategy*, sometimes called a logic of enquiry, provides a starting-point and set of steps by means of which 'what' or 'why' questions can be answered. Research strategies differ in their:

- ontological assumptions;
- starting-points;
- steps or logic;
- use of concepts and theory;
- styles of explanation and understanding; and
- the status of their products.

I shall discuss four research strategies; the *inductive, deductive, retroductive* and *abductive* (see figure 4.1). Each strategy has connections with particular philosophical and theoretical traditions, i.e. approaches to social enquiry (see Blaikie 1993a). As a preamble to their elaboration, the following parable is presented as a way of exploring the characteristics of the research strategies.

A Parable of Four Paradigms: Part I

Imagine you are a member of a group of social scientists that has just arrived on a strange planet inhabited by human-like creatures. It appears that these creatures have a sophisticated form of social life, although it bears little resemblance to that anywhere on Earth. The task of your group is to begin to describe and understand this totally different form of social life and to discover what kinds of social problems they experience. A major difficulty that confronts you is to know where to begin and how to proceed.

Perhaps, one day, social scientists may be faced with the same problem of understanding the social life of creatures from outer space. However, variations of this dilemma are encountered in much social research. This example just happens to be at the extreme end of a continuum, the other end of which is the everyday social world or worlds that the researcher inhabits. Between the very unfamiliar and the very familiar lies a range of forms of social life, each with its own challenges for the social researcher.

One of the dangers of conducting research in one's own society is to assume that, because it is familiar, research can proceed in a straightforward manner. However, societies of any size and complexity are heterogeneous in terms of worldviews, culture and lifestyles, and, in many cases, in language as well. In today's world, the fact of large-scale inter-country migration exacerbates this complexity. Normally, members of such societies, as well as social scientists, will experience only a limited range of this diversity. This means that social scientists are always likely to encounter unfamiliar social territory.

A consequence of this diversity and limited individual experience is that social research is much more complex than is frequently implied by textbooks on social research methods. The researcher has to develop an adequate acquaintance with the variety of sub-worlds that are present. The dominant ways of doing social research do not usually give this sufficient recognition.

To address the problem of where to begin and how to proceed, I want to explore the four major research strategies that are available in the social sciences, and to relate them to social research practice. These four strategies constitute four different ways of generating new social scientific knowledge. They provide fundamentally different procedures, with different starting-points and steps or stages that follow.

I believe that the choice of a research strategy is fundamental to any research design. This is because the research strategy has a large bearing on all the other decisions that have to be made in planning and designing a research project. To introduce the basic principles of the four research strategies, I have constructed a parable that reverses the situation in the opening paragraph of this section of the chapter. It reports a visit to Earth of some social scientists from outer space. The first part of the parable follows here; the second part will be found in chapter 7. If, after reading the first part of the parable, you feel you would like to read the two parts together, I invite you to do so. It was originally written that way. However, as some of the ideas may be unfamiliar, you may prefer to read each section in the context to which it relates. Of course, you may prefer to do it both ways!

Social Scientists from Outer Space

Once upon a time in the recent future, a craft arrived from outer space with a party of alien social scientists on board. Visits to Earth by inhabitants from the planet of Jarak Jauh (JJ) had occurred previously, but this was the first time that one had been made up of social scientists. Of course, the first visits to Earth had been greeted with both great alarm and curiosity. Obviously, it took some time before even elementary communication could be established, and then only with a few localized groups of Earthlings. Later visits were tolerated as the intentions of the Jarak Jauhans (JJans) turned out to be peaceful. Because visits to JJ were being planned, every effort was made to maintain good relations.

On this visit, the JJans landed in the spacious grounds of a university campus, and, after some difficult negotiations with the university authorities, due to communication problems, permission was given to roam freely about most of the campus. Because they were such a curiosity, the students tried to communicate with them in order to learn about life on JJ.[1]

As a result of their previous visits, the JJans had gained some ideas about the physical features and flora and fauna on Earth, and they were aware of the physical form and some individual behaviour of Earthlings. However, they had not achieved any understanding of their social and cultural forms and patterns, nor of how and why particular human behaviour and social relationships occur.

The aim of this expedition was to compare Earthly social life with that on JJ and to see if this would help the JJans to find new ways of dealing with their social problems. They had set themselves some very general questions.

What are the dominant patterns of social relationships on Earth?

Why do such patterns exist?

To what extent have these patterns changed over time?

What have been the consequences of these changes?

However, they realized that while these questions satisfied the authorities on JJ that were funding the expedition, they would need to focus their research on some more specific questions.

Some navigation problems on the final descent forced the JJans to land on an open area that turned out to be the sports fields of the campus. It was not immediately clear to them just where they had landed and what Earthly activities were taking place there.

---

[1] One area of curiosity was, of course, how JJans reproduce. The students decided to set up a demonstration and invited the JJans to participate. The JJans selected two members of the expedition, and the students found a willing married couple from among their colleagues. The JJan pair stood facing each other and rubbed their antennae together. After some time, a drawer opened in the front of one of them and a baby JJan was lifted out. The Earthling pair then provided their demonstration. After it was over, the JJans asked where the baby was; they were told it was necessary to wait nine months. They then asked what all the hurry was at the end. (Adapted with appreciation from the joke competition conducted by the BBC World Service and a listener from the south of France.)

This was only partially revealed in the course of their research. However, they decided to confine their investigations to the campus precincts as this allowed them to live on their spacecraft and to move about without needing to use their personal rocket transporters.[2]

For many years on JJ there had been raging debates about the best way to advance knowledge of their culture, social life, social institutions and social structures. The protagonists gradually formed themselves into four paradigmatic research communities known as the Inductivists, the Deductivists, the Retroductivists and the Abductivists. When the expedition to Earth was planned, the authorities agreed to include teams from each of these social scientific communities. The idea was to use the research on Earth to establish the relative merits of these paradigms, and their accompanying research strategies, for advancing knowledge of social life on JJ. Therefore, the visitors decided to do their research on the campus in the four teams, each one using what it regarded as the best strategy of social research.

Exploration

Before they started the serious stage of their research, the JJans sent out an exploratory party to select the aspects of human social life on which they would focus. They accepted the idea that any comparison of the four research strategies must be made on the same research problem. The exploratory party consisted of the leader and an elected representative from each of the four teams. They met and agreed to focus attention on the human activities in the confined spaces that the Earthlings inhabited on the campus, as well as on the types of Earthlings to be found in them. The members of the party made a number of excursions around the campus individually, recording what they observed on their wrist-communicating computers. After an agreed period, they met to consolidate their observations and to prepare a report for their colleagues.

The JJans had discovered that the inhabitants of this part of Earth ranged in age. However, most of the Earthlings appeared to be young, although a few were older. Some of the older Earthlings behaved differently from the younger ones. This was most evident in the spaces in which they met during the 'lights', and sometimes in the 'darks'.[3] The Earthlings usually met together for a 'chime', and sometimes for longer periods.[4]

These spaces varied in size, and, therefore, in the numbers of Earthlings that gathered in them. Some spaces were very large with up to 500 Earthlings present at

---

[2] JJan physiology had become adapted to this technology such that unaided movement over distances of more than a kilometre was no longer physically possible.

[3] On JJ, the alternating intervals between day and night are called 'lights' and 'darks', and a combination of one cycle is called a 'lark'. They had noted that the length of a 'lark' on Earth was very much shorter than on JJ.

[4] The exploratory party had observed some regularities in the duration that the groups of Earthlings met together and they decided to define a unit of time as being equivalent to the shortest normal duration. They had also noticed that the start of each interval usually corresponded with a chiming sound from a tall part of one structure. The number of chimes changed at the beginning of each period, starting with one and then increasing by one each time, until they reached twelve. Then the cycle repeated itself. They therefore decided to call each interval a 'chime', with the number of chimes identifying a particular period during the 'light' or 'dark'.

a time. At the other extreme, there were small spaces in which only two or three Earthlings would meet. However, for most of the time in these latter spaces there would be only one of the older Earthlings present. In between these two extremes, the exploratory party had found a variety of other spaces of different sizes and with different numbers of Earthlings present.

In most of the large spaces, the younger Earthlings sat in rows behind flat-topped objects on which they put things they had brought with them, and which they used during the time they were there. The rows rose in steps so that each row was a little higher than the one in front. An older Earthling usually stood at the front of these rows, facing the younger Earthlings, and behind an object on which it placed the things it had brought. The older Earthlings seemed to be trying to communicate something to the younger Earthlings that sat fairly quietly listening and, at the same time, making marks on the thin white sheets that they had brought with them.

The exploratory party also found three other kinds of specialized spaces. The first kind had flat floors on which flat-topped objects were arranged in rows and/or around the outside edges. The younger Earthlings stood or sat behind them. These flat-topped objects were larger and higher than those in the other spaces. On top were arranged objects of many shapes and sizes. The number of young Earthlings in these spaces was usually limited and their activities were different. While they sometimes faced the older Earthling that stood on one side of the space, for the most part they did things with the objects on the flat tops, either singly or in twos or threes. The older Earthling some-times faced the younger Earthlings, sometimes walked around the space, and was sometimes absent. The periods the Earthlings spent in these specialized spaces were found to be longer than those spent in the other spaces. The JJans also noticed that these spaces were concentrated in particular areas.

The second kind of specialized space was moderate in size. While it shared some things in common with some other spaces of this size, there were some special features. The floors were also flat, but the flat-topped objects behind which the younger Earthlings sat had on them what looked like very primitive and clumsy computers, with very primitive means of operating them. It was very rare to find the older Earthlings in these spaces, although one would sometimes wander around and seemed to offer help to the younger Earthlings. On rare occasions, they noticed that the behaviour in these spaces resembled that in some of the other similar-sized spaces, with the older Earthlings standing in front of the younger ones, apparently trying to communicate with them.

The third kind of specialized space was very different. Several of them were grouped together as well as being stacked on top of each other. They had many small flat-topped objects in them at which the younger Earthlings sat individually. Usually each object had a barrier around three sides that prevented neighbouring Earthlings from seeing what that particular Earthling was doing. These spaces also contained rows of tall narrow objects with limited space between them. These tall objects had a number of horizontal flat surfaces on each side, on which there were many bound sets of white sheets, almost all different. The younger Earthlings took these bound sheets, placed them on the objects where they sat, opened them, and spent a long time looking through them. At the same time, they also recorded strange symbols on their white sheets. There were usually no older Earthlings in these spaces, although the JJans noted that there were a few near the one opening through which the younger Earthlings went in and out.

The exploratory party spent many 'larks' gathering information. In addition to digital photographic evidence, they brought back some artefacts with them, for example some of the things that the younger Earthlings had taken with them to these spaces and had left behind, and a few of the bound sheets.

The JJans who had remained on the craft during this exploratory period of research were very impressed with what their colleagues had discovered. They asked many questions about what the Earthlings were doing. Apart from being able to describe what they had seen, the exploratory party was unable to answer most of the questions, although they offered comments based on their knowledge of JJan social life.[5]

After presenting the findings of this exploratory research to their colleagues, the JJan social scientists discussed what they thought should be investigated in the next stage of their work. They eventually decided to concentrate on the activities that occurred in the various spaces on campus. They settled on the topic:

'Social Interaction in Enclosed Spaces on Earth'

Because these activities continued for many hours nearly every 'light', and sometimes during the 'dark', and involved many Earthlings, although mostly younger ones, they concluded that they must be very important. Hopefully, they could learn something about a very common activity on the part of Earth on which they had inadvertently landed.

The Application of Four Research Strategies

The Inductive team

The Inductive team was feeling very confident because the exploratory work had already provided them with a great deal of information and some ideas about the range of things that they needed to observe. They decided to make many observations, to collect copious amounts of data, and then to produce some generalizations that they hoped would describe the patterns of life on this part of Earth. They believed that if their observations were systematic, and if they used objective procedures, they would be able to regard their generalizations as true descriptions of the laws of Earthly social life.

They formulated two general research questions to guide their activities:

What do Earthlings do in these confined spaces?

Why do they do it?

As they began their investigations, they tried to avoid making any assumptions about what was going on, and they certainly rejected the idea of working with any theories or hypotheses. They believed that in order to produce valid descriptions of what these Earthlings are doing, they must not interpret what they see. Rather, they must record

---

[5] We need to note here that what the exploratory party saw was expressed in their own language, using familiar JJan concepts. Their descriptions also contained many assumptions that were drawn from their everyday experiences and professional practices on JJ. Had they been able to translate their preliminary report into the language of the Earthlings, it is likely that the Earthlings would have found parts of it strange and unrecognizable.

what is happening with a completely open mind. To do otherwise would lead to a distorted account of this social life.

The Inductive team was a little suspicious of some of the observations made by the exploratory group because some members of it were not committed to this method of objective observation. Hence, they decided to re-observe the various situations that had been identified, to collect more detailed data in the process, and, of course, to observe any other similar situations they might come across. They were keen to record what they observed by using their own senses and also by using their recording equipment. In this way, they believed that they would capture the facts as objectively as possible.

They almost decided to dismiss the idea of talking to the Earthlings, as they believed that in their approach to social research they should not rely on what participants can tell them. Instead, they should look for external evidence of the social facts that constitute the observed regularities in behaviour. In any case, they were aware of the enormous communication difficulties they would face in attempting to question the Earthlings. However, they did decide to try to elicit some very basic information by using a simple structured questionnaire in which each question had a predetermined set of response categories. They based the questionnaire on a simple version of the standard one used in social research on JJ, as this would allow them to do comparative analysis. Of course, constructing the questionnaire required them to translate JJan concepts into the language spoken on this part of Earth. While they were able to make use of the limited knowledge of the language obtained by earlier expeditions, they had to do some basic work themselves.

Questionnaires were given to a random sample of Earthlings using four strata based on the main types of larger spaces as the initial sampling units; systematic sampling was then used within each stratum. They thought that the structured questionnaire might make it easier for the Earthlings to understand what the researchers wanted to know, and it would ensure that the same information was obtained from each one. The questions included: how often they visited each kind of space; what kinds of activities they engaged in; how long they had been doing these activities; how long they expected to continue to do them; and whether these activities had changed over time. Of course, they also wanted to know how old the Earthlings were, which one of the four sexes they belonged to,[6] how they had been educated,[7] how many journeys they had made into space,[8] and which research strategy they believed in.[9] These were the standard questions asked in all social research on JJ.

---

[6] On JJ, sex is a matter of choice rather than being biologically determined. There are four possible choices, to be a male, to be a female, to be neither (and thus not be involved in procreation) and to be both (and have a choice as to what part to play in procreation, perhaps different on different occasions). The choice that was made had social consequences, as there were prescribed roles for each sex. They assumed that Earthlings would have the same four choices.

[7] JJans can choose to rote learn from their book of knowledge, to learn from experience with the assistance of an old and wise JJan, or to learn by engaging in research. They assumed that Earthlings have the same options.

[8] Status on JJ is determined in this way, although extra status is achieved every time a JJan is a pilot or navigator on any of these journeys. They assumed that status on Earth is achieved in the same way, although they were not sure how often Earthlings had travelled into space.

[9] The adoption of a research strategy is a matter of faith on JJ. It entails beliefs about the nature of reality, the components that make it up, how these components behave, and what causes behaviour.

They considered asking the Earthlings to record the answers to the questions on the wrist-communicating computers that all JJans carried with them, but they thought this advanced technology might produce response resistance. The wrist computers could have both dictated the questions by synthesized voice and recorded the verbal responses onto the database. They therefore resorted to the long since abandoned manual recording method, realizing that this was going to create extra work in entering the data into the main computer on the spacecraft.

In addition to using the questionnaire, the Inductive team also made observations of the Earthlings' behaviour and the spaces in which this behaviour occurred. They used their wrist computers to provide a checklist of all the items to be observed and to record this information in a prepared format. Verbal comments were also entered. This structured method of recording their observations ensured that all observers paid attention to the same things and recorded their observations consistently. The checklist included a wide variety of items, as they did not want to prejudge what the important regularities might be.

The fact that the Inductive team had made a prior decision about what should be recorded caused some consternation in the group as some members saw it as preventing them from observing with a completely open mind. However, the pragmatists won the day by arguing that, as their time was limited, they could not observe 'all the facts', only the relevant ones. They consoled themselves with the defence that their wide selection was not based on hypotheses or prejudices, but consisted of a list of what the exploratory study had shown to be relevant. These were the most obvious things to observe, and, after all, they were also readily accessible.

As well as recording the kind of behaviour that occurred in these spaces, the Inductive team documented the starting and finishing time of each occasion on which a group of Earthlings gathered in a particular space. They also tracked the movements of as many individuals as possible and tried to see how often the same individuals met together. While this turned out to be a very complex task, they were determined to complete it as well as possible within the time limits because they did not want to miss data that might be important.

The team worked very systematically and efficiently accumulating data. Each evening they took turns to enter the questionnaire responses into the spaceship's computer. After a month of intensive work, they had accumulated a prodigious amount of data and felt confident that they would be able to produce objective generalizations about the regularities in the behaviour of the Earthlings in the spaces selected.

The Inductive team confirmed several of the exploratory party's findings, for example, the age distribution of Earthlings in the various spaces, and the kinds of activities that take place in them. In addition, they discovered that:

- not all the Earthlings visited all types of spaces;
- the Earthlings had regular patterns in their visits to these spaces;
- the modal period of the visits to the large spaces, and some of the smaller spaces, was one 'chime';
- the modal period of the visits to some other spaces was three 'chimes';
- the period of the visits to the spaces with the computers varied widely;
- there was a reasonably strong correlation between the size of a space and the number of Earthlings that met in it;

- in the spaces in which older and younger Earthlings met, the older Earthlings dominated the activities.

The Inductive team was confident that they had established the important regularities in the Earthling's behaviour and they believed that knowing these patterns allowed them to explain further observations that they, or future expeditions, might make. However, as they were not content to let their generalizations rest on this limited research, they decided to use whatever additional time they had to accumulate more data to strengthen their conviction that these generalizations were true.

The Deductive team

The Deductive team examined the results of the exploratory study carefully to see if there was sufficient evidence for the existence of regularities that needed to be explained. Before commencing their task of explanation, they decided that they needed to be more confident of the patterns of interaction that occur in these spaces. With the help of some of the Retroductive team, they set about designing a detailed descriptive study, using the results of the exploratory study as a guide. How they went about this was not very different from what the Inductive team had done; they used the same methods, but their research was more limited in scope. The focus of their attention was on the dominant forms of behaviour of the younger and older Earthlings, and on the patterns of relationships between these two kinds of Earthlings in the confined spaces. In short, they were looking for the external manifestations of the regularities in Earthling behaviour.

After satisfying themselves that they had a good grasp of these patterns, they proceeded to construct a number of theories that they hoped would explain them. One pattern that stood out in the spaces where an older Earthling stood in front of the younger ones was that the older one dominated the activities. The younger ones generally remained passive and made complex marks on many white sheets. In the bigger spaces where this behaviour occurred, a few young Earthlings appeared not to be paying attention to the older Earthling; they appeared to communicate quietly with each other, they seemed to be sleeping or they sometimes threw small objects at each other. This latter behaviour seemed to be confined to certain groups of young Earthlings, but they were not sure what distinguished them except that most of them had short hair on their heads.

The Deductive team set themselves the following research questions.

Why are there many more younger than older Earthlings meeting together in these enclosed spaces?

Why do the older Earthlings stand up and the younger ones sit down?

Why do the older Earthlings dominate the activity and the younger ones generally remain passive?

Why do the older Earthlings read from their white sheets and the younger ones make marks on theirs?

One member of the Deductive team was given the task of searching the databases they had brought with them for reports of all research conducted on JJ on interaction in confined spaces. This JJan was able to find a number of reports as well as some theories that had been well tested on JJ. However, these theories dealt neither with the standing and sitting of people of different ages in confined spaces, nor with behaviour associated with the use of white sheets. The reason for the latter is that these artefacts are not used on JJ. These differences posed some problems and forced the Deductive team to devise a new theory, in fact, a set of theories, one for each research question. They did get some help from a JJan theory about sitting and standing in open spaces, but it was younger JJans who were more likely than older ones to stand in such spaces. After much discussion, they were able to formulate three theories as arguments based on a logically related set of propositions. The first was on 'The Predominance of Younger Earthlings in Confined Spaces', the second on 'Sitting and Standing', and the third on 'Activity and Inactivity'. Only the first theory is reported here.

Theory A: On the Predominance of Younger Earthlings in Confined Spaces

1 Life on Earth in open spaces is nasty, brutish and short.
2 Few Earthlings survive beyond ten 'rounds'.[10]
3 In order to ensure their survival, younger Earthlings are required to spend most of their time in confined spaces.
4 As the survival of societies on Earth requires that some Earthlings spend time in open spaces, this is done during mid-life.
5 Those few Earthlings that survive their brief time in open spaces are allowed to return to the protection of confined spaces in their final 'rounds'.
6 Therefore, there are more younger than older Earthlings in confined spaces.

This theory was based on a meta-theoretical perspective about the physical conditions of JJan survival, and this was adapted to suit the Earthly context. They were not sure why Earthlings needed to spend time in open spaces or whether the reasons for a short life in open spaces would be the same as on JJ. However, they found the logic of the theory to be satisfactory and considered it to be worth testing. To do this, they predicted that in all the confined spaces on the university campus, young Earthlings would far outnumber older ones. While they were aware that the exploratory party had found some small confined spaces that did not conform to their prediction, they expected that this anomaly was simply an aberration in the selection of the places in which observations had been made.

To test the theory, they assigned two of their members to visit all confined spaces twice each 'lark', once during the 'light' and once during the 'dark'. The 'lights' and 'darks' were divided into ten equal intervals[11] within which an observation was to be made. The observation time for each space was randomized, and observations were

---

[10] JJans refer to the completion of an orbit of their planet around their sun as a 'round'. While they suspected that an Earthly 'round' might be shorter in length, for the moment they had no choice but to use the length of a JJ 'round' in their theory.

[11] These intervals corresponded to the way that JJan 'lights' and 'darks' were subdivided. It did not occur to these researchers that Earthlings worked with different intervals, or that the 'chimes' were a universal measure of time on Earth.

made for a period of twenty 'larks'. The observers were instructed to count the older and younger Earthlings present at the time. Ratios of older to younger Earthlings would then be calculated for each interval, for each space, for each 'lark', as well as for the grand total of all spaces.

The Deductive team found abundant evidence consistent with their theory about the different ratios of older and younger Earthlings in confined spaces. However, they discovered that the ratios varied depending on the sizes of the confined spaces; the larger the space the higher the ratio. In general, they found that there was only one older Earthling to many younger Earthlings in all the spaces, except in the very small ones. The exception that they had observed in their exploratory research turned out not to be an aberration. In these very small spaces the older Earthlings were usually found on their own, or, if not, the ratio was usually 1 : 1.

The Deductive team believed that by testing their conclusion to this theory they had tested the theory itself. After all, the conclusion had been derived logically from the abstract 'theoretical' premises; the premises cannot be false if the conclusion is true. They considered that the exception to the theory that was found in the very small spaces could be explained in terms of the few older Earthlings that had survived their time in open spaces being given a small space as a secure place in which to live. They were visited occasionally by younger Earthlings. What the Deductive team had failed to notice was that the older Earthlings were usually only in these small spaces during the 'lights'. This was because they had no similar situations on JJ that would have led them to expect fluctuating occupancy of such spaces.

The Retroductive team

Like the Deductive team, the Retroductive team also needed to begin its research with detailed descriptions of the regularities or patterns in Earthling behaviour and social interaction. Hence, they decided to join forces with the Deductive team for the first stage of their research. They were interested in the external manifestations of regularities in Earthling behaviour. Therefore, their descriptions of the behaviour of Earthlings in confined spaces were identical to those of the Deductive team. However, when it came to explaining this behaviour, the Retroductive team parted company with their colleagues. They believed that explanations had to be found in different places, using a different logic, that is, in the real structures and mechanisms that are responsible for producing observed regularities. They believed that these structures and mechanisms have an existence independent of social scientists. As these structures and mechanisms are not usually susceptible to direct observation, their nature and function has to be first imagined, or modelled, and then evidence for their existence sought. The process of building the model involves working back from the data obtained about the observable reality in order to hypothesize what the underlying reality might be like.

The Retroductive team postulated that Earthling society was based on a structure of power relations between younger and older members. Because the younger members outnumbered the older members, they could control the latter. This was based on the analogy that dominance among animals on JJ was always based on superiority of numbers and the fitness of younger animals.

The initial evidence for the truth of this model was that in the spaces where older and younger Earthlings meet, it appeared that the older Earthlings were being interrogated by groups of younger Earthlings. Perhaps they were being required to answer for their misdeeds while they were in the open spaces. Just as the exploratory party had found, the Deductive and Retroductive teams observed that when the older Earthlings were not with the younger Earthlings in the various spaces, they were to be found mainly on their own in their small spaces. They assumed that these were cells, although they did not seem to be locked and they had not seen any guards.

The Retroductive team's conception of this underlying power structure was reinforced by their interpretation of what was going on in some of the specialized spaces. Again, it appeared that the cases against the older Earthlings were being prepared and their answers to the questions were being taken from their white sheets and entered into a computer database.

The team then set about trying to establish the existence of these underlying structures by methods that are more systematic. They sought the permission of the university authorities to conduct an experiment in which two older Earthlings and twenty younger ones would be asked to volunteer to undertake problem-solving tasks. Their request was granted and a relatively small space was allocated for the purpose. However, before they could proceed with the experiment, they had to improve their command of the language in order to give the Earthlings instructions about the task. As the data were collected by observation only, it was not necessary to communicate with the Earthlings to produce their data.

The Earthlings were divided into two groups, one older and ten younger Earthlings in each one. Each group was set a different task and observations were made of the power relations that emerged. In both cases, it was the older Earthling that emerged as the leader and the decision-maker; the younger ones deferred to it and rarely challenged its authority.

The results of this experiment forced the Retroductive team to rethink their model of the underlying structure in Earthling society. As it did not appear to fit with their earlier attempt to understand the observed reality, they were forced to look at it differently and to postulate a different model. This time they based their model of the underlying structure on the universal idea held in JJan society that 'wisdom is power'. Their age and their outside experience would have provided the older Earthlings with superior wisdom. To test this idea, they devised a 'wisdom test' for the Earthlings, based on the one used on JJ. However, to adapt it, a great deal of work was required to establish what Earthlings regarded as wise judgements.

The test was administered to a random sample of both age groups. They were able to establish the wisdom superiority of the older members. This, together with their experimental evidence, gave them confidence in the existence of the underlying wisdom structure. They were then able to explain much of the observed behaviour of the Earthlings.

The Abductive team

The fourth team rejected the ways in which the Inductive and Deductive teams went about their research. They were interested in what the exploratory party had found but did not trust the methods they had used. Instead of just observing behaviour, the Abductive team considered that it was vital to find out how the Earthlings themselves interpret what they are doing; to grasp Earthling social reality as Earthlings understand it; to discover the everyday knowledge that they use in their social interaction. This team believed that social reality is socially constructed by the groups of people who inhabit it; it is *their* reality, not reality as conceived by researchers. Therefore, any descriptions of social reality must be based on the way it is viewed by the participants, not just the way it is viewed by the outside observer. This meant that the Abductive team needed to use very different methods to conduct their descriptive research. They needed to produce an account of the activities of the Earthlings in these confined spaces as they are 'known' to the participants. In short, they needed to talk to the Earthlings to discover their construction(s) of social reality.

The team assumed that they would encounter the same difficulties on Earth that they had to face on JJ. In particular, they expected that Earthlings would also live in largely taken-for-granted worlds, and, therefore, would not always be able to articulate the motives for their actions.

The need to discover these motives, and, more generally, the social stock of knowledge that Earthlings use in their everyday lives, posed a serious problem for the Abductive team, as their capacity to communicate with the Earthlings was very limited. They needed time to learn the Earthlings' form of communication and to discover something about their culture. The other social research teams were fully aware of this requirement and the additional time needed to do it; this had been built into the schedule for the expedition very reluctantly. The lack of sympathy from the other teams concerning this requirement was based on the extra costs involved. There had been a move to exclude this team from the expedition because of this, but a compromise was reached that allowed the members of the other three teams some time for sightseeing if they had finished their research early.

The Abductive team approached the university authorities and, after difficult negotiations, managed to get approval to spend four 'chimes' each day with a group of Earthlings who were expert in teaching the Earthling language that was used on the campus. For as much of the rest of each 'lark' that they could manage, the members of this team met with Earthlings to practise what they had learnt. As a very experienced Abductive team had been chosen for the expedition, they were able to pick up the rather primitive verbal language of the Earthlings very quickly.

The process of learning the language provided the Abductive team with the opportunity to begin to explore the concepts and meanings associated with activities in confined spaces, and, as language proficiency improved, this first stage of the research gathered momentum. The Abductive team set themselves some general questions.

What do Earthlings say is going on in these enclosed spaces?

What do the Earthlings say they are trying to achieve there?

As the research proceeded, they expected that these questions would be refined and supplemented.

The Abductive team began to discover a range of concepts that the Earthlings used to talk about their activities. In their conversations among themselves, the younger

Earthlings talked about going to 'lectures', to 'classes', to 'tutorials', to 'pracs', to 'labs', and to the 'library', the 'union', the 'cafe' or the 'canteen'. The younger Earthlings referred to themselves as 'students' and to the older Earthlings as 'lecturers' or 'professors'. They met together regularly in 'lecture theatres' and 'classrooms', and, occasionally, in a 'lecturer's' 'office', either one-to-one or in small groups, for 'consultations'. They also talked about 'assignments', 'essays', 'papers', 'tests', 'exams', 'marks' and 'grades', usually with a high level of anxiety. As these commonly used concepts were recorded, the Abductive team began to ask the Earthlings what they meant by them, and when and how they use them. Gradually, they began to piece together a core of shared meanings. However, they began to notice that the older and younger Earthlings did not always mean the same thing by some of the concepts. For example, they had different ideas about what 'lectures' were for, the younger ones seeing them mainly as providing clues about what they should learn for the 'exam', while the older ones talked about 'intellectual development' and 'critical thinking'.

The Abductive team recorded all their conversations with the Earthlings by means of their wrist computers. Later they made time to listen to the recordings, to search for common meanings, and to find gaps in their emerging understanding that might require further informal questioning. As this analysis proceeded, the Abductive team began to redescribe, in JJ social scientific language, what the Earthlings told them about their everyday reality. For example, they discussed abstract ideas about different processes of 'education', 'learning' and 'training' that went on in the enclosed spaces; they discussed the quality of the relationships between the 'lecturers' and the 'students' and how this is linked to 'learning'; and they discussed issues such as 'academic standards' and 'accountability'. In the end, they managed to produce very detailed accounts of the social realities present in this area of social life on Earth, both in the language of the participants, and in their own more abstract technical language. In the process, they began to produce descriptions of typical Earthlings who engaged in typical activities in typical social contexts. They found three types of younger Earthlings that they labelled as 'scholars', 'bludgers' and 'pragmatists'. The 'scholar' they saw as being interested in 'learning' for its own sake, the 'bludger' as engaging in the activities with the minimum of effort and the maximum of short-cuts, including getting as much help as possible, and the 'pragmatist' as engaging in the activity as a means to the end of security and advancement in the future. Similarly, other typologies were established to describe typical differences between 'lecturers' and 'students' and for the variety of confined spaces in which activities on campus took place.

While they were not able to produce a complete picture of all that went on in these confined spaces, they were able to understand a great deal, for example, the different motives and goals of the participants, and the variations in the nature of the social interaction. They could begin to answer their research questions. Their curiosity about this aspect of Earthly life had been largely satisfied, although they were aware that they had but scraped the surface.

We must leave the JJan research teams for the time being. In chapter 7 we will hear about the results of their research and their attempt to establish which is the best research strategy.

Four Research Strategies

The 'Parable of Four Paradigms' should have provided some clues about the core features of the four main strategies of social research available in the social sciences. However, before elaborating them, it is important to note that they must be regarded as ideal or constructed types (Patton 1988; Smaling 1994). They have been derived from the work of many writers and practitioners to identify clusters of characteristics that are typical of approaches to social research, and which highlight the differences between them. While the views of some writers may come close to the descriptions of the characteristics of each typical research strategy, other writers may not fit as well. Some writers may even include a mixture of the types in their work. The descriptions of these typical strategies are abstractions that are designed to make it possible to cope with the diversity of views and practices. They are heuristic tools rather than descriptions of watertight categories that researchers occupy, but, nevertheless, tools that have been derived from such descriptions. This distinction between abstraction and description makes it possible to use the research strategies to compare the writings or research of both theorists and practitioners. The four ideal types also allow for the possibility that a combination of two or more may occur in practice.

The method used to produce the research strategies partly follows the one described in this chapter as the *abductive* strategy, as it is applied to the analysis of texts. It allows for the possibility that other ideal typical research strategies may have existed in the past, and may exist now or in the future. Attempts to typify any aspect of the natural or social worlds are constrained by the range of resources available or selected. Therefore, while I am confident that these four research strategies broadly encompass the logics of enquiry that are available to social researchers, it is possible that other distinctive strategies have been used, are used now, or will be used in the future.

The research strategies provide different ways of answering research questions by specifying a starting-point, a series of steps and an end-point. It is the particular character of these points and steps that distinguishes the strategies. The *inductive* strategy starts with data collection, followed by data analysis, and then the development of generalizations that, with further testing, can become law-like propositions to be used to explain aspects of social life. The *deductive* strategy works in the reverse order. It begins with an observed regularity that needs to be explained; a tentative theory is acquired or constructed; then hypotheses are deduced and then tested by collecting appropriate data. Similarly, the *retroductive* strategy begins with an observed regularity, but this is followed by the construction of a hypothetical model of a possible structure or mechanism that could have produced this regularity. By observation and experiment, a search is then undertaken to establish whether the explanatory structure or mechanism exists. The *abductive* strategy begins by exploring through everyday language the knowledge that social actors use in the production, reproduction and interpretation of the phenomenon under investigation. This is followed by a redescription of this everyday account into a social scientific account, and, possibly, into a grounded explanation (see table 4.1).

Table 4.1 The logic of four research strategies

	Inductive	Deductive	Retroductive	Abductive
Aim	To establish universal generalizations to be used as pattern explanations	To test theories to eliminate false ones and corroborate the survivor	To discover underlying mechanisms to explain observed regularities	To describe and understand social life in terms of social actors' motives and accounts
From	Accumulate observations or data	Borrow or construct a theory and express it as an argument	Document and model a regularity	Discover everyday lay concepts, meanings and motives
	Produce generalizations	Deduce hypotheses	Construct a hypothetical model of a mechanism	Produce a technical account from lay accounts
To	Use these 'laws' as patterns to explain further observations	Test the hypotheses by matching them with data	Find the real mechanism by observation and/ or experiment	Develop a theory and test it iteratively

Each strategy has a philosophical and theoretical ancestry and foundation, and includes ontological assumptions about the nature of reality and epistemological assumptions about how that reality can be known. Only four major approaches to social enquiry are referred to here. For a detailed discussion of these and another seven approaches, see Blaikie (1993a) (see also Guba and Lincoln 1994). While there is overlap between the strategies on some of these, each has a unique combination. *Induction* is the logic of Positivism, the view of science propounded by Bacon (1620) and Mill (1879) in the period of the development of the natural sciences and, later, by Durkheim and others during the establishment of the social sciences. *Deduction* is the logic of Critical Rationalism, the alternative to Positivism developed by Popper in the 1930s. *Retroduction*, the logic of transcendental or Scientific Realism, has been advocated by Bhaskar and Harré as an alternative to both Positivism and Critical Rationalism; its proponents claim that it characterized good science from the beginning. *Abduction* has a long ancestry and comes in many versions; it has links with hermeneutics and social phenomenology and is based on various branches of Interpretivism, particularly the work of Schütz and Giddens.

Readers familiar with the broad range of social scientific approaches included under the label of 'Interpretivism' will recognize that I am advocating a particular 'middle-of-the-road' version which owes much to Weber, to contemporary hermeneutics, to the social phenomenology of Schütz, and to Winch, Rex,

Douglas and Giddens. What characterizes this particular version of Interpretivism is that, while it has a strong hermeneutical foundation, it does not eschew the possibility of developing and testing theory, but theory with time and space limitations (for further elaboration, see Blaikie 1993a).

The research strategies have been constructed so that the logic of enquiry used in each one is incompatible with the logics of the other three. This does not preclude the possibility that strategies may share common ontological assumptions. For example, the *inductive* and *deductive* strategies share the same ontology, and one version of the *retroductive* strategy shares the ontology of the *abductive* strategy (see e.g. Harré and Secord 1972). Nor does it preclude the possibility that they can be combined in practice, for example being used in sequence, as has been advocated for the *inductive* and *deductive* strategies by Wallace (1971, 1983) and de Vaus (1995) (see chapter 5).

These strategies and their foundations will now be examined. (For a more detailed review of the research strategies and their philosophical foundations, see Blaikie 1993a.)

Inductive Research Strategy

The *inductive* strategy is the commonsense view of how scientists go about their work. According to this view, meticulous and objective observation and measurement, and the careful and accurate analysis of data, are required to produce scientific discoveries. Bacon saw science as based on presuppositionless observation; by clearing the mind of all prejudices, the book of nature is to be read with fresh eyes (O'Hear 1989: 16). J. S. Mill, believing that the purpose of science was to establish general laws, proposed an elementary experimental method to identify possible causes and effects. Again, these causes are to be discovered by unprejudiced observation.

Positivism, on which the *inductive* strategy is based, entails *ontological assumptions* about an ordered universe made up of discrete and observable events. It assumes that this order can be represented by universal propositions, i.e. by generalizations about the relationships between concepts. Only that which can be observed, that is, experienced by the senses, can be regarded as real and therefore worthy of the attention of science. *Social reality* is viewed as consisting of a complex of causal relations between events. This is usually represented as an emerging network of relations between concepts. The causes of human behaviour are regarded as being external to the individual.

In its *epistemological assumptions*, knowledge is considered to be produced through the use of the human senses and by means of experimental or comparative analysis. The senses produce 'observations' or data. Concepts, and generalizations about their relationships, are regarded as shorthand summaries of particular observations. Trained humans are assumed to be able to produce 'objective' data. By adopting 'objective' observation procedures, it is assumed that reality can be recorded accurately. Hence, a correspondence is considered to exist between the record of 'objective' observations and the things that are observed. What you see is what is there. Regularities that are recorded through such observation are the basis for scientific laws. In other words, statements based on 'objective' observations become theoretical statements about the order in reality.

The *inductive* strategy has been described as consisting of three principles: accumulation, induction, and instance confirmation. Scientific knowledge consists of well-established regularities that are arrived at by the accumulation of much data. General laws are produced by applying inductive logic to the carefully accumulated observations and experimental results. The plausibility of any general law is proportional to the number of instances of it that have been observed (Harré 1972: 42). Hence, the researcher must begin by setting aside all preconceptions about how the world works and then proceed to gather data using 'objective' methods. Inductive logic is used to produce generalizations about the patterns or regularities that exist in the data obtained. The greater the number of instances of the regularity that has been observed, the greater is the confidence that the generalization corresponds to the timeless uniformities in the world.

The *inductive* strategy has also been characterized as consisting of four main stages.

1 All facts are observed and recorded without selection or guesses as to their relative importance.
2 These facts are analysed, compared and classified, without using hypotheses.
3 From this analysis, generalizations are inductively drawn as to relations between the facts.
4 These generalizations are subjected to further testing (Wolfe 1924: 450; Hempel 1966: 11).

The inductive strategy has been subjected to extensive criticism. The following of its claims have been contested:

- that preconceptions can be set aside to produce objective observations;
- that 'relevant' observations can be made without some ideas to guide them;
- that inductive logic has the capacity to mechanically produce generalizations;
- that universal generalizations can be based on a finite number of observations; and
- that establishing regularities is all that is necessary to produce explanations.

The uses of the concepts of 'objectivity', 'facts' and 'truth' have also been challenged. See chapters 4 and 5 of Blaikie (1993a) for a critical review, and Popper (1959, 1961), Hempel (1966), Medawar (1969), Hindess (1977) and Chalmers (1982) for general critiques.

In the light of these criticisms, it is necessary to make some amendments to the 'pure' form of the inductive research strategy in order for it to be useful in the social sciences today. Given that presuppositionless data collection is impossible, concepts, and the theoretical baggage that goes with them, are required before any observations or measurements can be made. The choice of concepts, and the way they are defined, will predetermine what data are collected. Therefore, the researcher will begin with some preconceptions and choices about what will be observed. While this procedure infringes the original requirements for the research strategy, if the definitions of the concepts are made explicit the conclusions can be evaluated in terms of them, and other researchers can attempt to replicate the findings.

With these modifications, the inductive strategy can be used for two purposes: to pursue exploratory and descriptive objectives to answer 'what' questions, i.e. to describe phenomena and establish regularities which need to be explained; or to pursue an explanatory aim, i.e. to discover laws or very general regularities that can be used to explain observed regularities. The limitations of this form of explanation, referred to as 'pattern explanation', will be discussed later.

In addition to its use in producing generalizations of characteristics or patterns from data accumulated within a project, the logic of induction can also be used across studies. Replication studies can be used to extend generalizations about characteristics and patterns. Cook (1998) has argued that attempts to establish the generality of a causal explanation must rely on *induction*. The process of random selection of respondents, or the random assignment of subjects to groups (as in experimental research), is always limited by the definition of the population from which the selection is made. The same limitations apply to the selection of units of analysis, measures of concepts, places, times, etc., to which random selection is rarely applied. The only way to go beyond these limitations is to use the logic of *induction*, to generalize from the results of different studies, assuming that the results are consistent.

Because induction is not a 'perfect' logic, all attempts to generalize must be tentative. In other words, consistent findings can support a generalization but never prove it to be true. Hence, in spite of the claims of some of its advocates, the status of the knowledge produced using the *inductive* research strategy must always be regarded as being subject to revision; further research may reveal contrary findings. Therefore, as we shall see, the status of knowledge derived from both the *inductive* and *deductive* research strategies is similar. (See Research Design 1 in chapter 8 for a practical application of the *inductive* strategy.)

Deductive Research Strategy

Notions of deduction go back to antiquity, to Euclidean geometry and Aristotelian logic. Known also as the hypothetico-deductive method, or falsificationism, the *deductive* strategy was developed by Popper, the founding father of the philosophy of science known as Critical Rationalism.[12] It is his attempt to overcome the deficiencies of Positivism and the *inductive* strategy. The core of his argument is that, as observations do not provide a reliable foundation for scientific theories and as inductive logic is flawed, a different logic is needed for developing theories. His solution was to accept that all data collection is selective

---

[12] Guba (1990) and Guba and Lincoln (1994) have identified a similar enquiry paradigm that they have labelled 'postpositivism'. However, they, unlike Phillips (1990), have not fully acknowledged Popper's (1959, 1972) contribution to it.

and involves interpretation by the observer, and then to develop an appropriate logic that is the reverse of that advocated by Positivism.

According to Popper (1972: 47), observations are always made from a point of view, with a frame of reference, with a set of expectations, thus making the notion of presuppositionless observation impossible. To collect any useful data, it is necessary first to have some ideas about what to look for. It is necessary to have some tentative answers to 'why' questions, some hypotheses that have been derived from a theory, to provide direction for data gathering. Then, rather than accumulating data, as in the *inductive* strategy, data are used to test the tentative answers. The aim is to see if the data match the hypotheses. Ideally, what the researcher would like to be able to develop is a theory that matches the behaviour of the phenomenon under study, i.e. a theory that matches reality. However, according to Popper, reality cannot be observed directly; all that can be done is to try to match the theory with the data.

The *deductive* research strategy derives its *ontological and epistemological assumptions* from Critical Rationalism; it shares some aspects of Positivism's ontological assumptions but rejects its epistemological assumptions. Nature and social life are regarded as consisting of essential uniformities, i.e. patterns of events. It is the aim of science to discover these uniformities, to find universal statements that are true because they correspond to the facts of nature, or, more correctly, to descriptions of observed states of affairs. However, the use of the senses is rejected as a secure foundation for scientific theories.

Critical Rationalism makes no distinction between observational and theoretical statements; all observations are considered to be theory-dependent and to occur within a 'horizon of expectations'. In other words, collecting any kind of data involves the use of some theoretical ideas; concepts about which data are collected have theoretical ideas associated with them. Data collection occurs against the background of certain expectations about what exists and how it behaves.

In this approach to the generation of new knowledge, data are used in the service of deductive reasoning, and theories are invented to account for observations, not derived from them. Rather than scientists waiting for the social world to reveal its regularities, they must impose theories on the world and, by a process of trial and error, use data to try to reject false theories. Theories that survive this critical process are provisionally accepted, but never proven to be true. All knowledge is tentative and subject to ongoing critical evaluation.

This view of the role of observation or data collection is accompanied by a different kind of logic. Instead of looking for confirming evidence to support an emerging generalization, as occurs in the inductive research strategy (known as 'justificationism'), Popper argued that the aim of science is to try to refute the tentative theories that have been proposed. The search for truth is elusive because we have no way of knowing when we have arrived at it. All that can be done is to eliminate false theories by showing that data do not fit with them. Theories that survive the testing process are not proven to be true as it is still possible that further testing will find disconfirming evidence; it may be necessary to discard the theory, or at least modify and retest it. Therefore, science is a process of conjecture and refutation, of trial and error, of putting up a tentative theory, and then endeavouring to show that the theory is false. The fittest theories will survive.

Popper's argument can be summarized as follows.

- The natural and social worlds consist of essential uniformities.
- The aim of science is to establish generalizations that correspond to these uniformities and theories that explain them.
- However, it is not possible ultimately to establish whether such generalizations or theories are true, i.e. that they correspond with reality.
- All that can be done is to eliminate false theories, thus getting closer to the truth.
- But we never know when we have arrived at true theories.
- Therefore, all theories that have survived testing, i.e. that have been *corroborated*, must remain tentative; they may be replaced in the future by better theories.

According to Popper, the *deductive* research strategy has a number of essential steps.

1 Begin by putting forward a tentative idea, a conjecture, a hypothesis or a set of hypotheses that form a theory.
2 With the help, perhaps, of other previously accepted hypotheses, or by specifying the conditions under which the hypotheses are expected to hold, deduce a conclusion, or a number of conclusions.
3 Examine the conclusions and the logic of the argument that produced them. Compare this argument with existing theories to see if it constitutes an advance in our understanding. If you are satisfied with this examination, then:
4 Test the conclusion by gathering appropriate data; make the necessary observations or conduct the necessary experiments.
5 If the test fails, i.e. if the data are not consistent with the conclusion, the theory must be false. If the original conjecture does not match the data, it must be rejected.
6 If, however, the conclusion passes the test, i.e. the data are consistent with it, the theory is temporarily supported; it is *corroborated*, but not proven to be true (Popper 1959: 32–3).

An example of what a deductive theory might look like comes from a reconstruction of Durkheim's theory of egoistic suicide. It consists of five propositions using three main concepts: 'suicide rate' (the number of suicides per thousand of a population); 'individualism' (the tendency of people to think for themselves and to act independently, rather than to conform to the beliefs and norms of some group)[13]; and 'Protestantism' (a collection of Christian religious groups formed following the Reformation and the subsequent fragmentation of Roman Catholicism).

---

[13] An alternative concept is 'social integration', which refers to the acceptance and practice of a group's beliefs and norms by its members. Durkheim discussed what he called a spirit of free enquiry that some religious groups may encourage, and which can lead to schisms within the group. In contrast, other groups require strict adherence to beliefs and practices and this has the consequence of socially integrating its members.

1 In any social grouping, the suicide rate varies directly with the degree of individualism (egoism).
2 The degree of individualism varies directly with the incidence of Protestantism.
3 Therefore, the suicide rate varies with the incidence of Protestantism.
4 The incidence of Protestantism in Spain is low.
5 Therefore, the suicide rate in Spain is low (Homans 1964: 951).

> The theory contains two universal propositions (1 and 2) which state the form of relationships between pairs of concepts. The meaning of each proposition could be elaborated and reasons given for including it. The third proposition follows logically from the first two and links the suicide rate with 'Protestantism', a less abstract concept than 'individualism'. On its own, each proposition explains nothing, but all three propositions together constitute an explanation for differences in suicide rates. What Durkheim wanted to explain was why Protestants have a higher suicide rate than Catholics; he claimed that these propositions provide such an explanation. The addition of proposition 4, a descriptive statement, allows for a prediction (proposition 5) that can be tested (assuming that relative suicide rates can be satisfactorily established). Similarly, predictions could be made about other countries (e.g., Republic of Ireland) to provide further tests of the theory. Alternatively, if proposition 5 needs to be explained, then the preceding propositions provide the explanation. In this particular theory it would be possible to test propositions 1 to 3 directly by gathering data on these pairs of concepts in various populations. Hence, when theories are structured in this deductive way, the differences between explanation, prediction and testing, as Popper has argued, is just a matter of emphasis. (Blaikie 1993a: 149)

Critical Rationalism and its *deductive* research strategy have also been severely criticized. The following list includes the major criticisms:

- If observations are interpretations, and we can never observe reality directly, how can regularities be established confidently and theories be refuted conclusively?
- The tentative acceptance of a yet unrefuted theory requires some inductive support.
- There is no interest in where tentative theories should come from, or how they might be constructed.
- Science needs to be less logical to allow for chance discoveries.
- Paying too much attention to logic can stifle scientific creativity.
- The process of accepting or rejecting theories involves social and psychological processes, not just logical ones.

See chapters 4 and 5 of Blaikie (1993a) for a critical review, and Hesse (1963, 1974), Medawar (1969), Kuhn (1970), Lakatos (1970), Hindess (1977), Chalmers (1982), Salmon (1988a, 1988b, 1988c), O'Hear (1989) and Pawson (1989) for specific critiques or suggested amendments. (A practical application of the deductive strategy can be found in chapter 8, Research Design 2.)

Retroductive Research Strategy

The *retroductive* strategy is the logic of enquiry associated with the philosophical approach of Scientific Realism, or, more particularly, the transcendental Realism of Bhaskar and the constructivist Realism of Harré. These authors have been very critical of both Positivism and Critical Rationalism and have presented what they consider to be a superior ontology, and a more appropriate logic of enquiry.

Scientific Realism is distinguished from other approaches to social enquiry by its particular ontology. In the Realist *ontology*, the ultimate objects of scientific enquiry are considered to exist and act independently of scientists and their activity. A distinction is made between the domains of the empirical, the actual and the real: the *empirical* domain consists of events that can be observed; the *actual* domain consists of events whether or not they are observed; and the *real* domain consists of the structures and mechanisms that produce these events. It is an ontology of intransitive structures and mechanisms that are distinguished from transitive concepts, theories and laws that are designed to describe them. These structures and mechanisms are the real essences of things that exist in nature, such essences being their power or tendency to produce effects that can be observed.

Social reality is viewed either as a socially constructed world in which social episodes are the products of the cognitive resources social actors bring to them (Harré 1977), or as social arrangements that are the products of material but unobservable structures of social relations (Bhaskar 1979). The aim of Realist science is to explain observable phenomena with reference to underlying structures and mechanisms.

Realist *epistemology* is based on the building of models of mechanisms such that, if they were to exist and act in the postulated way, they would account for the phenomena being examined. These models constitute hypothetical descriptions that, it is hoped, will reveal the underlying mechanisms. In other words, these mechanisms can only be known by constructing ideas about them. This is an epistemology of laws as expressing tendencies of things, as opposed to the conjunctions of events advocated by Positivism.

Bhaskar rejected Positivism's pattern model of explanation, i.e. that explanation can be achieved by establishing regularities, or constant conjunctions, within phenomena or between events. Both Bhaskar and Harré have argued that establishing such regularities is only the beginning of the process. What is then required is to locate the structure or mechanism that has produced the pattern or relationship. These structures and mechanisms are nothing more than the tendencies or powers of things to act in a particular way. The capacity of a thing to exercise its powers, or the likelihood that it will, depends on whether or not the circumstances are favourable.

This view of causation allows for the possibility that competing or cancelling mechanisms may be operating when no event or change is observed, i.e. lack of movement may be due to opposing forces at work. Therefore, the independence of an event and its associated structures or mechanisms can be demonstrated.

Bhaskar's brand of Realism consists of five principles (Outhwaite 1987: 45–6):

1 A distinction is made between *transitive* and *intransitive* objects of science. ✓ Transitive objects are the concepts, theories and models that are developed to understand and explain some aspects of reality, and intransitive objects are the real entities and their relations that make up the natural and social worlds.
2 Reality is stratified into three levels or domains, the empirical, the actual and ✓ the real.
3 Causal relations are regarded as powers or *tendencies* of things that interact ✓ with other tendencies such that an observable event may or may not be produced, and may or may not be observed. Social laws need not be universal; they need only represent recognized tendencies. This view contrasts with the Positivist view in which causal laws are regarded as universal connections between events.
4 In the domain of the real, definitions of concepts are regarded as *real defini-* ✓ *tions*, i.e. statements about the basic nature of some entity or structure. These are neither summaries of what is observed nor stipulations that a term should be used in a particular way.
5 Explanatory *mechanisms* in the domain of the real are postulated, and the task ✓ of research is to try to demonstrate their existence.

The logic of the *retroductive* strategy has some similarities to that of the *deductive* strategy, but there are also important differences. Both commence with an observed regularity that requires an explanation. Harré regarded this first stage, labelled *empirical studies*, as involving both 'exploration', to extend what is known by common observation, and 'experiment', to check critically the authenticity of what is thought to be known. A researcher may have some idea of the direction to go in this exploration but no clear idea of what to expect. This is followed by a second stage, labelled *theoretical studies*, which is concerned with producing an explanation for the regularity established by the empirical study. Explanation is achieved by identifying the generative mechanisms that produced the regularity (Harré and Secord 1972: 69–71).

When these structures and mechanisms have not been observed previously, they are initially proposed as hypothetical entities. The researcher 'uncovers' them by first constructing a hypothetical model of their nature and tendencies. This model building is a creative activity involving disciplined scientific imagination and the use of analogies and metaphors. If the mechanism exists and acts in the postulated way, it would explain the regularity (Bhaskar 1979: 15). Put rather too simply, the researcher's task is then to establish whether the mechanism exists. This may involve testing predictions based on the assumption that it does exist, and perhaps devising new instruments to observe it. The major value of the hypothetical model is that it gives direction to the research; the *retroductive* researcher, unlike the *inductive* researcher, has something to look for.

Many searches for explanatory mechanisms will have been unsuccessful, or only partially successful. In the natural sciences, successful examples are the discovery of the elliptical orbits of the planets of the solar system, and the existence of atoms and viruses. They all began as ideas in the minds of their discoverers and could not have been produced by accumulating data. The process used to establish their existence was slow and painstaking.

Constructing models of mechanisms may involve the use of analogies. Analogies involve borrowing ideas from other fields with which the researcher is familiar, and transferring the principles to the area being investigated. A natural science example of this can be found in the early stages of the process of understanding electricity when the analogy of water flowing in pipes was used. In the social sciences, a classical example is to be found in a number of theories that regard societies as being like huge organisms. The extent to which such analogies are fruitful is a matter of experience and usually much debate; some, like the organismic analogy, while initially useful, eventually imposed limits on understanding. (See chapter 6 for a discussion of the use of analogies as models.)

> Scientific method, as it is practised in the advanced sciences, consists then of the exploration of certain fields of natural phenomena in the attempt to discern non-random patterns in those fields, and critically to check them. This is followed, accompanied, or even preceded by the work of the creative imagination, in the course of which iconic models of the generative mechanisms at work in the field of natural phenomena are conceived. The invention of such models is essential to the scientific enterprise and their appearance is what distinguishes real science from critical description, for it is through them that we come to form some idea of why events happen as they do, and why things manifest the structures, powers and qualities that they do. (Harré and Secord 1972: 76–7)

The *retroductive* research strategy can be summarized as follows.

1 In order to explain observable phenomena and the regularities that obtain between them, scientists must attempt to discover appropriate structures and mechanisms.
2 Since these structures and mechanisms will typically be unavailable to observation, it is necessary to first construct a model of them, often drawing upon already familiar sources.
3 A model is such that, were it to represent correctly these structures and mechanisms, the phenomena would then be causally explained.
4 The model is then tested as a hypothetical description of actually existing entities and their relations. To do so, it is necessary to work out further consequences of the model (that is, additional to the phenomena to be explained), that can be stated in a manner open to empirical testing.
5 If these tests are successful, this gives good reason to believe in the existence of these structures and mechanisms.
6 It may be possible to obtain more direct confirmation of these existential claims, by the development and use of suitable instruments.
7 The whole process of model-building may then be repeated, in order to explain the structures and mechanisms already discovered (Keat and Urry 1975: 35; Harré 1961).

However, the *retroductive* strategy requires more than the discovery of mechanisms. A mechanism produces a regularity only under certain conditions; i.e. a pattern or regularity will be generated only if the conditions are conducive. The social conditions in which a social episode occurs, or within which any social group or community exists, is not entirely the result of the activities of the participants. This means that social actors may have little or no awareness of the mechanisms, and, in particular, the structures, which are involved in the production of the regularities in their social activities.

The notion of *retroduction* appears to be more easily applied in the natural sciences than in the social sciences. There is a dearth of social research that has explicitly used retroductive logic. However, as has been done in the natural sciences, it is possible to reconstruct classic studies in the social sciences within the retroductive strategy. There are probably many reasons for the lack of use of this research strategy, an important one being the different character of mechanisms in the social sciences (see Blaikie 1994, 1996). In the natural sciences, *retroduction* is used to search for unknown and more 'fundamental' underlying phenomena.

> The chemistry of substances demands the mechanisms of atoms, the physics of atoms demands the mechanisms of proton and electron structures, the physics of these entities demand the mechanisms of quarks, and so on, extending as far as technological proficiency and human ingenuity can lead. (Harré and Secord 1972: 77)

In the social sciences, as the nature of explanatory mechanisms is usually well known, the task becomes one of discovering which of a number of possible mechanisms is responsible for producing a particular regularity. The structuralist version of Scientific Realism in the social sciences hypothesizes the role of an underlying social structure, such as a Marxian version of the class structure. The constructivist version assumes that regularities in social behaviour are the result of social actors following rules and conventions in a self-monitoring process. Thus, explanatory mechanisms consist of 'the rules, plans, conventions, images and so on that people use to guide their behaviour' (Harré and Secord 1972: 151).

> In general social behaviour is the result of conscious self-monitoring of performance by the person himself [*sic*], in the course of which he contrives to assess the meaning of the social situations in which he finds himself, and to choose amongst various rules and conventions, and to act in accordance with his choice, correcting this choice as further aspects of the situation make themselves clear to him. (Harré and Secord 1972: 151)

Access to these rules and meanings is from participants' accounts. However, these mechanisms need to be distinguished from the reasons or justifications that social actors can also give for their actions.

Therefore, the arguments for hypothetical model building in the natural sciences do not seem to transfer well to the social sciences, where the notion of 'hidden' mechanisms has a rather different meaning. In the natural sciences, mechanisms are hidden because they reside in the *real* domain of reality that has still to be 'discovered'. If mechanisms in the social sciences are regarded as social constructions, then their 'hidden' character refers to the fact that the social researcher cannot observe them directly, and that social actors may not be aware of them. Hence, complex and sometimes time-consuming procedures are needed to

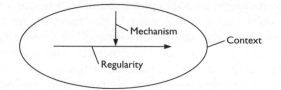

Figure 4.2   Realist social explanation

(*Source:* Pawson and Tilley 1997: 72)

unearth them. Social actors may have come to take them so much for granted that they are not readily 'available', and may even be unconscious. In spite of these difficulties, considerable knowledge of possible social mechanisms is available.

An important recent development in the application of the *retroductive* research strategy to the social sciences has been presented by Pawson and Tilley (1997). Drawing on Giddens's (1979, 1984) discussions of the duality of *agency* and *structure*, they have endeavoured to bring together elements of the *structuralist* and *constructivist* versions of realism. They have argued that explanation is not achieved by the action of independent variables on dependent variables, by the operation of intervening variables, or by the chain reaction of such variables. Rather, explanation of social regularities, rates, associations, outcomes or patterns come from an understanding of mechanisms acting in social contexts. *Regularity = Mechanism + Context* (see figure 4.2).

> The basic task of social inquiry is to explain interesting, puzzling, socially significant regularities (*R*). Explanation takes the form of positing some underlying mechanism (*M*) which generates the regularity and thus consists of propositions about how the interplay between structure and agency has constituted the regularity. Within realist investigation there is also investigation of how the workings of such mechanisms are contingent and conditional, and thus [are] only fired in particular local, historical or institutional contexts (*C*). (Pawson and Tilley 1997: 71)

Pawson and Tilley have argued that all social regularities are embedded in a wider range of social processes, within different layers of social reality. For example, interaction between teacher and students occurs within a classroom, that is located within a particular school, that has a geographical location, with parents of particular social backgrounds, within a particular sector of educational administration, etc., etc. To understand the patterns of academic success in the classroom, these sectors of reality must be taken into account.

'Causal social mechanisms' refers to the *choices* that social actors make and the *capacities* or resources they derive from group membership (I would also add *cognitive resources* as they are likely to have some degree of independence from these socially derived resources). A child's success in the education system will depend on a combination of mechanisms: their decisions, their individual abilities and their socially derived resources. However, such mechanisms will only fire, i.e. lead to academic success, if the context is conducive. The context includes the social rules, norms, values and relationships within which the child is located. For example, if a dominant norm among students is that no individual should stand out from the crowd, or alternatively, that the expression of superior ability must be constrained within narrow limits, then outstanding academic perform- ance is unlikely to occur. The immediate conditions have to be conducive for an individual's resources and choices to be able to produce a particular outcome.

Pawson and Tilley have added a realist reconstruction of Durkheim's theory of egoistic suicide. As we have seen, Durkheim thought he was an *inductivist* while Homans and Merton have regarded his theory as being *deductivist*. Well, now we have a *retroductivist* rendition.

> Durkheim (1951), whilst accepting that the decision to commit suicide was, of course, a matter of the individual's misery, desperation, isolation and so on, was able to show that such dispositions are socially structured and thus vary with the social cohesion and social support which different communities, localities, organizations, family group- ings and so on are able to bring to marginalized members. He demonstrated that the supremely 'individual' act of suicide is in fact 'socially' structured and so produced the famous research cataloguing differences in suicide rates: higher in (individualistic) Protestant communities than in (collectivist) Catholic communities; higher for widowers in their competitive (public) male networks than widows in their communal (private) female networks; higher for the childless in their (restricted) family roles than for parents with their (extended) family ties; higher on (insouciant) weekends than (well-structured) weekdays; and so on. (Pawson and Tilley 1997: 65–6)

To put this another way, individual choices (e.g. to take one's life) are constrained or enabled by characteristics of the social context in which the individual is located. In this way, both agency and structure enter the explanation.

It is possible to confuse the testing of models in the *retroductive* strategy with the testing of theories in the *deductive* strategy. The latter tests for relationships between events, or variables, while the former tries to establish the existence of a particular generative mechanism. Explanation in the *deductive* strategy is achieved by means of a deductive argument made up of various kinds of propositions that postulate relationships between concepts. In contrast, explanation in the *retro- ductive* strategy is achieved by establishing the existence of the structure or mechanism that produces the observed regularity. Another important difference concerns the use of prediction. In the *deductive* strategy, scientific prediction is regarded as being possible by the use of deductive arguments, and can be part of the testing process. However, in the *retroductive* strategy, it is argued that prediction is impossible in the social sciences because of the open nature of social systems.

As *retroduction* and Realism are relatively new in the social sciences, the same intensity of criticism that has been levelled at *induction* and *deduction* has, perhaps, still to emerge. There has been a rearguard attack from a modified form of Positivism, called constructive empiricism (van Fraassen 1985), but this has been directed at all realist philosophies of science[14] rather just the form of

---

[14] A realist philosophy is one that is based on the assumption that reality exists independently of social actors and observers. Positivism, Critical Rationalism and the structural version of Realism all adopt this ontological assumption. However, they differ in their epistemologies, in how knowledge of this reality can be obtained, and how close it is possible to get to it.

Scientific Realism being discussed here. Another line of criticism has suggested that the notion of 'unobservable' cannot be applied to mechanisms in the social sciences in the same way as in the natural sciences. The structural branch of Realism in the social sciences deals with entities that are theoretical and therefore cannot be perceived by direct observation. It is only from their effects that they can be known. In the constructivist branch of Realism, the self-monitoring of social actors is not open to sensory experience but to communicative experience. See chapters 4 and 5 in Blaikie (1993a) for a critical review, and van Fraassen (1980), Benton (1981), Stockman (1983), and Churchland and Hooker (1985) for specific criticisms. (See Research Design 3 in chapter 8 for an application of one version of the *retroductive* strategy.)

Abductive Research Strategy

The idea of *abduction* refers to the process used to generate social scientific accounts from social actors' accounts; for deriving technical concepts and theories from lay concepts and interpretations of social life. The concept of *abduction* has had limited use in philosophy and social science. I know of only two writers who have used it. Peirce (1931a, 1931b, 1934a, 1934b) used *abduction* and *retroduction* synonymously to refer to the process of inventing a hypothesis to explain some observed phenomenon in somewhat the same way as *retroduction* is being used in this book. Following Peirce, Willer (1967) referred to *abduction* as the process used for generating theories. Peirce discussed three levels of abduction. The first involves guessing initial hypotheses after an examination of the data. The second level requires the use of mental experiments to simplify the hypotheses. At the third level, a model is abducted to provide a point of view, or rationale, as an organizing idea to integrate the hypotheses. My use of *abduction* includes some of these ideas but has a different emphasis because of its exclusive application within the Interpretive approach to social enquiry (see Blaikie (1993a) for further elaboration).

Unlike the other three research strategies, whose advocates claim are equally applicable to the natural and the social sciences, the *abductive* strategy is peculiar to the social sciences. It takes various forms and is associated with a range of Interpretive approaches to social enquiry.[15] Because of its rejection of Positivism and Critical Rationalism, Interpretivism is often referred to as 'anti-naturalist' (meaning against the methods of the natural sciences) or 'anti-positivist' (meaning the rejection of Positivism and Critical Rationalism as discussed here). However, the constructivist version of Scientific Realism has some overlap with Interpretivism.

---

[15] This approach has been labelled in many ways. During the paradigmatic debates in sociology in the 1960s and 1970s it was commonly called 'phenomenology', 'symbolic interactionism' or even 'ethnomethodology', although each of these has a different ancestry. It is now commonly called 'constructivism'. 'Interpretivism' is being used here to include all or a part of a number of traditions that share similar ontological assumptions. These include hermeneutics, phenomenology, symbolic interactionism, existential sociology and social constructivism. See Schwandt (1994) for a review of the varieties of interpretivism and constructivism.

Positivists are concerned with establishing the fundamental patterns or relationships in social life and Critical Rationalists are concerned with using such patterns to form explanatory arguments. However, Interpretivists argue that statistical patterns or correlations are not understandable on their own. It is necessary to find out what meanings (motives) people give to the actions that lead to such patterns. What leads people of one religion to have a higher chance of committing suicide than people of another religion? What leads young people from dysfunctional families to engage in criminal activities? According to Interpretivists, these relationships, between religion and suicide, or juvenile delinquency and broken homes, can only be understood once the connection between these concepts has been established in terms of motives of the people concerned.

Interpretivism takes what Positivism and Critical Rationalism ignore – the meanings and interpretations, the motives and intentions, that people use in their everyday lives and that direct their behaviour – and it elevates them to the central place in social theory and research. For Interpretivism, the social world *is* the world interpreted and experienced by its members, from the 'inside'. Hence, the task of the Interpretive social scientist is to discover and describe this 'insider' view, not to impose an 'outsider' view on it.

Interpretive social science seeks to discover why people do what they do by uncovering the largely tacit, mutual knowledge, the symbolic meanings, motives and rules, which provide the orientations for their actions. Mutual knowledge is background knowledge that is largely unarticulated; it is constantly being used and modified by social actors as they interact with each other; and it is produced and reproduced by them in the course of their lives together. It is the everyday beliefs and practices, mundane and taken for granted, which have to be grasped and articulated by the social researcher in order to provide an understanding of these actions.

Interpretivists have a very different view of social life to that held by Positivists and Critical Rationalists. Interpretivists are concerned with understanding the social world people have produced and which they reproduce through their continuing activities. This everyday reality consists of the meanings and interpretations given by the social actors to their actions, other people's actions, social situations, and natural and humanly created objects. In short, in order to negotiate their way around their world and make sense of it, social actors have to interpret their activities together, and it is these meanings, embedded in language, that constitute their social reality.

However, these subjective meanings are not private; they are *intersubjective*. Members of a particular group or society share common meanings and interpretations, and they maintain them through their ongoing interaction together. Therefore, social explanations need to go beyond the specific meanings that a social actor gives to his/her actions and needs to deal with typical meanings produced by typical social actors. This involves the use of approximations and abstractions.

Hence, the *abductive* research strategy entails *ontological* assumptions that view social reality as the social construction of social actors. It is their creation and does not exist independently of their social activities together. Social reality is regarded as the product of processes by which social actors together negotiate the meanings for actions and situations; it is a complex of socially constructed mutual knowledge – meanings, cultural symbols and social institutions. These meanings and interpretations both facilitate and structure social relationships. Social reality *is* the symbolic world of meanings and interpretations. It is not some 'thing' that may be interpreted in different ways; it is those interpretations. Hence, in contrast to physical reality, which has to be interpreted by scientists, social reality is pre-interpreted; it has already been interpreted before social scientists begin their task of interpretation.

These *ontological* assumptions can be regarded as 'relativist' rather than 'absolutist'; the idea that there is single social reality is rejected in favour of the idea that there may be multiple and changing social realities. The implication is that there is no independent or neutral way of establishing the 'truth' of any of them; each social reality may be 'real' to its inhabitants.

The *epistemological* assumptions of the *abductive* research strategy regard social scientific knowledge as being derived from everyday concepts and meanings, from socially constructed mutual knowledge. The social researcher enters the everyday social world in order to grasp these socially constructed meanings. At one level, the accounts of a social world produced by the social scientist are redescriptions in social scientific language of the social actors' everyday accounts. At another level, these redescriptions can be developed into theories that go beyond everyday knowledge to include conditions of which social actors may be unaware.

The distinguishing features of the *abductive* research strategy are:

- its view of the nature of social reality;
- the origin of answers to 'why' questions; and
- the manner in which those answers are obtained.

It is based on the following principles.

1 The basic access to any social world is the accounts that people can give of their own actions and the actions of others.
2 These accounts are provided to the social scientist in the language of the participants and contain the concepts that the participants use to structure their world, the meanings of these concepts, and the 'theories' that they use to account for what goes on.
3 However, much of the activity of social life is routine and is conducted in a taken-for-granted, unreflective manner.
4 It is only when enquiries are made about their behaviour by others (such as social scientists) or when social life is disrupted, and/or ceases to be predictable, that social actors are forced to consciously search for or construct meanings and interpretations.
5 Therefore, the social scientist may have to resort to procedures that encourage this reflection in order to discover the meanings and theories.
6 Ultimately, it is necessary to piece together the fragments of meaning that are available from their externalized products.

It is to the process of moving from lay descriptions of social life to technical descriptions of that social life that the notion of *abduction* is applied. In other words, the *abductive* strategy involves constructing theory that is grounded in everyday activities, and/or in the language and meanings of social actors. It has two stages:

- describing these activities and meanings; and
- deriving categories and concepts that can form the basis of an understanding or an explanation of the problem at hand.

The logic of *abduction* that is elaborated here draws primarily on the work of Schütz (1963a, 1963b), but also shares much in common with the work of Winch (1958), Douglas (1971), Rex (1971, 1974), and, particularly, Giddens (1976). (See Blaikie 1993a: 176–93 for a review of these writers.)

Schütz claimed that all scientific knowledge of the social world is indirect. The social sciences cannot understand people as living individuals, each with a unique consciousness. Rather, they can only be understood as personal ideal types existing in an impersonal and anonymous time which no one has actually experienced or can experience.

Schütz insisted that social scientists' ideal types (second-order constructs) must be derived from everyday typifications (first-order constructs) which constitute social actors' social reality.

> The thought objects constructed by the social scientist, in order to grasp this social reality, have to be founded upon the thought objects constructed by the common-sense thinking of men [sic], living their daily life within their social world. Thus, the constructs of the social sciences are, so to speak, constructs of the second degree, that is, constructs of the constructs made by the actors on the social scene, whose behaviour the social scientist has to observe and to explain. (Schütz 1963a: 242)

The critical difference between first- and second-order constructs is that they are constructed with different purposes in mind and within different contexts. First-order constructs take a particular social stock of everyday knowledge for granted and are designed to deal with a social problem – to make social interaction possible and understandable to the participants. Second-order constructs are designed to deal with a social scientific problem – to explain social phenomena – and have to relate to a social scientific stock of knowledge (Schütz 1963b: 337–9).

The move from first-order to second-order constructs requires the social scientist to select from the activities and meanings of everyday life those considered to be relevant to the purpose at hand, and to construct models of the social world – typical social actors with typical motives and typical courses of action in typical situations.

> Yet these models of actors are not human beings living within their biographical situation in the social world of everyday life. Strictly speaking, they do not have any biography or any history, and the situation into which they are placed is not a situation defined by them but defined by their creator, the social scientist. He [sic] has created these puppets or homunculi to manipulate them for his purpose. A

merely specious consciousness is imputed to them by the scientist, which is constructed in such a way that its presupposed stock of knowledge at hand (including the ascribed set of invariant motives) would make actions originating from it subjectively understandable, provided that these actions were performed by real actors within the social world. (Schütz 1963b: 339–40)

While Schütz did not set out the *abductive* strategy as a set of principles or steps, it is possible to extract this from his work.

1 The social scientist 'observes certain facts and events within social reality which refer to human action' (1963a: 247).
2 'He [*sic*] constructs typical behaviour or course-of-action patterns from what he has observed' (1963a: 247; 1963b: 339).
3 'He co-ordinates to these typical course-of-action patterns a personal type, a model of an actor whom he imagines as being gifted with consciousness' (1963a: 247; 1963b: 339).
4 'He thus ascribes to this fictitious consciousness a set of typical notions, purposes, goals (in-order-to motives corresponding to the goals of the observed course-of-action patterns and typical because-motives upon which the in-order-to motives are founded), which are assumed to be invariant in the mind of the imaginary actor-model' (1963a: 247; 1963b: 340).
5 This puppet 'is invested with a system of relevances originating in the scientific problem of his constructor and not in the particular biographically determined situation of an actor within the world' (1963b: 341).
6 The puppet 'is interrelated in interaction patterns to other . . . puppets constructed in a similar way' (1963a: 247).
7 This constitutes a model of the social world of everyday life (1963a: 247).
8 The system of typical constructs designed by the social scientist must be formed in accordance with the following postulates:
    (a) the postulate of *logical consistency* – they must supersede first-level constructs by conforming to the principles of formal logic and by being clear and distinct (1963b: 342);
    (b) the postulate of *subjective interpretation* – it must be possible to refer 'all kinds of human action or their result to the subjective meaning such action or result of an action had for the actor' (1963b: 343); and
    (c) the postulate of *adequacy* – 'A human act performed within the life-world by an individual actor in the way indicated by the typical construct would be understandable for the actor himself as well as for his fellow-men [*sic*] in terms of commonsense interpretations of everyday life' (1963b: 343; 1963a: 247).
9 In much the same way as social actors test first-level constructs, ideal types can be verified by predicting 'how a puppet or system of puppets might behave under certain conditions' (1963a: 248). In this way propositions can be developed which state relations between sets of variables.

What Schütz, Winch (1958), Douglas (1971), Rex (1971, 1974) and Giddens (1976, 1984) have in common is their belief that social science accounts of the social world must be derived, at least initially, from the accounts that social actors can give of the aspect of their world of interest to the social scientist. They differ, however, in what is done with these accounts. There is one tradition that argues that reporting everyday accounts is all that is possible or necessary in order to understand social life (see e.g. Garfinkel's ethnomethodology). Others are prepared to turn these accounts into social scientific descriptions of the way of life of a particular social group (community or society), but they would insist on keeping these descriptions tied closely to the social actors' language. Such descriptions lend themselves to two other possibilities. The first is to bring some existing theory or perspective to bear on them, thus providing a social scientific interpretation or critique of that way of life. The second is to generate some kind of explanation, using as ingredients the ideal types that are derived from everyday accounts. There are disagreements on both of these latter possibilities, in the first case about whether criticism of another way of life is legitimate, and, in the second case, about what else can or should be added to the everyday account to form a theory. (A practical application of the *abductive* strategy can be found in chapter 8, Research Design 4.)

Ontological and Epistemological Comparisons

While the four research strategies are based on unique combinations of ontological and epistemological assumptions, there are some overlaps. For example, the *inductive* and *deductive* strategies both adopt 'realist' ontologies. They assume that social phenomena exist independently of both the observer and social actors; it is the regularities or patterns in this reality that social research endeavours to discover and describe, and it is elements of this reality that determine social behaviour. However, while these two strategies may share a common ontology, they differ in their epistemologies, in their assumptions about how this reality can be described, and, particularly, how it can be explained. In the *inductive* strategy, the activity of observing, and the possibility of establishing the truth of a theory, are accepted uncritically, whereas in the *deductive* strategy, the inherent limitations of observations and the impossibility of knowing whether a theory is true are recognized. In the *inductive* strategy, faith is placed in 'objective' procedures to arrive at the truth, while the *deductive* strategy involves the use of rigorous and critical evaluation of any theory that is proposed. The logics of their procedures are fundamentally different, as are their products. The *inductive* strategy produces descriptions of regularities that form a hierarchy of generality; lower-level 'conjunctions' or correlations are explained as being specific cases of higher-level regularities. The *deductive* strategy, on the other hand, involves a search for causal explanation based on deductive arguments, the conclusions of which are rigorously tested.

Because the *retroductive* strategy is based on the idea that reality consists of three domains, it is possible to adopt different ontological assumptions in each domain, particularly the 'empirical' and the 'real' domains. In the structuralist version, the empirical domain can be regarded as being an 'external' reality, while in the constructivist version, reality is socially constructed. Both forms of reality are observable. In the structuralist version, the structures and mechanisms that produce regularities reside in the real domain. These structures can have an influence on social actors and are regarded as part of reality that is 'external' to them. In the constructivist version, the explanatory mechanisms are cognitive rather than social structural in nature. In both versions of the *retroductive* strategy, the epistemological assumptions of the *inductive* strategy are rejected. However, the *retroductive* strategy is faced with the same dilemma as the *deductive* strategy, i.e. how to make contact with the hypothesized structures and mechanisms of the real domain.

The *abductive* research strategy entails radically different ontological assumptions from those of the *inductive* and *deductive* strategies. The *abductive* strategy is not only based on a constructivist view of social reality, but the source of its explanatory accounts is also located there. The epistemological assumptions of *abductive* strategy distinguish it sharply from *inductive* and *deductive* strategies, and the structuralist version of the *retroductive* strategy. However, it shares a great deal in common with the constructivist version; it is only in the location of the explanatory accounts that differences are evident and, even then, they are somewhat illusory. For example, Harré's use of models and Weber's notions of ideal types are very similar (see Blaikie 1994).

In spite of the differences in ontological and epistemological assumptions between the research strategies, there is a methodological problem that confronts the users of all four. This concerns the relationship between data and social reality. Data are produced by the activities of social researchers acting on some version of social reality. In the *inductive* and *deductive* research strategies, concepts are used to make contact with social reality. 'Measuring' these concepts is a major way of producing data. Concepts are also used in the *retroductive* research strategy to initially describe social reality, and postulated structures or mechanisms provide the path to 'unknown' parts of it. Data about structures or mechanisms are produced by 'observation' and experiment. In the *abductive* strategy, social reality is socially constructed and is seen to reside in lay language. Knowledge of this reality is produced by 'immersion' in it.

A problem encountered in using any of the research strategies is that social researchers can only collect data from some point of view, by making 'observations' through spectacles with lenses that are shaped and coloured by the researcher's language, culture, discipline-based knowledge, past experiences (professional and lay), and the expectations that follow from these. It is possible to introduce some controls on these factors, such as having multiple investigators, but, ultimately, all 'observation' is interpretation – all observation is theory-dependent. Therefore, there will always be a gap of some kind between the data that are collected and the reality that they are supposed to represent.

However, in the case of the *abductive* research strategy, and the constructivist version of the *retroductive* strategy, the situation is somewhat different. The reason is that the ontological and epistemological assumptions are very different. In these two cases, social reality has no independent existence apart from the 'knowledge' of it held by the social actors who produce and reproduce it. If the social researcher can learn to inhabit their social reality as a 'native', then they will be as close as any person can be to that social reality. To the extent that a researcher chooses to maintain some distance from such social realities, or cannot avoid doing so, a gap will be created between the social reality and any under-standing of it. Similarly, if in the process of redescribing the social actors' accounts of their activities in social scientific language the researcher fails to 'retain the integrity of the phenomenon', for example by introducing concepts and ideas that are foreign to that social reality, a bigger gap will be created. In this case, a 'distorted' view of a social reality will be produced. Hence, it is inevitable that distance will also be present when the *abductive* research strategy is used, although its nature and degree will usually be different from that in the other strategies.

In short, social researchers are constantly plagued with the problem of creating 'sociological' realities that may not represent the 'social' realities they claim to be studying, whatever those realities are assumed to be. The choice of research strategy, and how it is used, has a large bearing on this problem.

Research Strategies and Research Questions

As we have seen, the four research strategies provide different ways of answering 'why' questions; each one sets out a logic of enquiry for generating an account of some phenomenon; a starting-point, a series of stages and a concluding-point. It has been argued that the *inductive* strategy is weak on answering 'why' questions, and it is recognized that only some versions of the *abductive* strategy are used for it. The *inductive* strategy explains by means of well-confirmed generalizations that can be expected to hold across space and time. The *deductive* strategy explains by means of well-tested theories that represent the current state of knowledge. The *retroductive* strategy explains by means of real mechanisms, the existence of which has been established. Lastly, the *abductive* strategy produces understanding based on 'thick' descriptions and ideal types that have been derived from everyday accounts.

The *inductive* and *abductive* research strategies are the only ones that can answer 'what' research questions, but they do so in quite different ways. If a 'realist' rather than a 'relativist' ontology is desired, then the alternative is the *inductive* strategy. However, it is necessary to accept the assumptions of the inductive strategy, and the methods for overcoming its limitations.

The pragmatic solution to the limitations of the *inductive* research strategy is well known and is commonly referred to as 'operationalism'. It has its founda-tions in Durkheim's injunction to define concepts in advance of the research being undertaken. Operationalism traditionally requires two levels of definition: a for-mal definition that states what the concept means; and an operational definition that states how the concept will be measured. For example, the concept of 'social status' might be formally defined as 'a position within a social hierarchy', and then measured in terms of occupational prestige. This will be discussed further in chapter 5.

Operationalism infringes the strict requirements of the *inductive* strategy because it involves both focusing attention on specific phenomena and limiting the conception of them. To the purists, this is introducing preconceptions. The process of formally defining any concept, in a way that will relate it to the current state of knowledge, involves locating it in a network of concepts and their accepted definitions. This introduces a background of theoretical assumptions as all concepts carry theoretical baggage.[16] Therefore, all description involves some point of view, and pure description is impossible.

Both the *deductive* and *retroductive* research strategies accept these restrictions. Therefore, they have no difficulty in using answers to 'what' questions derived in this way as topics for which answers to 'why' questions are sought. The same is also the case for many *abductivists*; while being suspicious of the ontological assumptions on which such answers to 'what' questions are based, they may be prepared to use these descriptions as a starting-point for research.

Answering a 'how' question requires a different kind of description which is built on previous answers to both 'what' and 'why' questions. Answers to 'how' questions require a description of a desired state of affairs, and the specification of stages and procedures for getting from an existing situation to the desired situation. Clearly, this type of description is complex and requires a great deal of knowledge of the social phenomenon and the context. All four strategies would claim to be able to answer 'how' questions, although there are disagreements about which ones are the most effective. In some cases, a combination of strategies might be an advantage.

Choosing a Research Strategy

The principal aim in choosing a research strategy, or strategies, is to achieve the best procedure(s) for dealing with a research topic, and, particularly, for answering research questions. However, it is important to note that it may be necessary to use different strategies for different research questions. For example, the *inductive* strategy can be used to answer 'what' questions, and the *deductive* and *retroductive* strategies are used to answer 'why' questions. The *abductive* strategy has the advantage that it can be used to answer both 'what' and 'why' questions, depending on the branch of Interpretivism within which the researcher works.

To arrive at a decision on what will be the best research strategy or strategies, the capabilities and the relative strengths and weakness of each strategy must be understood. This requires a reasonably sophisticated understanding of the philosophies of social science and the approaches to social enquiry with which each research strategy is associated (see Blaikie 1993a, particularly chapter 7).

Research questions can usually be answered by using more than one research strategy. For example, in the research topic 'Absenteeism in the Public Sector' (see the Appendix), the research question – 'Why does absenteeism occur?' – could be answered by selecting an appropriate theory and putting it to the test in this context (the *deductive* strategy), or, alternatively, by trying to understand work and life from the nurses' points of view (the *abductive* strategy).

---

[16] These problems are related to what is known as the 'theory dependence of observations' (Hanson 1958). If there is no theory-neutral observation language, then pure inductivism is impossible.

The two strategies are likely to produce different kinds of accounts of absentee-ism, and it will be difficult, if not impossible, to decide which is the best one. One criterion might be to see which account leads to interventions that produce the greatest reduction in absenteeism. However, situations like this are always com-plex and changing, interventions are never simple, and outcomes may not be easy to establish conclusively. It has been argued that there are no completely neutral criteria for making such choices (see e.g. Kuhn 1970). Hence, ultimately, the choice of research strategy has to be a matter of judgement, and judgements involve both acceptable criteria and personal preferences.

A number of other factors can influence the choice of research strategy. When a researcher is contributing to a particular research programme, a decision might be made to select the strategy or strategies already in use. This may be a conscious choice or may simply be taken for granted, particularly if the researcher is trained in the research traditions used in that research programme, and in the particular paradigm within which it is located. Not to follow these traditions may lead to conflict with colleagues and, ultimately, to reduced career prospects.

It is also possible that a preference for, or familiarity with, certain research methods will influence the choice of strategy. For example, if a researcher believes that particular quantitative methods are best, and has received training in only these methods, they may opt for a strategy in which it is believed these methods are used. For example, the *deductive* strategy might be selected because it is believed that quantitative methods, such as questionnaires, are used in this strat-egy. Similarly, students who have received training in the use of a new computer package for analysing textual data may assume that it must be used within the *abductive* strategy.[17]

Another set of possible influences has to do with the audiences that a researcher considers important and the assumptions that are made about their methodo-logical preferences. These audiences can include funding agencies, publishers and journal editors, discipline colleagues and consumers of the research, such as book buyers, journal readers, clients and respondents. In the case of research students, there is the very important group that includes supervisors/advisers and ex-aminers. Perceptions of the preferences of these audiences may need to be taken into account. However, conflict between audience expectations can obviously be a problem.

In the last analysis, practical considerations, such as time, cost and availability of equipment, may have an influence. While these factors are more directly associated with research methods, views about links between strategies and methods, whether correct or not, may lead to the rejection of a particular strategy. For example, in-depth interviewing may be seen to be associated with the *abduc-tive* research strategy, and as this method can be time-consuming, both the method and the strategy may be rejected.

The possible influence of all these factors, and the difficulty involved in estab-lishing the relative merits of the four research strategies, would seem to undermine my case for a detailed knowledge of the strategies and the need to give careful

---

[17] I have heard it said that some postgraduate students have even chosen their research topic, as well as their research strategy, so that they could use such software.

consideration to their selection. My concern is about making informed choices based on adequate knowledge of what is being selected and rejected and on an understanding of the ontological and epistemological assumptions that go with such choices. The fact that personal, social and practical factors may also have an influence makes it necessary not only to be aware of these, but also of the consequences of allowing them to influence the choices.

Research Design and Research Strategies

The selection of a research strategy does not predetermine the kind of research design that is adopted. While some research strategies tend to be associated with particular types of research, such as the *inductive* strategy and social surveys, the *deductive* strategy and the experimental method, and the *abductive* strategy and case studies, there is no necessary connection. The logic of any of the four research strategies can be implemented using a variety of research designs.

Differences exist between the research strategies in the kinds of objectives they are able to pursue (see table 4.2). *Exploration* and *description* are confined to the *inductive* and *abductive* strategies. While the *deductive* and *retroductive* strategies need description as their starting-point, they must rely on the other two strategies for them. The major task of the *deductive* and *retroductive* strategies is *explanation*, although *inductivists* also claim to be able to do it, and some *abductivists* would like to be able to do it. *Prediction* is confined to the *inductive* and *deductive* strategies, again being achieved in different ways. Some *abductivists* may be interested in *prediction*, based on 'thick' descriptions, but this is of minor concern. The objective of *understanding* is the exclusive preserve of the *abductive* strategy. Some users of the *retroductive* and *abductive* strategies are interested in *change*,

Table 4.2 Research strategies, objectives and questions

| Objective | Research strategy | | | | Type of research question |
	Inductive	Deductive	Retroductive	Abductive	
Exploration	***			***	What
Description	***			***	What
Explanation	*	***	***		Why
Prediction	**	***			What
Understanding				***	Why
Change		*	**	**	How
Evaluation	**	**	**	**	What and Why
Assess impacts	**	**	**	**	What and Why

Key: *** = major activity; ** = moderate activity; * = minor activity. These 'weightings' of the connections between objectives and research strategies are indicative only.

particularly researchers concerned with emancipation. *Evaluation* research is
practised by followers of all four research strategies, with a common division
between positivist and constructivist approaches (Guba and Lincoln 1989) and
quantitative and qualitative methods. Social impact assessment can use the *inductive* strategy, perhaps in combination with the *deductive* strategy, the *retroductive*
strategy or the *abductive* strategy.

As we shall see in chapter 7, while there may be conventions about quantitative
methods being used in some strategies, for example the *inductive* and *deductive*,
and qualitative methods being used in others, for example the *abductive*, there is
no necessary association. Methods can be used in the service of a number of
research strategies. However, they will need to be used, and can be used, with
different ontological assumptions. For example, observation can be used in
the service of all four research strategies, although just how it is used might
vary; the same is true in the case of interviewing. The critical issue is the need to
be aware of the ontological and epistemological assumptions within which the
method is used.

Research Strategies and the Role of the Researcher

To conclude this discussion of the four research strategies, we need to return to an
issue raised in chapter 2 regarding the role of the researcher. Because of its
particular ontological and epistemological assumptions, each research strategy
entails a position with regard to objectivity and validity and, hence, affects the
choice of role.

In the *inductive* research strategy, it is argued that the researcher must take a
detached observer position and avoid allowing personal values or political commitments to contaminate the research. If objectivity cannot be achieved, then the
generalizations produced cannot be trusted as representing the regularities in
social life; it would not be possible to achieve the aim of arriving at true statements about the world.

While the aim of the *deductive* research strategy is also a search for the truth, it
is recognized that the culture, including language, together with knowledge and
previous experiences, make presuppositionless data collection impossible. However, even though 'observation' may be theory-laden, it is still necessary to
endeavour to exclude personal values and political commitments from the
research process. Detachment remains the ideal, even though it is recognized
that its complete achievement is impossible.

The two branches of the *retroductive* research strategy, the 'structuralist' and
the 'constructionist', deal with this issue differently. The 'structuralist' version
essentially follows the role of the researcher adopted in the *deductive* strategy. The
aim is to establish the existence of real structures and mechanisms even in the face
of the 'theory-dependence of observation' (see Pawson 1989). In the 'constructionist' version, the view of the role of the researcher is likely to be one of those
adopted in the *abductive* strategy.

It is in the *abductive* research strategy that very different views of the role of the researcher are adopted. These include the *faithful reporter*, the *mediator of languages*, the *reflective partner*, the *conscientizer*, and the postmodern 'narrative dialogue'. The reflexive nature of this type of social research casts the researcher in very different roles to that required by both the *inductive* and *deductive* research strategies (see chapter 2, 'Roles for Researchers').

In spite of their sympathy for one or more of these latter roles, some writers have expressed reservations about their implications for the social scientific enterprise (e.g. Geertz 1988; Hammersley and Atkinson 1995). The acceptance of these roles can lead the researcher in a number of directions, including the abandonment of any concern with the production of new social scientific knowledge. The fear is that research will just become a form of journalism or part of a political programme, or will lead to 'methodological paralysis'. While I sympathize with the view that social science should include emancipatory concerns, I am also committed to seeking better understanding of social life, preferably by incorporating the social actors' point of view. In any case, without sound understanding, emancipation becomes problematic. Of course, it is necessary to accept the idea that such knowledge will be limited in its relevance in terms of both time and space. However, accepting this degree of relativity in the nature of the knowledge we produce does not invalidate the social research enterprise. An example of the adoption of a middle position can be found in Hammersley and Atkinson (1995: 1–22).

Conclusion

When social researchers set out to answer their research questions, they are faced with the task of choosing the best research strategy or strategies to answer them. Four fundamentally different strategies are available, each with its particular combination of ontological and epistemological assumptions, and its unique logic of enquiry.

The research strategies differ in the types of research objectives and research questions they can answer. The *inductive* and *abductive* strategies are the only ones that are useful for *exploration* and *description*, although they each achieve these objectives in different ways and with different outcomes. The *deductive* and *retroductive* research strategies are the most suitable for pursuing the objective of *explanation*. Likewise, they achieve this using different procedures based on different assumptions. The *abductive* research strategy is the only one that can pursue the objective of *understanding* because of its particular ontological and epistemological assumption, and its peculiar logic of enquiry. The four research strategies have different capacities with regard to the other research objectives and types of research questions.

While the considerations in the previous paragraph are very important in the choice of research strategy, other factors can have an influence. Although not always recognized, chief among them is the researcher's preference for certain ontological and epistemological assumptions. However, there is also a range of pragmatic and (small 'p') political factors that can play an important role.

Before proceeding to a consideration of the research methods that may be suitable for selecting, collecting and analysing data to answer research questions, within a particular research strategy, we need to backtrack to consider a set of fundamental issues. These are the roles of concepts, theories, hypotheses and models in social research.

5

Concepts, Theories,
Hypotheses and Models

To speak of a science without concepts suggests all sorts of analogies – a carver without tools, a railroad without tracks, a mammal without bones, a love story without love. (Blumer 1969)

Contemporary sociologists have been preoccupied with 'theory,' yet have seldom tried to make clear what theory is. (Homans 1964)

Research without theory is blind, and theory without research is empty. (Bourdieu and Wacquant 1992)

Introduction

The social science literature is replete with ideas about the role of concepts, theories, hypotheses and models in social research. Some of these ideas have come to be accepted uncritically. For example, many textbooks on social research methods regard the core of social research as being the definition and measurement of concepts, with theories stating relationships between concepts and models consisting of a network of such relationships. Hypotheses are regarded as potential relationships between concepts that can be tested by measuring the key concepts in them and analysing the data so produced. This view is attractive because of its simplicity. However, while it is very common, it is only relevant to two of the research strategies, the *inductive* and *deductive*, and then it is used differently in each one. Other views also need to be considered.

This chapter will examine:

- views on how concepts are used in social research;
- ideas on the nature and use of theory;
- classical and contemporary views on the relationship between theory and research;
- the role of hypotheses and their connection with theory;
- types of models and their uses; and
- the role of concepts, theories, hypotheses and models in the four research strategies (see figure 5.1).

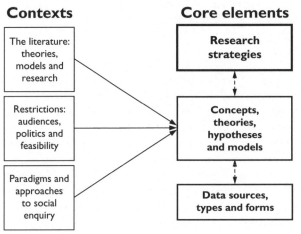

Figure 5.1   Concepts, theories, hypotheses and models

The Role of Concepts

A concept is an idea that is expressed in words or as a symbol. Technical concepts in any discipline form the language, or jargon, by means of which it deals with its subject-matter. They range in generality from the very specific to the highly abstract and from the simple to the complex. Concepts are regarded as the building blocks of social theories. Theories, in turn, specify the relationships between concepts and why these relationships exist. Good theories are supposed to represent what happens in the social world.

> Theory is of value in empirical science only to the extent to which it connects fruitfully with the empirical world. Concepts are the means, and the only means of establishing such connection, for it is the concept that points to the empirical instances about which a theoretical proposal is made. If the concept is clear as to what it refers, then sure identification of the empirical instances may be made. With their identification, they can be studied carefully, used to test theoretical proposals and exploited for suggestions as to new proposals. Thus, with clear concepts theoretical statements can be brought into close and self-correcting relations with the empirical world. (Blumer 1969: 143)

In addition to this role of establishing some kind of link with the social world, Blumer saw concepts as being important in the theoretical framework that sets a context for the research, as being involved in the statement of the research problem, as determining the data that will be collected and how they will be categorized, and as being essential in describing the findings.

> Throughout the act of scientific inquiry concepts play a central role. They are significant elements in the prior scheme that the scholar has of the empirical world; they are likely to be the terms in which his [sic] problem is cast; they are usually the

categories for which data are sought and in which the data are grouped; they usually become the chief means for establishing relations between data; and they are usually the anchor points in interpretation of the findings. Because of such a decisive role in scientific inquiry, concepts need especially to be subjected to methodological scrutiny. (Blumer 1969: 26)

Blumer's depiction of the role of concepts is intended to represent their place in the Positivist paradigm that dominated at the time of writing. However, he proceeded to scrutinize this view, in particular, to question whether concepts used in this paradigm actually match the empirical world to which they are supposed to refer (Blumer 1969: 28). His solution was to use sensitizing rather than definitive concepts. This distinction will be discussed shortly.

A concept consists of both a word (or symbol) and a definition. It is differences in views about the sources of these words and their definitions that distinguish the research strategies. For example, in the *inductive* and *deductive* research strategies, it is the researcher's responsibility to select the relevant concepts and to define them before the research commences. However, in the *abductive* research strategy, the concepts and their definitions may be derived initially from those used by social actors in the context of the topic under investigation. Technical concepts are derived from these lay concepts by a process of abstraction during the course of the research. Because of these different usages, we cannot set out with just a single view of the role of concepts in social research.

In the *inductive* and *deductive* research strategies, concepts and their definitions have various origins. For example, they may come from:

- a theoretical perspective that is dominant within a discipline or social scientific community (e.g. conflict theory);
- a specific research programme (e.g. social mobility);
- commonly used theoretical concepts that are given a new definition (e.g. social class); or
- everyday concepts that are given precise meanings.

All of these sources involve the researcher in deciding what concepts and definitions are the most appropriate.

To explore these differences, four traditions in the use of concepts in the social sciences will be discussed: the *ontological*, the *operationalizing*, the *sensitizing* and the *hermeneutic*. The *ontological* tradition is concerned with establishing the main features of social reality, the *operationalizing* tradition with specifying and measuring concepts to produce variables for a particular research project, the *sensitizing* tradition with refining an initial flexible concept in the course of the research, and the *hermeneutic* tradition with deriving technical concepts from lay language.

The Ontological Tradition

The *ontological* tradition is concerned with establishing a set of concepts that identify the basic features of the social world, and that are essential for

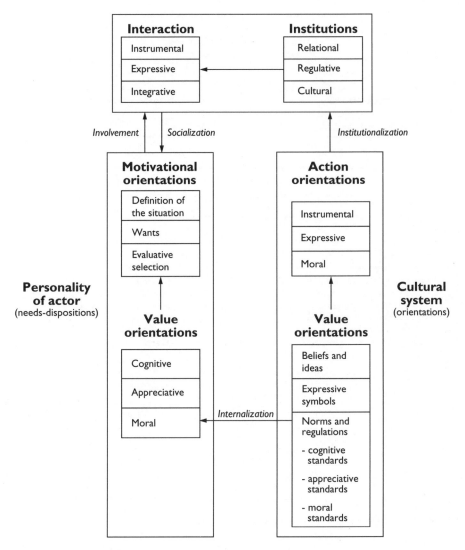

Figure 5.2   Parsons's theory of the system of action

(*Source:* Waters 1994: 145)

understanding society, major social institutions or, perhaps, small-scale social situations. Elements of the ontological tradition can be found in the work of classical and modern social theorists. Classical theorists, such as Marx, Weber and Durkheim, each developed a battery of key concepts that provided a view of reality and were used in their theorizing. However, it is modern theorists, such as Parsons, who have turned the ontological analysis of concepts into a major preoccupation. A modification of part of Parsons's conceptual scheme will serve as an illustration of this tradition (see figure 5.2).

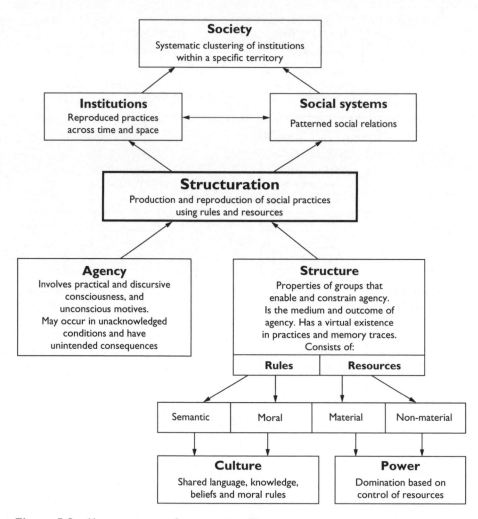

Figure 5.3   Key concepts in Structuration Theory

Merton was critical of this type of theorizing. He argued that conceptual analysis that deals with the specification and clarification of key concepts, while essential to theoretical work, does not itself constitute theory.

> It is only when such concepts are interrelated in the form of a scheme that a theory begins to emerge. Concepts, then, constitute the definitions (or prescriptions) of what is to be observed; they are the variables between which empirical relationships are to be sought. When propositions are logically interrelated, a theory has been instituted. (Merton 1968: 89)

More recent attempts at theoretical synthesis, such as those of Habermas and Giddens, also include a strong ontological emphasis. Giddens, for example, has reorganized and redefined some of the basic concepts used by Parsons and others (e.g. society, social system, institution, structure), and has arranged them around the concept of 'structuration'. The foundation concepts in his scheme are 'agency' and 'structure', and the interplay of these leads to the process of structuration. While it is not possible to elaborate Structuration Theory here (see Giddens 1979, 1984; Cohen 1989; Bryant and Jary 1991; Craib 1992; Blaikie 1993a; Layder 1994; Scott 1995), I have attempted to set out the relationships between the basic concepts (see figure 5.3).

The Operationalizing Tradition

The operationalizing tradition is concerned with turning concepts into variables, with identifying the key concepts to be used in a particular study in order to define them and to develop ways of measuring them.

From Durkheim on, it has been argued that, as concepts are the basic building blocks of theory, they must be defined precisely and consistently. The imprecision of ordinary language must be superseded by a technical use of concepts. This has led to the view that science has two languages (see e.g. Blalock 1968a; Babbie 1992; Sedlack and Stanley 1992; Neuman 1997): one is the language of *conceptualization* and the other is the language of empirical testing, or the language of *operationalization*.

The language of *conceptualization* is the language which social scientists use to communicate their theoretical ideas and research findings to each other; it is the language of both abstract theoretical notions as well as a means of identifying observable phenomena. In the context of a research project, this language is used to identify key concepts and to state relationships between these concepts; it is the language used to state research questions and hypotheses. Thus, some authors refer to this language as 'theory'. For example: 'Theories are built from concepts [and]...concepts are constructed from definitions' (Turner 1991: 5).

Researchers are required to define these concepts precisely in terms of how they will be used in a particular research project. The aim is to produce a consistent theoretical language, although this is unlikely to be achieved. Turner has certainly adopted an optimistic view on this.

> Hence the verbal symbols used to develop a concept must be defined as precisely as possible in order that they point to the same phenomenon for all investigators. Although perfect consensus may never be obtained with conventional language, a body of theory rests on the premise that scholars will do their best to define concepts ambiguously. (Turner 1991: 5)

These meanings are usually referred to as *formal definitions*.

The second language, *operationalization*, is used to transform theoretical language into empirical concepts. This is done by specifying the procedures by which the 'theoretical' concept will be measured, by indicating what will count as an example of, or what will have to change to produce different values for, the theoretical concept, i.e. the indicators that will be used to measure the concept to produce data related to it. These are commonly called *operational definitions*. '*Conceptualization* is the refinement and specification of abstract concepts, and *operationalization* is the development of specific research procedures (operations) that will result in empirical observations representing those concepts in the real world' (Babbie 1992: 137).

When a concept can have a number of values, the measurement of it produces a *variable*. Stinchcombe (1968: 28–9) has defined a variable as 'a *concept* which can have *various values*, and which is defined in such a way that *one can tell by means of observations which value it has in a particular occurrence*'. Hence, he defined variables as observational contrasts. Therefore, in research that stresses the importance of operationalism, variables are the focus of research activity.

The concept of 'social class' is an example of such an abstract concept. Social class might be defined as 'a category of individuals who occupy a similar position in a structure resulting from the distribution of economic resources'. While there may be other meanings, this is what social class could mean in a particular research project. Thus defined, the concept might then be measured in terms of the income a person receives from wages or salary. This operationalization relates to only one part of the total economic resources to which an individual may have access, such as interest on savings, dividends from shares, rental income from property, capital gains from property or other assets, a pension or superannuation. To faithfully measure the concept as defined, these and maybe other data would be required. However, the researcher might decide that some sources of income (e.g. capital gains) are too difficult to measure reliably, or the individuals in the study may have little or no idea how much of such income they receive. Hence, the operationalization may be kept to something that is readily measured (although experienced researchers will know that obtaining accurate information about a person's annual wages or salary is far from straightforward).

A great deal of attention has been given to the problems of operationalizing some of the major concepts in social science. Debates about defining and operationalizing concepts have sometimes been regarded as a theoretical activity. For example, some time ago, discussions on the appropriate meaning of the concept of 'role' kept many writers busy. The purpose seems to have been to arrive at the 'right' definition and to somehow persuade others to use it.

Biddle (1979), for example, discussed what he called 'role theory', 'a science concerned with the study of behaviors that are characteristic of persons within contexts' (1979: 4). The theory consisted of identifying a set of concepts related to 'role', such as 'social position', 'expectations', 'context', 'role playing', 'role taking', 'role set', 'role conflict', 'role overload', 'role strain', 'role discontinuity' and 'role malintegration'. Roles were also set within 'social systems', and this involved the elaboration and definition of another collection of concepts, mainly within a functionalist framework. This scheme could be regarded as having an ontological intention, but there is also a strong emphasis on definitions.

About as close as this book comes to any kind of theory is the specification of a set of 'underlying propositions'. However, these do nothing more than assert that the behaviour of some persons within contexts is patterned, that these 'roles' are associated with social positions and expectations, that they persist because they have consequences and are embedded in social systems, and that people have to be socialized into them (Biddle 1979: 8). What theory there is, is at best deterministic, and at worst trivial. What is missing is a theory of social action to bring the 'role players' to life, and to deal with social actors' meanings and motives.[1]

A major difficulty encountered in defining and operationalizing concepts is that they differ in their level of abstractness. Some concepts relate to concrete phenomena in specific times and places (e.g. the suicide rate). Other concepts deal with phenomena that span time and place, that are very general (e.g. deviant behaviour). These latter concepts may be difficult to operationalize unless they are translated into more specific concepts.

This tradition of two languages also identifies a particular relationship between theory and research. Theoretical activity is essentially about identifying the most useful concepts and finding the right formal meaning for them, while research is about selecting the best method of operationalizing a concept and then proceeding to collect the appropriate data and then analyse them. As C. Wright Mills pointed out many years ago, this is a very restricted view of both theory and research.

> 'Theory' becomes the variables useful in interpreting statistical findings; 'empirical data'... are restricted to such statistically determined facts and relations as are numerous, repeatable, measurable.... There are no philosophical grounds, and certainly no grounds in the work of social science... so to restrict these terms. (Mills 1959: 66)

The relationship between theory and research will be taken up later in this chapter.

Blumer was a major critic of the operational tradition. He depicted the tradition thus.

> 'Operational procedure' rests on the idea that a theoretical assertion or a concept can be given both empirical reference and validation by developing a specific, regularized procedure for approaching the empirical world. The given procedure or operation may be the use of a test, a scale, a measuring instrument, or standardized mode of inquiry. The procedure 'operationalizes' the theoretical proposition or concept. If the given operation meets tests of reliability the operation is taken as a sound instrument for disengaging specific empirical data. In turn, these data are thought to be valid empirical referents of the concept or proposition that is operationalized. (Blumer 1969: 30–1)

He objected to the idea of measuring concepts by selecting only a limited aspect of the relevant phenomenon and assuming that it reflected all aspects. Take the measurement of intelligence for example. In everyday life, intelligence manifests itself in many ways and is

> present in such varied things as the skilful military planning of an army general, the ingenious exploitation of a market situation by a business entrepreneur, effective

---

[1] In 1969 I attended a series of seminars at Melbourne's Monash University at which the author presented draft chapters of the book for discussion. At the time I, and others, voiced this criticism. The author subsequently recognized that the 'theory' is weak on motivation (Biddle 1979: 345), but was unable to incorporate an adequate account of it, no doubt because of the deficiencies of his functionalist framework.

methods of survival by a disadvantaged slum dweller, the clever meeting of the problems of his world by a peasant or a primitive [*sic*] tribesman, the cunning of low-grade delinquent-girl morons in a detention home, and the construction of telling verse by a poet. It should be immediately clear how ridiculous and unwarranted it is to believe that the operationalizing of intelligence through a given intelligence test yields a satisfactory picture of intelligence. To form an empirically satisfactory picture of intelligence, a picture that may be taken as having empirical validation, it is necessary to catch and study intelligence as it is in play in actual empirical life instead of relying on a specialized and usually arbitrary selection of one area of its presumed manifestation. (Blumer 1969: 31)

As a symbolic interactionist, Blumer argued that an adequate understanding of social life requires recognition of the fact that individuals and groups find their way about by defining and interpreting the objects, events and situations that they encounter. The operational tradition ignores this.

When current variable analysis deals with matters or areas of human group life which involve the process of interpretation, it is markedly disposed to ignore the process. The conventional procedure is to identify something which is presumed to operate on group life and treat it as an independent variable, and then to select some form of group activity as the dependent variable. The independent variable is put at the beginning part of the process of interpretation and the dependent variable at the terminal part of the process. The intervening process is ignored or, what amounts to the same thing, taken for granted as something that need not be considered. (Blumer 1969: 133)

Blumer was not completely against the operational tradition as long as it was only used 'for those areas of social life and formation that are not mediated by an interpretive process' (Blumer 1969: 139). For Blumer, and fellow interpretivists, it is necessary for a researcher to get as close as possible to the everyday world under investigation and not to rely on procedures that are loaded with assumptions and keep the social world at arm's length. However, he was prepared to accept that even in areas where interpretation is involved, variable analysis might unearth patterns that cannot be detected by the direct study of people as is required in the interpretive approach to social enquiry. These patterns can then be investigated for the interpretations that lie behind them.

The Sensitizing Tradition

Blumer's major solution to the deficiencies of the operational tradition was to suggest the use of sensitizing concepts.[2] He argued that in getting close to the social world we discover what social phenomena have in common. However, these similarities are usually expressed in a distinctive manner, with individual and group variations. Therefore, concepts need to be sensitizing rather than definitive in order for the researcher to be able to explore the nature of what is common.

---

[2] Writers in this tradition differ in terms of whether they regard sensitizing concepts as an alternative to the operationalizing tradition or as a complement to it.

Sensitizing concepts provide clues and suggestions about what to look for. The task is to reshape the concept to identify the nature of the common aspects within the diversity of other features. Until this is done, it is premature to impose predefined (definitive) concepts on the phenomenon.

> It seeks to improve concepts by naturalistic research, that is, by direct study of our natural social world wherein empirical instances are accepted in their concrete and distinctive form.... As such its procedure is markedly different from that employed in the effort to develop definitive concepts. Its success depends on patient, careful and imaginative life study, not on quick shortcuts or technical instruments. While its progress may be slow and tedious, it has the virtue of remaining in close and continuing relations with the natural social world. (Blumer 1969: 152)

In the sensitizing tradition, the researcher sets out with one or a few rather general and vaguely defined concepts that are needed to provide an orientation to the research topic. Initially, their meaning will be established by exposition rather than by definition. However, as the research proceeds, the meaning of the concepts will be refined to make them more relevant for their purpose.

Advocates of this tradition argue that, at the outset of a research project, it may not be possible to be definite about what concepts are relevant or to be precise about their meaning. While a researcher needs some guidance, it is necessary to view the research itself as a process in which meanings of concepts are developed. Goffman (1963) claimed to work this way in developing the concept of 'stigma'. Thus, this type of research develops concepts that can become the basis of formal theory, i.e. theory that synthesizes the commonalities or similarities in generically different phenomena into a coherent theoretical framework (Denzin 1970: 15).

In their exposition of grounded theory, Glaser and Strauss (1967) referred to theoretical sensitivity as the continual development of theory from data. Grounded theory combines 'concepts and hypotheses that have emerged from the data with some existing ones that are clearly useful.... Potential theoretical sensitivity is lost when the sociologist commits himself [*sic*] exclusively to one specific preconceived theory' (1967: 48). The notion of *sensitivity* here refers to openness on the part of the researcher to different ideas, to a process of inter-relating theoretical insights and data.

Drawing on the ideas of Glaser and Strauss (1967) about grounded theory, Denzin has taken the middle ground with regard to sensitizing concepts. He has argued that within his version of symbolic interactionism, the use of sensitizing concepts precedes operationalization. In fact, he defined sensitizing concepts negatively: 'By *sensitizing concepts* I refer to concepts that are not transformed immediately into *operational definitions* through an attitude scale or check list' (Denzin 1970: 14). He illustrated his position with regard to the concept of 'intelligence'.

> Thus if I offer an *operational definition* for 'intelligence,' I might state that intelligence is the score received on an I.Q. test. But if I choose a *sensitizing approach* to measuring intelligence, I will leave it nonoperationalized until I enter the field and learn the processes representing it and the specific meanings attached to it by the

persons observed. It might be found, for example, that in some settings intelligence is not measured by scores on a test but rather by knowledge and skills pertaining to important processes in the group under analysis.... Once I have established the meanings of a concept, I can then employ multiple methods to measure its characteristics. Thus, closed-ended questions, direct participation in the group being studied, and analysis of written documents might be the main strategies of operationalizing a concept. Ultimately, all concepts must be operationalized – must be measured and observed. The sensitizing approach merely delays the point at which operationalization occurs. (Denzin 1970: 14)

Two points need to be noted here. First, Denzin included the meanings that social actors give to the concept being investigated (although they might use some other concept than, say, 'intelligence' to refer to what the researcher is concerned with) in order to arrive at his meaning for it. Second, the subsequent *operationalizing* of the concept may be looser and much more diverse that would normally be the case in the operationalizing tradition.

The defining characteristic of the *sensitizing* tradition is that the researcher sets out with a concept that is loosely defined and then refines its meaning during the course of the research. While some help might be obtained from the people involved in the study, the concept remains the researcher's. Even if another concept is substituted, the concept and its ultimate meaning are based on the researcher's decisions. The final conceptual tradition to be discussed here presents a radical alternative to this view.

The Hermeneutic Tradition

The *hermeneutic* tradition differs from the *sensitizing* tradition in that concepts that the researcher uses to describe and understand any social phenomenon (i.e. technical concepts) have their origin in the everyday language of the social actors under investigation, not in the language of the discipline.

Advocates of this tradition argue that accounts of social life need to be derived, initially, from the accounts that social actors give of their activities; the language used by the social scientist must be derived from everyday language. As Schütz stated it, second-order constructs must be derived from first-order constructs. This requires a hermeneutic process in which the researcher tries to grasp the meaning of everyday language by becoming immersed in the relevant sector of the social world (Giddens 1976). As the process advances, the researcher has to mediate between the particular everyday language and some version of the technical language of social science in order to produce concepts that are relevant to the research topic. The process of mediation is akin to the hermeneutic reading of a text; it is a matter of interpretation rather than translation (Gadamer 1989).

While a researcher may need sensitizing concepts at the outset, the search is for the everyday concepts that social actors use to discuss and relate to this phenomenon. For example, if the topic for investigation is the 'care of the aged', then a researcher has to discover what language old people, their families and professionals use to discuss the problem of what should be done about old people who have lost the capacity to care for themselves. A range of concepts might be used by different actors in different contexts, and none of these may correspond to the ones a researcher has derived from the literature. The researcher's task is to make sense of this diversity of language by producing a typology, a set of categories (types) that capture the different concepts and their meanings. The labels for the types may be invented or borrowed from the literature, but their meaning will be generalized from those used by the social actors (see Stacy 1983; see also Blaikie and Stacy 1982, 1984).

Hence, the *hermeneutic* tradition also differs from the *operational* tradition in terms of the source of the concepts. The *operational* tradition works 'top down' in the sense that it imposes the researcher's concepts on everyday life, the assumption being that the researcher is in a position to judge what concepts will be relevant because of the theoretical model or perspective that has been adopted. In the *hermeneutic* tradition, the researcher works 'bottom up' by adopting the position of learner rather than expert. The social actors have to teach the researcher how they understand their world, i.e. what everyday concepts and interpretations (lay theories) they use to make sense of it. By a complex process, the researcher can use these lay concepts and methods of understanding as the ingredients for their account. From lay concepts technical concepts can be generated. This may require the invention of new concepts, the adaptation of existing technical concepts, or the borrowing of the latter. In the process, a more general and abstract account than the individual accounts of social actors is produced.

To use concepts as advocated by this tradition is to be reflexive: to allow concepts to evolve through a process of re-examination and reflection. The meaning of a concept does not remain static; it changes as the concept evolves from the data and is applied to them. Whether concepts developed in this way can be applied in other contexts is a matter for investigation. Of course, a researcher has to stop somewhere and freeze the meaning of a concept for a while. However, this does not prevent other researchers from using such concepts in their own work, and furthering their development. The aim of all this is to generate concepts that fit the problem at hand and work to provide useful description and understanding.

Concepts and Research Strategies

There are some connections worth noting between the research strategies outlined in chapter 4 and these four conceptual traditions. The ontological tradition provides a background to all research, although it is less relevant to, and may be rejected by, researchers who use the *abductive* research strategy. While *deductivists* may find conceptual schemes very useful as a source of variables, *abductivists* may resist the imposition of such 'top down' schemes and prefer to generate their own concepts in a 'bottom up' manner.

As we have seen, the originators of the *inductive* strategy in the natural sciences insisted that researchers begin with no preconceptions or prejudices. This means that not only were hypotheses regarded as being inappropriate, but so also was the conscious adoption of concepts. They considered that concepts were somehow revealed in the process of making observations; the world was regarded as being already divided into discrete categories of things and events. These categories must be used to avoid distorting reality. However, when Durkheim introduced this research strategy into sociology, he recognized the need to have concepts at the outset in order to be able to make observations, to collect data. By insisting that the researcher define these concepts, he opened up the possibility that a variety of definitions of concepts might be used.

It was then an easy step from Durkheim's ideas to the operationalizing tradition, and to the idea of networks of relationships between variables. However, in spite of the close connection between Positivism and Structural Functionalism in American sociology, particularly in the decades following World War II, and the strong ontological tradition in the latter, the operationalizing tradition has tended to develop independently of this theoretical perspective. In other words, concepts in conceptual schemes were not directly operationalized, no doubt because they were too abstract. As we shall see later in this chapter, there was a chasm at this time between abstract theorizing and empirical research.

It is in the *deductive* research strategy that the operationalizing tradition has been most evident. In this strategy, hypotheses are deduced from a theory, and the concepts in a hypothesis are measured in order to test whether or not a hypothesized relationship exists. While it is possible to test hypotheses using other methods, this research strategy has been dominated by the operationalizing tradition. However, we need to note that the sensitizing tradition might also be used in the *deductive* strategy, for example, in an exploratory phase when relevant concepts and their definitions are being sought.

The connection between the *retroductive* research strategy and the conceptual traditions is rather complex. Strictly speaking, concepts are not operationalized in this research strategy; structures and mechanisms are hypothesized and discovered by direct and indirect observations and experiments. Of course, to hypothesize the existence of a structure or mechanism requires the use of language; you have to have some idea of what you are looking for. This may involve adapting an existing concept, or inventing a new one, to identify it. In this regard, it would be interesting to know how concepts such as 'atom' and 'virus' came to be used.

These comments on the *retroductive* strategy apply particularly to the structuralist version. The situation is rather different in the constructivist version, and is similar to that in the *abductive* research strategy. It is in this latter strategy that both the sensitizing and hermeneutic traditions are used, but in different branches. Nevertheless, it is the hermeneutic tradition that is most appropriate for genuine *abductive* research. This is because the generation of technical concepts from lay concepts is a hermeneutic process.

Clearly, these four views of the role of concepts in social research are very different. As a result, researchers have to make choices about which tradition or traditions to use and, in the process, to make sure that their use is consistent with other research design decisions. The choice of research strategy will have a big influence on the way concepts are used. However, a researcher may use concepts in more than one way in a particular research project.

The Role of Theory

One of the most vexed problems for novice researchers is how to use theory in research. Atheoretical research is condemned; good research is supposed to involve the use of theory in some way. However, there are many views, and much confusion, about where and how theory should be involved in the research process. No doubt, part of the reason for this uncertainty is the fact that the concept 'theory' itself refers to a variety of activities and products.

> Like so many words that are bandied about, the word theory threatens to become meaningless. Because its referents are so diverse – including everything from minor working hypotheses, through comprehensive but vague and unordered speculations, to axiomatic systems of thought – use of the word often obscures rather than creates understanding. (Merton 1968: 39)

The problem is what kind of theory to use, and for what purpose. The situation is further complicated by the existence of a diversity of perspectives in social theory, and differences in the ways in which theory is used in the four research strategies.

Some Definitions of Theory

In order to examine the role of theory in research, we must first be clear about what constitutes social or sociological theory. While the answer to this question may appear to be self-evident, an examination of the literature indicates that there are numerous uses of the concept.

The *Shorter Oxford Dictionary* defines *theory* as

> a scheme or system of ideas or statements held as an explanation or account of a group of facts or phenomena . . . a statement of what are held to be general laws, principles, or causes of something known or observed.

At the more general end of the continuum are definitions that identify theory with the current state of knowledge about why something happens.

> Theories are nets cast to catch what we call 'the world': to rationalise, to explain and to master it. (Popper 1959: 59)

> A theory we take to be a heuristic device for organizing what we know, or think we know, at a particular time about some more or less explicitly posed question or issue. (Inkeles 1964: 28)

> Theory is a 'story' about how and why events in the universe occur. (Turner 1991: 1)

> A theory highlights and explains something which one would otherwise not see, or would find puzzling. (Gilbert 1993: 21)

The next two definitions begin to move to the more specific end of the continuum. They introduce the idea that theories provide explanations by establishing connections between the subject of interest and other phenomena.

> Explanations and predictions are provided by theories. Theories attempt to answer the why and how questions. Theorizing can be defined as the process of providing explanations and predictions of social phenomena, generally by relating the subject of interest (e.g., riots) to some other phenomena (e.g., heat and crowding). (Bailey 1994: 41)
>
> [Theory] explains the relationships among observed activities. (Lin 1976: 15)

At the specific end of the continuum we can find a collection of definitions that concentrate on theory as a set of propositions that state relationships between concepts.

> A theory is an integrated set of relationships with a certain level of validity. (Willer 1967: 9)
>
> A scientific theory is a set of concepts and propositions asserting relationships among concepts. (Land 1971: 180)
>
> A theory is a general and more or less comprehensive set of statements relating different aspects of some phenomenon. (Babbie 1975: 76)
>
> A theory is a set of concepts plus the interrelationships that are assumed to exist among these concepts. (Seltiz et al. 1976: 16)

Two further definitions take this idea a bit further, suggesting that a set of propositions should form a deductive argument.

> A theory is a deductively connected set of general statements, some of which, the premises or axioms, logically imply others, the theorems. ... [The] purpose is to show what else must be true *if* the premises are true. (Brodbeck 1968: 385–6)
>
> Sociological theory refers to logically interconnected sets of propositions from which empirical uniformities can be derived. (Merton 1968: 39)

Out of this diversity it is possible to identify two types of theory in terms of the activities engaged in by the practitioners: *theoreticians'* theory and *researchers'* theory (Menzies 1982). *Theoreticians'* theory is that produced by writers whose aim is to develop an understanding of social life in terms of basic concepts and ideas. These can be about macro- or micro-social phenomena. Such concepts and ideas are produced with little or no direct reference to the findings of research, and they are not systematically tested by means of research. Their status may be so abstract that they constitute a broad perspective on social life rather than explanatory accounts of it. The *ontological* conceptual tradition discussed earlier in this chapter is an example of *theoreticians'* theory, as is most of the work usually discussed as classical and modern social/sociological theory. Various views of *theoreticians'* theory will be outlined later in the chapter.

Researchers' theory, on the other hand, is either theory that the researcher uses as a source of hypotheses to be tested, or theory that is generated in the course of the research. From the definitions of theory discussed earlier, it is possible to construct a composite definition of *researchers'* theory as consisting of:

- a related set of statements
- about relationships between concepts

- with a certain level of generality
- which are empirically testable; and which,
- when tested, have a certain level of validity.

These characteristics of a theory describe its *form*. It is also possible to define a theory in terms of its *functions*. An important function of social theory is 'to make things that were hidden visible, to define some patterns and give some meaning to the sorts of observations that social researchers continually make when investigating society' (Gilbert 1993: 11). Thus, theories provide:

- explanations
- of some aspects of human experience
- that form non-random patterns.

In other words, *social theories are explanations of recurrent patterns or regularities in social life*. They are answers to questions or puzzles about why people behave in the way they do in particular social contexts, and why social life is organized in the way it is.

The distinction between *theoreticians'* theory and *researchers'* theory helps us to understand the common complaint that there is a gap between theory and research in the social sciences. This gap refers to the lack of connection between what theoreticians and researchers do, between the ideas discussed in books on social theory and the theoretical ideas that are used in research. Some researchers try to bridge this gap by setting their research within a theoretical perspective. However, the connection is often very tenuous; a perspective may be reviewed in a theory chapter of a thesis and then largely ignored as the research proceeds. Alternatively, an attempt may be made at the end of the research to interpret the results within a theoretical perspective in the hope of staving off accusations of the research being atheoretical. But, according to Merton (1968), *post hoc* theorizing is an unsatisfactory use of theory.

In the context of research design, *a theory is an answer to a 'why' question*; it is an explanation of a pattern or regularity that has been observed, the cause or reason for which needs to be understood.

Levels of Theory

Some writers have classified theoretical activity into a number of levels. Denzin (1970), for example, has slightly elaborated the scheme developed by Parsons and Shils (1951) by proposing five levels: *ad hoc* classificatory systems; categorical systems or taxonomies; conceptual frameworks; theoretical systems; and empirical-theoretical systems. These five levels are intended to move from 'mere' description, through patterns of relationships, to explanatory schemes, and then to empirical testing of the theoretical ideas.

Ad hoc classificatory systems are used to summarize data. The classes or categories are more or less arbitrary and no attempt is made to establish relationships between them. They are just labels for particular observations or data, and are normally not derived from any theory. For example, students might be classified as 'bright', 'serious', 'average', 'lazy' and 'dull', as well as 'older' and 'younger', and 'female' and 'male'. Such classifications are not theoretical but may later be incorporated into a theoretical scheme.

A categorical system or taxonomy moves beyond the *ad hoc* classification, although it is still tied closely to a particular context or limited range of phenomena. Now the relationships between the classes or categories are stated. For example, the classification of students into their level of ability and attitude to their work (a mixed classification that would need to be refined into at least two separate 'dimensions') could be related to their age or gender. Research might then match the relationships with some data, but the activity remains at the level of description.

Conceptual schemes take us to a higher level by presenting a systematic image of the world (as in the *ontological* tradition). These schemes lend themselves to the development of propositions about relationships between concepts, and are intended to apply to a wide range of situations. Some conceptual schemes claim to represent society and its constituent parts (see figures 5.2 and 5.3). A more limited example might deal with concepts involved in predicting 'academic performance': 'level of ability', 'attitudes to study', 'age', 'gender', 'social class background', 'type of schooling' and 'career aspirations'. These concepts could be developed into a scheme of relationships, including some assumptions about causal connections.

Theoretical schemes bring together combinations of taxonomies and conceptual schemes into a theoretical argument. Now explanation is the aim. However, these schemes are likely to be rather abstract and not in a form that can be used directly in research. This requires another step, the establishment of empirical-theoretical schemes that are formulated precisely and in such a way that they can be tested. Hence, only these last two levels in the list can be regarded as being truly theoretical, and only the last connects theory with research.

Another basis for differentiating between levels of theory is to consider their scope. Again, Denzin (1970) has proposed four main levels: *grand* theories, *middle-range* theories, *substantive* theories and *formal* theories. *Grand* theories, or system theories, present a master conceptual scheme that is intended to represent the important features of a total society. These are often referred to as macro-theories because they apply to large-scale social phenomena. Merton referred to these as 'general sociological orientations' that

> involve broad postulates which indicate *types* of variables which are somehow to be taken into account rather than specifying determinate relationships between particular variables. . . . The chief function of these orientations is to provide a general context for inquiry; they facilitate the process of arriving at determinate hypotheses. (Merton 1968: 88)

Middle-range theories, a notion coined by Merton, lie between grand theories and empirical generalizations.

> Middle range theories have not been logically *derived* from a single all-embracing theory of social systems, though once developed they may be consistent with one.

Furthermore, each theory is more than a mere empirical generalization – an isolated proposition summarizing observed uniformities of relationships between two or more variables. (Merton 1968: 41)

Nevertheless, these theories (e.g. a theory of reference groups – Merton's example) are intended to apply to a variety of contexts and research problems. I shall elaborate Merton's ideas on middle-range theories in the next section of this chapter.

The third level referred to by Denzin, *substantive* theories, does apply to specific problem areas such as race relations and juvenile delinquency. Both middle-range theories and substantive theories are stated at a level that a researcher can use. They can also be combined, for example by using reference group theory as part of a theory of race relations.

Finally, the development of *formal* theory is based on the now contested idea that universal explanations of social life can be developed. While the content may be different in different contexts, the form of these theories will be the same. They constitute a synthesis of commonalities in different phenomena into a unified theory: 'Basic to formal theory will be universal interactive propositions that are assumed to apply to all instances of the phenomenon studied. ... these propositions ... describe relationships between processes that mutually influence one another' (Denzin 1970: 18). Simmel, Goffman and Homans were all committed to the idea that the development of formal theory was possible. Homans, for example, claimed that social behaviour could be explained in terms of a few psychological principles. One of his principles was that: 'The more rewarding men [*sic*] find the results of an action, the more likely they are to take this action.'

These two examples of classifications of social theories into levels contain suggestions about how theory can be used in research. I now want to examine four examples of how this issue of the relationship between theory and research has been dealt with. The first two, by Merton and Mills, are now regarded as classical discussions, and still worthy of attention. The other two, by Turner and Wallace, are examples of more recent contributions. They provide an interesting contrast between linear and cyclical linkages.

Relationship between Theory and Research

The relationship between theory and research was a topic of considerable interest in the United States during the 1950s and the 1960s, largely as a result of the seminal work of Merton (1968, and earlier editions of the same work in 1949 and 1957), the provocative writings of C. Wright Mills (1959) and, later, the systematic scheme developed by Willer (1967). Merton and Mills lamented the state of the sociological enterprise at that time and proposed their own broad solutions, 'middle-range theory' and the 'sociological imagination' respectively. Later, Willer elaborated a methodological framework in which the concepts of 'theory' and 'model' were given precise meanings. His work was followed immediately by a spate of rather technical writing on theory construction by, for example, Stinchcombe (1968), Dubin (1969), Blalock (1969), Reynolds (1971) and Hage (1972). Later editions of some of these works (e.g. Dubin 1978), and other contributions (e.g. Chafetz 1978), followed a decade later to consolidate a particular view of the relationship between theory and research.

More recent attempts to link theory and research have done so either in a series of *linear* steps or levels, or in a *cyclical* process used to construct and test theories. Both approaches are used to move from abstract theory to the empirical products of research, or from data to theory. Turner (1991) and Alexander (1982) have discussed the linear view of the relationship, and Wallace (1971, 1983), Lin (1976) and de Vaus (1995) the cyclical view.

I will limit the discussion here to a consideration of Merton's advocacy of middle-range theory, Mill's use of the sociological imagination, Turner's scheme of levels, and Wallace's proposal to integrate induction and deduction into a cyclical process.

Merton: middle-range theory

Merton's arguments were directed towards the two unsatisfactory extremes that he had observed in the practices of sociologists about fifty years ago. This is captured in his oft-quoted passage from the beginning of the chapter in which he discusses the various uses of the concept of theory.

> The recent history of sociological theory can in large measure be written in terms of an alternation between two contrasting emphases. On the one hand, we observe those sociologists who seek above all to generalize, to find their way as rapidly as possible to the formulation of sociological laws. Tending to assess the significance of sociological work in terms of scope rather than the demonstrability of generaliza-tions, they eschew the 'triviality' of detailed, small-scale observation and seek the grandeur of global summaries. At the other extreme stands a hardy band who do not hunt too closely the implications of their research but who remain confident and assured that what they report is so. To be sure, their reports of facts are verifiable and often verified, but they are somewhat at a loss to relate these facts to one another or even to explain why these, rather than other, observations have been made. For the first group the identifying motto would at times seem to be: 'We do not know whether what we say is true, but it is at least significant.' And for the radical empiricist the motto may read: 'This is demonstrably so, but we cannot indicate its significance.' (Merton 1968: 139)

Throughout his work on the nature of sociological theory, Merton's main target was theorists such as Marx, Parsons and Sorokin and their concern for all-embracing theory. What he wanted was theories that were of use to the researcher who was trying to deal with more practical problems, theories that could be part of the research process.

> A large part of what is now described as sociological theory consists of general orientations toward data, suggesting types of variables which theories must some-how take into account, rather than clearly formulated, verifiable statements of relationships between specified variables. We have many concepts but fewer con-firmed theories; many points of view, but few theorems; many 'approaches' but few arrivals. (Merton 1968: 52)

Merton's solution to the excesses of these two contrasting positions was to advocate what he called *theories of the middle range*,

> theories that lie between the minor but necessary working hypotheses that evolve in abundance during day-to-day research and the all inclusive systematic efforts to develop a unified theory that will explain all the observed uniformities of social behavior, social organization and social change.
>
> Middle-range theory is principally used in sociology to guide empirical inquiry. It is intermediate to general theories of social systems which are too remote from particular classes of social behavior, organization and change to account for what is observed and to those detailed orderly descriptions of particulars that are not generalized at all. Middle-range theory involves abstractions, of course, but they are close enough to observed data to be incorporated in propositions that permit empirical testing. Middle-range theories deal with delimited aspects of social phenomena, as is indicated by their labels. (Merton 1968: 39–40)

Merton's examples of such labels are 'reference group theory', and theories of 'social mobility' or 'role-set'. He considered the core idea of these theories to be basically simple, and from them theoretical problems and hypotheses could be generated.

While he was concerned with the gap between practical problems and comprehensive theories, Merton was not against the sociologist trying to develop general theories or work on pressing problems. What he was most concerned about was the retarding effect on the advancement of the discipline of giving primary attention to 'developing total sociological systems'.

> Sociological theory, if it is to advance significantly, must proceed on these interconnected planes: (1) by developing special theories from which to derive hypotheses that can be empirically investigated and (2) by evolving, not suddenly revealing, a progressively more general conceptual scheme that is adequate to consolidate groups of special theories.
>
> To concentrate entirely on special theories is to risk emerging with specific hypotheses that account for limited aspects of social behavior, organisation and change but that remain mutually inconsistent.
>
> To concentrate entirely on a master conceptual scheme for deriving all subsidiary theories is to risk producing twentieth-century sociological equivalents of the large philosophical systems of the past. (Merton 1968: 51)

Merton summarized his arguments as follows:

1 Middle-range theories consist of limited sets of assumptions from which specific hypotheses are logically derived and confirmed by empirical investigation.
2 These theories do not remain separate but are consolidated into wider networks of theory...
3 These theories are sufficiently abstract to deal with differing spheres of social behavior and social structure, so that they transcend sheer description or empirical generalization...
4 This type of theory cuts across distinctions between micro...and macro social problems...

5 Total sociological systems of theory – such as Marx's historical materialism, Parsons' theory of social systems and Sorokin's integral sociology – represent general theoretical orientations rather than the rigorous and tightknit systems envisaged in the search for a 'unified theory' in physics.

6 As a result, many theories of the middle range are consistent with a variety of systems of sociological thought.

7 Theories of the middle range are typically in direct line of continuity with the work of classical theoretical formulations...[3]

8 The middle range orientation involves the specification of ignorance. Rather than pretend to knowledge where it is in fact absent, it expressly recognizes what must still be learned in order to lay the foundation for still more knowledge...(Merton 1968: 68–9)

When Merton presented his ideas on middle-range theory, he was, understandably, criticized by the grand theorists. In time, the notion of *middle-range theory* has entered the consciousness of many sociologists and lip-service has been paid to it by succeeding generations. It has become the flag under which many self-respecting researchers would wish to be seen marching. However, it would appear that many have neither read nor understood the full implications of what Merton was saying. They are prepared to salute the flag but have not read the constitution. Their research practice has fallen short of Merton's ideal and has tended to become ritualized in the testing of isolated or trivial hypotheses. The linking of research to theory has tended to be achieved through theories being reduced to simple and isolated statements of relationships. As Glaser and Strauss (1967) lamented in the early part of this period, sociologists have become overconcerned with the testing of theories and have neglected the process of generating them.

A major critic of Merton's idea of middle-range theory has argued that grand theory and small-scale empirical research are not really at ends of a continuum, and, even if they were, middle-range theory is not intermediate between them (Willer 1967: p. xiv). Willer has suggested that Merton equated a middle range of generality with the scientific adequacy and testability of a theory. For concepts to be testable, they do not need to be at a middling level of generality, or modest in scope; what they need to be is precise and measurable, and it must be possible to connect them in a meaningful way. Willer supported Merton's call for testable theory but was critical of him for not providing a methodology for constructing and testing theory (Willer 1967: xvi).

This latter criticism seems to be rather unfair, as Merton had very clearly advocated the use of the *deductive* research strategy; he constantly reiterated the need to derive hypotheses from theory. While his ideas of theory testing are consistent with those of Popper, as a practical researcher, and unlike Popper, he paid attention to the process of theory generation. His ideas on this may have been too 'woolly' for Willer as they reflect the rather messy process that seems to be inevitable in most research.

What Merton clearly recognized was the complex interplay between theory and data, and he saw research findings as being a major source of stimulus for theory

---

[3] He would have regarded Weber's work on the Protestant Ethic, and Durkheim's work on suicide and his concept of anomie as good examples of middle-range theory.

development. His views were made clear in his paper entitled 'The Bearing of Empirical Research on Sociological Theory', a paper that has been given less attention than his statements on middle-range theory. Merton has suggested that: 'Under certain conditions, a research finding gives rise to social theory' (1968: 157). He called this the *serendipity* pattern, the 'experience of observing an *unanticipated, anomalous and strategic* datum which becomes the occasion for developing a new theory or for extending an existing theory' (1968: 158). The observation of something that is inconsistent with existing theory provokes curiosity, stimulates the researcher to try to make sense of it in terms of a broader theoretical framework, and leads to new observations. 'The more he [*sic*] is steeped in the data, the greater the likelihood that he will hit upon a fruitful direction of inquiry' (1968: 159). However, Merton suggested that it is not the data themselves that provide the stimulation but the application by the researcher of some general theoretical ideas: 'For it obviously requires a theoretically sensitized observer to detect the universal in the particular' (1968: 159). Therefore, serendipity is not the discovery of a new idea accidentally, but the presence of an unexpected anomaly which excites curiosity and puts pressure on the researcher to think creatively in new directions by matching different theoretical ideas to the situation. This process is at the core of the theory generation use of the later stages of the *abductive* research strategy.

Another stimulus to theory construction which Merton discussed concerns data overlooked by the conceptual framework being used. The repeated recording of these data can stimulate the researcher to extend the conceptual framework to include other concepts. 'Whereas the serendipity pattern centers in an apparent inconsistency which presses for resolution, the reformulation pattern centers in the hitherto neglected but relevant fact which presses for an extension of the conceptual scheme' (1968: 162). Merton gave the example of how Malinowski observed the differences in the way the Trobriand Islanders went about fishing in the inner lagoon, compared to the open sea. This led Malinowski to incorporate new elements into existing theories of magic. The theory was extended by an observant, curious and creative researcher recognizing that the existing theory had something missing, and using his observations to stimulate the filling of the gap.

A third way in which empirical data affect theory occurs when new research procedures shift the foci of theoretical interest by providing previously unavailable data.

> After all, sound theory thrives only on a rich diet of pertinent facts and newly invented procedures help provide the ingredients of this diet. The new, and often previously unavailable, data stimulate fresh hypotheses.... The flow of relevant data thus increases the tempo of advance in certain spheres of theory whereas in others, theory stagnates for want of adequate observation. (Merton 1968: 166)

However, there is the danger that these new research techniques will divert attention to problems that are theoretically and socially less important.

Finally, Merton has suggested that the process of doing research can lead to the clarification of concepts. He regarded a large part of theoretical work as involving such clarification. 'For *a basic requirement of research is that the concepts, the variables, be defined with sufficient clarity to enable the research to proceed*, a requirement easily and unwittingly not met in the kind of discursive exposition which is often miscalled social theory' (1968: 169). He argued that research stimulates this clarification as the result of the need to establish indices of the variables being used, i.e. the need, in the kind of quantitative research with which he was familiar, to find the best, the most precise way to operationalize a concept. It is this pressure to measure concepts that is instrumental in clarifying them in a way that cannot occur in purely theoretical activity.

In summarizing these four ways in which the process of research stimulates theoretical development, Merton argued that

> an explicitly formulated theory does not invariably precede empirical inquiry, that as a matter of plain fact the theorist is not inevitably the lamp lighting the way to new observations. The sequence is often reversed. Nor is it enough to say that research and theory must be married if sociology is to bear legitimate fruit. They must not only exchange solemn vows – they must know how to carry on from there. Their reciprocal roles must be clearly defined. (Merton 1968: 171)

Given that Merton wrote some time ago (his work was first published in 1949 with a major revision in 1957), the reader may be curious as to why so much space has been devoted to his three short articles. The reason is that not only have they been common reference points over recent decades, but they have also provided some practical methodological wisdom that is still very relevant today. The problems with which Merton was wrestling, of how to relate theory and research, and what kind of theory is relevant to research, are matters that still perplex researchers and cause disputes among the proponents of the various theoretical, methodological and research traditions. While Merton's commitment was clearly to the *deductive* research strategy and quantitative methods, his view of theory construction shares much in common with that used in the *abductive* research strategy. His view of research is not that of a rigid, linear set of stages, but involves the researcher as an active and creative agent in the complex interplay between ideas and data. He was reflecting on his own research experience in attempting to understand important and practical problems, and that is why he objected so strongly to the work of the 'armchair' theorists.

Mills: sociological imagination

A slightly later attempt to discuss similarly conceptualized extremes in sociology can be found in the writing of C. Wright Mills (1959). Mills lamented the state of sociology in the 1950s because of the two extreme tendencies that had developed. On the one hand, there was the interest in what he called 'grand theory' and, on the other hand, there was the concern with research methods and empirical studies, what he called 'abstracted empiricism'. He acknowledged that considerations of theory and method are essential to the task of the sociologist, but he argued that these two dominant versions of them were a hindrance to understanding and resolving 'the personal troubles of milieu' and 'the public issues of the social structure' (Mills 1959: x).

> *Troubles* occur within the character of the individual and within the range of his [*sic*] immediate relations with others; they have to do with his self and with those limited areas of social life of which he is directly and personally aware. Accordingly, the statement and the resolution of troubles properly lie within the individual as a biographical entity and within the scope of his immediate milieu – the social setting that is directly open to his personal experience and to some extent his wilful activity. A trouble is a private matter: values cherished by an individual are felt by him to be threatened.
>
> *Issues* have to do with matters that transcend these local environments of the individual and the range of his inner life. They have to do with the organisation of many such milieux into the institutions of an historical society as a whole, with the ways in which various milieux overlap and interpenetrate to form the larger structure of social and historical life. An issue is a public matter: some value cherished by publics is felt to be threatened. . . . An issue, in fact, often involves a crisis in institutional arrangements. (Mills 1959: 8–9)

Mills divided grand theory into two types, both of which have been discussed earlier in this chapter. The first, in the work of Comte, Marx, Spencer and Weber, tried to develop 'a theory of man's [*sic*] history'. He described this kind of sociology as

> an encyclopedic endeavor, concerned with the whole of man's [*sic*] social life. It is at once historical and systematic – historical, because it deals with and uses the materials of the past; systematic, because it does so in order to discern 'the stages' of the course of history and the regularities of social life. (Mills 1959: 22)

The second type of grand theory is concerned with producing a systematic theory of the nature of man and society, as in the work of Simmel and von Weise.

> Sociology comes to deal in conceptions intended to be of use in classifying all social relations and providing insight into their supposedly invariant features. It is, in short, concerned with a rather static and abstract view of the components of social structure on a quite high level of generality. (Mills 1959: 23)

Mills was critical of both of these traditions: the first because it can become distorted into 'a trans-historical strait-jacket' into which human history is forced and which is used to predict the future; and the second because it can become 'an elaborate and arid formalism in which the splitting of Concepts and their endless rearrangement becomes the central endeavour' (1959: 23).

Mills regarded Parsons as the leading exponent of the second tradition. To illustrate how this kind of grand theory makes unnecessarily complex what are essentially simple ideas, he reduced Parsons's classic text, *The Social System*, to four paragraphs that take up no more than a page. In fact, he claimed it could be summarized in two sentences – 'How is social order possible? Commonly accepted values.' Mills was simply trying to illustrate what he thought was the limited value that such a theoretical endeavour has in aiding our understanding of the human condition, of the intersection of 'biography and history, and the connections of the two in a variety of social structures' (1959: 32). Another aspect of his criticism was that grand theorists have attempted to produce one universal scheme by which to understand the nature of society and social life. This, he argued, is impossible.

It would be easy to conclude from his damning criticisms that Mills was developing an argument for the use of systematic research rather than grand theory as the central activity of sociology. However, this was not his intention, as he was equally critical of the dominant kind of social research that was conducted in his day. Both, he argued, are ways of avoiding the task of the social sciences, dealing with personal troubles and public issues. The former he described as producing a 'fetishism of the Concept' and the latter as leading to 'methodological inhibition'.

For Mills, abstracted empiricism is equivalent to crude survey research, atheoretical data gathered by interview or questionnaire from a sample of individuals. 'As a style of social science, abstracted empiricism is not characterized by any substantive propositions or theories. It is not based upon any new conception of the nature of society or of man [*sic*] or upon any particular facts about them' (Mills 1959: 55). It is an activity that can be done by administrators and research technicians, although the practitioners like to regard themselves as scientists. The problems selected for consideration, and the way they are formulated, are severely limited by what the practitioners regard as 'the scientific method', which means some version of Positivism. Mills regarded the work of Lazarsfeld (e.g. Lazarsfeld and Rosenberg 1955) as being typical of this tradition of research. In it, theory is equated with variables that help to interpret statistical findings, and data are restricted to statistically determined facts and relations. This is the *operationalizing* conceptual tradition discussed earlier in this chapter.

According to Mills, the major characteristic of the abstracted empiricists is that they are methodologically inhibited, and this is what accounts for the thinness of their results.

> Those in the grip of the methodological inhibition often refuse to say anything about modern society unless it has been through the fine little mill of The Statistical Ritual. It is usual to say that what they produce is true even if unimportant. I do not agree with this; more and more I wonder how true it is. I wonder how much exactitude, or even pseudo-precision, is here confused with 'truth'; and how much abstracted empiricism is taken as the only 'empirical' manner of work. (Mills 1959: 71–2)

Mills did not deny the value of statistical procedures, when they are appropriate, but he argued that there are also other ways of doing research.

> What has happened in the methodological inhibition is that men [*sic*] have become stuck, not so much in the empirical intake, as in what are essentially epistemological problems of method. Since many of these men, especially the younger, do not know very much about epistemology, they tend to be quite dogmatic about the one set of canons that dominate them.
> What has happened in the fetishism of the Concept is that men have become stuck way up on a very high level of generalisation, usually of a syntactical nature, and they

cannot get down to fact. Both of these tendencies or schools exist and flourish within what ought to be pauses in the working process of social science. But in them what ought to be a little pause has become, if I may put it so, the entrance into fruitfulness.

Intellectually these schools represent abdications of classic social science. The vehicle of their abdication is pretentious over-elaboration of 'method' and 'theory'; the main reason for it is their lack of firm connection with substantive problems. (Mills 1959: 74–5)

In spite of the fact that it is now forty years since Mills expressed these concerns, what he had to say can still be applied to a great deal of social research. The techniques may have become more sophisticated, and there may be more effort to avoid the appellation of being atheoretical, but methodological inhibition is still rampant. With the advent of postmodernism, 'methodological paralysis' has taken over.

Mills's solution to these extremes was rather different from Merton's. For Mills, it was not a case of finding some middle ground between the lofty heights of theory and the mundane activities of data collection. Rather, he argued for the use of the *sociological imagination* as a way of understanding personal troubles and public issues.

The sociological imagination enables its possessor to understand the larger historical scene in terms of its meaning for the inner life and the external career of a variety of individuals. It enables him to take into account how individuals, in the welter of their daily experiences, often become falsely conscious of their social positions. Within that welter, the framework of modern society is sought, and within that framework the psychologies of a variety of men and women are formulated. By such means the personal uneasiness of individuals is focused upon explicit troubles and the indifference of publics is transformed into involvement with public issues.

The first fruit of this imagination – and the first lesson of the social science that embodies it – is the idea that the individual can understand his own experience and gauge his own fate only by locating himself within his period, that he can know his own chances in life only by becoming aware of those of all individuals in his circumstances. In many ways it is a terrible lesson; in many ways a magnificent one.... We have come to know that every individual lives ... out a biography, and that he lives it out within some historical sequence. By the fact of his living he contributes, however minutely, to the shaping of his society and to the course of its history, even as he is made by society and by its historical push and shove.

The sociological imagination enables us to grasp history and biography and the relations between the two within society. That is the task and its promise. (Mills 1959: 5–6)

Turner: linear elements

According to Turner (1991), theory is constructed from several basic elements: concepts, variables, statements and formats (see figure 5.4). *Concepts*, he argued, are the basic building blocks of theory. They are the means by which we endeavour to identify phenomena in the social world, both in everyday language and social scientific or technical language. In theory, but more particularly in research, concepts need to be defined; we need to state what we mean by them and we need

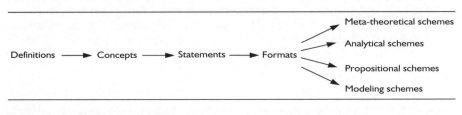

Figure 5.4 Elements of theory

(*Source:* Turner 1991: 8)

to identify the phenomena to which we wish them to apply. This is supposed to ensure that researchers will use a particular concept in the same way; that they will refer to the same phenomenon (Turner 1991: 5).

Theories consist of a set of statements of relationships. Turner (1991: 7–12) described such a set of statements as a *theoretical format*, and used this concept as a general term for a variety of ways in which theoretical statements are organized: *as meta-theoretical* schemes, *analytical* schemes, *propositional* schemes, and *modelling* schemes. Each format can be developed in a variety of ways, and they are not mutually exclusive; it is possible to move from one to another in the process of theory construction. However, as Turner has pointed out, the proponents of these formats have engaged in a great deal of debate about which one is the best.

Meta-theory is concerned with discerning underlying ontological and epistemo-logical assumptions that a body of theory or a theoretical perspective uses. However, as Turner has pointed out, some writers (e.g. Alexander 1982) have argued that the ontological and epistemological issues should be settled before theorizing commences. However, this reflection can become an end in itself and may not get beyond long-standing philosophical debates; it may not contribute very much to the explanation of specific puzzles or problems.

By *analytical* schemes, Turner referred to conceptualizations of the key proper-ties of and relationship in the social world; they give the social world a sense of order. This is equivalent to the *ontological* conceptual tradition discussed earlier in the chapter. Turner has divided *analytical* schemes into two types: *naturalistic* schemes and *sensitizing* schemes. *Naturalistic* schemes 'try to develop a tightly woven system of categories that is presumed to capture the way in which the invariant properties of the universe are ordered' (e.g. the work of Parsons). They assume that there are timeless and universal processes in the social world just as there are in the natural world. The aim is to produce an abstract conceptual scheme that corresponds to these processes.

Sensitizing schemes are 'more loosely assembled congeries of concepts intended to sensitise and orient researchers and theorists to certain critical processes' (Turner 1991: 10). Apart, perhaps, from some very general concepts, the authors who advocate sensitizing schemes do not assume that they apply across time and space. They accept that as social arrangements are subject to change, concepts and their arrangements may also have to change; it must be possible to revise conceptual schemes over time. While the schemes can provide ways of understanding events and social processes, this understanding is always provisional.

Some writers have argued that *analytical* schemes are a prerequisite for the development of theory to be used in research; they provide a framework and an orientation to a research problem. Turner, on the other hand, has argued that the *naturalistic* variety of concepts may be too rigid and elaborate to stimulate theorizing, and that *sensitizing* schemes may be more useful.

Turner's third type of format, *propositional* schemes, is more directly related to the business of research. A proposition is a statement of a relationship between two or more concepts; it claims that a variation in one concept is associated with a variation in another concept. For example, as Durkheim might have argued, an increase in the level of individualism among members of a group or society is associated with a rise in the suicide rate. Propositional schemes vary along two dimensions, in their level of abstraction and in the way the propositions are organized. Some are highly abstract and do not relate to any empirical instance, while others may simply summarize relations between observed phenomena. Turner has suggested that these two dimensions lead to three main types of propositional schemes: *axiomatic*, *formal* and *empirical* (Turner 1991: 11–15).

In an *axiomatic* organization of propositions, a theory is expressed in formal language using strict logical argument. The propositions in the argument form a hierarchical order, with axioms or highly abstract statements at the top, from which lower-level statements are derived. There will also be one or more conditional statements that indicate the scope of the conditions under which these abstract statements apply, and they will influence the conclusions, or theorems, that can be drawn. An axiomatic theory is the form used in the *deductive* research strategy (see Homans's (1964) reconstruction of Durkheim's theory of anomic suicide that was discussed in chapter 4).

According to Turner, *formal* theories are watered-down versions of *axiomatic* theories.[4] Highly abstract and general propositions are used to explain observed events or relationships, by viewing the latter as instances or examples of the former. If deductions are made from these general propositions, they do not conform to the strict rules of logic as in *axiomatic* theory. When extraneous facts cannot be excluded, these theories will use the well-known disclaimer 'other things being equal'. This is the more common form of theories in sociology.

Turner referred to his third type of propositional scheme as *empirical generalizations*, although he has some reservations about calling them theories. They are derived from specific events in particular social contexts. Such propositions are usually not very abstract and are filled with empirical content. They may be nothing more than statements of empirical regularities that need to be explained,

---

[4] Freese (1980) had a very different view of formal theories. He referred to them as deductive theories that are expressed in the symbols and rules of formal logic or mathematics, either as translations of theories expressed in ordinary language, or as theoretical expressions in their own right. In the former case, the use of the language of logic or mathematics is designed to remove the vagueness and imprecision from ordinary language. We shall discuss these views later in this chapter under 'The Role of Models'.

and are therefore precursors to theoretical activity. However, Turner has acknowledged that if the concepts are relatively abstract, if they relate to basic or fundamental properties of the social world, and if they can be applied across a number of substantive areas, they may be considered theoretical. This is the form of theory used in the *inductive* research strategy.

Turner's fourth type of scheme involves the use of diagrammatic or pictorial representations of social events or processes. These have been labelled *modelling* schemes and will be discussed later in this chapter.

Turner has expressed some strong views on the value to the researcher of the various approaches to theorizing just reviewed. At one extreme, he regarded *meta-theory* as interesting but counterproductive. At the other extreme, he regarded

> empirical generalisations and causal models of empirically operationalized variables as not theory at all. They are useful summaries of data that need a theory to explain them. Some would argue that theory can be built *from* such summaries of empirical regularities. That is, we can induce from the facts the more general properties that these facts illustrate. I doubt this, but many disagree. I grant that familiarity with empirical regularities is crucial to developing more abstract and comprehensive theoretical statements, but I doubt if this process of mechanically raising the level of abstraction from empirical findings will produce interesting theory. A much more creative leap of insight is necessary, and so I do not suggest that theory building begin with a total immersion in the empirical facts. I suspect that, once buried in the facts, one rarely rises above them. (Turner 1991: 23–4)

Between the extremes of *meta-theory* and *empirical generalization* Turner has placed six steps with gradations in the level of generality (see figure 5.5). He has argued that the most productive area for theory building lies in the interchange between formal propositions and analytical models, between translating propositions into diagrams and translating diagrams into propositions. This is the level at which he wished theory to be stated. Middle-range propositions can stimulate analytic models and these, in turn, can encourage the development of more abstract propositions. However, he has argued that middle-range theorists need abstract propositions to encourage them to raise their empirically laden statements to a more abstract level. On the other hand, middle-range theories and causal models can provide vehicles by means of which abstract propositions can be empirically tested (Turner 1991: 27). In this way, Turner has regarded the various components of theorizing as serving each other rather than being in conflict.[5]

Schemes such as that of Turner imply a relationship between theory and research that is facilitated by a series of levels or steps from data produced by research, through theory at different levels of abstraction, to general ideas and assumptions. Turner clearly saw the movement between these levels as occurring in both directions, although his preference was for working from the middle to the ends: 'Start with sensitizing schemes, propositions and models, and

---

[5] Alexander (1982) has presented a similar scheme to that of Turner, but uses a different array of categories. However, his scheme adds little to our understanding of the relationship between theory and research.

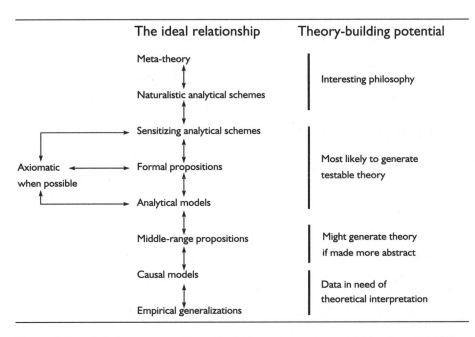

Figure 5.5   Relations among theoretical approaches and potential for theory-building

(*Source*: After Turner 1991: 26)

only then move on to the formal collection of data or to metatheorizing and scheme-building' (Turner 1987: 167).

Turner's reference to 'models' here anticipates the discussion in the next section. In it I will discuss the views of another writer (Willer 1967) who, somewhat earlier, set out a more specific scheme for linking theory and research. As it presents a particular view of models in research, it will be reviewed as an example of such. However, the discussion of his ideas could just as easily have been included here.

Wallace: ongoing cycles

Wallace first developed the idea of research as a cyclical process in his *Logic of Science in Sociology* (1971) and modified it in a later publication (1983). The idea has been taken up by a number of writers (e.g. Lin 1976; de Vaus 1995). Wallace argued that the logics of *induction* and *deduction* should be combined in an ongoing cycle. Or, to put this in my language, the *inductive* and *deductive* research strategies should be combined to provide an explicit link between theory and research. While these two research strategies can be viewed as presenting opposing logics of enquiry, these authors have suggested that, in practice, theory and research can be combined in a never-ending alternation between induction, deduction, induction, and so on. The process of theory construction and theory testing are seen to occur in this cyclical process (see figure 5.6).

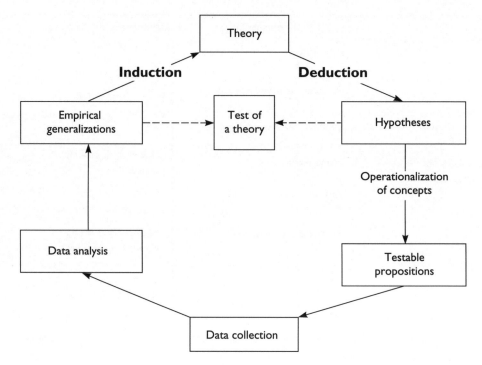

Figure 5.6   The cycle of theory construction and testing

(*Source*: Adapted from Wallace 1971, 1983; de Vaus 1995)

The starting-point for theory construction could be data collection, at the bottom of the diagram, to be followed by data analysis, from which empirical generalizations are derived. According to the *inductivists*, a new theory is constructed from these generalizations, by the use of inductive logic, and further testing could follow.

The starting-point for theory testing is at the top of the diagram with the 'theory' box. Hypotheses are deduced, their concepts operationalized, the data collected and analysed, and the results compared with the original hypothesis (represented by the 'test of a theory' box). In other cycles around this process, the step from 'empirical generalizations' to 'theory' can be used to refine an existing theory. Hence, the process can be used in at least three ways: to generate a new theory, to test a theory, or to refine a theory.

The extent to which researchers follow these processes is an open question; much research is done in less systematic ways than the diagram would require. Perhaps researchers who use the *deductive* research strategy might benefit from recognizing the cyclical rather than linear nature of their kind of research, and for those who use the *inductive* strategy it is important to recognize that induction cannot stand on its own as a method of theory development.

The strength of this scheme is the recognition of the developmental nature of theory construction. However, I would argue that the *inductive* phase of the cycle is a much too simplistic representation of the creative side of research. What should occur is a complex trial and error process, more akin to that used in the *abductive* research strategy and by grounded theorists. The other major deficiency of the scheme is that it provides no place for the social actors' concepts and meanings to enter into the process; it uses the ontology of both positivism and critical rationalism, and a combination of their epistemologies.

Theoreticians' Theory

As we have seen, *theoreticians'* theory can be defined as the products of attempts to understand social life, both at the macro- and micro-levels. This intellectual activity usually occurs with little or no reference to the findings of social research. Rather, theoreticians feed off each other in the sense that much of their work attempts to synthesize and/or build on earlier theorizing.

Theoreticians' theory can be examined from a number of points of view.

- *The history of social thought*: developments in the understanding of social life and society (e.g. Becker and Barnes 1938; Bogardus 1940; Barnes 1948; Martindale 1960).
- *The work of great theorists*: original works, plus reviews and commentaries (e.g. Aron 1965, 1968; Raison 1969; Coser 1971; Giddens 1971; Beilharz 1991).
- *Theoretical schools or perspectives*: clustering of classical and contemporary theorists into schools based on common ontological assumptions (e.g. Cuff and Payne 1979; Ritzer 1980, 1996a, 1996b; Jones 1985; Giddens and Turner 1987; Turner 1991; Craib 1992, 1997; Scott 1995; Cuff et al. 1998; Wallace and Wolf 1999).
- *Theorizing strategies*: the establishment of broad categories of theorizing in terms of both ontological and epistemological assumptions (e.g. Johnson et al. 1984; Blaikie 1993a; Waters 1994; Ritzer 1996a).

As the most relevant aspect of *theoreticians'* theory in the present context is *theoretical perspectives*, only these will be discussed here.

Theoretical perspectives

In this approach to social theory, classical and contemporary theorists who share common ontological assumptions and ways of understanding social life are grouped together, and the common elements of their theories are abstracted. A theoretical perspective provides a way of looking at the social world; it highlights certain aspects while at the same time making other aspects less visible. A shift in theoretical perspective changes the shape of the social world (Gilbert 1993: 11).

The concept of *theoretical perspective* (Cuff and Payne 1979) is equivalent to the notions of 'general theoretical orientation' (Merton 1968), 'general model' (Willer 1967), 'meta-theory' (Turner 1991), 'foundationalist theory' or 'formal theory' (Waters 1994), and even 'paradigm' (Freidrichs 1970; Kuhn 1970; Krausz and Miller 1974).

A *theoretical perspective* provides a particular language, a conceptual framework, or collection of 'theoretical' concepts and related propositions, within which society and social life can be described and explained. Some perspectives attempt to establish a set of principles that provide the ultimate foundation for social life and a basis for its explanation. In general, theoretical perspectives provide images of society or social life (ontologies), but they do not provide rigorously developed and logically organized theoretical statements (Turner 1991: 29–30).

Theoretical perspectives are sometimes regarded as paradigms because they include ontological and epistemological assumptions, and associated practices for the pursuit of social knowledge (Friedrichs 1970; Kuhn 1970). The advocates of these perspectives differ in the kinds of 'stories' that they tell about social life. They tend to disagree on:

- what the social world looks like and how it works (ontological assumptions);
- what kind of knowledge about human interaction and social organization is possible (ultimate reference);
- how this knowledge can be developed (epistemological assumptions);
- what topics should be studied and what kinds of questions can be asked (subject-matter); and
- what this knowledge should be used for (objectives) (Wallace and Wolf 1999: 5–13).

The ontological assumptions that are invariably implicit include:

- the basic components of social life, including individuals, social processes or social structures;
- how these components relate to each other;
- what human nature is like, i.e. whether human behaviour is essentially determined and therefore predictable, or whether human beings are relatively autonomous and create their own social life, thus making prediction difficult; and
- whether human beings are motivated essentially by interests or by values.

A simple set of major theoretical perspectives has been arrived at by using two overlapping dichotomies, structural vs. interpretive and consensus vs. conflict. This is mainly a British way of viewing social theories and has been used in introductory texts on sociology and social theory (e.g. Cuff and Payne 1979; Haralambos and Holborn 1980; Jones 1985; Cuff et al. 1998). Three perspectives are commonly identified in these texts:

- structural-consensus (Functionalism);
- structural-conflict (Marxism);
- interpretive (Interpretivism).[6]

---

[6] Some versions of this classification subdivide the interpretive perspective, for example, into symbolic interactionism and ethnomethodology.

Theoretical perspectives have been categorized in a number of ways. A common set of categories can be found in texts from the United States on social/sociological theory (e.g. Turner 1991; Ritzer 1996a, 1996b; and Wallace and Wolf 1999), in more recent British texts (e.g. Craib 1992; Scott 1995), and in the North Atlantic collaboration by Giddens and Turner (1987). These classifications include categories such as:

- *functionalism* (Durkheim, Malinowski, Radcliffe-Brown, Parsons, Merton);
- *neo-functionalism* (Luhmann, Alexander);
- *conflict theory* (Marx, Weber, Dahrendorf, Coser, Collins, Rex);
- *rational choice and exchange theory* (Frazer, Malinowski, Mauss, Weber, Homans, Blau, Elster);
- *phenomenology* (Husserl, Schütz, Tiryakian, Bruyn, Berger, Luckmann, Douglas, Psathas);
- *ethnomethodology* (Garfinkel, Cicourel, Sacks, Schegloff, Zimmerman);
- *symbolic interactionism* (Mead, Dewey, Cooley, Thomas, Blumer, Strauss, Becker, Denzin);
- *dramaturgy* (Goffman);
- *structuralism and post-structuralism* (Saussure, Lévi-Strauss, Foucault, Lacan, Althusser, Derrida);
- *critical theory* (Adorno, Horkheimer, Marcuse, Habermas, Fay);
- *structuration theory* (Giddens); and
- *feminist theory* (Barnard, Smith, Harding).

The Role of Theoreticians' Theory in Research

In spite of the division of labour between *theoreticians'* theory and *researchers'* theory, the former, and, particularly, theoretical perspectives, has much to offer the researcher. It can provide:

- a way of viewing the social world, including ontological and epistemological assumptions;
- a language with which to describe and explain aspects of the social world;
- general theoretical ideas to set the context and direction for research; and
- possible explanations or tentative hypotheses.

The first contribution, to provide a perspective or way of looking at the social world, involves making a commitment to a set of ontological assumptions about the nature of the social world and human nature. For example, social reality may be viewed as either 'material' or 'ideal' (Johnson et al. 1984), or as either 'subjective' or 'objective' (Waters 1994; Ritzer 1996a). People's actions may be regarded as the result of either choice or constraint (humanistic vs. deterministic assumptions), and their relationships based either on agreement about norms and values or on different interests (consensus vs. conflict assumptions). Perspectives also include different epistemological assumptions about how the social world can be known. Social reality can be approached from a nominalist or realist epistemology (Johnson et al. 1984), or explained in individualistic or holistic terms (Waters 1994).

While such ontological commitments are not always fully recognized, the consequences of the paradigmatic disputes of the 1960s and 1970s now make it essential that researchers be aware that a choice of ontological assumptions is needed. This choice should be made explicit.

The second role of theory in research, to provide a language, facilitates the statement of research questions and the answers to them. Like everyday language, theoretical language provides a vocabulary and meanings for concepts. While the meanings may be more precise than in everyday language, they are still subject to multiple definitions and disputes within and between paradigms. There are fashions in theoretical perspectives, and, therefore, in theoretical language. Such language both facilitates dialogue between adherents to a perspective and excludes the outsider.

The adoption of a theoretical language is necessary to establish a way of relating to the social world. However, while the relationship between a theoretical language and everyday language is regarded as the most fundamental methodological issue in the social sciences (Bhaskar 1979; Blaikie 1993a), it is also a highly contested one. All researchers need a language both to formulate a research project and to report its outcomes. While the level of theoretical sophistication of the language used may vary, that some technical language is necessary to understand and explain any social phenomenon cannot really be disputed. Some Interpretivists, for example ethnomethodologists, argue that all that is necessary to achieve such understanding is to report social actors' accounts in their language. However, this is a minority view, and, in any case, is impossible to sustain. Any discussion of such accounts needs a technical language, and the language of ethnomethodology, for example, is certainly technical. Even in grounded theory, with its aim of generating theory largely free of theoretical preconceptions and language, it is necessary to borrow or invent technical concepts.

The third role of theory is an extension of the second. It provides a context of ideas, or a theoretical framework, that is the source of the focus and direction for the research. The review of a theorist's ideas on an issue, such as Marx's discussion of 'alienation', can set the scene for the collection of particular types of data from particular sources, for example from factory workers who were formerly rural peasants in a developing country. While the theoretical ideas may not suggest specific hypotheses, they provide the inspiration to pursue the research in a particular way.

The final role of theory concerns the source of hypotheses. Theory can be used either to provide general explanatory ideas to guide research, or, more specifically, to provide answers to 'why' questions, i.e. as a source of hypotheses to be tested. The *deductive* research strategy has taken the latter to the limit by requiring that hypotheses be logically deduced from a set of theoretical propositions. In this case, a hypothesis is the conclusion to a theoretical argument that provides a tentative answer to a 'why' question. Of course, hypotheses can come from other sources, including previous research.

It is clear that researchers must rely on *theoreticians'* theory in a number of ways. However, the extent to which theoreticians use the results of research is much less clear. Certainly, there would appear to be few explicit connections in the literature. The exceptions are the rare cases where a researcher is also a theoretician (e.g. Bourdieu).

Researchers' Theory

Earlier in this chapter I defined *researchers'* theory as a related set of general statements of relationships between concepts. These theories provide explanations of regularities in social life at a level that is directly relevant to research.

Each of the research strategies gives a particular interpretation of this definition. In the *inductive* research strategy, general statements are related in networks, while in the *deductive* strategy, these statements are related logically and have different levels of generality. Although the *retroductive* research strategy only requires a description of the generative structure or mechanism, it may require discursive support for their operation. This may take the form of a theoretical argument, but less formalized than in the *deductive* strategy. In the *abductive* research strategy, theory may take many forms, from tight logical arguments to loose discussions. However, in the end, theories in all four research strategies need to be reduced to statements of relationships between concepts. We will return to these differences between the research strategies towards the end of the chapter.

An important issue for a researcher is where to get a suitable theory. In the absence of a good existing theory, Stinchcombe has argued that you should make them up yourself, a task that he regarded as being manageable even for students: 'A student who has difficulty thinking of at least three sensible explanations for any correlation that he [*sic*] is really interested in should probably choose another profession' (Stinchcombe 1968: 13).

The Role of Hypotheses

It should be clear by now that hypotheses play a specific and limited role in social research. They are only relevant when 'why' questions are being investigated and, then, mainly when the *deductive* research strategy is being used to answer them. Hypotheses are not appropriate in the *inductive* strategy and are generally regarded as inappropriate in the *abductive* strategy, at least in the initial stages.

To recapitulate, in the *deductive* research strategy, hypotheses are derived from theory to provide a possible answer to 'why' questions. This very traditional approach to social research has been succinctly summarized by Blumer.[7]

> One starts with the construction of a scheme, theory, or model of the empirical world or area of study. The scheme, theory, or model represents the way in which one believes the empirical world to be structured and to operate. One then deduces from this scheme an assertion as to what one would expect to happen under such and such

---

[7] Blumer was in fact critical of this approach to social research and set up this description as a kind of 'straw man' against which to present his own views.

a set of circumstances. The assertion is the hypothesis. One then arranges a study of a given empirical area that represents these circumstances. If the findings from such a study verify the hypothesis one assumes that the scheme, the model, or the theory from which the hypothesis has been drawn is empirically valid. Logically, this view rests on an 'as if' notion; that is, one approaches the empirical world *as if* it had such and such a makeup, deduces narrow specific consequences as to what one would find if the empirical world had the makeup attributed to it, and then sees if in fact such consequences are to be found in the empirical world. (Blumer 1969: 29)

If quantitative methods are being used, a hypothesis will be tested by operationalizing the concepts in the hypothesis, collecting the appropriate data, and then exploring the nature of the relationship between the measures of the concept by some form of statistical analysis, such as correlation or regression. For some kinds of testing, it is a convention to express hypotheses in the null and alternative forms. A null hypothesis states that there is no relationship between two variables, i.e. that a position on, or a value for, one variable does not predict the position on or the value for the other variable. Alternative hypotheses state that there is some kind of relationship; it may be linear, either positive or negative, or curvilinear. In a positive linear relationship, the values on the variables correspond; a high value on one variable is associated with a high value on the other, and vice versa. In a negative linear relationship, a high value on one variable is associated with a low value on the other, and vice versa. A curvilinear relationship can be in the form of a 'hump' or a 'hollow'. In the former, a high value on one variable is associated with a moderate value on the other, and a low value on the first variable is associated with both high and low values on the second. In the latter, a low value on one variable is associated with a moderate value on the other, and a high value on the first variable is associated with both high and low values on the second. A researcher will try to reject the null hypothesis in favour of one of the alternatives. It is also common practice just to state the preferred alternative hypothesis.

If qualitative methods are being used in the *deductive* research strategy – and there is no reason why they should not be – the testing process will be less formal and is likely to rely more on arguments from evidence and the manipulation of concepts and categories in textual data.

Hypotheses also have a role in the *abductive* research strategy, and in grounded theory in particular. However, their use here is less formal and is an integral part of the process of generating theory from data. Questions will arise from the analysis of some of the data, and hypotheses may be used to explore these questions, within the same body of data, or to stimulate further data collection. This will not involve either the measurement of concepts or the statistical testing of relationships.

To reiterate a point made in chapter 3, 'what' questions do not require hypotheses to guide the data collection, and they may also not be necessary for 'how' questions. 'What' questions need concepts, but descriptions can be produced using these concepts, with either quantitative or qualitative data, without the need to guess at what the outcome might be. Such guessing of answers to 'what' questions adds nothing to the quality or sophistication of the research.

The Role of Models

Like *theory*, the concept of *model* has a variety of meanings and uses in the context of creating new knowledge and understanding social life. Using a model seems to be regarded as adding sophistication or legitimacy to one's research. A discussion of the role of *models* and *theory* in research is complicated by the fact that the concepts are sometimes used interchangeably. Some writers even combine them to produce 'theoretical models'.

In this section of the chapter, I will review the major types of models used in the social sciences. However, before doing this, it is necessary to set aside two every-day uses of *model* that are not relevant to our discussion: three-dimensional representations of objects, and ideals of some kind. Examples of the representations include model aeroplanes, or an architect's model of a proposed building. The first is a model *of* an actual aeroplane, while the second is a model *for* a new building. If the model *of* is to scale, i.e. if there is a 'one-to-one correspondence between the elements of the model and the elements of the thing of which it is a model' (Brodbeck 1968: 80), then the thing and the model are said to be isomorphic; the model is a smaller representation of the original thing. If it is a working model, such as a steam engine, and if it works on the same principles as the thing itself, then the isomorphism is complete. However, this is rarely achieved; working models frequently use different principles. Because of this, such models have limited theoretical or research value and may even be misleading.

The other everyday use of model, again not relevant to research, is in the normative or ideal sense, for example a model parent or a model organization. Such models may never exist in reality but are presented as ideals for which to strive. This type of model is sometimes confused with ideal types. This may be due, in part, to Weber's discussion of ideal types and his construction of an ideal type of bureaucracy. What Weber intended by an ideal type was the accentuation of particular features of a social phenomenon into a kind of model that can be used to analyse and compare existing examples of the phenomenon. In this sense, an ideal type is like a measurement standard. Because Weber also argued that a bureaucratic form of organization is the most rational way to co-ordinate the administrative activities of a large number of people, his ideal type of bureaucracy has been regarded as the best form of large-scale administration. Even he was not entirely innocent in perpetuating this view. The fact that the German has been translated as 'ideal' type has not helped; the notion of 'constructed' type (Becker 1940, 1950) overcomes these connotations. The idea of a model as a comparative 'yardstick' may be appropriate, but its use in the normative sense is not relevant to social research.

Types of Models

Models have been used in social research in a variety of ways. They provide a conceptual or theoretical framework, they can represent a hypothetical explanatory structure or mechanism, perhaps derived by the use of analogies, or they can be a method of organizing research results, and communicating them.

Abstract descriptions

The most elementary but not trivial use of models in social research is as abstract descriptions. While not usually thought of as models, abstract descriptions can be regarded as models *of* some aspects of social reality. Casual or systematic observation and data may inform them, but their purpose is different from that of an abstract model.

Two examples of models as abstract descriptions can be found in the work of Schütz and Harré. Schütz elaborates how models are used in the *abductive* research strategy and Harré how they are used in the constructivist version of the *retroductive* strategy. Schütz's project (1963a, 1963b), like that of Weber and Dilthey before him, was to find a way 'to form objective concepts and objectively verifiable theory of subjective meaning structures' (Schütz 1963a: 246). He attempted to do this by establishing a bridge between the meanings social actors use in everyday activities and the meaning the social scientist must attribute to these activities in order to produce an adequate theory. He argued that social life is possible to the extent that social actors use typifications. Typifications are everyday categorizations of typical persons, social actions and social situations. They are socially constructed and transmitted, and they are refined and changed by processes of trial and error in everyday activities. The typifications, or everyday ideal types, that social actors use are related to their biographically and situationally determined system of interests and circumstances (Schütz 1963a: 243). According to Schütz, the intersubjective meanings that social actors use – motives, goals, choices and plans – can only be experienced in their typicality (1963a: 244). It is these typical meanings that the social scientist must discover, describe and use as the ingredients in sociological ideal types.

> **Types of Models**
>
> **Abstract descriptions**
>
> **Synonym for theory**
>
> **Conceptual models**
>
> **Theoretical models**
>
> **Analogues of mechanisms**
>
> **Diagrammatic representations**
>
> **Mathematical representations**

As we saw in the discussion of the *abductive* research strategy in chapter 4, Schütz referred to everyday typifications as first-order constructs and to sociological typifications, or ideal types, as second-order constructs. The critical difference between first- and second-order constructs is that they are constructed with different purposes in mind. First-order constructs are part of the social stock of knowledge which, while often taken for granted, makes social life possible. Second-order constructs are constructed by the social scientists to supersede first-order constructs and to understand some aspects of social life (Schütz 1963a: 246).

Schütz argued that all knowledge of the social world is indirect; people cannot be understood theoretically in their uniqueness but only as impersonal ideal types existing in impersonal and anonymous time. He regarded these second-order constructs, his kind of ideal types, as models of typical social actors, typical social action and typical social situations, not as descriptions of actual human beings, actions and situations. The elements of Schütz's models of the social world can be manipulated and the logical outcomes compared. They are the building blocks of theory and the source of testable hypotheses.

In their version of social psychology, Harré and Secord (1972) have emphasized the use of ordinary language as a source of concepts to be used in any study. However, they do not confine ordinary language to that used by social actors, as Schütz does; they are willing to be guided by the work of linguistic philosophers and psychologists. This broader approach to the source of concepts is tempered by their insistence, as in phenomenology and symbolic interactionism, that the explanation of behaviour should be made from the social actors' point of view.

> Those who wish to study people as they really live their lives have a ready-made conceptual scheme for expressing the results of their observations in the accounts people ordinarily give of their behaviour. This is why we have emphasized the essential rightness of the discoveries of the linguistic philosophers for psychology. And since one important feature of the conceptual scheme is that it allows for the explanation of behaviour of people from the point of view of the actors themselves ... some insights into the genesis of that behaviour can be obtained by studying the accounts that are given by the social actors themselves. (Harré and Secord 1972: 152)

The focus of this social psychology is on 'episodes' involving one or more people, in which there is a beginning and an end and some internal structure or unity. 'Everything of interest that occurs in human life, happens in the course of, or as the culmination of, or as the initiation of an episode' (Harré and Secord 1972: 153). In order to grasp such an episode it is necessary to construct a model of it, a critical or abstract description of its structure and its principle of unity, of the pattern of relationships and social processes. This type of model has been referred to as a *homeomorph* (Harré and Secord 1972; Harré 1977). However, the explanation of the episode requires the use of a different kind of model, a *paramorph*, which identifies the mechanism(s) that produced it. This kind of model is based on the use of analogies and will be discussed shortly.

Synonym for theory

The concept of *model* has been used by some writers as a synonym for *theory*, or, more particularly, for a particular view of theory. For example, Lave and March (1975) regarded *model* as being not only interchangeable with 'theory' but also 'paradigm', 'hypothesis' and even 'ideas'. Another example can be found in Inkeles's (1964) discussion of evolutionary, structural-functional and conflict *theories* as *models* of society. The sociologist 'carries in his [sic] head [models that] greatly influence what he looks for, what he sees, and what he does with his observations by way of fitting them, along with other facts, into a larger scheme of explanation' (Inkeles 1964: 28). However, he went on to suggest that a *model* is a general theory with a strong ontological component, while a *theory* is an answer to a specific research question.

> It is not always possible to distinguish precisely between a scientific model and a scientific theory, and the terms are sometimes used interchangeably. A model may generate a host of theories but one theory may be so powerful as to become, in effect, a general model.... we use model to refer to a rather general image of the main outline of some major phenomenon, including certain leading ideas about the nature of the units involved and the pattern of their relations. A theory we take to be a heuristic device for organising what we know, or think we know, at a particular time about some more or less explicitly posed question or issue. A theory would, there-fore, be more limited and precise than a model. A theory can ordinarily be proved wrong. In the case of a model, it can usually only be judged incomplete, misleading, or unproductive. (Inkeles 1964: 28)

To use *model* and *theory* synonymously is to add confusion to concepts that already have a variety of other uses. This practice is to be avoided.

Conceptual models

Model is also associated with the idea of a conceptual scheme. This usage is closely related to both 'theoretical perspectives' and the *ontological* tradition in the use of concepts in research, discussed earlier in this chapter. A *conceptual model* attempts to represent the social world in terms of an array of related concepts, or a conceptual scheme (see e.g. Krausz and Miller 1974: 5). Further examples of conceptual schemes will be discussed in the section 'Diagrammatic representations' later in this chapter.

A *conceptual model* may be an important component of a theoretical perspec-tive. However, theoretical perspectives tend to use different sets of concepts. If the same concepts are used, they will usually be given different meanings. For exam-ple, structural-functionalism uses concepts such as norms, values, roles, socializa-tion, social control, equilibrium, adaptation and system, while the conflict perspective uses concepts such as economic base, superstructure, alienation, con-tradiction, interests, class, power and structure. These two theoretical perspec-tives share some concepts, such as institution, and may use them in a similar way, but, overall, the concepts in each perspective entail very different assumptions about and ways of viewing the social world. The former is based on the idea that consensus on norms and values is the basis of social order, and the latter that conflict and power are characteristic of all social relationships, including those between social classes. 'Role' is a good example of a concept that is used very differently in two perspectives such as structural-functionalism and symbolic interactionism. In the former, roles are occupied by social actors whose behaviour is determined by the associated norms. In the latter, roles are negotiated and renegotiated as social interaction proceeds; they are not predetermined.

Theoretical models

Another common use of *model* is to combine the word with *theory* to form *theoretical model*. Willer (1967) has attempted to use the combined concept precisely in an elaboration of the relationship between theory and research. His scheme falls within the *deductive* research strategy (see figure 5.7).

In arguing that social theory needs to be developed through the use of models, Willer has placed 'theoretical models' between 'general models' and research. 'General models' provide a background for 'theoretical models' that are essential in theory construction and testing. A 'theoretical model' contains concepts and explanatory ideas related to a particular phenomenon. It is the source of specific hypotheses that can be tested in the course of research. Willer defined a 'theoretical model' as 'a conceptualization of a group of phenomena, constructed by means of a rationale, where the ultimate purpose is to furnish the terms and relations, the propositions, of a formal system which, if validated, becomes a theory' (Willer 1967: 15). A 'general model' refers to a wider range of phenomena than do 'theoretical models'. The former is equivalent to what Merton called a 'general theoretical orientation' and Inkeles called 'model'. For example, 'general model' might refer to a total society while a 'theoretical model' may refer to only one subgroup. 'General models' may be a source, but not the only one, of 'theoretical models'. However, Willer argued that a 'theoretical model' is not equivalent to middle-range theory. The latter is much broader and would include what he called a 'formal system', an 'operational system' and 'theory'.

A 'formal system' is the simplest set of statements that represent the key relationships within a phenomenon; it is a compact, systematized and internally consistent set of statements of relationships that identify the core ingredients of a 'theoretical model'. It may be, but need not be, deductive in form. An 'operational system' translates the nominally defined concepts and the statements of the relationships of the 'formal system' into measurable relationships between concepts. (See the earlier discussion on the *operationalizing* tradition.)

As well as containing nominally defined concepts, a 'theoretical model' contains a rationale and a mechanism. The rationale is a point of view about a phenomenon, a way of looking at the social world, an organizing idea, that comes from the imagination of the researcher and not from data. The structure of the relationships between the concepts, which is determined by the definitions used, forms the mechanism of the model.[8] The presence of a mechanism distinguishes a 'theoretical model' from a 'general model'. Willer illustrated this with reference to Durkheim's theory of the division of labour and social solidarity.

> To conceive of societies according to the extent of their division of labour and their solidarity, whether mechanical or organic, as Durkheim did, is to employ a rationale.

---

[8] This use of 'mechanism' needs to be distinguished from its use in the *retroductive* research strategy. The former is a much weaker method of establishing causation as it relies only on a network of relationships, while in the latter use, a mechanism is supposed to generate the regularity to be explained.

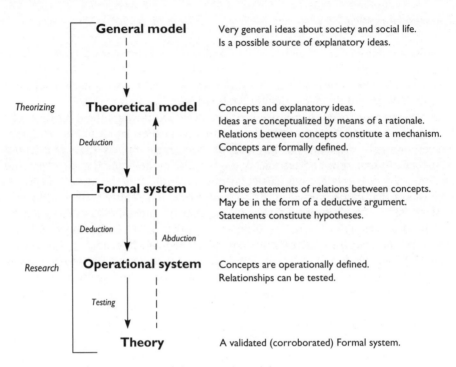

Figure 5.7 Willer's scheme of theory and models

> The relationship between the extent of division of labor and the type of solidarity, as well as the further relations which are implied, compose the mechanism. (Willer 1967: 17)

In short, 'general models' can be the source of ideas for the 'theoretical model' which, in turn, provides concepts and explanatory ideas that can be stated as relationships between concepts. These relationships form the mechanism through which an explanation is achieved. When these relationships are stated more precisely and systematically, they constitute the 'formal system'. When the concepts in the relationships of the 'formal system' are operationally defined it becomes the 'operational system' and can be tested. If the 'operational system' survives the testing, the 'formal system' can be called a 'theory'.

> A model contains a rationale and nominally defined concepts which are structured in the form of a mechanism. A model is cumbersome and complex in comparison to the purity and parsimony of a formal system.... There is a one-to-one correspondence between the relationships developed in the mechanism of the model and those of the formal system. It is the function of the model, through its mechanism, to furnish the relationships of the formal system. Since a theory is a validated formal system, it can be seen that it stands in direct logical relationship to its model. The theory can be deduced from the model while the model can be induced from the theory. (Willer 1967: 18)

Willer argued that models are constructed on the basis of extensive knowledge and through the use of imagination, in the *context of discovery*. They cannot be deduced from data, nor by induction conceived as a process of generalizing from data. It is, rather, a process of *abduction* involving imagination and creativity, not logic in a narrow sense.

While this scheme of 'general models', 'theoretical models', 'formal systems', 'operational systems' and 'theory' may seem to be rather eccentric, Willer has argued that it is consistent with many accepted ideas in philosophy (he has drawn heavily on Braithwaite 1953) and practices in the social sciences. Certainly, the idea contained in his use of 'general models' is well accepted, and operationalism has a long history. What he has tried to do is to show how models are used in theory construction, and to separate theoretical ideas and assumptions from the empirical testing of specific statements of relationships. If 'theory' is restricted to mean 'an integrated set of relationships with a certain level of validity' (Willer 1967: 9), then it can only get its meaning from the 'theoretical model' from which it was deduced. However, as Inkeles has also argued, the testing of a theory does not also test the model. It is not possible to establish whether models are true or false, valid or invalid. The only judgement that can be made about models is whether they are useful or productive.

> Since models stand in an inductive relation to their theories it is incorrect to speak of valid or invalid models. Models are never validated, even if their theories are validated; nor can models be proven invalid, even when they result in invalid theories.... Since the validation of a formal system never implies the validation of the model from which it was derived, it is best to speak of useful or 'good' models when they produce valid formal systems or when it is felt probable that they will produce valid formal systems. (Willer 1967: 20–1)[9]

Clearly, Willer's view of theory construction and testing is consistent with, and provides an elaboration of, the *deductive* research strategy.

Some time ago, I attempted to apply Willer's scheme in a study on the occupational choices of university students (Blaikie 1971). The theoretical model used is as follows:

(1) Individuals have goals and seek means to realize them; action is goal oriented.
(2) The values which an individual holds determine the relative importance given to these goals; individuals give highest priority to those goals which accord with the values they hold.
(3) Values are internalized, initially, during primary socialization as part of an individual's symbolic universe, and are subsequently either modified by processes of secondary socialization, or largely replaced by re-socialization.
(4) Individuals choose an occupation in which they perceive they can realize the occupational goals which they give the highest priority.
(5) When individuals perceive restrictions related to their possible employment in occupations which are seen to accord best with their high priority occupational

---

[9] As the arguments behind these claims are rather complex, they have not been included here. See Willer (1967: 20–1) for details.

goals, they will choose an occupation which they perceive will be least likely to hinder the realization of their high priority occupational goals; they will minimize value deprivation.

(6) Students enter university as inhabitants of diverse symbolic universes.

(7) During their university course secondary socialization, and perhaps, re-socialization occurs, entailing a change in goal priorities.

(8) Therefore, changes in occupational choice between entering and leaving university may be determined by:

    (a) changes in goal priorities;

    (b) changes in the perception of the possibility of realizing high priority goals in the occupation chosen initially;

    (c) changes in the perception of the possibility of obtaining employment in an occupation. (Blaikie 1971: 316)

Some hypotheses were derived from this theoretical model to form part of what Willer called the 'formal system'. Here are two examples.

- The goal priorities of students choosing a particular occupation tend to be similar even when restrictions related to entry and necessary qualifications, as perceived by them, are taken into account.
- Compared with restricted choice conditions, when restrictions are set aside there is a greater similarity in the goal priorities of students choosing a particular occupation.

Analogues of mechanisms

In both the natural and social sciences, many theories have been developed by drawing on ideas from another field of science. An example from the natural sciences occurred when physicists tried to understand the structure of the atom. They developed the idea of electrons and neutrons by drawing from astronomy the idea of the orbits of the planets around the sun. In sociology, Spencer's (1891) evolutionary theory of social change viewed society as being like an evolving organism. He argued that evolutionary growth is accompanied by changes in society's structure and functions, that an increase in size produces an increase in differentiation and structural complexity. His theory has employed what is commonly called the 'organismic analogy'; an idea that can be traced back to ancient and medieval writings. Hence, as the discipline of sociology developed to provide a 'scientific' understanding of human societies, it drew on familiar and well-established ideas from the discipline of biology. A theory in biology was used as a model for a theory of society.

Many other examples can be found of the use of a theory from a better-developed field as a model for a theory in a field where knowledge is still limited. The process is one of taking the concepts, and the established relationships between them, from the better-developed field and translating them into concepts and statements of relationships in the new field. For the model to be most useful, a one-to-one correspondence has to be established between the concepts and statements of relationship in both fields. If this is achieved, then hypotheses can be developed and tested in the new field. For example, in order to understand how rumours spread, it is possible to use as a model a theory about the spread of diseases. If the resulting hypotheses are corroborated, theories in the two fields will have the same form. In fact, as theories of the spread of rumours are advanced, the reverse process might then be useful, i.e. to use a theory developed about the spread of rumours as a model to advance knowledge about the spread of disease.

Representations of real or imagined things have been referred to as *iconic* models (Harré and Secord 1972: 74). Harré's second type of model, the iconic *paramorph*, relies on the use of analogies. Their function is to hypothesize plausible generative mechanisms, i.e. explanations, for the observed patterns identified by a *homeomorph*.

> The most important function of iconic models in science is as plausible analogies of the unknown causal, generative mechanisms of the non-random patterns discovered in critical explorations of fields of natural phenomena. In this role they serve as a basis both for existential hypotheses as to the reality of certain classes of entities, and further hypotheses as to their nature and behaviour. In this role they are indispensable, since if we depend only upon formal criteria for explanation, such as the deductibility from a theory of what is to be explained, then there will be indefinitely many theories which satisfy that criterion for any given set of facts. (Harré and Secord 1972: 76)

Some writers (e.g. Black 1962; Brodbeck 1968) have argued that analogies are the only genuine kinds of models in science. They considered all other uses of the term are unnecessary, because there are perfectly good alternative concepts available; other uses simply create ambiguity and confusion.

Diagrammatic representations

Models of this type are designed to indicate patterns of relations, time sequences, or causal connections between aspects of social life. Concepts are arranged in a visual space to reflect their ordering in the social world, and symbols, such as lines and arrows, are used to represent the form and direction of the relationships. These models include arrangements of abstract concepts about generic aspects of the social world, and more specific summaries of relations among a number of variables. The former have been described as *abstract-analytical* models and the latter as *empirical-causal* models (Turner 1987: 164–5; 1991: 17) (see figure 5.8).

Abstract-analytical models deal with generic properties of the social world, and depict a complex set of connections among context-free concepts. Explanation is achieved by the ability of the model to map the crucial connections (perhaps weighted) among basic properties of some social process or phenomenon. *Empirical-causal* models are designed to represent the influence, in a temporal sequence, of a set of independent variables on a dependent variable. Explanation is achieved by tracing the causal connections among measured variables that are assumed to

Analytical models

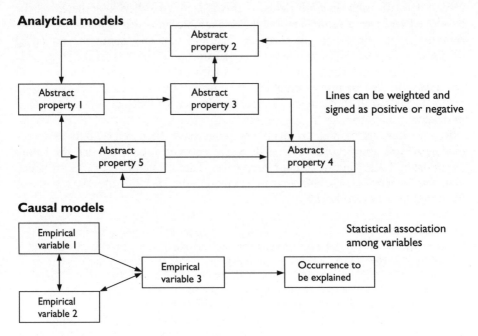

Lines can be weighted and
signed as positive or negative

Causal models

Statistical association
among variables

Figure 5.8   Types of modelling schemes

(*Source*: Turner 1991:19)

account for the occurrence that needs to be explained (Turner 1991: 17–19).
However, Turner has argued that the lack of abstraction in empirical-causal
models makes them much less useful in theory building; they essentially represent
regularities in data and require more abstract theory to explain them (Turner
1987: 165). A typical use of such models can be found in path analysis.

Turner (1988) has attempted to present the theories of fourteen major theorists
using thirty-nine separate diagrammatic representations. He has also produced his
own analytical theories of interpersonal motivation, the dynamics of interaction,

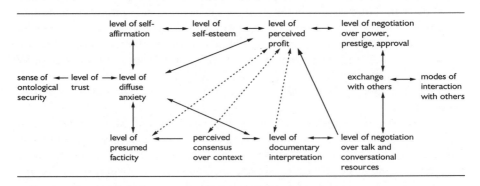

Figure 5.9   The dynamics of interpersonal motivation

(*Source*: Turner 1987: 172)

and processes of structuring (Turner 1987). These figures attempt to integrate systematically the work of many theorists. One example, on interpersonal motivation, will serve as an illustration: see figure 5.9.

Mathematical representations

While this is not the place for a detailed discussion of the role of mathematics in the social sciences, a few comments are in order. The use of mathematics is well accepted in physics, and to a certain extent in biology, but social scientists are very divided about the extent and manner in which it should be used in the social sciences. Of course, the application of mathematics to the social sciences is not completely new: economics is very dependent on the use of mathematical models, and psychologists have applied mathematics to certain aspects of their work, particularly in psychometrics. It is in the areas of social psychology, sociology and political science that the use of mathematics is a more recent and controversial development.

At a very basic level, however, whenever we count some aspect of the social world, and then apply some form of statistical analysis to the data, we are assuming that regularities in the social world conform to the rules of arithmetic. However, this kind of mathematical modelling is largely taken for granted.

It is other activities to which the label of *mathematical modelling* is usually applied, such as:

- formalizing theories by providing a language that clarifies assumptions and consequences embedded in the use of ordinary language;
- organizing, sifting through and finding systematic patterns in data;
- proving substitutes for theories from which consequences can be drawn and tested; and
- playing 'what if' games with sociological ideas (Lazarsfeld and Henry 1966; Leik and Meeker 1975).

The first of these activities is concerned with developing a precise language for social theory. However, this has not been the major use of mathematics in sociology (Sorensen 1978). The second use is the more common. It includes descriptive, correlational and inferential statistics at one extreme, and, at the other extreme, attempts to achieve causal explanations. The latter includes the use of regression and other forms of structural equation modelling (e.g. path analysis). In this activity, the aim is either to find a line or curve that represents a relationship in data, or to establish the extent to which a network of relationships conforms to a perfect model of them. The third and fourth uses involve constructing a theory in the form of a set of mathematical (algebraic) equations, exploring its implications by substituting parameters (possible values for the variables), and seeing what the model would predict.

From the time of its enthusiastic application in sociology in the 1970s, mathematical modelling has had its advocates and critics. The advocates claim that if there are regularities in social phenomena, and if these can be described precisely in abstract terms, then mathematical analysis is possible. The critics claim that it is not appropriate to impose mathematical principles on social life, as the two fields are unrelated. Some critics have decried the excessive concern with all techniques of quantitative measurement and analysis, while for others, mathematical modelling is seen as a fetish that is both far removed from the reality of social life and is an inadequate representation of it. The fascination with sophisticated data manipulation, including model building, is seen to remove the researcher from real-world concerns.

In a polemical presidential address to the American Sociological Association, Coser (1975) offered a critique of this tradition of research in particular, and of the sectarian enthusiasm for new tools of research in general. He was concerned about the excessive fascination with techniques of measurement and analysis, to the neglect of theoretical concerns.

> The fallacy of misplaced precision consists in believing that one can compensate for theoretical weakness by methodological strength. Concern with precision in measurement before theoretical clarification of what is worth measuring and what is not, and before one clearly knows what one is measuring, is a roadblock to progress in sociological analysis. (Coser 1975: 695)

The editor of *The American Sociologist* invited responses from two of the major exponents of path analysis in social stratification research. Featherman (1976) and Treiman (1976) both mounted a strong defence.

> I am of the conviction that structural equation models are helpful instruments in the systemization and formalization of theory, in the explication of concepts and their measurement, and in the representation of collateral hypotheses and their derivative implications....In my view, path analysis, as an adjunct to an array of other quantitative research instruments, is an example of *properly* placed precision and has *removed* many of the barriers to our theoretic thinking by helping to organize it.... path analysis and its genre of statistical analysis...force their users to precision of thought and explicitness of meaning in ways which other analytic tools and strictly verbal constructions do not. (Featherman 1976: 25)

> First, that from being a substitute for theoretical analysis, path analysis and other sophisticated procedures increasingly utilized in sociological research constitute powerful aids to theorizing; second, that our substantive understanding of social stratification has been furthered by these procedures in a way quite impossible without their use...It does no good to formulate hypotheses about, for example, differences in the rate and pattern of social mobility in capitalist and socialist societies if we do not have a clear idea about exactly what we mean by social mobility and precisely how we can measure it. (Treiman 1976: 28)

Responses to these arguments will depend on the reader's preferences in ontological and epistemological assumptions and research strategies.[10]

It is hard to find an article in any issue of *The American Sociological Review* over recent years that does not use some form of structural equation modelling,

---

[10] For another debate on the same kind of issue see Blaikie (1977) and the replies by Jones et al. (1978), Cass and Resler (1978), Daniel (1978) and Blaikie (1978).

particularly regression. Generally, the aim is to find a set of independent variables that can best predict variations in a dependent variable. Usually the independent variables are suggested by some theory. In regression analysis, independent variables are progressively added or manipulated in various combinations, each combination being described as a model. The other dominant form of modelling involves the use of mathematical equations of various kinds, including log linear and logit variations, to express a complex theoretical statement (such as that involved in rational choice theory) or the relations among dependent and independent variables.

Whether or not consideration needs to be given to mathematical modelling in a research design will depend on a number of other choices. These choices are likely to be influenced by the various audiences that a researcher needs or wishes to take into account as well as the paradigms that are regarded as being appropriate in one's discipline or research community. In some kinds of research, the development of a mathematical model may only be relevant after the data have been collected. In other kinds of research, such as most qualitative studies, mathematical models will be completely irrelevant.

Theories, Models and Research Strategies

To summarize the discussion in this chapter, I shall review the role of theory and models in each of the research strategies. Two issues will be discussed. The first is

Table 5.1   Research strategies, theory and models

Research strategy		Nature of theory	Use of models
Inductive	Form:	Generalizations/laws	Abstract descriptions
		Networks of propositions	Mathematical representation
	Process:	Generated by induction from data	Conceptual frameworks
Deductive	Form:	Deductive argument	Theoretical models
		produces hypotheses	Diagrammatic representation
	Process:	Hypotheses tested by	Mathematical representation
		matching against data	
Retroductive	Form:	Generative structures or	Abstract descriptions of
		mechanisms	episodes (homeomorphs)
	Process:	Modelling mechanisms	May involve use of
		Establishing their existence	analogies (paramorphs)
Abductive	Form:	Social scientific accounts	
		Ideal types	Abstract descriptions
	Process:	Generated from everyday	(ideal types)
		concepts/meanings/accounts	

the contrast between theory development and theory testing; whether research sets out with a well-developed theory or whether theory is the end product of research. The second is concerned with the way explanation or understanding is achieved. The four research strategies present us with contrasting positions on these issues (see table 5.1).

Inductive and Deductive Strategies

The relationship between theory and research is viewed differently in the *inductive* and *deductive* research strategies. In the *inductive* research strategy, theory consists of generalizations derived by induction from data. Hence, research is about theory development, starting with the collection of data and, hopefully, ending up with abstract descriptions of patterns in the data, i.e. with generalizations. If sufficient support is achieved for a generalization from many studies, its status as a 'true' representation of social reality is enhanced. Inductivists search for universal 'laws' of social life. Such propositions are regarded as both describing the essential characteristics of the social world and providing the basis for explanations of it. Specific instances of a particular phenomenon can be explained by regarding it as an instance of such universal regularities, i.e. they are seen to fit the pattern. Hence the idea of *pattern* explanations. In short, research within the *inductive* strategy involves collecting data by operationalizing concepts, and then searching for patterns in the data. Patterns become generalizations, and networks of generalizations become a theory. Theory development consists of accumulating generalizations and producing further support for them. However, the possibility of establishing universal regularities in the social sciences is a contested issue and is now widely rejected.

The use of models in the *inductive* research strategy is confined to abstract descriptions and mathematical representations. The former consists of relatively low-level generalizations and possible networks of such generalizations, while the latter involves the mathematical modelling of data. This modelling can range from basic statistical summaries, such as measures of central tendency, dispersion and association, to more complex mathematical simplifications of patterns of relationships.

In the *deductive* research strategy, theory not only has a different form, but it is also arrived at in a very different way. The logic of the *deductive* research strategy is the reverse of the *inductive* strategy. Rather than theory being the outcome of research, it has to be produced, borrowed or invented, at the outset. Theory takes the form of a deductive argument. Theoretical ideas are connected in such a way that, from one or more very general propositions that state relationships between abstract concepts, plus some conditions under which they apply, and, perhaps, some descriptive statements, a specific conclusion can be drawn. Depending on the purpose at hand, the conclusion to the argument can be a hypothesis, a prediction, or the regularity that is to be explained. Hence, this strategy requires a great deal of theoretical work before data are collected.

The task of research using the *deductive* research strategy is to put theories to the test, to establish whether or not what the theory proposes matches the available data. In order to do this, it is necessary to deduce one or more hypotheses from the theory and to collect data relevant to the hypothesis or hypotheses. A lack of match between the data and the hypothesis means that the theory is at best inappropriate, and is probably false. On the other hand, a match lends some support to the theory but it can never establish conclusively that it is the only or true explanation for the regularity. Therefore, theory development is a trial and error process of proposing theories and rejecting those that are inconsistent with data; theories that survive this process will be retained until they may be replaced with a better theory. Again, as we have seen, this process matches the theory to data, not to social reality. The theory dependence of observations makes any matching between data and reality impossible. For the same reason, theories cannot be rejected conclusively.

A *deductive* theory can come from many sources, or a combination of them. An existing *researchers'* theory could be used in its original or a modified from. Alternatively, theory might be constructed using elements from *theoreticians'* theory and/or the findings of previous research. The latter clearly requires a great deal of knowledge of the field, as well as creativity. However, according to Popper, it matters not whence a theory comes; it is the logic of its construction and the rigour of its testing that are important.

In the *deductive* strategy, the theory provides a very clear focus for the research. The concepts in the hypothesis or hypotheses that have been deduced from the theory determine the data that need to be collected. These hypotheses will also state relationships between concepts, and their testing is achieved by comparing the relationships between the measures of the concepts with the form of the relationship that was hypothesized. While the *inductive* strategy requires the collection of large quantities of data, perhaps the measurement of many concepts in order to justify a generalization, the *deductive* strategy only requires the measurement of specific concepts in the hypotheses.

The *deductive* strategy lends itself to the use of various types of models. It is possible to regard a deductive argument as a 'theoretical model' and to set it in the context of a 'general model', a 'formal system' and an 'operational system' (Willer 1967). Alternatively, it is possible to represent the relationships between the concepts contained in the propositions of the argument in diagrammatic and/or mathematical form. This is now common practice among quantitative researchers.

As we have seen earlier, the claims made about the status of the theories in these two research strategies are very different. Inductively produced theories are supposed to be true as long as theoretical preconceptions and prejudices have not contaminated the research, and so-called objective methods have been used. However, critics have argued that as neither of these requirements can be fully met, inductively produced generalizations must be regarded not only as limited in scope but also as subject to modification by subsequent research. The pragmatic position is that some preconceptions and 'subjectivity' must be involved, as research cannot get started without concepts. The selection of concepts, and decisions on how they are defined and measured, will 'prejudice' the findings. However, as an advocate of *inductivism*, Durkheim (1951, 1962) insisted that concepts must be defined at the outset. While this is clearly necessary, it is a deviation from the earlier arguments about the need to start with a completely open mind and to simply describe the world as it 'really' is. Nevertheless, researchers have no option but to compromise the ideals of this strategy in answering 'what' questions, and then to recognize the consequent limitations.

The *deductive* strategy, on the other hand, accepts that all theories are tentative and subject to either revision or replacement. While the aim is to produce theories that match reality, the researcher can never know when the match has been achieved. According to Popper, all that can be achieved with confidence is the rejection of theory that does not match reality. As we have seen in chapter 4, this claim cannot be made in the way that Popper insisted. The result is that pragmatic judgements must be made about when to keep or dispose of a theory. In other words, all theories are under-determined by data.

Retroductive and Abductive Strategies

The *retroductive* and *abductive* research strategies do not lend themselves to conceptual or logical ways of linking theory and research. In the *retroductive* strategy, a theory or explanation is achieved by establishing the existence of the hypothesized structure or mechanism that is responsible for producing an observed regularity. Alternatively, and probably more commonly in the social sciences, the task is one of establishing which one of a number of possible known structures or mechanisms is responsible, and the conditions under which it operates. Whether it is a structure or a mechanism on which the researcher focuses will depend on whether the structuralist or the constructionist version is used.

Models play a vital role in the *retroductive* strategy. They are used to provide abstract descriptions of the regularities or episodes under consideration (homeo-morphs), and they are then used to construct 'images' of mechanisms (para-morphs). It is in this latter use that analogies may be employed as a stimulus to the creative process involved in discovering unknown mechanisms.

The process of constructing a model of a possible structure or mechanism can be extremely demanding, requiring extensive knowledge and involving the use of creativity and imagination. The process of establishing the existence of a structure or mechanism is demanding in a different way, in this case requiring ingenuity and skill. In the end, the connection between a hypothetical model, and the process of establishing its existence, is more a matter of arguing from evidence than of engaging in the statistical testing of hypotheses (as in the *deductive* strategy).

To demonstrate the existence of a particular structure, for example, may involve documenting many possible consequences of its existence, and then arguing for the plausibility of the connection between the evidence and the theory. For example, to establish the existence of a particular type of class structure as an explanation for patterns of alienated behaviour at work will require an argument of the kind that connects evidence other than the work behaviour in question to both that behaviour and a possible class structure. Such arguments will obviously be a matter of persuasion and contention.

The relationship between theory and research in the *abductive* research strategy is very different from that in the other three strategies. In this case, the two are intimately intertwined; data and theoretical ideas are played off against one another in a developmental and creative process. Regularities that are discovered at the beginning or in the course of the research will stimulate the researcher to ask questions and look for answers. The data will then be reinterpreted in the light of emerging theoretical ideas, and this may lead to further questioning, the entertainment of tentative hypotheses, and a search for answers. Research becomes a dialogue between data and theory mediated by the researcher. Data are interpreted and reinterpreted in the light of the emerging theory, and, as a result, change in the process. The emerging theory is tested and refined as the research proceeds. While this dialogue could continue forever, a satisfactory explanation will have been produced when theoretical saturation is achieved and satisfying answers to the research questions have been arrived at.

The process used to generate theory in the *abductive* research strategy is some-times described as inductive. However, this is misleading for a number of reasons. *Abduction* is a process by means of which the researcher assembles lay accounts of the phenomenon in question, with all their gaps and deficiencies, and, in an iterative manner, begins to construct their own account. The central characteristic of this process is that it is iterative; it involves the researcher in alternating periods of immersion in the relevant social world, and periods of withdrawal for reflec-tion and analysis. This alternating process means that theory is generated as an intimate part of the research process; it is not invented at the beginning nor is it just produced at the end. The form of this theory can vary, depending on the particular branch of interpretivism within which the researcher is working. Fol-lowing Weber, Schütz and Becker, my preference is for the construction of ideal types as the abstract second-order descriptions. The rich detail in ideal types can then be used to produce theoretical propositions, which, in turn, may be tested by the further use of the *abductive* strategy, or, possibly, within the *deductive* strategy. The latter case does not necessarily entail the use of quantitative methods; it is possible to test deductively derived hypotheses using any type of data.

Ideal types can be regarded as models of social actors, social situations or social processes; Schütz certainly viewed them this way. They are a particular kind of abstract description that is derived from the everyday, tacit knowledge that social actors use to find their way about in their social world, and to communicate and interact with other social actors. Ideal types as models can look very much like the models of mechanisms developed in the constructionist version of the *retroductive* research strategy. I have argued (Blaikie 1994) that Weber's ideal type of the Protestant work ethic, particularly the typical meaning given to work by the early Calvinists, is equivalent to a model of a mechanism. In this case, the mechanism explains the relationship between religion and occupation that Weber claimed existed in Germany about a hundred years ago. However, it is not clear whether Weber arrived at this ideal type cum model by *abduction* or *retroduction*. Given the historical nature of his study, his ability to use *abduc-tion* was rather restricted; perhaps he used a combination of both, thus reinforcing the idea of the possible close association between these two research strategies.

Summary and Conclusion

This excursion into the diverse and complex roles of concepts, theories, hypotheses and models in research has taken us down many paths. Just how any researcher decides to deal with these issues will, no doubt, be the result of many influences at work. What is clear is that it is not possible to avoid dealing with them.

In addition to the need to achieve consistency between the elements of a research design, there are other possible influences on the way concepts, theories and models are used. Commitment to a particular paradigm or approach to social enquiry, with its accompanying ontological and epistemological assumptions and theoretical preferences, will lead to some uses being regarded as legitimate and others as inappropriate. Such commitments are sanctioned by academic peer groups and other audiences.

To a large extent, the nature of the research questions, and the choice of research strategy or strategies, will determine how concepts are used, whether hypotheses are used, and the role of theory and models. 'What' questions will be much less demanding theoretically than 'why' or 'how' questions. It may be possible to use the *inductive* or *abductive* research strategies to produce descriptions that have little theoretical content. However, when 'why' questions are entertained, there is no escaping theory. The research strategy selected largely determines how theory will be dealt with, i.e. what kind of *researchers'* theory will be used. Nevertheless, the process of generating or testing theory also requires knowledge of *theoreticians'* theory. To achieve this knowledge may be a daunting task for the uninitiated, and a potentially distracting one for others.

This discussion of the use of theory and models in the four research strategies needs to be viewed in the light of the methodological criticisms that have been made of all four of them. Among many other considerations, to be of practical value to the social researcher, the following modifications need to be adopted.

- The *inductive* strategy needs to begin with specific concepts that are defined by the researcher. Whether concepts are operationalized or used to sensitize will depend on the researcher's preferences.
- It is necessary to recognize that in the *deductive* strategy it may not be possible to conclusively reject hypotheses just as it is not possible to conclusively prove them.
- In using the *retroductive* strategy, it may be necessary to establish the relevance of one of a number of possible known mechanisms rather than be searching for a unique unknown mechanism.
- The *abductive* strategy may be extended beyond ideal types and 'thick' descriptions to testable theoretical propositions. Whether these propositions are tested by use of the *deductive* strategy, or by the further use of the *abductive* strategy, is a matter of choice.

6

Sources and Selection of Data

A common error has been to equate sampling with survey research and to assume that field research does not involve any form of sampling. (Burgess 1982b)

Introduction

Before decisions can be made about how to collect the data required to answer research questions, consideration needs to be given to the kind of data to be collected, where they will come from, and how they will be selected. Hence, this chapter discusses:

- types of data used by social researchers, i.e. primary, secondary and tertiary;
- forms in which data are produced in the social sciences, i.e. in either words or numbers;
- sources of data in terms of the settings from which they will be obtained, i.e. natural social settings, semi-natural settings, artificial settings, and social artefacts;
- selection of data, with particular reference to sampling; and
- the role of case studies in social research.

Types of Data

Data used in social research can be of three main types: *primary, secondary* and *tertiary*. *Primary data* are generated by a researcher who is responsible for the design of the study, and the collection, analysis and reporting of the data. This is 'new' data, used to answer specific research questions. The researcher can describe why and how they were collected. *Secondary data* are raw data that have already been collected by someone else, either for some general information purpose, such as a government census or other official statistics, or for a

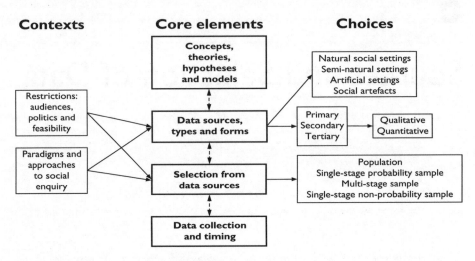

Figure 6.1   Data sources and selection

specific research project. In both cases, the original purpose in collecting such data is likely to be different from that of the secondary user, particularly in the case of a previous research project. *Tertiary* data have been analysed either by the researcher who generated them or by an analyst of secondary data. In this case the raw data may not be available, only the results of this analysis (see figure 6.1).

It is important to note that in the discipline of history, 'primary' and 'secondary' have quite different meanings from those being used here. Primary sources are the original social artefacts, while secondary sources are the result of someone having worked on or from the primary sources, or even from someone else's secondary sources. However, the concern in this usage is the same as in the social sciences, i.e. how far the researcher is removed from the 'original' source, and the possible consequences of this for the quality of the data.

While primary data can come from many sources, they are characterized by the fact that they result from direct contact between the researcher and the source, and that they have been generated by the application of particular methods by the researcher. The researcher, therefore, has control of the production and analysis, and is in a position to judge their quality. This judgement is much more difficult with secondary and tertiary types of data.

Secondary data can come from the same kind of sources as primary data; the researcher is just one step removed from these data. The use of secondary data is often referred to as secondary analysis. It is now common for data sets to be archived and made available for analysis by other researchers. Such data sets

Types of Data

Primary
Generated by the researcher

Secondary
Generated by another researcher

Tertiary
Analysed by another researcher

constitute the purest form of secondary data. Most substantial surveys have potential for further analysis because they can be interrogated with different research questions.

> Secondary information consists of sources of data and other information collected by others and archived in some form. These sources include government reports, industry studies, archived data sets, and syndicated information services as well as traditional books and journals found in libraries. Secondary information offers relatively quick and inexpensive answers to many questions and is almost always the point of departure for primary research. (Stewart and Kamis 1984: 1)

While there are obvious advantages in using secondary data, such as savings in time and costs, there are also disadvantages. The most fundamental drawback stems from the fact that this previous research was inevitably done with different aims and research questions. It may also have been based on assumptions, and even prejudices, which are not readily discernible, or which are inconsistent with those of the current research. Secondly, there is the possibility that not all the areas of interest to the current researcher may have been included. Thirdly, the data may be coded in an inconvenient form. Fourthly, it may be difficult to judge the quality of secondary data; a great deal has to be taken on faith. A fifth disadvantage for some research stems from the fact that the data may be old. There is always a time lag between collection and reporting of results, and even longer before researchers are prepared to archive their data set. Even some census data may not be published until at least two years after they were collected. However, this time lag may not be a problem in some research, such as historical, comparative or theoretical studies.

With *tertiary* data, the researcher is two steps removed from the original primary data. Published reports of research and officially collected 'statistics' invariably include tables of data that have summarized, categorized or otherwise manipulated raw data. Strictly speaking, most government censuses report data of these kinds, and access to the original data set may not be possible. When government agencies or other bodies do their own analysis on a census, they produce genuine tertiary data. Because control of the steps involved in moving from the original primary data to tertiary data is out of the hands of a researcher, such data must be treated with caution. Some sources of tertiary data will be more reliable than others. Analysts can adopt an orientation towards the original data, and they can be selective in what is reported. In addition, there is always the possibility of academic fraud. The further a researcher is removed from the original primary data, the greater the risk of unintentional or deliberate distortion.

Forms of Data

Data are produced in two main forms, as *numbers* or *words*. There seems to be a common belief among researchers, and the consumers of their products, that numerical data are needed in scientific research to ensure objective and accurate results. Somehow, data in words tend to be regarded as being not only less precise but also less reliable. These views still persist in many circles, although non-numerical data are now more widely accepted. As we shall see later in this chapter, the distinction between words and numbers, between qualitative and quantitative data, is not a simple one (see figure 6.1).

Forms of Data

Words
At source
During analysis
For reporting

Numbers
Soon after source
For analysis
For reporting

It can be argued that all primary data start out as words. Some data are recorded in words, they remain in words throughout the analysis, and the findings are reported in words. The original words will be transformed and manipulated into other words, and these processes may be repeated more than once. While the level of the language may change, say from lay language to technical language, throughout the research the medium is always words.

In other research, the initial communication will be transformed into numbers immediately, or prior to the analysis. The former involves the use of pre-coded response categories, and the latter the post-coding of answers provided in words, as in the case of open-ended questions. Numbers are attached to both sets of categories and the subsequent analysis will be numerical. The findings of the research will be presented in numerical summaries and tables. However, words will have to be introduced to interpret and elaborate the numerical findings. Hence, in quantitative studies, data normally begin in words, are transformed into numbers, are subjected to different levels of statistical manipulation, and are reported in both numbers and words; from words to numbers and back to words. The interesting point here is whose words were used in the first place and what process was used to generate them? In the case where responses are made to a predetermined set of categories, the questions and the categories will be in the researcher's words; the respondent *only* has to interpret both. However, this is a big 'only'. As Foddy (1993) and Pawson (1995, 1996) have pointed out, this is a complex process that requires much more attention and understanding than it has normally been given.

Sophisticated numerical transformations can occur at the data reduction stage of analysis. For example, responses to a set of attitude statements, in categories ranging from 'strongly agree' to 'strongly disagree', can be numbered, say, from 1 to 5. Subject to some test of unidimensionality, these scores can be combined to produce a total score for an attitude scale. Such scores are well removed from the respondent's original reading of the words in the statements and the recording of a response in a category with a label in words.

In studies that deal with large quantities of textual data, as in the case of transcribed in-depth interviews, manipulation can occur in two main ways: in the generation of categories in which segments of text are coded (as in grounded theory); or in the abstraction of technical language from lay language (as in the case of Schütz's and Giddens's versions of the *abductive* research strategy). In both of these forms of analysis, it is possible to do simple counting, for example to establish the number of times a category occurs in a body of text, or the number of respondents who can be located in each of a set of ideal types.

So far, this discussion of the use of words and numbers has been confined to the collection of primary data. However, these kinds of manipulations may have already occurred in secondary data, and will certainly have occurred in tertiary data.

The controversial issue in all of this is the effect that any form of manipulation has on the original data. We need to be clear at the outset that it is impossible to produce any data without the researcher having an influence. Perhaps the more fundamental question is, is it possible to collect 'pure' data? If all observation is interpretation, and all concepts are theory-laden, then manipulation is involved from the very beginning. Even if a conversation is recorded unobtrusively, any attempt to understand what went on requires the researcher to make interpretations and to use concepts. How much manipulation occurs is a matter of choice. Researchers who prefer to remain qualitative through all stages of a research project may argue that it is bad enough manipulating lay language into technical language without translating either of them into the language of mathematics. A common fear about such translations is that they end up distorting the social world out of all recognition, with the result that research reports based on them become either meaningless or, possibly, dangerous if acted on. We shall encounter arguments in favour of quantification later in the chapter.

Sources of Data

Regardless of whether data are primary, secondary or tertiary, they can come from four different types of settings: *natural social settings*, *semi-natural settings*, *artificial settings* and from *social artefacts* (see figure 6.1). Research conducted in a *natural social setting* involves the researcher in entering an area of social activity and studying people going about their everyday lives. In a *semi-natural setting*, individuals are asked to report on their activities that occur in natural settings, while in an *artificial setting*, social activity is contrived for experimental or learning purposes. The fourth kind of social setting is in the past and involves the examination of records or traces left by individuals or groups. A fundamental distinction here is whether social activity is studied as it occurs *in situ*, or whether it will be artificially or historically reconstructed in some way. This fourth type of research setting introduces a time dimension, and this will be examined shortly.

Natural Social Settings

Natural social settings involve three main levels of analysis: micro-social phenomena, meso-social phenomena, and macro-social phenomena.[1] These levels vary in scale from individuals and small social groups, through organizations and communities, to institutions and large-scale social situations, such as cities and

[1] These categories closely resemble Layder's (1993) stratified model of society.

Sources of Data

Natural social settings

Micro
   Individuals
   Small groups
   Social episodes
Meso
   Organizations
   Communities
   Crowds
   Social movements
Macro
   Social institutions
   Social structures
   Nations
   Multinational bodies
Quasi-experiments

Semi-natural settings

Individuals' characteristics
Individuals as informants
Representative individuals
Life histories
Individuals as case studies

Artificial settings

Experiments
   Categories of individuals
   Groups
Simulation and games

Social artefacts

Official statistics
Public documents
Private documents
Personal records

regions, nations and multi/transnational bodies. However, it is very difficult to use 'naturalistic' methods in large-scale social units. In these cases, it may be possible to regard the unit of analysis as social, i.e. as involving continuing social activity, but accept that it may not be possible to study this activity directly; indirect methods may have to be used.

Micro-social phenomena

Micro-social phenomena begin with individuals in their everyday social setting. There are many reasons for focusing on individuals, for example because they have a significant or typical role. However, unlike a great deal of research in psychology, this interest in the individual is more a matter of focus within some field of everyday social life, rather than a study of an individual *per se*. Then follow other basic social units, such as the dyad, and small primary social groups.[2] These micro-social relations are normally characterized by face-to-face social interaction in which social actors give meaning to their own actions, and the actions of the others involved, and take these others into account when making decisions about their own actions. Another important feature of these small groups is their continuity; they have a history and, usually, a relatively permanent membership, and they develop and reproduce patterns, structures and institutions.

The other major type of micro-social phenomenon is the social episode, those social interactions that are limited in time and space, such as crowds and social gatherings. Most of the participants in these situations may not meet again, or certainly not in the same circumstances or with the same membership. The intersubjective meanings develop and then dissipate, and the structuring of social relations is fleeting. The number of people involved in social episodes can vary considerably, from two to hundreds, thus making their inclusion under this category of social phenomenon somewhat arbitrary. However, the processes involved in understanding such phenomena are likely to be social-psychological in nature and similar to those used for small groups.

---

[2] In using such distinctions as *micro*, *meso* and *macro*, as well as primary and secondary social groups, we encounter problems of definition and boundaries. It is not the intention here to try to be definitive about such distinctions, but, rather, to distinguish broadly between a range of social phenomena.

Meso-social phenomena

Meso-social phenomena include organizations, communities, crowds and social movements. Organizations are relatively permanent, large social groups which are established to achieve goals. The organizations can be public or private, for business or pleasure, legal or illegal. The social relationships in organizations are largely secondary in nature, with membership that may be compulsory (e.g. in a prison) or voluntary (e.g. in a sporting club), full-time or part-time, paid or unpaid, long-term or short-term. While organizations change, at times rapidly, the structure of relations and forms of authority and leadership are likely to be relatively enduring.

'Community' has been included to refer to a diverse range of social phenomena. Like 'society', this concept has many uses; for example, we refer to 'local' communities, 'the' community, 'ethnic' communities, 'regional' communities and 'the world' community, all of which are very different. The notion of community being used here refers to looser forms of social organization in which either space or common interests are the defining characteristics. These social collectivities are different from organizations, and remove us one step further from primary and even secondary relationships.

Within the broad field of collective behaviour are two important types of social settings, 'crowds' and 'social movements'. A crowd is a reasonably large collection of people gathered together in a public place. Four types of crowds have been identified: *casual, conventional, expressive* and *active* (Goode 1992). *Casual* crowds are loosely structured and are made up of people who just happen to be in the same place at the same time. Members are united by physical proximity, and they can enter and leave at any time. Such crowds are only marginally examples of collective behaviour. A *conventional* crowd comes together for a specific purpose, for example for a lecture or a concert. It is governed by normative rules. Members of an *expressive* crowd gather for the specific purpose of belonging to the crowd itself, to cheer, clap, scream or stomp. Membership is an end in itself. An *acting* crowd engages in overt behaviour, such as a demonstration or a riot. While a crowd can be regarded as a type of group, it is frequently characterized by emergent behaviour that can spread rapidly from one person to another, and from one situation to another. Even though crowds form and change suddenly and unexpectedly, their members may have a high degree of personal engagement (Marx and McAdam 1994).

'Social movements' lie somewhere between crowds and organizations or institutions. They are reasonably organized collectivities, fairly long-lasting and stable, with emerging rules and traditions, and with an indefinite and shifting membership. Leadership positions are 'determined more by the informal response of the members than by formal procedures for legitimating authority' (Turner and Killian 1972: 246). Social movements are 'organized efforts by a substantial number of people to change, or to resist change, in some major aspect of society' (Goode 1992: 399). They are collective attempts to pursue a common interest, or achieve a common goal, outside established institutions. Four types of social movements have been proposed (Aberle 1966): *transformative* movements that seek major and violent changes (e.g. revolutionary and radical religious movements; *reformative* movements that try to alter some aspects of the social order (e.g. social justice movements); *redemptive* movements that try to rescue people from what are seen as corrupting ways of life (e.g. many religious movements); and *alternative* movements that try to change an aspect of an individual's life (e.g. Alcoholics Anonymous) (Giddens 1997: 511–13).

Macro-social phenomena

Macro-social phenomena are either very abstract and/or much larger social entities than those already discussed. Examples of such abstract phenomena are social institutions and social structures, both of which are the products of the theorizing by experts about the social world. While institutions and structures are usually discussed in the context of some society, or nation,[3] it is also possible to use them in the analysis of cross/inter/multinational bodies, such as transnational corporations, international non-government organizations, and the United Nations.

At the macro level, it is becoming increasingly necessary in social science to move beyond nations, or even comparisons between nations, to deal with social phenomena that span the globe. We are witnessing a developing paradox in which national and regional boundaries are becoming both less important and more important at the same time. In terms of world economics and migration, national boundaries have become less significant, but in terms of politics and social identity, national and regional boundaries are assuming greater significance. Ethnic identity provides an interesting illustration. The fragmentation of the Soviet Union and the former Yugoslavia are examples of the desire of ethnic communities to assert their independence. At the same time, migration since the discovery of the New World, and particularly since World War II, has created worldwide ethnic communities, or potential communities, of groups such as the Chinese, Irish, Jews, Greeks, Italians and Vietnamese. Nations and multinational bodies have been included as social phenomena to reinforce, firstly, that societies are not coincident with nations, and secondly, that social analysis must also go beyond national boundaries. It is now desirable to both engage in cross-national comparative research, and to deal with the growing phenomenon of regional and multi/transnational bodies and organizations.

The boundaries between micro, meso, and macro social settings are not rigid; the three categories are intended to indicate a range of possible research sites that

---

[3] The concept of 'society' is not included here as a social phenomenon, partly because of the diversity of its uses and the vagueness of its meaning, but also because it adds nothing to the range of concepts being discussed, i.e. organizations, communities, social movements and nations. Differences between 'society' and 'nation' hinge on both political and geographical criteria. However, the details of these differences need not concern us here. Some writers, perhaps economists, use 'economy' instead of 'nation'. While an 'economy' may be a large social unit with relatively autonomous political and legal institutions, globalization and regional trading blocks are reducing this autonomy.

vary in terms of the number of people involved, the nature of their social relationships and their relative geographical concentration or dispersion.

The category of quasi-experiment is included under *natural social settings* ✓ to identify research in which experimental procedures are used outside the laboratory. Rather than contriving an experiment, the researcher may use opportunities as they arise in natural settings. An example comes from a before-after study of a town in which a change of circumstances was introduced that was outside the researcher's control. Many years ago, I participated in a study of an isolated town on the west coast of the South Island of New Zealand. A thriving gold-mining centre in the late nineteenth century, the town was located on a narrow plane between mountains and the sea. It was isolated at the end of a road. A decision was made to extend the road across a mountain pass to a popular tourist resort area, thus creating the potential for the town to be included in a tourist route. A project was designed to study the town before and some time after the road was constructed to assess the impact of tourism. While the design of this study did not satisfy experimental ideals, the natural setting and fortuitous timing made a quasi-experiment possible. Many social impact studies are of this kind.

Semi-natural Settings

Probably the most common form of research in the social sciences involves asking individuals to report either on their own or other people's activities, attitudes and motives, or on social processes and institutionalized practices.

Individuals' characteristics

Three main kinds of data are collected in these studies: demographic characteristics; orientations to the world; and reported behaviour. Demographic char- ✓ acteristics are an essential part of data collected in censuses and social surveys. These include age, gender, marital status, education, income, occupation, place of residence, ethnic background and religion. While these characteristics may have social origins and social consequences, the analysis undertaken on them searches for connections between such variables and other variables. The social processes or structures on which these connections might depend are left very much in the background, although assumptions about them may be made.

The second common focus in studies of individuals is their orientation to the world or, more narrowly, their perceptions, knowledge, attitudes, beliefs, values, etc. The aim is usually to use this information to explain reported behaviour. Not only are such data taken out of the context in which they might be relevant, but the connection between attitudes and behaviour is often extremely tenuous.

The third feature of this type of research is to ask individuals to report behaviour. This is either the individual's own behaviour (e.g. the number of times they make a call on the telephone, or the number of hours they watch television in a particular week), or the behaviour of others (e.g. the number of times particular categories of people telephoned them, or the number of hours their children watched television in a particular week).

A major difficulty in asking people about themselves is the gap between what they say they do and what they actually do (Deutscher 1973). In addition, the reports individuals give about their views and behaviour are likely to be interpreted differently by the researcher if they had studied the social actors in their natural setting. For example, a respondent may be asked about their occupation, which is then used by the researcher to establish a status hierarchy. In everyday life, social actors might use occupation quite differently to structure their relationships. What goes on in the natural setting may be either ignored or distorted by the researcher.

Individuals as informants or representatives

Individuals can also be studied as special persons (e.g. in the case of political biographies), as being representative of a particular type of social actor (e.g. 'indulgent parent' or 'rebellious teenager'), or are used as informants to report on beliefs, values, norms, social activities and, possibly, the motives of the participants. They can also be studied as categories (e.g. youth, pensioners, members of the working class, tertiary-educated), as populations (e.g. residents 18 years old and over living in the city of Montreal on 1 August, 1998, or all newly enrolled full-time students at the University of London in the 1998/99 academic year) or as samples from a population (either probability or non-probability).

Individuals as case studies

The study of single persons, perhaps as in-depth case studies, lies on the boundary of *social* science, particularly if the person's social context is given little or no attention. It is possible to assess an individual's perceptions of the social world and to get them to report their social experiences, i.e. their interaction with other people. However, when the emphasis is placed more on cognitive processes, as in psychoanalytic studies of political leaders, the research might be more correctly classified as psychological or behavioural rather than social.

Artificial Settings

A limited range of social research places people in experimental or simulated conditions in order to study some form of social behaviour in a controlled environment.

Experiments

Some social scientists who prefer to use the *inductive* and, particularly, the *deductive* research strategies may regard experiments as the ultimate way of establishing causation, and, hence, of answering 'why' questions.[4] To be able to hold some variables constant while others are manipulated, and then to observe the outcome, is considered to be the only way to explain any social phenomenon conclusively. These social scientists regard all other research designs as deviations. However, in practice, very little social research involves the use of genuine experiments. Rather, pseudo-experimental language is used in other types of research such that 'independent' and 'dependent' variables have become almost universally adopted in survey research.

In view of the limited use of experiments, they will be given only a brief treatment here. It is in psychological research that their use is most common.

> The purpose of the simple experiment is to test whether a treatment causes an effect.... To determine that a treatment causes an effect, you must create a situation where you show that the treatment comes before the effect, that the effect occurs after the treatment is introduced, and that nothing but the treatment is responsible for the effect.... The ideal for doing a psychological experiment to demonstrate causality would be to find two identical groups of subjects, treat them identically except that only one group gets the treatment, test them under identical conditions, and then compare the behavior of the two groups. (Mitchell and Jolley 1988: 112)

Simple experiments are particularly suitable where a single cause is assumed to produce an effect. However, it is possible to extend an experimental design to deal with different levels of treatment, and with more than one kind of treatment.

All experiments with human subjects are attempts to approximate these ideal conditions and to try to determine the influence of deviations from them. The use of random assignment to groups, instead of trying to match the members of the groups, is such a compromise that lends itself to statistical interpretation. Quasi-experiments 'have treatments, outcome measures, and experimental units, but do not use random assignment to create the comparisons from which treatment-caused change is inferred' (Cook and Campbell 1979: 6). Another way has to be found to demonstrate that other variables have not produced the relationship between the treatment and the effect.

There are a number of possible threats to the validity of this relationship, commonly referred to as *internal validity*.

1 *Selection bias*: without random assignment, there is a risk that groups will not be equivalent.
2 *History*: specific events that occur during the experiment may influence the experimental variable.
3 *Maturation*: biological, psychological or emotional changes, like growing older, or becoming hungry, tired or bored, can occur if experiments extend over long periods.
4 *Testing*: the effects of taking a test on the scores on a second test.
5 *Instrumentation*: changes in the calibration of a measuring instrument, or in the observers or scorers used.

---

[4] See Campbell and Stanley (1963a) and Cook and Campbell (1979) for classic discussions of experiments in social research, and Kidder and Judd (1986: chs 4 and 5) and Neuman (1997: ch. 8) for useful reviews.

6 *Statistical regression*: the tendency of subjects who receive extreme scores on the pre-test to receive less extreme scores on the post-test, and thus move the results towards the average.
7 *Selection*: comparing groups that are different.
8 *Mortality*: subjects dropping out of the study.
9 *Selection-maturation interaction*: groups naturally maturing at different rates. Because they scored similarly at the beginning of the study does not mean that they would have scored identically at the end of the study, had the treatment not been applied to one group.
10 *Diffusion of treatment*: subjects in different groups may communicate and learn about the other's treatment.
11 *Compensatory behaviour*: a specific example of the diffusion of treatment occurs if one group receives something of greater value than another group; if this becomes known, resentment may lead to a distortion in responses.
12 *Experimenter expectancy*: unintentional, perhaps non-verbal, communication between the experimenter and the subjects can give clues about what the experimenter hopes to find. This can be reduced by the use of assistants, who have limited knowledge of the logic of the experiment, to do the measurements (Campbell and Stanley 1963a: 5; Mitchell and Jolley 1992: 242–3; Neuman 1997: 182–5).

The effects of the experimental process on the subjects can also threaten the representativeness (external validity) of the results. However, the most serious threat to the possibility of generalizing results obtained in social experiments comes from the fact that people may behave differently in experimental situations than they do in natural situations. This threat is the greatest concern of critics of the use of experiments.

Simulation and games

Social life has been simulated for a number of reasons, perhaps the most common being for educational purposes. Such *simulations* or *games* allow the participants to:

- experience features of social life under controlled conditions;
- experience and be involved in initiating co-operation and conflict;
- experience what it is like to be a particular type of person, for example to be wealthy or poor, to have high status or low status; and
- learn about how power is acquired and used.

However, it is the use of simulation and games as a way of modelling some aspect of social life and as a research technique that is of interest here.

Games can be used to model some aspects of social life in terms of a set of rules. They put together not only a limited set of factors or variables, but they also specify relationships between some of these, and allow other relationships to be explored. While some factors are held constant by the controller of the activity, the participants are able to manipulate others in the course of their activity together. The effects of changing what is controlled and what can be manipulated can be observed and analysed. Therefore, games are a form of experimentation in artificial settings. However, they differ from experiments in that they attempt to replicate some real social situation; they may be less concerned with establishing causation and more concerned with recognizing and understanding the complexities of social processes.

Some games involve just two persons and explore the dilemmas of decision-making. A commonly used example is the Prisoner's Dilemma in which two prisoners who are accused of being accomplices in a crime have to separately, without the knowledge of the other's responses, decide whether or not to confess. They have been promised a lenient sentence if they do confess. The four different combinations of decisions the prisoners can make have different consequences for the way they will be treated by the courts: whether both might receive the minimum sentence (neither confesses); whether one receives a maximum sentence and the other a minimum sentence (one confesses and the other does not); or whether both receive a moderate sentence (both confess). The logic of this game has been used in a number of studies reported in the *Journal of Conflict Resolution*. (See e.g. Baxter 1973; Behr 1981; Murnigham and Roth 1983; Lindskold et al. 1983; Carment and Alcock 1984; Diekmann 1985; Levy 1985; Thomas and Feldman 1988; Lichbach 1990; Bendor et al. 1991; and Marinoff 1992. See also Axelrod 1984 for the use of a computerized version of the game.)

Games for more than two players explore such issues as the conditions under which co-operation rather than conflict is likely to develop (see e.g. Oliver 1980, 1984; Michener, et al. 1980; Michener and Yuen 1983; Michener et al. 1989; Ward 1990; McDaniel and Sistrunk 1991; and Michener 1992).

The use of simulation as a method for investigating social phenomena has been stimulated in recent years by the advent of small powerful computers and developments in computer science and information technology. Now people need not be involved; social processes that are not directly accessible, or are of too large a scale to be observed directly, can be modelled. The logical possibilities of a set of specifications or assumptions can be explored when the values of certain variables are changed. An early example of such a simulation was conducted by Markley (1964) in which he simulated Caplow's theory of organizational behaviour to test the claim that the system would reach a stable equilibrium. Through a series of iterations Markley discovered the reverse.

Another form of computer simulation involves a theoretically informed selection of aspects of some social phenomenon that are then manipulated by means of a selected computer language. Simulations are run and the output compared with data from such a social situation. The model of the phenomenon can be modified gradually by running a series of simulations to provide the best approximation to the data. Unlike statistical analysis, where the data are manipulated, computer simulation is a process by which a simplified and abstract representation of some part of the social world is developed to fit the data as closely as possible. A recent development in computer modelling of relevance to the social sciences is the simulation of cognitive processes and communication between people using techniques drawn from artificial intelligence. (See also Gullahorn and Gullahorn

1963; Inbar and Stoll 1972; Hanneman 1988; Ragin and Becker 1989; Brent and Anderson 1990; Garson 1990; Anderson 1992; Gilbert and Doran 1993; Lee 1995; Gilbert 1995.)

Social Artefacts

The fourth main source of data, *social artefacts*, involves neither natural nor artificial situations. Rather, it involves the traces of social activities left behind by the participants. Records of past social activities can be found in various places. Some are kept officially, such as censuses, publicly available minutes of meetings, or biographies and autobiographies, while others have been kept for private purposes, such as internal reports and correspondence of a company or organization, and diaries, private letters or family photographs and genealogies. Unlike public records, these latter records are defined as 'private' because there is no legal obligation to provide open access to them. In addition, some individuals keep personal records, such as diaries or journals, which, during their lifetime, are intended for no one else's eyes but the author's. It is usually only after their death, or by special permission, that access to them can be gained. Typically, these are the sources on which the historian has to rely, but they can also be invaluable, and, in some cases, the only data available to other social scientists.

A Dilemma

A major dilemma which researchers face in studying any social phenomenon is the assumptions that are to be made about its ontological status. As we have seen, there are essentially two choices here. One is for the researcher to define the phenomenon in terms of the technical concepts and ideas of some theoretical perspective within a discipline. The other is to adopt the social actors' construction of reality, at least as the starting-point in the investigation. For example, what constitutes a social episode or a social group is not simply a matter of observation; it is either a product of the way social actors consider their social world to be organized, or it is the result of a social scientist's way of organizing the social world; it is either a *social* construction or a *sociological* construction. In both cases, information may be sought from the social actors; the difference is how that information is regarded.

More abstract social entities, such as social institutions and social structures, are *sociological* constructions, the inventions of social scientists. Nevertheless, as with social groups and social processes, data can be obtained both from the researcher's observations and experience, as well as from the social participants' knowledge, perceptions and experiences. However, there is no guarantee that social actors will see their world in the same way as the social scientist. In fact, their views are invariably different because they are coming from different directions and have different purposes. For example, social scientists have conceptualized structures of inequality in various ways, for example as three social classes (upper, middle and lower), or as a hierarchy of occupations, but the social actors concerned may not share these conceptions. They may have a very different way of 'structuring' their world (e.g. in terms of 'insiders' and 'outsiders', or as a set of concentric circles around their own position in society). Differences between *social* constructions and *sociological* constructions pose a fundamental methodo-logical problem for researchers. It is on this issue that the four research strategies adopt different positions. In short, the issue is whose construction of reality should provide the foundation for understanding social life.

Selection of Data

All social research involves decisions about how to select data from whatever the source or sources may be. This is true regardless of the objectives of the research, the research setting, the time dimension, the type of social phenomenon being studied, the type of data, the form of the data, and the methods of data collection, reduction and analysis. When data are obtained separately from a number of individuals, social units or social artefacts, the researcher has a choice of either taking a whole population, or selecting a sample from a population. However, whether a population or a sample is used, a selection must be made. If sampling is used, then a choice must be made from a variety of methods.

Sampling is a common but not universal feature of social research. However, even if sampling is used, other forms of selection will precede it, such as the research site and the population. When a decision has been made to include sampling in the selection process, the concern is with the choice of sampling method.

Sampling is frequently the weakest and least understood part of research designs. The type of sample selected, and the method used to do so, can have a bearing on many other parts of a research design, and these decisions can determine the kind of conclusions that can be drawn from a study.

This section begins with a discussion of some of the key concepts in sampling, in particular, distinguishing between the technical meanings of 'population' and 'sample'. This will be followed by a review of the major sampling methods, commonly referred to as random and non-random methods, but which will be identified here as probability and non-probability methods. The concepts of 'prob-ability' and 'non-probability', rather than 'random' and 'non-random', more correctly identify the differences between the two major types of sampling methods. Referring to them as 'random' methods has the disadvantage of being associated with 'accidental' sampling rather than with the idea of representativeness and the ability to statistically estimate population characteristics from a sample.

As part of this review, consideration will be given to how different methods can be combined, and how the size of a sample can be established. In addition, some comments will be made on the connection between the use of tests of significance and probability sampling methods. Details of the techniques used in the major methods of probability sampling, and the associated mathematics, will not be elaborated here. (See e.g. Kish 1965 and Scheaffer et al. 1996 for technical details.) Rather, an overview will be provided of the major sampling methods, and consideration will be given to the implications that the choice of sampling method can have for other research design decisions.

Populations and Samples

First, it is necessary to clarify the concepts of *population* and *sample*. In order to apply a sampling technique, it is necessary to define the population (also called the target population, universe or sampling frame) from which the sample is to be drawn. A *population* is an aggregate of all cases that conform to some designated set of criteria. Population elements are single members or units of a population; they can be such things as people, social actions, events, places, time or things. The researcher is free to define a population in whatever way is considered appropriate to address the research questions. For example, a population might be defined as:

- the citizens of a country at a particular time;
- first-year university students at a particular university;
- telephone subscribers in a particular city;
- people of a particular age;
- all the issues of a newspaper published over a twelve-month period;
- only the Saturday issues of this newspaper during this period; or
- only articles in these newspapers that report domestic violence.

A *census* is a count of all population elements and is used to describe the characteristics of the population.

A *sample* is a selection of elements (members or units) from a population; it is used to make statements about the whole population. The ideal sample is one that provides a perfect representation of a population, with all the relevant features of the population included in the sample in the same proportions. However, this ideal is seldom achieved. In a probability sample, *every population element must have a known and non-zero chance of being selected*. Most types of probability samples will also give every element an equal chance of being selected. Non-probability samples do *not* give every population element a chance of selection. The relationship between the size of the sample and the size of the population is the *sampling ratio*.

While sampling can introduce many complexities into the analysis of data, it is used for a variety of reasons. Studying a whole population may be slow and tedious; it can be expensive and is sometimes impossible; it may also be unnecessary. Given limited resources, sampling can not only reduce the costs of a study, but, given a fixed budget, it can also increase the breadth of coverage.

Methods of Sampling

A range of types or methods of drawing a sample is available. Some methods aim to represent the population from which the sample is drawn, while other methods involve a compromise on this ideal. The nature of the research, the availability of information, and the cost will determine the selection of a particular method.

Sampling methods have been divided along two dimensions: probability versus non-probability, and single-stage versus multi-stage.

Single-stage probability sampling

One of the major sampling design choices is between probability and non-probability sampling. If a decision is made to use probability sampling, then a choice of methods must be made.[5] *Simple random sampling* is the standard against which all other methods are judged. It involves a selection process that gives every possible sample of a particular size the same chance of selection. Formally defined, 'simple random sampling is a sample scheme with the property that any of the possible subsets of n distinct elements from the population of N elements is equally likely to be the chosen sample' (Kalton 1983: 8). In other words, every combination of population elements that can be drawn by this method has an equal chance of being selected. However, even simple random sampling does not guarantee that a sample drawn by such procedures will be an exact representation of the population; it is possible to draw very 'biased' samples. What simple random sampling does is to allow the use of probability theory to provide an estimate of the likelihood of such 'deviant' samples being drawn. The other probability sampling methods provide different kinds of compromises with simple random sampling, each with its own advantages in terms of cost or convenience. However, each one also entails some sacrifice in terms of accuracy.

> **Sampling Methods**
>
> **Single-stage probability**
> Simple random
> Systematic
> Stratified
> Cluster
>
> **Multi-stage**
>
> **Single-stage non-probability**
> Accidental/Convenience
> Quota
> Judgemental/Purposive
> Snowball

Simple random samples require that each element of a population be identified and, usually, numbered. Once the size of the sample has been determined, a list of computer-generated columns of random numbers can be used to make the selection from the population.[6] For samples between 10 and 99, two columns of numbers will be used; between 100 and 999, three columns; between 1,000 and 9,999, four columns, and so on. Not all combinations of digits in the selected columns will be relevant as they may lie outside the range of the desired sample size. However, by scanning the column, the numbers that are relevant can be noted until the desired sample size is reached. These numbers then determine the population elements to be selected.

---

[5] In addition to Kish (1965) and Scheaffer et al. (1996), Moser and Kalton (1971: chs 3–7) provide a comprehensive discussion, and Hoinville and Jowell (1977), Kalton (1983), Henry (1990), Arber (1993) and de Vaus (1995) have brief, readable overviews.

[6] Textbooks on social research methods often include a table of random numbers. See, for example, de Vaus (1995) and Neuman (1997).

2   ✓   *Systematic sampling* provides a method that avoids having to number the whole population. If the population elements can be put in a list, they can be counted and a sampling ratio decided to produce the desired sample size, for example, one in five, or one in sixteen. In effect, the list is divided into equal zones the size of the denominator of the sampling ratio (e.g. five or sixteen), and one selection is made in each zone. The only strictly random aspect to this method of selection is determining which element in the first zone will be selected. Then it is a matter of counting down the list in intervals the size of the denominator (e.g. five or sixteen).

The *systematic sampling* procedure is simple and foolproof. However, it does have some potential dangers. Should the size of the zone correspond to a regular pattern in the list, the method may produce a very biased sample. For example, if houses in a regular pattern of city blocks are being selected, with a sampling ratio of one in sixteen, and if there happened to be sixteen houses in each block, and if the first house was randomly selected in the first zone, then the sample would consist only of corner houses. The subject of the study, for example traffic noise pollution, may affect corner houses differently than others in the block. There are two ways to protect a sample from such bias. One is to make a random selection more than once, thus changing the selection within the zones from time to time. Another is to double or treble the size of the zones and then to make two or three random selections within each zone. It is desirable to use either or both of these methods as they introduce a greater degree of randomness into the selection.

3   ?   ✓   *Stratified sampling* is used for two main purposes. Firstly, when the researcher wishes to ensure that particular categories in the population are represented in the sample in the same proportion as in the population, for example age categories, or religious affiliation. In order to do this, it must be possible to identify the population elements in terms of the relevant characteristic. If this is possible, the population elements can be grouped into the desired categories, or strata, before selections are made. By using the same sampling ratio in each stratum, the population distribution on this characteristic will be represented proportionately
?   in the sample. The second major use of stratified sampling is to ensure that there are sufficient numbers in the sample from all categories that are to be examined. For example, if people are to be compared in terms of their religious background, and a particular minority religion is considered to be important for this purpose, simple random sampling, and stratified sampling with the same sampling ratio in each stratum, may produce insufficient numbers from this category for later analysis. Assuming that this is the only underrepresented stratum, one solution is to lower the sampling ratio for this stratum (say, $1:3$ rather than $1:15$ for the other strata). Another solution is to draw equal numbers from each stratum, by varying the sampling ratios. Once the number that is required from each stratum is decided, the denominator of the sampling ratio is arrived at by dividing that number by the number in the stratum. For example, if there are four strata of 5,000, 1,500, 1,000 and 100, and 50 are required from each stratum, the sampling ratios would be $1:100$, $1:30$, $1:20$ and $1:2$.

It is important to note that if the same sampling ratios are not used in all strata, the resulting sub-samples cannot be combined for analysis, as every member of the population did not have an equal chance of being selected. This can be overcome by weighting each stratum in the sample to restore it to the original relative proportions of the population strata. In the example just used, as the ratios between the population strata are $50:15:10:1$, the numbers on which the data in each stratum are based would need to be multiplied by its respective ratio figure, or some multiple of it. Thus, the 'reconstituted' sample could have weighted strata of 2,500, 750, 500 and 50. If the original numbers are required, the ratios of $100:30:20:2$, multiplied by the stratum sample size of 50, will produce them. The main disadvantage with this procedure is that any lack of representativeness in the initial sample will be magnified in the 'reconstituted' sample, particularly in the cases where large weights are used. This kind of weighting procedure can also be used in simple random sampling when the population proportions on some variable are known, and the sampling proportions differ considerably from these.

All other forms of probability sampling will use one or a combination of simple random sampling, systematic sampling or stratified sampling. The fourth common sampling method is *cluster sampling*, one version of which is known as *area sampling*. A cluster is a unit that contains a collection of population elements. Cluster sampling selects more than one population element at a time, for example a classroom of students, a city suburb of households, a street or block of residences, a year of issues of a newspaper, or a month of applications for citizenship. Cluster sampling is generally used when it is impossible or very difficult to list all population elements. It also has the advantage that it can reduce the cost of data collection by concentrating this activity in a number of areas, rather than being scattered over a wide area. However, as clusters are unlikely to be identical in their distribution of population characteristics, cluster sampling will normally be less accurate than simple random sampling; it is not difficult to select a very biased set of clusters, and this problem is exacerbated if only a few are selected.

Before leaving the discussion of probability sampling methods, it is necessary to refer to the practical issue of *response rate*. Ultimately, the usefulness of any sampling design will be determined by the extent to which all sampling units can be included in the study. A poor response rate can destroy all the careful work that has gone into devising an appropriate sampling design. Many years ago a statistician colleague advised me that there is no point in trying to estimate population parameters from sample statistics if the response rate is below about 85 per cent. Lower response rates, he suggested, make nonsense of the application of probability theory because of the possible biases that can be introduced. When I have quoted this figure to my students, they usually reel in horror as they have little confidence in achieving anything like this response. A casual reading of research reports will show that this level of response is very rarely achieved.[7] What my colleague was claiming was that it is pointless to apply tests of significance to sample data that are based on poor response rates. Nevertheless, this statistical ritual *is* applied to samples with response rates of well below 50 per

---

[7] I once managed an 87 per cent response rate in a survey using mailed questionnaires, a method renowned for low response rates. In this case, a population was studied, thus eliminating the need for estimation procedures. This was achieved by the use of very elaborate and time-consuming procedures with a very particular population.

cent. To use probability sampling is one thing; to achieve a high response rate is another. Both are needed to estimate population parameters from samples. It is therefore essential that every effort be made to achieve as high a response rate as possible, whether the study is based on a sample or a population, but particularly for samples.

As human populations have become saturated with social surveys and opinion polling, low response rates have become increasingly common. What can a practising social researcher do? The problem with low response rates is the risk of unrepresentativeness. If data are available on population distributions on critical variables (e.g. as from the census), sample distributions can be compared with them. If the distributions are similar, then tests of significance can be used with some confidence. When a very poor response rate is anticipated, it may be better to use a carefully designed non-probability quota sample (to be discussed shortly). This will at least ensure that sample distributions will be similar to those in the population, even if representativeness cannot be guaranteed.

Multi-stage sampling

Cluster sampling is often the first stage, or perhaps one of the stages, of multi-stage sampling designs. The selection of the clusters themselves, and later selections within clusters, can use any of the three probability sampling methods. It is preferable that clusters are of equal size, otherwise each population element will not have an equal chance of being selected. However, this is not always achievable as natural clusters may vary considerably in size. One rather complex method for overcoming this is to stratify the clusters roughly according to size, and use a sampling ratio in each cluster that will give each population element a more or less equal chance of selection. Weighting can also be used, although this makes make multi-stage sampling rather complex.

Multi-stage sampling is commonly used in surveys of householders. For example, if householders of a large metropolitan area have been defined as the population, the first stage could be a random selection of administrative areas (e.g. local city councils), perhaps stratified by size, and/or mean socio-economic status of the residents. The second stage could be based on subdivisions that are used in census collection (perhaps using simple random procedures, or stratified procedures if the areas vary considerably in size). This could be followed by a random sample of households (perhaps using the systematic method while walking along each street). Finally, a member of the household could be selected by a random procedure. This sampling design does not require the identification of households and householders until the very last stages, and even then they need not be listed. Efficiencies in data gathering can be achieved as interviewers can concentrate their efforts and save a great deal of time and money in travelling. However, at each stage in this sampling design sampling errors can creep in. In order to compensate for this, a larger than the minimum desirable sample could be used. Nevertheless, this design represents an example of how practical problems (e.g. not having access to lists of householders) can be overcome, and how a compromise can be struck between precision and cost.

It is possible to combine probability and non-probability methods in a multi-stage sample. For example, the selection of initial clusters, such as areas of a city based on the demographic characteristics of the residents, could be based on a judgement of how typical each area is of the range of these characteristics. Subsequent sampling in each cluster could then use probability methods. Judgemental sampling will be discussed shortly.

Single-stage non-probability sampling

So far I have concentrated on issues related to probability sampling. Such sampling may be necessary in order to answer certain kinds of research questions with large populations. However, in addition to the use of populations rather than samples, some studies either do not need to generalize to a population, or cannot adequately identify the members of a population in order to draw a sample. For example, research on people who are infected with HIV/AIDS faces the problem that lists of such people are unlikely to be available. To insist on the use of random sampling would make the research impossible. Therefore, in such cases, it will be necessary to compromise with the ideal and use a non-probability sampling method. This research design decision can be justified in the terms of it being better to have some knowledge that is restricted because of the type of sample than to have no knowledge of the topic at all.

However, having said this, it must be stressed that social researchers usually hope that what they find in a sample or group has some kind of relevance or value further afield. This issue will be taken up in the next main section on 'Case Studies'. Therefore, even when non-probability samples are used, they can be selected in such a way that it is possible to make a *judgement* about the extent to which they represent some population or group. What the researcher hopes to achieve is a sound basis for making such a judgement.

Decisions about whether or not to use a probability sample, and how it should be done, are not confined to quantitative studies; they are also necessary in studies that intend to gather qualitative data.[8] Invariably, because qualitative methods are resource-intensive, smaller samples must be used. Here the compromise is between having data that can be applied to large populations, or having in-depth and detailed data on, perhaps, an unrepresentative sample or just a single case. Qualitative researchers may argue that they are not really involved in a compromise, and that their methods can produce a richer understanding of social life than is possible by more superficial methods used by quantitative researchers. The relative merits of qualitative and quantitative methods will be discussed in chapter 7. In the meantime, we need to confine our attention to the role of sampling in both types of data gathering and analysis.

There is no necessary connection between the type of research method used (quantitative or qualitative) and the type of sample that is appropriate. As in quantitative studies, qualitative studies can also work with populations,

---

[8] See Burgess (1982b) and Honigmann (1982) for useful reviews of the use of sampling in field research.

although they are likely to be much smaller. For example, it would be possible to study neighbouring behaviour through participant observation in a city street (block) in a middle-class suburb. Defining a population in this way may restrict the statistical generalizability of the results, but the richness of the data may allow generalizations, based on a judgement about how typical the chosen research site is, or whether other suburbs in other cities are similar in important respects. If the research also included a variety of sites in the same city (e.g. working-class, upper-class, ethnically homogeneous, etc.), the generalizability may be enhanced. Here the sampling issue becomes one of which city, and which streets/blocks, to select. The method of selection may be *judgemental* rather than being based on probability, although probability sampling should not be overlooked.

The idea of randomness in sample selection should not be confused with the selection of respondents by accident. The method of *accidental* or *convenience sampling* is the most extreme and unsatisfactory form of non-probability sampling; it is likely to produce very unrepresentative samples. The use of such methods may be an indication of laziness or naivety on the part of the researcher, or may be used in 'quick and dirty' research. A typical convenience sample is obtained when an interviewer stands on a street and selects people accidentally as they pass. Such respondents are representative of no particular population, not even of people who passed that spot during a particular period of a particular day. The views obtained in such a study do not even represent the mythical 'person in the street'. Doing accidental interviews at a random selection of spots in a city is no help; the population can neither be defined adequately nor its members be given an equal or known chance of selection.

A similar kind of accidental sample is obtained when readers of a newspaper or magazine are asked to complete a short questionnaire that is then cut out and mailed in. While the population might be defined as the readers of that particular issue of the newspaper or magazine, the self-selection process gives no guarantee that the respondents are representative. A similar process can occur when a researcher advertises in the print media for people with particular characteristics to volunteer to participate in a study; there is no way of knowing how representative they might be of that population. However, in some circumstances a researcher may have to use such a sampling method as a last resort. Results from such a study would need to be heavily qualified.

A commonly used non-probability method is *quota sampling*. It is certainly an improvement on accidental sampling and is commonly practised when it is impossible, difficult or costly to identify members of a population. This method has the advantage that it can produce a sample with a similar distribution of characteristics to those that are considered to be important in the population that it is supposed to represent. A set of selection criteria is identified because of their relevance to the research topic, although the establishment of these criteria may not be a simple matter. For example, in a study of undergraduate university students, three selection criteria might be used: gender (male and female), year at university (e.g. 1, 2, 3 and 4 or more), and degree being under-taken (e.g. arts, social science, science, engineering, medicine, law, economics/business, or education). These three criteria would produce sixty-four selection categories.[9] The researcher would then have to decide how many respondents are to be selected in each category. There are two main possibilities: equal numbers in each category, or numbers proportional to incidence in the population (if this is known). The first option can ensure sufficient numbers for analysis, while the second option has some of the advantages of proportional stratified random sampling. However, in neither case can the population characteristics be estimated statistically, as the selection into each category will be accidental; in an interview survey, for example, interviewers are only required to fill up the categories with the quota of respondents who meet the selection criteria. The advantages of quota sampling are that it is economical, easy to administer and quick to do in the field. It can also produce adequate results, although the degree to which it does this may not be known. As has already been mentioned, it may be no worse than using a probability sample with a poor response rate.

Judgemental or *purposive sampling* is another commonly used non-probability ✓ method with a number of uses. One use is to deal with situations where it is impossible or very costly to identify a particular population, i.e. where there is no available list of the population elements. For example, a study of intravenous drug users could find respondents by a number of means: by contacting users in the field, through police and prisons, and through public and private agencies such as drug rehabilitation centres. Depending on the particular research questions being investigated, it would be possible to contact a significant number of drug users from a variety of contexts, and to include at least some of most types of such drug users. A second use of the judgemental sampling method is for selecting some cases of a particular type. For example, a study of organizational behaviour may use a few cases of organizations that have been particularly successful in achieving what the researcher is interested in. The selection will be a matter of judgement as to which organizations would be most appropriate. A variation on this would be to select cases that contrast in some way, for example successful and unsuccessful organizations. Another use would be to select a variety of types of cases for in-depth investigation. For example, a study of 'problem' families could seek the assistance of experts in a social welfare agency to provide a list that includes a variety of such families, or, perhaps, families that differ on a set of criteria. The expert, with directions from the researcher, will make a judgement about the appropriateness of families for the study. These judgements may be informed by theoretical considerations.

A fourth type of non-probability method is *snowball sampling,* also known as ✓ 4 network, chain referral or reputational sampling. The analogy is of a snowball growing in size as it is rolled in the snow. This method has two related uses. In a difficult to identify population, such as intravenous drug users, it may be possible to contact one or two respondents who can then be asked for names and addresses of other users, and so on. Another example would be in a study of people who regard themselves as social equals; the respondents' definitions of social equality can be used to build up a sample. Snowballing can also be used to locate natural social networks, such as friendship networks. Once contact is made with one

---

[9] I have used a similar set of categories, but such a large number can create difficulties for interviewers. A simpler set could be based on gender and age (say, four categories) which would create only eight quota categories.

member of the network, that person can be asked to identify other members and their relationships. In this way a sociogram can be built up and, perhaps, the members of the network interviewed.

Finally, a common sampling method used in qualitative research is *theoretical sampling*. When the researcher collects, codes and analyses data in a continuous process, as in grounded theory, decisions about sample size are made progressively. Glaser and Strauss defined theoretical sampling as 'the process of data collection for generating theory whereby the analyst jointly collects, codes and analyzes his [*sic*] data and decides what data to collect next and where to find them, in order to develop his theory as it emerges' (1967: 45). The initial case or cases will be selected according to the theoretical purposes that they serve, and further cases will be added in order to facilitate the development of the emerging theory. As theory development relies on comparison, cases will be added to facilitate this. An important concept in this process is 'theoretical saturation'. Cases are added until no further insights are obtained; until the researcher considers that nothing new is being discovered. Another grounded theory concept related to sampling is 'slices of data', defined as 'different kinds of data [that] give the analyst different views or vantage points from which to understand a category and to develop its properties' (Glaser and Strauss 1967: 65). A variety of slices is desirable to stimulate theory development. Just what slices are selected, and how many, is a matter of judgement. An important point about this method of sampling is that any notion of representativeness is irrelevant.

Accuracy, Precision and Bias

Three important sampling concepts need to be discussed briefly.[10] They are concerned with the ability of a particular sample, and a particular method of sampling, to be able to estimate a population parameter from a sampling statistic. A population parameter is the actual value of a particular characteristic, such as the percentage of females, or the mean age. A sample statistic is the value of such characteristics obtained from the sample. The aim, of course, is to draw a sample in which the value of the characteristic is the same as that in the population.

The concept of *accuracy* refers to the degree to which a particular sample is able to estimate the true population parameter. A sample value is inaccurate to the extent that it deviates from the population value. This is sometimes referred to as the *sampling error*. While it is usually not possible to establish the level of accuracy of an estimate, it is possible to calculate from any one sample value the likely distribution of all possible sample values. This possible distribution indicates the fluctuations in sample values that result from random selection. In other words, the probable accuracy or *precision* can be calculated and used as a basis for estimating the population parameter.

Sampling *bias* refers to the systematic errors of a particular sampling *method*. These errors affect the capacity of the method to estimate population parameters.

---

[10] See Moser and Kalton (1971: 63–9) or Kish (1965: chs 1 and 13) for more details.

Here we are dealing with not just one sample estimate, but with all possible samples that the method can produce. The mean value of all sample statistics produced by a particular method is compared with the population parameter. If this mean corresponds to the population parameter, the sampling method can be regarded as being unbiased. Some of the methods we have discussed are better at this than others; the compromises made against the method of simple random sampling may be responsible.

There are, therefore, two important considerations in selecting a sampling method. The first is the likely *bias* of the method itself, and the second is the possible *accuracy* of its estimates of population parameters. The researcher can deal with the former by selecting a method that minimizes bias, and with the latter by making sure that the sample size is appropriate. In general, the larger the sample, the narrower is the distribution of possible sample values, and hence the more precise the estimates. Sample size will be discussed shortly.

Sampling and Tests of Significance

Tests of significance are designed to apply probability theory to sample data in order to make judgements as to whether characteristics, differences or relationships found in the sample can be expected to have occurred, other than by chance, in the population from which the sample was drawn. Of course, these statistical tests are only relevant when probability sampling has been used, and then only when there is a very good response rate.

There appears to be a great deal of misunderstanding about the use of tests of significance with populations and samples. It is not uncommon for social researchers to call whatever units they are studying a sample, even when the units constitute a population. This can lead to the use of certain statistical tests (e.g. the chi-square test for nominal data and the *t* test for interval or ratio data) with population data (parameters) when they are only necessary if sample data (statistics) are being analysed. The fact that these tests are called 'statistical' is the clue that they should be applied only to sample 'statistics'.

It is because tests of significance are frequently misinterpreted as indicating whether there is any difference or relationship worth considering in the data, that they are applied inappropriately to data from populations. Any differences or relationships found in a population are what the data tell you; applying a test of significance is meaningless. The researcher has to decide on the basis of the evidence if the difference or relationship is worthy of consideration. It is the strength of association between variables, in both samples and populations, that is relevant to this decision, and then it is a matter of judgement about whether the relationship is important.

> Unfortunately, the *statistical* significance of research findings (which is determined in large part by the size of the sample used in the study) is, quite wrongly, regularly confused and conflated with the *substance* or *practical* importance of research results, which is a matter for judgement and cannot be determined mechanically by statistical techniques. (Hakim 1987: 7)

A critical research design decision for the researcher is whether to use a population or sample. This decision will be influenced by the need to strike a compromise between what would be ideal in order to answer the research questions, and what is possible in terms of available resources and other practical considerations, such as accessibility of population elements. The decision will then have a big bearing on the kinds of analysis that will be necessary.

Sample Size

This brings us to the research design question that I have been asked more than any other: 'How big should my sample be?' Of course, the question might mean, 'How big should my population be?' There is no easy answer to this question, as many factors have to be considered. In addition, the answer will vary depending on whether probability or non-probability samples are being used.

Probability sample size

There are three important factors to be considered in deciding the size of probability samples:

- the degree of accuracy that is required, or, to put this differently, the consequences of being wrong in estimating the population parameters;
- how much variation there is in the population on the key characteristics being studied;
- the levels of measurement being used (nominal, ordinal, interval or ratio) and, hence, the types of analysis that can be applied; and
- the extent to which subgroups in the sample will be analysed.

A common misunderstanding in sampling is that a sample must be some fixed proportion of a population, such as 10 per cent.[11] In fact, it is possible to study very large populations with relatively small samples. While large populations may need larger samples than smaller populations, the ratio of population size to an appropriate sample size is not constant. For example: for populations around 1,000, the ratio might be about 1 : 3 (a sample of about 300); for populations around 10,000, the ratio may be about 1 : 10 (1,000); for populations around 150,000, the ratio may be 1 : 100 (1,500); and, for very large populations (say over 10 million), the ratio could be as low as 1 : 4,000 (2,500) (Neuman 1997: 221–2). It is not uncommon for opinion pollsters to use samples of 1,000 with populations of 5–10 million. For such populations, increases beyond 1,000 produce only small gains in the accuracy with which generalizations can be made from sample to population, and beyond 2,000 the gains are very small. However, the analysis undertaken in opinion polls is usually very simple. The factors mentioned in the previous paragraph may require larger samples. It is in small populations that care must be taken in calculating the sample size, as small increases in size can produce big increases in

---

[11] I have no idea why 10 per cent is regarded as some magical figure to determine sample size. It is quoted to me *ad nauseam* by colleagues and students.

accuracy, or alternatively, samples that are too small can produce inaccurate generalizations. *It is the absolute size of a sample, not some ratio to the population size, which is important in determining sample size.*

In any attempt to generalize from a sample to a population, it is necessary to decide on what is technically called a 'level of confidence'. What this means is the degree to which we want to be sure that the population parameter has been accurately estimated from the sampling statistic. All such estimates of population parameters have to be made within a range of values around the sample value. This is known as the 'confidence limits'. Just how big this interval is depends on the level of confidence set. If you want to have a 95 per cent chance of correctly estimating the population parameter, the interval will be smaller than if you want to have a 99 per cent chance. For example, if in a sample of 1,105 registered voters, 33 per cent said they would vote for a particular candidate at the next election, we can estimate the percentage in the population to be between 30.2 and 35.8 (a range of 5.6 per cent) at the 95 per cent level of confidence, and between 29.4 and 36.6 (a range of 7.2 per cent) at the 99 per cent level.[12] Therefore, setting the level of confidence high will reduce the chance of being wrong but, at the same time, will reduce the accuracy of the estimate as the confidence limits will have to be wider. The reverse is also true. If narrower confidence limits are desired, the level of confidence will have to be lowered. For example, if you only want to be 80 per cent sure of correctly estimating the population parameter, you can achieve this with very narrow confidence limits, i.e. very accurately. In the example above, the confidence intervals would be between 31.2 per cent and 34.8 percent (a range of 3.6 per cent). However, this more accurate estimate has limited value, as we cannot be very confident about it. Hence, there is a need to strike a balance between the risk of making a wrong estimate and the accuracy of the estimate.

Unfortunately, there is no other way of generalizing from a probability sample to a population than to set a level of confidence and estimate the corresponding confidence limits. The commonly used levels of confidence are 95 per cent (0.05 level) or 99 per cent (0.01 level), but these are conventions that are usually used without giving consideration to the consequences for the particular study. It is worth noting again that these problems of estimation are eliminated if a population is studied; as no estimates are required no levels of confidence need to be set. The data obtained *are* the population parameters.

Various formulae are available to calculate a suitable sample size. However, they are limited in their ability to take into account all the factors mentioned above. One approach in studies that work with sample statistics in percentages is to estimate the likely critical percentage as a basis for the calculation. For example, if we have an idea that the voting between two candidates at an election is going to be very close, then a poll prior to the election could select a sample to give the best estimate assuming each candidate will get about 50 per cent of the votes. Foddy (1988) has provided a formula for this.

$$\text{Sample size} = \frac{pqZ^2}{E^2}$$

---

[12] Formulae are available for calculating these intervals. They can vary depending on the sampling method used and the type of data, for example means or percentages (see Kish 1965).

Table 6.1   Sample size based on population homogeneity and desired accuracy

Acceptable sampling error*	Per cent of population expected to give particular answer					
	5 or 95	10 or 90	20 or 80	30 or 70	40 or 60	50/50
1%	1,900	3,600	6,400	8,400	9,600	10,000
2%	479	900	1,600	2,100	2,400	2,500
3%	211	400	711	933	1,066	1,100
4%	119	225	400	525	600	625
5%	76	144	256	336	370	400
6%	—**	100	178	233	267	277
7%	—	73	131	171	192	204
8%	—	—	100	131	150	156
9%	—	—	79	104	117	123
10%	—	—	—	84	96	100

* At the 95 per cent level of confidence.
** Samples smaller than this would normally be too small to allow meaningful analysis.
Source: de Vaus 1995: 72.

where p is the expected percentage (say 50), q is p subtracted from 100 (in this case 50), Z is the t value for the chosen confidence level (say 95 per cent), and E is the maximum error desired in estimating the population parameter (say 5 per cent). In this example the sample would need to be 384, say 400. Table 6.1 gives a range of such calculations, given different acceptable levels of error in estimating the population parameter (sampling error) and different proportions of the population expected to answer a particular question. While this table provides a useful guideline, it deals with only some of the factors being considered here.

The second factor that has a bearing on the decision about sample size is the dispersion of the population on the characteristics being studied. The parameters of a homogeneous population can be estimated with much smaller samples than one in which there is a wide dispersion. Take age for example. If the population is all the same age, it is possible to estimate that age from a sample of one. However, if a population has a wide age distribution, a relatively large sample will be required. Similarly, if a population is likely to equally support two political parties (i.e., 50 per cent vote for each party), the sample size needed to estimate this at an acceptable level of error will be larger than that required in the case where most people are likely to support one party. This is also illustrated in table 6.1 in terms of expected answers to a survey question.

The third factor is the effect of the level of measurement, and the associated method of analysis. In general, the more precise or higher the level of measurement, the smaller the sample required, and vice versa. Interval and ratio measures require smaller samples than nominal measures. The reason for this is that nominal measures have to use cumbersome forms of analysis and, therefore, usually need larger samples to achieve satisfactory results. However, the distribution of population characteristics affects all levels of measurement, but they are more difficult to deal with when lower levels are used. There is no simple rule of thumb for making this decision. What is necessary is to know before the study commences what levels of measurement are going to be used and what methods of analysis can be applied to them (assuming they are both quantitative). Most good statistics textbooks will indicate what the minimum number is for using a particular statistical procedure, particularly for parametric statistics. When non-parametric statistics are applied to nominal and ordinal data, and the results are presented in tabular form (usually cross-tabulations), a rule of thumb is that the sample size needs to be ten times the number of cells in the table. This rule is based on the requirement for chi-square analysis and the measures of association derived from chi-square. The number of cells will be determined both by the number of categories on each variable, and the need to meet chi-square requirements in terms of minimum expected frequencies. Other methods of analysis will have different implications for sample size. However, the complicating factor in all of this is the possibility that in any study a variety of levels of measurement will be used. The sample size will have to meet the requirements of the lowest level of measurement.

The fourth factor is partly related to the second and third. If it is intended that analysis will be undertaken on a sub-sample, then the total sample must be big enough to make this possible. For example, if a study is conducted with a population of ethnic communities whose members migrated to the country before the age of 18, and if analysis is to be done on each group separately, then there must be a sufficient number of people from each group to do the analysis. Clearly, the size of the smallest community becomes important. The actual numbers required in this group will depend on the levels of measurement to be used and on the kind of analysis to be undertaken. If some of the variables are nominal, and three of these are to be used in a three-way cross-tabulation, the size of the group would need to be about ten times the number of cells in this table. For example, if country of birth (coded into three categories) is to be cross-tabulated with political party preference (three categories), and if the first variable is to be controlled by year of migration (coded into three time periods), then a table of twenty-seven cells will be produced requiring a sub-sample of 270. If the smallest ethnic community makes up 10 per cent of the population, then a total sample of 2,700 would be required. Of course, one way to reduce the total sample size would be to use a stratified sample by ethnic community, and different sampling ratios in each stratum, to make all sub-samples of 270. If there were five ethnic communities, the total sample would be exactly half (1,350), thus producing a considerable reduction in the cost of the study. However, if the variables to be analysed are interval or ratio, much smaller numbers can be used. One rule of thumb is to have a minimum of fifty in each subgroup, but, clearly, many things should be considered in making this decision.

It will be clear from this discussion that a decision on sample size is rather complex. The best a researcher can do is to be aware of the effects of accuracy requirements, population characteristics, levels of measurement, and the types of analysis to be used. The latter consideration reinforces the need to include in any research design decisions about how the data will be analysed. In my experience, researchers resist pushing their design decisions this far. It is easy to think that this can be put off until later, but it cannot. Failure to make the decision is likely to lead to samples that are the wrong size, and to data that cannot be sensibly analysed. In some studies, it is not possible to know in advance how the population is distributed on the characteristics being studied. Even rough estimates may be impossible to make. In this case, the researcher must be conservative and use a sample that will cope with the worst possible situation, which means making it larger.

Having said all this, one other major consideration enters into the equation. It is the practical issue of resources. The ideal sample needed to answer a set of research questions may be beyond the scope of the available resources, both time and materials. *Sample size decisions are always a compromise between the ideal and the practical, between the size needed to meet technical requirements and the size that can be achieved with the available resources.* In the end, the researcher must be able to defend the decision as being appropriate for answering the research questions, given the particular conditions. If resources require that the sample size be reduced beyond minimum practical limits, then the design of the study would need to be radically changed, or the project postponed until sufficient resources are available.

It is always important to discover what conventions are used for your kind of research in your discipline or sub-discipline, in your university or research organization, and what the consumers of the research, including thesis examiners, find acceptable. These conventions do not always fit well with the technical requirements, but, in the end, may be politically more important. I have a few conventions of my own which I use when students ask me about sample size for surveys. After going through the points that have just been discussed, I may say something like: 'A sample of 1,000 would be ideal, or 2,000 if you can manage it, but 500 might be enough and even 300 if your resources are very limited.' Students are invariably horrified by the idea of having to work with samples of this size. However, if resources are not available to achieve samples of this size, then a different kind of research design will be required, or the research questions may have to be changed.

Non-probability sample size

As it is not possible to estimate population parameters from the data acquired using a non-probability sample, the discussion in the previous section on confidence levels and acceptable errors in estimates is not relevant. If, however, quantitative analysis is to be undertaken, then sample size *will* be influenced by the requirements of the type of analysis to be undertaken.

When a research project involves the use of time-intensive, in-depth methods, particularly when directed towards theory development, the issue of sample size takes on a very different complexion. As we saw in the case of *theoretical sampling*, sampling decisions evolve along with the theory. It is not possible to determine in advance what the size should be. However, time and resource limitations will inevitably put some restrictions on sample size. In this kind of research, it may be more useful to think of selecting cases for intensive study, rather than getting distracted by sampling concerns that are irrelevant. It is to the discussion of case studies that we now turn.

Case Studies

Throughout the history of social research, *case studies* have been regarded in a variety of ways:

- as a particular kind of research design;
- as involving the use of particular kinds of research methods, usually qualitative; and
- as being a method of selecting the source of data.

Their discussion has been included here because their role in data selection will be emphasized.

The idea of a case study has some relationship to the notions of both clinical studies in medicine and psychology, and to case histories as used in the helping professions, such as social work. However, there are some important differences that should become evident as this discussion proceeds.

The case study has a long history. It has been used extensively in social anthropology, and it is now used in political science (e.g. policy and public administration research), sociology (e.g. community studies), management (e.g. organizational studies), and planning (e.g. research on cities, regions and neighbourhoods). A large number of theses in the social sciences have used case studies (Yin 1989: 13).

Some writers have suggested that case studies are suitable for single-person research on a limited budget, and that the study of one case provides a manageable opportunity for a researcher to study one aspect of a problem in some depth within a limited time-scale (e.g. Bell 1993; Blaxter et al. 1996). It is implied that they are appropriate for student research, particularly for postgraduate theses, and that most researchers are capable of doing a case study. However, according to Yin (1989: 22), good case studies are very difficult to do.

Case studies have been used for various purposes: exploratory, descriptive and explanatory research (Yin 1989: 15–16), and to generate theory and initiate change (Gummesson 1991). These uses will depend on the research questions asked, and the extent to which the researcher has control over the events being studied (Yin 1989).

It has become a common practice in many textbooks on social research methods to include case studies as a type of research design, alongside surveys, experiments, and ethnography or field research. As we saw in chapter 2, this way of classifying research designs is completely inappropriate.

Background

The case study has had a chequered career in the social sciences. We need to go back to the 1920s, to the period prior to the social survey becoming the dominant style of social research in the United States, to find the case study being used as an acceptable way of doing research. This occurred mainly in the Chicago tradition of sociology (e.g. Thomas, Znaniecki, Cooley, Park and Burgess, Zorbaugh, and Blumer). There followed a period in which case studies were contrasted with the social survey, as the latter became the dominant social research method. The arguments centred on which of the two 'methods' was the most scientific, i.e. came closest to the methods used in the natural sciences. Hence, the late 1920s and the 1930s saw a period of defence of the case study (e.g. Shaw 1927; Jocher, 1928; Queen 1928; Znaniecki 1934; Young 1939) and debates about the relative merits of 'statistical methods' and 'case studies' (e.g. Burgess 1927).

Following World War II, debates continued between advocates of 'surveys' (and sometimes 'experiments') and 'participant observation', essentially between supporters of quantitative and qualitative methods. In the eyes of many, the former were scientific, but not the latter (Lundberg 1929; reviewed by Hammersley 1992). By the 1950s, the discussion of case studies had all but disappeared from textbooks on social research methods, although considerable attention was still given to specific techniques, such as participant observation. This decline in interest was no doubt due to the expansion in the use of quantitative and statistical methods, and the increasing availability of computers to speed up this type of analysis (Mitchell 1983).

Thirty years later, as a result of a revival of interest in qualitative methods, particularly in educational and evaluation research, and in much British sociology, the discussion of case studies re-emerged (e.g. Mitchell 1983; Yin 1989; Platt 1988). Case studies were now identified with methods that had been commonly used in anthropological research, with techniques of data collection such as participant observation, the use of informants, interviewing, and the study of personal documents and records. The general tenor of the discussion of such qualitative methods was that they were inferior to quantitative methods, that they were only really useful in the exploratory stages of research, and that researchers were unfortunate if they had no alternative but to use them as major methods (Goode and Hatt 1952; Platt 1988).

A major deficiency of the early discussions of case studies was that an approach to research design was confused with techniques of data collection and analysis. Any research using qualitative methods and data was assumed to be a case study. This view may have been derived from the conjunction in early social anthropology between the study of single small-scale societies and the use of a variety of qualitative methods. Here is an example of this view.

> The case study uses a mixture of methods: personal observation, which for some periods or events may develop into participation; the use of informants for current and historical data; straightforward interviewing; and the tracing and study of

relevant documents and records from local and central governments, travellers, etc. (Cosley and Lury 1987: 65)

However, *the case study is not one or a number of specific techniques.*

Definitions

The literature abounds with various definitions of the case study. It is still common to use the concept as 'an umbrella term for a family of research methods having in common the decision to focus on inquiry around an instance' (Adelman et al. 1977). While some methods may be used frequently, such as observation and interviewing, any method is regarded as being legitimate. Even a survey may be used in a case study. What, then, is peculiar about case studies?

Goode and Hatt focused their definition on the notion of a social unit and the manner in which it is studied.

> The case study, then, is not a specific technique. It is a way of organizing social data so as to preserve the *unitary character of the social object being studied.* Expressed somewhat differently, it is an approach which views any social unit as a whole. Almost always, this means of approach includes the *development* of that unit, which may be a person, a family, or other social group, a set of relationships or processes (such as family crisis, adjustment to disease, friendship formation, ethnic invasion of a neighborhood, etc.), or even an entire culture. (Goode and Hatt 1952: 331)

There are two important elements in this definition: it refers to a *social* unit, a 'real' individual, social event or group of people; and it treats the individual, group or event as a whole. What this means in practice is that the case study attempts 'to keep together, as a unit, those characteristics which are relevant to the scientific problem being investigated' (Goode and Hatt 1952: 333). This is in contrast to survey research that deals with individuals, but only as a collection of traits or variables.

Goode and Hatt avoided identifying the case study with a particular technique for collecting data. Rather, they regarded it as

> a *mode of organizing data* in terms of some chosen unit, such as the individual life history, the history of a group, or some delimited social process. In order to obtain such holistic data, one may use all the techniques which any other mode of organization uses: intensive interviews, questionnaires, self-histories, documents, case reports by others, letters, etc. Maintenance of the unitary character of the case is aided by the breadth and added levels of data gathered, the use of indexes and typologies, and the emphasis on interaction in a time dimension. There is, then, some attempt to make each case a research in itself. (Goode and Hatt 1952: 339)

Creswell (1994) has provided a similar definition with five components. A case study is a single, bounded entity, studied in detail, with a variety of methods, over an extended period. In case studies, 'the researcher explores a single entity or phenomenon ("the case") bounded by time and activity (a program, event, process, institution, or social group) and collects detailed information by using a variety of data collection procedures during a sustained period of time' (Creswell 1994: 12). While being sympathetic with this emphasis on the unitary character of a case, Mitchell (1983) has been critical of it on two counts. First, the authors give no place for extrapolation from case studies, leaving this activity to studies using statistical analysis. Second, the stress on the whole appears to ignore the context in which the case is located. In other words, Mitchell objected to case studies being limited to social descriptions in social isolation.

In the context of a discussion of the relationship of case studies to comparative, clinical and experimental studies, Eckstein has produced a particular definition that also takes the emphasis away from the use of multiple and qualitative methods. He had problems with the idea of establishing a single entity, even with treating an individual as such. In a clinical context, he argued that it is possible to apply a number of treatments to a single individual, and then to compare the effects of the treatments (as against having experimental and control groups). He wanted to regard each treatment as a case, not the individual on which they are carried out. Hence he defined a 'case' as '*a phenomenon for which we report and interpret only a single measure of any pertinent variable*' (Eckstein 1975: 85). He regarded a 'measure' as including either precise, quantitative measurement or imprecise observation. With this definition, Eckstein then defined comparative research as

> the study of numerous cases along the same lines, with a view to reporting and interpreting numerous measures of the same variables of different 'individuals.' The individuals . . . can be persons or collectivities, or the same person or collectivity at different points in time, in different contexts, or under different treatments. (1975: 85)

The issue raised by Eckstein, about what constitutes the unit of analysis in a case study, has been dealt with in some detail by Yin (1989). Yin has suggested that the key to resolving the problem is the way the research questions are stated. For example, a research question might ask: 'What internal and external changes are related to changes in religious practices and orientation to the world adopted by new religious movements?' (see the Appendix). In this example, the emphasis is on new religious movements, one or more of which could be treated as case studies. If, however, the research question was 'What kinds of religious movements arise in times of rapid social change?', then one or more rapidly changing societies could be selected as case studies.

Yin has also advised that in defining the unit of analysis, attention needs to be given to the definitions used in other studies. This will allow for comparative analysis.

> Most researchers will want to compare their findings with previous research; for this reason, the key definitions should not be idiosyncratic. Rather, each case study and unit of analysis should be either similar to those previously studied by others, or should deviate in clear, operationally defined ways. (Yin 1989: 33)

Yin's (1989) definition distinguished a case study from other types of research design, or what he called research strategies: experiment, survey, archival analysis and a history. More specifically, he has defined a *case study* as

an empirical inquiry that:

- investigates a contemporary phenomenon within its real-life context; when
- boundaries between phenomenon and context are not clearly evident; and
- multiple sources of evidence are used.

NB

An experiment . . . deliberately divorces a phenomenon from its context, so that attention can be focused on a few variables . . . A history, by comparison, does deal with the entangled situation between phenomenon and context, but usually with *non*contemporary events. Finally, surveys can try to deal with phenomenon and context, but their ability to investigate the context is extremely limited. (Yin 1989: 23)

By defining the case study as a research strategy, Yin has been able to argue that there is no connection between case studies and qualitative research: 'case studies can include, and even be limited to, quantitative evidence' (Yin 1989: 24).

In the context of anthropological research, Mitchell has argued that case studies have a theoretical aim: 'we may characterise a case study as a detailed examination of an event (or series of related events) which the analyst believes exhibits (or exhibit) the operation of some identified general theoretical principle' (Mitchell 1983: 192). Therefore, a case study is not just a narrative account of an event or a series of related events; it must also involve analysis against an appropriate theoretical framework, or in support of theoretical conclusions. A case study documents a particular phenomenon or set of events 'which has been assembled with the explicit end in view of drawing theoretical conclusions from it' (Mitchell 1983: 191).

NB

Hammersley (1992) has provided a much more limited definition of the case study. Like Yin, he has contrasted the case study with the experiment and the social survey and has confined the comparison to the manner in which each one selects its units for study. The case study is viewed as just one method of selection. In the process, Hammersley has rejected the view that case studies use certain kinds of methods of data collection, or a particular logic of enquiry.

There is no implication here that case studies always involve the use of participant observation, the collection and analysis of qualitative rather than quantitative data, that they focus on meaning rather than behaviour, or that case study inquiry is inductive or ideographic rather than deductive or nomothetic etc. Nor do I believe that case studies display a distinctive logic that sets them apart from surveys and experiments. . . . the same methodological issues apply to all three; the different strategies[13] simply vary in how they deal with these issues. From this point of view, each of these strategies might often be usable to pursue the same research problem, though they would have varying advantages and disadvantages, depending on the purposes and circumstances of the research. (Hammersley 1992: 185)

[13] Hammersley's use of 'strategy' here is more akin to what other writers call research designs, and is different from my use of it, which is confined to what he has referred to as a 'logic', i.e. inductive and deductive.

According to Hammersley, what distinguishes case studies from both experiments and surveys is that they use a comparatively small number of units in naturally occurring settings.

> What is distinctive about an experiment, in my view, is that the researcher creates the cases to be studied through the manipulation of the research situation, thereby controlling theoretical and at least some relevant extraneous variables. The distinctiveness of surveys is that they involve the simultaneous selection for study of a relatively large number of naturally occurring cases. From this perspective, case study combines some features of these two strategies. It involves the investigation of a *relatively small* number of *naturally occurring* (rather than researcher-created) cases. (Hammersley 1992: 185)

Criticisms of Case Studies

There have been three major criticisms of case studies that have arisen from their comparison with quantitative methods (Yin 1989: 21–2). The first and greatest concern is the possibility of sloppy research and biased findings being presented. What this criticism boils down to is a prejudice that quantitative researchers have had against qualitative data, a view based on the mistaken belief that only numbers can be used to describe and explain social life validly and reliably. Part of this prejudice is that qualitative research, unlike quantitative research, cannot be replicated because there is too much scope for the researcher to influence the results. These issues are taken up in chapter 7.

The second concern is that case studies are not useful for generalizing. There are two aspects of this position: that it is not possible to generalize from a single case, and that if a number of cases are used for the purpose, it is extremely difficult to establish their comparability. Each case has too many unique aspects. However, the same criticisms could be raised about a single experiment, or the study of a single population, whether or not a sample has been used to do so. I will return to this issue in a moment.

A third criticism of the case study is not so much methodological as practical. The complaint is that case studies take too long and produce unmanageable amounts of data. This criticism confuses the case study with specific methods of data collection that are time-consuming, for example, participant observation in particular and ethnography in general. Yin has argued that case studies need not take a long time and that they can now be conducted in a manageable way (1989: 21).

Uses of Case Studies

According to Gluckman (1961), the anthropological notion of the case study has had three main uses: as 'apt illustrations', as 'social situations' and as 'extended case studies'. The *apt illustration* is a description of an event in which some general principle is in operation. To illustrate mother-in-law and son-in-law avoidance in daily life, Gluckman used the example of the young man who stepped off the path and hid himself as his mother-in-law approached.

The analysis of a *social situation* involves a more complex collection of connected events that occur in a limited time span, and which demonstrate the operation of general principles of social organization. Gluckman referred to the situation of the opening of a new bridge in Zulul and that brought together representatives of the diverse segments of the population. Their behaviour before, during and after the bridge opening were regarded as being characteristic of the wider social structure.

An even more complex use can be found in the *extended case study* that follows a sequence of events over an extended period. Usually, the same social actors will be involved in a series of situations and events that are linked together and through which they move. Thus it is possible to identify structural features, for example kinship, by describing social processes over time.

While Gluckman's classification was based mainly on differing degrees of complexity, and to a lesser extent on duration of time, Eckstein's (1975) five-way classification focused on the different uses of case studies in theory development: *configurative-ideographic* studies, *disciplined-comparative* studies, *heuristic* case studies, *plausibility probes*, and *crucial-case* studies.

Configurative-ideographic studies use descriptions to provide understanding. The configurative element depicts the overall gestalt of the unit under investigation. The ideographic element either allows facts to speak for themselves or for intuitive interpretation. The intensity of such studies and the empathetic feeling that they can produce is their claim to validity. The major weakness of this type of case study is that the understanding or insight produced by each study cannot be used to generate theory. They tend to stand alone and are usually not designed by their authors for this purpose.

Eckstein's second type of case study, the *disciplined-comparative*, requires that each case be viewed in the context of an established or at least a provisional theory. Ideally, the findings of a particular case study should be able to be deduced from such a theory, or could be used to challenge it. As such, these cases are not used to build theory, apart from serendipitous 'discoveries'.

> The chain of inquiry in disciplined-configurative studies runs from comparatively tested theory to case interpretation, and thence, perhaps, via *ad hoc* additions, newly discovered puzzles, and systematic prudence, to new candidate-theories. Case study thus is tied into theoretical inquiry – but only partially, where theories apply or can be envisioned; passively, in the main, as a receptacle for putting theories to work; and fortuitously, as a catalytic element in the unfolding of theoretical knowledge. (Eckstein 1975: 100)

The third type, the *heuristic* case study, is deliberately used to stimulate theoretical thinking.

> Such studies, unlike configurative-ideographic ones, tie directly into theory building, and therefore are less concerned with overall concrete configurations than with

potentially generalizable relations between aspects of them: they also tie into theory building less passively and fortuitously than does disciplined-configurative study, because the potentially generalizable relations do not just turn up but are deliberately sought out. (Eckstein 1975: 104)

Heuristic case studies do not usually exist in isolation. They will usually be conducted in a series to facilitate theoretical development.

> One studies a case in order to arrive at a preliminary theoretical construct. That construct, being based on a single case, is unlikely to constitute more than a clue to a valid general model. One therefore confronts it with another case that may suggest ways of amending and improving the construct to achieve better case interpretation: and this process is continued until the construct seems sufficiently refined to require no further major amendment or at least to warrant testing by large-scale comparative study. (Eckstein 1975: 104)

Therefore, the *heuristic* case study does not guarantee a theoretical outcome; comparative studies may be more fruitful.

Plausibility probes, Eckstein's fourth type of case study, are used in the intermediate stage between the development of a theory, whether by heuristic case studies or some other means, and the testing of that theory. A plausibility probe attempts to establish whether a theoretical construct is worth considering at all, by, perhaps, finding an empirical instance of it.

> In essence, plausibility probes involve attempts to determine whether potential validity may reasonably be considered great enough to warrant the pains and costs of testing, which are almost always considerable, but especially so if broad, painstaking comparative studies are undertaken. (Eckstein 1975: 108)

Finally, *crucial-case* studies are similar to crucial experiments; they are designed to challenge an existing theory. If a theory survives a test that is loaded against it, confidence in it will be increased. Such a case

> *must closely fit* a theory if one is to have confidence in the theory's validity, or, conversely, *must not fit* equally well any rule contrary to that proposed.... In a crucial case it must be extremely difficult, or clearly petulant, to dismiss any finding contrary to theory as simply 'deviant' ... and equally difficult to hold that any finding confirming theory might just as well express quite different regularities. (Eckstein 1975: 118)

These principles are easy to express, but finding crucial case studies is clearly difficult.

Mitchell has also championed the view that case studies in anthropology are used for theoretical purposes. He has argued that such case studies are not simply descriptions of the life of these people. Although he did not differentiate such a range of theoretical activities, he claimed that they are used to generalize and to develop theories.

> Nearly the whole of the respectable body of anthropological theory has been built up over the years from a large number of separate case studies from which anthropologists have been prepared to draw inferences and to formulate propositions about the nature of social and cultural phenomena in general. (Mitchell 1983: 189)

While some writers (e.g. Eckstein) have distinguished case studies from comparative research on the basis of whether one or a number of cases are used, Yin (1989) has included both single and multiple cases within case-study research. Single-case studies have a number of uses. In the first, the case study is analogous to a single experiment, like Eckstein's crucial-case studies. It provides a critical test of a theory, to corroborate, challenge or extend it. The second use of the single-case study is as an extreme or unique case. This is common in clinical psychology and can also be used in sociology for the study of deviant or unusual groups of any kind. The third use of the single-case study occurs in a situation where some phenomenon has not been studied before; where an opportunity arises to research something that has been previously inaccessible. Yin referred to these as *revelatory cases*.

In all three uses, the single-case study will be a complete study. However, Yin has divided them into two types: holistic and embedded case studies. The holistic case study has only one unit of analysis while the embedded case study may have a sub-unit or a number of sub-units. For example, an organization could be studied as a holistic case if the main research question was concerned with the type of cultural change that could follow from the use of different technology. In an embedded case study, organizational change associated with technological change might be studied at various levels: change in management style, change in work practices and change in organizational structures, as well as change in organizational culture. The embedded study requires research at different levels within the organization, while still treating the organization as a single-case study.

In contrast to single-case studies, Yin has argued that the main use of multiple-case designs is analogous to conducting a series of experiments. He has claimed that a well-developed theory can be tested by carefully selecting a series of cases in the same way as theories are tested experimentally. This, as we shall see shortly, requires the use of replication rather than sampling logic.

Just how many cases should be included in a multiple-case design will depend on the complexity of the phenomenon and the conditions in which it occurs; the greater the complexity, the greater the number of cases that will be necessary to achieve confidence in the testing of the theory. Notions of sample size used in association with sampling logic are not relevant to multiple-case study designs.

The use of multiple-case studies has both advantages and disadvantages compared to the use of single-case studies. All three types of single-case designs, critical, extreme or revelatory, serve useful purposes on their own. While the use of a number of cases may add greater weight to a study, and make its findings more convincing, their use is only appropriate when replication rather than sampling logic is used. In addition, as case studies are expensive to conduct, multiple-case studies should not be undertaken lightly.

Generalizing and Theorizing from Case Studies

Mitchell, Eckstein and Yin have all raised the issue of whether it is possible to generalize or theorize from case studies. This issue will now be explored further. Must the findings from a case study remain just interesting description, or can they be used to generalize and to generate and test theory?

The question of whether it is possible to generalize from case studies has to do with how cases are selected. Researchers may feel more comfortable generalizing if they work with 'typical' cases, i.e. if the case being studied can be shown to be similar to other cases in terms of relevant characteristics. However, it is difficult to demonstrate whether a particular case study is typical rather than unique. Certainly, this was not the guiding principle when anthropologists selected small-scale societies to study.

Mitchell has argued against trying to find typical cases.

> There is absolutely no advantage in going to a great deal of trouble to find a 'typical' case: concern with this issue reflects a confusion of enumerative and analytic modes of induction. For general purposes any set of events will serve the purpose of the analyst if the theoretical base is sufficiently well developed to enable the analyst to identify within these events the operation of the general principles incorporated in the theory. (Mitchell 1983: 204)

It follows that researchers should not be concerned with the issue of representativeness and generalizability in the narrow sense, but, rather, with appropriateness, or what Bassey (1981) has called 'relatability'. In the practical context of educational research,

> an important criterion for judging the merit of a case study is the extent to which the details are sufficient and appropriate for a teacher working in a similar situation to relate his [sic] decision making to that described in the case study. The relatability of a case is more important than its generalisability. (Bassey 1981: 85)

I shall come back to this issue in the next chapter in the context of generalizing in qualitative research.

In contrast to arguments in favour of using typical cases, Eckstein (1975), Mitchell (1983), Yin (1989) and Platt (1988) have argued for the use of the extreme, deviant or least likely cases in theory testing. If a general theoretical principle can be shown to hold in these types of cases, the degree of corroboration is stronger than in cases that might be regarded as typical.

Eckstein has identified five theory-related roles, each linked to one of his five uses of case studies:

- understanding – configurative-ideographic studies;
- linked to theory – disciplined-comparative studies;
- theory building – heuristic studies;
- exploring theoretical possibilities – plausibility probes; and
- testing theory – crucial-case studies.

Platt went further when she claimed that 'a single case may be a useful source of hypotheses, or refute a universal generalization, or demonstrate the existence of a phenomenon which needs to be taken into account' (Platt 1988: 17). 'Case studies can be used to generalize even in some of the ways less often accepted' (1988: 19). However, she supported Diesing's (1972) idea that Kaplan's (1964) pattern model of explanation should be used rather than the deductive one.

This issue of case selection has also been dealt with in terms of the logic appropriate for case studies. As Mitchell and Yin have argued, the concern about the representativeness of case studies is based on a mistaken view of the logic appropriate for case studies. The critics of the case study were operating from the logic of statistical inference appropriate to sample surveys. This is a very narrow view of generalizing, in which the selection of a number of individuals or units is used to represent the population from which they are drawn. This allows the use of statistical procedures to generalize the sample findings to the population. On the other hand, a different kind of logic is required to test a theory. This has been called 'logical inference' (Mitchell), 'analytic generalisation' (Yin) or replication logic.

Mitchell has dealt with this issue in terms of the distinction between statistical and logical inference.

> Statistical inference is the process by which the analyst draws conclusions about the existence of two or more characteristics in some wider population from some sample of that population to which the observer has access.... logical inference is the process by which the analyst draws conclusions about the essential linkage between two or more characteristics in terms of some systematic explanatory schema – some set of theoretical propositions. (Mitchell 1983: 199–200)

It is logical not statistical inference that is appropriate for case studies. 'We infer that the features present in the case study will be related in a wider population not because the case is representative but because our analysis is unassailable' (Mitchell 1983: 200).

Yin has argued for the use of 'analytic generalisation' as an alternative to 'statistical generalisation' in case studies.

> A fatal flaw in doing case studies is to conceive of statistical generalization as the method of generalizing the results of the case. This is because cases are not 'sampling units' and should not be chosen for this reason. Rather, individual case studies are to be selected as a laboratory investigator selects the topic of a new experiment. Multiple cases, in this sense, should be considered like multiple experiments (or multiple surveys). Under these circumstances, the method of generalization is 'analytic generalization,' in which a previously developed theory is used as a template with which to compare the empirical results of the case study. If two or more cases are shown to support the same theory, replication may be claimed. The empirical results may be considered yet more potent if two or more cases support the same theory but do not support an equally plausible, *rival* theory.... Analytic generalization can be used whether your case study involves one or several cases. (Yin 1989: 38)

Hence, Yin has given a theory development and testing role to both single-case studies and multiple case studies. In either a one-off or a series of tests, case studies are viewed as being equivalent to one or more experiments. Conclusions can only be drawn in the context of an existing theory.

As all cases necessarily occur in a specific context, the common and unique features of that context need to be acknowledged. Researchers need to give readers a sufficient account of the context to enable them to evaluate the conclusions drawn. However, detailed knowledge of the context is also an important element in the researcher's capacity to draw conclusions from a case study.

> The case study, because of the observer's intimate knowledge of the connections linking the complex set of circumstances surrounding the events in the case and because of the observer's knowledge of the linkages among the events in the case, provides the optimum conditions in which the general principles may be shown to manifest themselves even when obscured by confounding side effects. (Mitchell 1983: 206)

It is Platt's view that, to strengthen their theoretical role, case studies need to be specifically designed rather than being chosen as a matter of convenience or by accident. A case study needs to be located in the context of relevant knowledge and appropriate theory.

> Thus case studies are just as good a basis for such inference as other sorts of study, although its justification will also depend upon the adequacy of the theory and the corpus of related knowledge. This argument suggests that a strategic choice of types is likely to be of more use than either a single case or a representative sample. (Platt 1988: 18)

Platt concluded:

> In some areas case studies can make the same sort of contribution as other types of research, while in other areas they can do things better or worse, or equal though different. Whatever the area, case studies have in common with other methods that they are only part of a larger enterprise transcending the individual work, and can only be used or evaluated against that background which, whether or not this is explicitly acknowledged, is a component in the research design. (Platt 1988: 20)

While it must be acknowledged that Mitchell's view of case studies is derived from their use in social anthropology, or in related disciplines working in similar contexts, his summary of his argument in favour of the use of case studies provides a useful conclusion to this discussion.

> Case studies of whatever form are a reliable and respectable procedure of social analysis and . . . much of the criticism of their reliability and validity has been based on a misconception of the basis upon which the analyst may justifiably extrapolate from an individual case study to the social process in general. A good deal of the confusion has arisen because of a failure to appreciate that the rationale of extrapolation from a statistical sample to a parent universe involves two very different and even unconnected inferential processes – that of statistical inference which makes a statement about the confidence we may have that the surface relationships observed in our sample will in fact occur in the parent population, and that of logical or

scientific inference which makes a statement about the confidence we may have that the theoretically necessary or logical connection among the features observed in the sample pertain also to the parent population.

In case studies statistical inference is not invoked at all. Instead the inferential process turns exclusively on the theoretically necessary linkages among the features in the case study. The validity of the extrapolation depends not on the typicality or representativeness of the case but upon the cogency of the theoretical reasoning.

In terms of this argument case studies may be used analytically – as against ethnographically – only if they are embedded in an appropriate theoretical frame-work. The rich detail which emerges from the intimate knowledge the analyst must acquire in a case study if it is well conducted provides the optimum conditions for the acquisition of those illuminating insights which make formerly opaque connections suddenly pellucid. (Mitchell 1983: 207)

Conclusion

This chapter has dealt with three basic issues: the kinds of data that can be collected in the social sciences; the contexts from which data can be collected; and the processes by which individuals, social units and social artefacts can be selected.

The discussion of types and forms of data was included to highlight some research design choices that are often glossed over. While they are elementary, consideration needs to be given to them, as well as to the implications of the choices. Similarly, the discussion of the range and contexts from which data can be obtained is really basic introductory sociology. However, it is necessary to be clear about the differences in the kinds of social settings in which social research can be conducted, and the range of social units that are available. The choice made from among these needs to match the nature of the research questions. Alternatively, when research questions leave the choice of data source reasonably open, the choice will have consequences for the research outcomes. However, these choices, like many others, are also influenced by pragmatic factors, such as proximity, access and cost. While compromises may be necessary, care must be taken not to jeopardize the possibility of answering the research questions.

Regardless of the decision made about the source of data, it is usually necessary to make selections, either between social settings (e.g. certain organizations) or from within a social setting (e.g. families in a village, or householders in a city). This applies to research that uses both populations and samples. A population is arrived at by definition, by using a set of criteria. It is here that the researcher has considerable scope to determine the nature and size of the study. Frequently, it is necessary to make selections from within a population. The purpose of this selection is determined by the research objectives and the research strategy or strategies adopted. Hence, the various sampling methods, both probability and non-probability, have to be considered very carefully to ensure that the selection will make it possible to answer the research questions. However, once again, a compromise between the ideal and the practical may be necessary.

Considerable attention has been given to case studies in this chapter, partly because there is a great deal of confusion and many misconceptions about what they are and what they can be used for. It was argued that case studies should not be seen as the poor relation in social research as they have some very special uses, particularly in theory development. As a great deal of research uses case studies, explicitly or implicitly, it is important to be clear about their possible uses and their limitations. Finally, the case study is very relevant to student research at all levels.

Now we are in a position to get to what is usually regarded as the heart of social research, data collection and analysis. However, the choice from among these methods is very dependent on choices made on all the other research design elements discussed so far. It is only in the context of these choices that consideration can be given to the methods of data collection and analysis.

7

Methods for Answering Research Questions

To quantify or not to quantify. Is that the question?

Introduction

With research questions in place, one or more research strategies selected, ontological assumptions made explicit, and, perhaps, hypotheses specified, the next
step in the development of a research design is to decide how to collect the data to
answer the research questions. However, the kind of data that are considered to be
appropriate, and their source and method of collection, will depend on a variety
of factors. On the one hand, there are methodological considerations that are
linked to research strategies, and, on the other hand, there is a range of pragmatic
factors to be considered. These might include the nature of the research topic, the
research objectives, the kind of research questions being investigated, the context
of the research, the expertise and personality of the researcher, time and budget
considerations, the availability of equipment (including computer hardware and
software), and the expectations of funding bodies, clients, colleagues and/or the
consumers of the research findings (Smaling 1994).

Back in the 1950s and 1960s there were debates about the relative merits of
what was then considered to be the major research methods, social surveys
and participant observation (see the section on case studies in chapter 6). For the
past thirty years, the debates have moved to a more general level to cover the full
gambit of research methods and to include disputes about the appropriateness
of particular paradigms or approaches to social enquiry. It is interesting to note
that many of the contributors to these debates have worked in evaluation and
policy research, particularly in education. Their motivation has been to counter
the dominance of quantitative methods and to establish a legitimate place for
qualitative methods.

This chapter covers six main topics. It:

- considers the role of timing of data collection in determining the character of a
  research design;

- reviews the characteristics of qualitative and quantitative methods and the preoccupations of researchers who use them;
- reviews the debates about the relative merits of qualitative and quantitative methods;
- provides a critique of the use of the concepts of 'qualitative' and 'quantitative' beyond the description of methods, i.e. using the concepts to identify different paradigms;
- critically reviews arguments for combining both types of methods; and
- discusses the nature of the links between research strategies and research methods.

From simple beginnings about fifty years ago, there is now a vast and complex literature on these topics. There is a tendency in some textbooks on research methods to oversimplify this complexity. Should you prefer this, you may want to consult one of these books (e.g. Creswell 1994). However, because these issues have loomed large in the methodological literature in recent years, and because they are of vital importance to contemporary researchers, I believe it is necessary to explore them in some detail.

The Timing of Data Collection

All social research adopts a position with regard to the timing of the data collection (see figure 7.1). In fact, some writers regard time as the critical defining characteristic of all types of research designs. This appears to stem from the classic experimental design in which variables in experimental and control groups are measured at two points in time, the experimental group having been subjected to some kind of treatment in between. All other designs are seen as variations of this kind of experiment. De Vaus (1995), for example, has discussed six variations.

- *Panel design*: only uses an experimental group that is measured before and after the intervention.
- *Quasi-panel design*: applies an intervention to a population but measures one sample before and another sample after.
- *Retrospective panel design*: a measurement is made at the present time and the group is asked to recall its position on the variable at an earlier time, assuming the effects of some events in between.
- *Retrospective experimental design*: a matched control group that does not experience the effects or intervention is added to the retrospective panel design; both are asked to recall their earlier position.
- *Cross-sectional or correlational design*: at least two groups are measured in the present and their positions compared; the consequences of the passage of time are absent here.
- *One-shot case study design*: only one group is measured in the present.

There are three basic choices for the social researcher with regard to time. A study may:

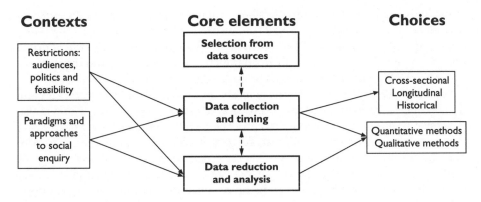

Figure 7.1 Data collection, reduction and analysis

- be confined to the present time – *cross-sectional*;
- extend over a period of time – *longitudinal*;
- be confined to the past – *historical*.

Cross-sectional studies are designed to capture a still picture of aspects of social life, including population (demographic) characteristics, individual attitudes, values, beliefs and behaviour, social interaction, and aspects of social groups, organizations, institutions and structures. However, this type of study is not well suited to research on social processes and social change, as these require the collection of data over time.

Some *longitudinal* studies involve only two points in time and are referred to as *before-and-after* designs. These include experiments and evaluation studies, i.e. any situation that involves an intervention to bring about change. In addition, before-after designs can be used to examine naturally occurring changes, in which case they are nothing more than two cross-sectional studies at different points in time.

Other longitudinal studies involve a number of points in time, or a series of cross-sectional studies on the same or a similar population or group. There are three variations, all of which can be regarded as *prospective* studies as they begin in the present and plan further stages in the future. The first is referred to as *time series* research. For example, a study may be done of people who happen to be living in a particular street at different points in time. The situation remains constant although there may be some changes in the residents. The second, a *panel* study, involves continuous or regular contact with the same people, group or organization over a period of time. A variation of the panel study is *cohort analysis* in which categories of people, rather than the same

Time Dimension

Cross-sectional
In the present

Longitudinal
Before and after
   Impact of an intervention
Change over time
   Prospective: looking forward
      Time series
      Panel study
      Cohort study
   Retrospective: looking back

Historical
In the past

individuals, are studied over time. A cohort is defined in terms of a specific criterion that identifies people who have had similar life experiences due to having had a critical life event in common. Examples of cohorts include people who were born in the same year (birth cohorts), who are in the same year in educational institutions, or who joined or left an organization at around the same time.

Each of these three latter versions of a *longitudinal* study has its advantages and disadvantages. *Panel* studies may be the ideal but they are expensive. There is also the constant difficulty of keeping track of the members and dealing with the fact that people will drop out for various reasons. *Cohort* designs are easier to conduct, but their results are less powerful. *Time series* designs are different from the other two. *Panel* studies track the changes in a sample or group of people over time, while a *time series* study may be more concerned with the changing effects over time on people who have some circumstances in common. Therefore, *cohort* and *time series* studies are compromises on *panel* studies; the first two avoid the complex and expensive process of keeping track of people over an extended time period, but have to sacrifice some ability to draw reliable conclusions.

Retrospective studies take the present as a base and seek information about recent history. A common form of this research, oral and life histories, gets people who lived through a particular period to recall those experiences, or uses the traces that such people have left behind, such as diaries. There are clearly some limitations to this kind of research as memory is fallible and its use always involves a possible reconstruction of the past under the influence of subsequent experiences.

Historical studies, by definition, deal with social events or phenomena in the past. Such studies are very different in character to those that can collect data about and from people in the present. While historical studies may seek information about the past from people who have lived through a particular time period, or who have known people who have, data normally have to come from written records of some kind, or from other traces of past social activity. Historical research may be confined to the past, but some social scientists may want to connect the past to the present. However, when a researcher's concerns are essentially in the present, it is usually necessary or desirable to locate the experiences of contemporary individuals, and social events and processes, in some kind of historical context. Therefore, research in the present may need to be linked to the past. Whether this is necessary will depend on the nature of the topic and the research questions.

Of course, actual research designs can be made up of a combination of these approaches to the time dimension. For example, a *cross-sectional* study conducted today can become a *longitudinal* study if it is replicated, say, in five years' time. A *retrospective* or a *prospective* study can be used in combination with a *cross-sectional* study to produce a *longitudinal* study. Also, a *historical* study can be either *cross-sectional* or *longitudinal*.

It follows that research design choices related to the time dimension will be determined largely by the objectives of the study and the type of research questions to be answered. Some objectives and research questions can be pursued successfully using a *cross-sectional* study, whereas others, ideally, require a *longitudinal* design. While exploratory and descriptive studies are likely to be concerned with the present, longitudinal description is certainly a legitimate research activity. Similarly, while the objectives of *explanation* and *understanding* may be more easily achieved in *longitudinal* research, the potential costs involved may lead to the common compromise of trying to establish explanation using a *cross-sectional* design. The applied objectives of *change* and *evaluation*, and their associated research questions, might also be better achieved in a *longitudinal* study. However, the tension between achieving the ideal research design to answer the research questions, and the costs involved in doing so, is ever present at the research design stage. A major characteristic of *longitudinal* studies is that they are usually more costly than *cross-sectional* studies to undertake. Hence, the time dimension is a critical consideration.

A typical dilemma for researchers is how to answer research questions that deal with the passage of time using only a *cross-sectional* design. For example, we may be interested in the effect on students of exposure to a particular three-year educational programme. One method would be to follow a cohort of students over the three years, making measurements of their position on relevant variables at the beginning and end of the programme and, possibly, at intervals in between. However, if the programme has been in operation for at least three years, a compromise would be to measure these variables at one time for each year cohort of students, and see if they differ. This is a compromise design as it lacks random assignment to each year cohort. It also lacks controls for the fact that each cohort enters the programme, and passes through the three years, over a different time period, thus making it possible that its members have been subjected to the influence of different social conditions. Nevertheless, versions of this compromise are commonly used, and the passage of time is dealt with statistically.

Some writers (e.g. Neuman 1997) have suggested that both *cross-sectional* and *longitudinal* studies are quantitative because they involve a limited number of measurements on many individuals or social units. These two types of studies are contrasted with *case studies* that are considered to involve the use of qualitative methods with one or a few cases over a limited time period. However, I shall argue that both *cross-sectional* and *longitudinal* studies can use either quantitative or qualitative methods and data in the study of individuals, groups and communities, and social processes, institutions and structures. The extent to which the research focuses on a few or many aspects, and a few or many individuals or social units, is a matter of choice. Similarly, *case studies* can use both types of methods and can either focus on the present, or trace changes over time. Perhaps the best examples of longitudinal, qualitative case studies can be found in the anthropological studies of small-scale societies in which the researcher may revisit the society over many years. However, as we saw in chapter 6, *case studies* have many forms and uses.

Qualitative and Quantitative Techniques

It has become common practice to divide research methods into two broad types, *quantitative* and *qualitative*. However, the concepts have also been used to contrast five different aspects of the social research enterprise:

- *methods*, that cover the techniques of data collection and analysis;
- *data*, that are produced by particular types of methods;
- *research*, in which particular types of methods are used;
- *researchers*, who use particular methods; and
- *paradigms*, approaches or perspectives, that adopt different ontological and epistemological assumptions.

The first four aspects are closely related; a method produces a particular form of data, and research and researchers are related to the use of particular methods. The association of the concepts of qualitative and quantitative with *paradigms* is distinctive and different; to refer to paradigms in this way is to elevate a distinction between types of data and methods to the level of research strategy and even paradigm or approach to social enquiry (Blaikie 1993a). I regard this latter usage as unhelpful and inappropriate (see also Guba and Lincoln 1994: 105).

As we saw in chapter 6, when the quantitative/qualitative distinction is associated with data, the contrast is usually between data in numbers and words. Data, both at their source, and during and following analysis, can be produced in either form. In studies commonly labelled as quantitative, data are collected in numbers, or are very soon converted into them, and are subsequently analysed and reported in the same form. In qualitative studies, the original data are produced in one of two languages, the technical language of the researcher or the everyday language of the respondents. These languages are used to describe behaviour, social relationships, social processes, social situations, and, in particular, the meanings people give to their activities, the activities of others, and to objects and social contexts. Qualitative analysis, which may occur in conjunction with data collection, and the reporting of results from this analysis, can involve the use of both languages.

Quantitative methods are generally concerned with counting and measuring aspects of social life, while qualitative methods are more concerned with producing discursive descriptions and exploring social actors' meanings and interpretations.

> By quantitative methods, researchers have come to mean the techniques of randomised experiments, quasi-experiments, paper and pencil 'objective' tests, multivariate statistical analyses, sample surveys, and the like. In contrast, qualitative methods include ethnography, case studies, in-depth interviews, and participant observation. (Cook and Reichardt 1979)

While this is a convenient way to classify research methods, and I will use *qualitative* and *quantitative* this way in the first part of this chapter, there is a growing body of literature that has questioned the legitimacy of this dichotomy. These arguments will be reviewed later in the chapter.

Data Collection Techniques

The term *method* is used here to refer to ways in which evidence is obtained and manipulated, or, more conventionally, to techniques of data collection and analysis. This chapter will provide an overview of techniques for data collection, data reduction and data analysis, using the qualitative/quantitative distinction. However, as there are countless books that describe the nature and use of social research methods, no attempt will be made to provide details. The list in the box below is only intended to be indicative of the common methods used in both quantitative and qualitative research. Many refinements have been made to this classification.

The most commonly used quantitative data-gathering methods in the social sciences are undoubtedly the self-administered *questionnaire* and the *structured interview*, both of which keep the researcher at a distance from natural social processes. There is a great deal of confusion, particularly in the popular literature, about the way these two methods are identified. The commonest practice is not to distinguish between them, and, therefore, to assume that they are identical. Sometimes 'survey' will be used to refer to questionnaires, and questionnaires are seen to be used in structured interviews. De Vaus (1995) used 'questionnaire' as the generic term and then distinguished between face-to-face, telephone and mail as different methods of administration.

> # Data Collection Techniques
>
> ## Quantitative
> Observation: structured
> Questionnaire (self-administered)
> Structured interview
> Content analysis of documents
>
> ## Qualitative
> Participant observation
> Observation: semi-structured and unstructured
> Focused interview
> In-depth interview
> Oral/Life histories
> Focus groups/Group interviews
> Content analysis of documents

Oppenheim (1992), on the other hand, made the distinction between 'standardized interview' and 'questionnaire' very clear.

As the processes by which data are collected differ in important ways, it is necessary to distinguish between these two methods. Ideally, the format of the instruments should be different. They also have their own particular advantages and disadvantages. Questionnaires have to be prepared in such a way that respondents can complete them without any assistance other than built-in and/ or separate written instructions. An interview schedule, on the other hand, will usually contain instructions to the interviewer, and the interviewer will provide other instructions to the respondent. Samples of an interview schedule and a questionnaire format can be found in Smith (1981: appendices C and D). There are a number of discussions in the literature on the strengths and weaknesses of both methods (see e.g. Groves and Kahn 1979; Oppenheim 1992; de Vaus 1995).

The use of *structured observation* is much less common and is confined largely to experiments and observational studies in artificial settings. Examples of the former would be observing the response of individuals to periods of social isolation, or their reaction to an authority figure acting in an aggressive manner. Examples of the latter would be observing a group of children at play, or applicants for a leadership position undertaking a problem-solving task. In both cases, video recording may be used, but all this means is that the numerical coding of the behaviour can be delayed and the 'original' data revisited. Structured observation may be combined with other methods of data collection, such as the structured interview.

Some form of *participant observation* is regarded as the classic 'anthropological' method and the qualitative method *par excellence*. It involves the researcher in one or more periods of sustained immersion in the life of the people being studied (see e.g. Spradley 1980; Jorgensen 1989). This anthropological method is commonly referred to as 'field research' (Burgess 1984) or 'ethnography' (Fetterman 1989; Hammersley and Atkinson 1995). The latter literally means producing a picture of the way of life of some group. Both of these, however, involve a combination of methods, of which participant observation may be the main one.

Participant observation can be practised in a variety of ways, ranging from total participation (e.g. Whyte 1943) to mainly observation, and various combinations in between. It is not uncommon for a researcher to use both extremes as well as some combination in the same study (e.g. Gans 1967). Therefore, participant observation is not a single method, and it can combine different styles of observation (Bryman 1984: 48–9).

Contemporary social science is more likely to use some form of unstructured or semi-structured *interviewing*, in-depth, focused or group, rather than participant observation, to collect qualitative data (see e.g. Spradley 1979; McCracken 1990; Minichiello et al. 1995). Just as with structured interviews, any form of qualitative interview keeps the researcher removed from the natural setting; individual behaviour and social interaction will be reported rather than observed. However, the qualitative interview, particularly the in-depth variety, can get close to the social actors' meanings and interpretations, to their accounts of the social interaction in which they have been involved. Interviewing, in combination with reasonably extensive observation of actual social situations, provides a useful alternative to participant observation.

A special use of unstructured interviewing is *oral history*. One or more individuals are asked to recount aspects of their lives and/or the lives of their contemporaries, and to discuss their perceptions of the processes involved and the changes they have seen (see e.g. Thomas and Znaniecki 1927; Douglas et al. 1988; Yow 1994). The personal stories produced by this method can either stand on their own, or can be subjected to some type of qualitative analysis. A related method, but one that works with very different data, is the *life history* (Bertaux 1981; Plummer 1983). In this case, secondary rather than primary data are used to reconstruct the lives of individuals, and, perhaps, to produce an account of a particular historical period from the participant's experience of it. Diaries and autobiographies are the major sources.

Group interviews or discussion, or what is increasingly being referred to as *focus groups*, are gaining popularity as a method of data collection (e.g. Krueger 1988; Morgan 1988; Stewart and Shamdasani 1990; Berg 1995). Focus groups, which are the predominant qualitative method used in marketing research, have been adapted to more traditional social research, particularly evaluation research. Their purpose is different from that of individual interviews. They allow for group interaction and provide greater insight into why certain opinions are held.

Krueger has defined the focus group as 'a carefully planned discussion designed to obtain perceptions on a defined area of interest in a permissive, non-threatening environment' (1988: 18).

> Focus groups are communication events in which the interplay of the personal and the social can be systematically explored....The assumption...is that people will become more aware of their own perspective when confronted with active disagreement and be prompted to analyse their views more intensely than during the individual interview. Attempting to resolve differences is one of several mechanisms whereby participants build comprehensive accounts to explain their various experiences, beliefs, attitudes, feelings, values and behaviour. (Millward 1995: 277)

Documents as a data source can be used differently in conjunction with either quantitative or qualitative methods. Textual material can be coded into categories that are assigned numbers, counted and manipulated statistically. Alternatively, they can be treated qualitatively as identifying phenomena among which patterns of relationships are established. The ontological assumptions involved, and the end products in these two practices, tend to be different.

Compared with quantitative techniques most qualitative methods, if used diligently, are relatively time-consuming. This is no doubt a major reason for the attractiveness of quantitative methods, as well as their greater manageability and predictability in terms of outcomes. I have long suspected that each group of methods attracts different kinds of personalities, with level of comfort in being close to people an important factor.

Data Reduction Techniques

Data produced by most methods of collection require some manipulation to get them into a suitable form for analysis, using what is commonly referred to as data reduction techniques. This process is most obvious when the analysis is quantitative. Much less work is involved if *coding* frames are established before the data are collected, such as in a questionnaire or in observational methods. However, even in these cases, some reorganization of the coding categories, for example changing the order or combining categories, will usually be required. If the data are recorded in non-numerical form, such as in open-ended questions, the establishment of a set of coding categories will be necessary (see e.g. Oppenheim 1992; de Vaus 1995).

It is also possible to combine answers to a number of questions into a composite measure, such as an *index* or a *scale*. The major difference between them is that scales usually involve a demonstration of unidimensionality while an index does not (see McIver and Carmines 1981; de Vaus 1995).[1] Guttman scaling, factor

---

[1] Scaling is a relatively ancient art in social science and the classic references are still useful. See, for example, Thurstone and Chave (1929), Likert (1970), Bogardus (1933), Stouffer et al. (1950), Goode and Hatt (1952), Eysenck (1954), and Edwards (1957). The last reference provides a useful review of the state of the art at the time.

analysis and cluster analysis are alternative and sophisticated ways of establishing unidimensionality, each one being based on very different assumptions (see e.g. Stouffer et al. 1950; Lorr 1983; Oppenheim 1992; Lewis-Beck 1994). Simpler methods, such as item analysis, involve an assessment of the degree to which responses to a statement or item in a scale are correlated with the sum of responses to all statements or items (see Cronbach 1990). Factor analysis and cluster analysis also have other uses in data analysis.

> ## Data Reduction Techniques
>
> **Quantitative**
> Coding: pre-coding and post-coding
> Index construction
> Scaling: e.g. Likert and Guttman
> Factor analysis
> Cluster analysis
>
> **Qualitative**
> Coding: open and axial coding
> Developing themes
> Typology construction

Data reduction techniques are also used with qualitative methods, for example open and axial *coding* in grounded theory, and typology construction in the *abductive* research strategy. However, in these cases, it is impossible to separate data reduction and analysis; in fact, data collection, data reduction and data analysis can blend into one another in a cyclical process (see e.g. Eckett 1988; Minichiello et al. 1995).

Data Analysis Techniques

All that will be attempted here is to provide a brief overview of a range of commonly used quantitative and qualitative techniques. Techniques of quantitative analysis are well developed and are very diverse. In contrast, however, techniques of qualitative analysis are still being developed.

Quantitative methods of analysis fall into four main categories: description, association, causation, and inference. *Descriptive* methods are used to report the distributions of a sample or population across a range of variables (using all four levels of measurement), and to produce summary measures of the characteristics of such distributions. These measures include frequency counts (which can also be represented graphically), measures of central tendency (such as mode, median and mean, depending on the level of measurement), and measures of the dispersion of the distribution (such as the inter-quartile range and standard deviation).

Measures of *association* are used to establish the degree to which two variables covary, i.e. whether positions on one variable are likely to be consistently associated with positions on another variable, for example the extent to which people with high-status occupations identify with a particular type of religion, and people with low-status occupations identify with a different type of religion. The way in which association is established depends on the level(s) of measurement involved and whether there are two, or more than two, variables being analysed.

In order to answer 'why' questions, an attempt may be made to establish *causation*. There are three popular methods for doing this: factor analysis, path analysis and regression, the latter being the contemporary favourite. The aim in this kind of analysis is to deal with a network of relationships in the hope that causation can be demonstrated.

Inferential statistics are used for two purposes: to make estimates of population characteristics (parameters) from sample characteristics (statistics); and to establish whether differences or relationships within a sample (such as an association between occupation and religion) can be expected to exist, other than by chance, in the population from which the sample was drawn. It is for these purposes that the ubiquitous *tests of significance* are used (see the discussion in chapter 6).

Compared to quantitative methods of analysis, qualitative methods are less well developed. However, the literature on the latter is increasing rapidly as they become more popular (see e.g. Glaser and Strauss 1967; Lofland 1971; Turner 1981, 1994; Miles and Huberman 1984, 1994; Martin and Turner 1986; Richards and Richards 1987, 1991, 1994; Dey 1993; Silverman 1993; Bryman and Burgess 1994; Coffey and Atkinson 1996; Strauss and Corbin 1999). While there is no one dominant method, various versions of grounded theory have become popular, particularly as software is now available to aid the process, such as, Ethnograph, NUD*IST, ATLAS.ti and WinMAX (see Seidel 1984; Richards and Richards 1987, 1991, 1994; Pfaffenberger 1988; Tesch 1990; Fielding and Lee 1991; Miles and Huberman 1994).

An earlier method, *analytical induction* (Znaniecki 1934; Robinson 1951) has received some attention as a process for generalizing from a small number of cases. It involves six main steps.

> ## Data Analysis Techniques
>
> **Quantitative**
> Description
>   Distribution: numerical and graphical
>   Central tendency and dispersion
> Association
>   Correlation: simple, partial and multiple
>   Analysis of variance and covariance
>   Regression: simple, partial and multiple
> Causation
>   Factor analysis
>   Path analysis
>   Regression: simple, partial and multiple
> Inference
>   Sample statistic to population parameter
>   Sample differences to population differences
>
> **Qualitative**
> Description
> Theory generation
>   Analytic induction
>   Grounded theory: open and axial coding
>   Categorizing and connecting
>   From everyday typifications to typologies

1 Defining the phenomenon to be explained.
2 A hypothetical explanation of the phenomenon is formulated.
3 One case is studied to see whether the hypothesis relates to the particular case.
4 If the hypothesis does not fit the case, it is either reformulated or the phenomenon is redefined in order to exclude the particular case.
5 Practical certainty is achieved with a small number of cases, but negative cases disprove the explanation and require a reformulation.

6 The examination of cases, redefinition of the phenomenon and reformulation of hypotheses is continued until a universal relationship is established. (Burgess 1984: 179)

Analytic induction has many similarities to the trial and error process of the *deductive* research strategy, the major exception being that deductively derived theories have a more tentative status than is implied in the last step above. It is on this point that Robinson (1951) and Turner (1953) have been critical of analytic induction. Examples of its use can be found in Lindesmith (1947, 1952) and Sutherland and Cressey (1966).

The advocates of grounded theory have argued for the use of the constant comparative method as being superior to analytic induction (Glaser and Strauss 1967: 101–13). In grounded theory and its variants, an ongoing process of data collection, data analysis and theory construction is undertaken.

> In social research generating theory goes hand in hand with verifying it...the adequacy of a theory...cannot be divorced from the process by which it is generated ....Generating a theory from data means that most hypotheses and concepts not only come from the data, but are systematically worked out in relation to the data during the course of the research. *Generating a theory involves a process of research.* By contrast, the *source* of certain ideas, or even 'models', can come from sources other than the data. (Glaser and Strauss 1967: 2–6)

Turner (1981) has systemized grounded theory into a sequence of nine stages, although it is clear that these refer to a developmental process rather than linear steps.

(1) After some exposure to the field setting and some collection of data, the researcher starts to develop 'categories' which illuminate and fit the data well.
(2) The categories are then 'saturated', meaning that further instances of the categories are gathered until the researcher is confident about the relevance and range of the categories for the research setting. There is a recognition in the idea of 'saturation' that further search for appropriate instances may become a superfluous exercise.
(3) The researcher then seeks to abstract a more general formulation of the category, as well as specifying the criteria for inclusion in the category.
(4) These more general definitions then act as a guide for the researcher, as well as stimulating further theoretical reflection. This stage may prompt the researcher to think of further instances which may be subsumed under the more general definition of the category.
(5) The researcher should be sensitive to the connections between the emerging general categories and other milieux in which the categories may be relevant. For example, can categories relating to the dying in hospital (Glaser and Strauss's main research focus) be extended to encapsulate other social settings?

(6) The researcher may become increasingly aware of the connections between categories developed in the previous stage, and will seek to develop hypotheses about such links.

(7) The researcher should then seek to establish the conditions in which these connections pertain.

(8) At this point, the researcher should explore the implications of the emerging theoretical framework for other, pre-existing theoretical schemes which are relevant to the substantive area.

(9) The researcher may then seek to test the emerging relationships among categories under extreme conditions to test the validity of the posited connection. (Turner 1981, as summarized by Bryman 1988: 83–4)

The central activity in qualitative data analysis is a special form of coding. Such coding can facilitate description, but it is also used for analysis and theory generation.

> The analyst starts by coding each incident in his [*sic*] data into as many categories of analysis as possible, as categories emerge or as data emerge that fit an existing category.... Coding...should keep track of the comparison group in which the incident occurs. To this procedure we add the basic, defining rule for the constant comparative method: *while coding an incident for a category, compare it with the previous incidents in the same and different groups coded in the same category.* (Glaser and Strauss 1967: 105–6)

Coding involves the use of concepts (labels placed on discrete happenings, events, and other instances of phenomena) and categories (a more abstract notion under which concepts are grouped together). The coding process involves two stages. The first stage, known as *open coding*, involves breaking the data down into categories and sub-categories, that is, 'taking apart an observation, a sentence, a paragraph, and giving each discrete incident, idea, or event, a name, something that stands for or represents a phenomenon' (Strauss and Corbin 1990: 63). This is a process of breaking down, examining, comparing, conceptualizing and categorizing data. The second stage, known as *axial coding*, is used to find relationships between these sub-categories and categories and, thus, puts the data back together in a new way. Axial coding is done by using a 'coding paradigm' which involves thinking about possible causal conditions, contexts, intervening conditions, action/interaction strategies used to respond to a phenomenon in its context, and the possible consequences of action/interaction not occurring. A core category is then selected and a descriptive narrative constructed about it (Strauss and Corbin 1999).

> In essence, this approach involves: first, the 'chunking and coding' of data, dividing facets of the available data into segments which are given labels, names or codes; second, the accumulation of those central codes which recur, and the development of abstract definitions to specify the properties associated with these core codes; and third, identifying links between the codes, links which may merely be associational, but which in some cases will be causal. Exploration and elaboration of these links

make it possible to develop 'local' and 'grounded' theoretical patterns to account for aspects of the data under scrutiny. (Turner 1994: 196)

Dey (1993) has formulated this as a circular or spiral process involving three activities: describing, classifying and connecting. The first step is to produce 'thick' or 'thorough' *descriptions* of the phenomenon being studied (Geertz 1973; Denzin 1978). 'Thin' description merely states 'facts', while 'thick' description includes the context of the action, the intentions of the social actors, and the processes through which social action and interaction are sustained and/or changed. In the next part of the process, *classifying*, Dey has dealt with the activities referred to as open and axial coding of grounded theory. In the same way, he has argued that classifying data is an integral part of the analysis, and without this there is no way of knowing what is being analysed. Classification is achieved by creating categories, assigning categories to the data, and splitting and splicing categories.

> Classification is a conceptual process. When we classify, we do two things. We don't just break the data into bits, we also assign these bits to categories or classes which bring these bits together again, if in a novel way. Thus all the bits that 'belong' to a particular category are brought together, and in the process, we begin to discriminate more clearly between the criteria for allocating data to one category or another. Then some categories may be subdivided, and others subsumed under more abstract categories. The boundaries between these categories may be defined more precisely. Logic may require the addition of new categories, not present in the data, to produce a comprehensive classification. Thus the process of classifying the data is already creating a conceptual framework through which the bits of data can be brought together again in an analytically useful way. (Dey 1993: 44–5)

Classification is not a neutral process; the researcher will have a purpose in mind that will provide direction and boundaries.

The third part of the process is making *connections* between categories. The aim is to discover regularities, variations and singularities in the data and thus to begin to construct theories. Following Sayer (1992), Dey has distinguished between formal and substantive relations.

> Formal relations are concerned with how things relate in terms of similarity and difference – how far they do or do not share the same characteristics. Substantive relations are concerned with how things interact. Things that are connected through interaction need not be similar, and vice versa. (Dey 1993: 152)

Formal relations are equivalent to those established by correlational analysis in quantitative research. An example of such a formal relation is that 'active environmentalists have had intimate experiences with nature in their early years'. *Substantive* relations are regular sequences of events, processes or activities, and these sequences may entail ideas of causation.

Methods of qualitative analysis differ in the extent to which they attempt to 'retain the integrity of the phenomenon'. That is, the extent to which the researcher remains close to the language, the concepts and meanings of the social actors rather than imposing their own concepts and categories on lay accounts. There is a choice between a *high* stance, in which the researcher imposes concepts and meanings, and a *low* stance, in which the researcher derives concepts and meanings from lay language. In its purest form, the *abductive* research strategy involves a *low* stance because it develops technical concepts and theoretical propositions from accounts provided in lay language (see chapter 4). Technical concepts generated in this way are designed to be more abstract and generalizable than is possible with lay concepts.

Grounded theory, on the other hand, is much more a process of the researcher 'inventing' and imposing concepts on the data; it adopts a *high* stance. The various forms of coding are a search for technical concepts that will organize and make sense of the data. While these concepts can be either those that are already in use, or can be developed by the researcher for a particular purpose, there appears to be little attempt to derive them from lay concepts, to make use of lay meanings associated with the concepts, or to tie them to lay concepts. For this reason, grounded theory is not strictly an *abductive* research strategy.

Another major variation in qualitative analysis is whether the researcher is satisfied with description, or whether the goal is the development of theory. There is, however, no clear divide between these two activities. Some would argue that description is all that a researcher can legitimately do; others would argue that description, particularly 'thick' description, already provides understanding and possibly explanation, and that nothing more is needed, while others seek to develop 'bottom-up' theories consisting of testable propositions (Hammersley 1985). For grounded theorists, the testing of these theoretical propositions is tied intimately to the process of their generation. Others may be willing to subject their theories to independent post-testing, although this may consist of examining the relevance of the theory in other contexts, still using 'bottom-up' techniques rather than the formal testing that is advocated by the *deductive* research strategy. Researchers interested in combining research strategies, and qualitative and quantitative methods, may develop their theory by some kind of grounded method and then test it deductively using quantitative methods. Clearly there is a range of possibilities here, and if qualitative methods are used, a decision has to be made as to what will constitute understanding or explanation, and how these will be developed and tested.

There is as yet no clearly articulated method for using the pure version of the *abductive* research strategy as advocated by Schütz. I began working on this in 1974 (Blaikie 1974) and committed some preliminary ideas to paper about ten years later (Blaikie and Stacy 1982; 1984). Over the years, a number of my postgraduate students have successfully used versions of it in a variety of studies (Kelsen 1981; Stacy 1983; Drysdale 1985; Balnaves 1990; Smith 1995) and other students and colleagues have worked with it.

There is now recognition of a diversity of traditions in what I call the Interpretive approach to social enquiry. These include a very mixed bag, such as hermeneutics, phenomenology, ethnomethodology, ethnography, grounded theory and biography (see e.g. Lancy 1993; Denzin and Lincoln 1994; Morse 1994; Moustakas 1994; Creswell 1998). Each has its particular emphasis in terms of research objectives, logic of enquiry and methods of data collection and analysis.

Uses of Quantitative and Qualitative Methods

When quantitative methods are used, the researcher is likely to have very limited or no contact with the people being studied. The use of some quantitative methods, such as mailed questionnaires, structured observation, and unobtrusive methods that involve the use of secondary data, require no face-to-face or verbal contact at all. When there is contact, such as in structured interviewing and experiments, it is formal and of limited duration. However, even in these cases, the researcher may have no contact if assistants are employed to carry out these tasks. This maintenance of distance from the people being studied, and the fanatical resistance to any form of personal disclosure or emotional involvement by the researcher, is largely practised in the belief that it will ensure that objectivity is achieved. What constitutes objectivity, and why it must be achieved, is, of course, related to the epistemological assumptions (probably from either Positivism or Critical Rationalism) which the researcher has explicitly or implicitly adopted.

The use of qualitative methods, on the other hand, usually requires an extended and intensive period of involvement in some social world. The most extreme form is participant observation in which the researcher can become fully immersed in the social actors' world with all the levels of personal involvement that this entails. Such qualitative methods allow the researcher to become an 'insider' and to discover the social actors' culture and worldviews. The contact and involvement in in-depth, unstructured interviewing lies somewhere between participant observation and structured interviewing, and will involve varying degrees of personal involvement and disclosure on the part of the researcher. When a series of in-depth interviews is conducted with the same person, the level of involvement is likely to be higher. Rather than attempt to adopt the position of a detached 'scientific' observer, qualitative researchers may deliberately choose to 'go native', to allow themselves to become part of the world of the researched, to be seduced by the social actors' constructed reality. Some would argue that, without a period of immersion in a social world, no adequate understanding of it can be achieved. While it is probably not possible for a researcher to go completely native, a test of whether the social actors' meanings have been 'discovered' can only be based on whether the researcher has developed the capacity to interact successfully in a particular social context. To achieve this, it is necessary for the researcher to become as subjective as possible rather than to try to adopt some kind of objective stance, at least at the data collection stage.

Some preconceived notions of what concepts are relevant, and how they should be defined, usually accompanies the use of quantitative methods. This applies whether the research objectives are *descriptive* or *explanatory*. In the latter case, particularly within the *deductive* research strategy, the methods used to collect data related to concepts, and the postulated relationships between them, will have been derived from some theory. In other words, the methods serve some preconceived ideas about the nature of some part of the social world, and why it is the way it is.

In contrast, qualitative methods may be used deliberately without any theory in mind and with only sensitizing concepts as a guide. In the quest to take the social actors' point of view, everyday concepts that emerge as being relevant to the phenomenon under investigation will be identified and their everyday meanings explored. For those qualitative researchers who wish to go beyond *description* to some kind of *understanding* or *explanation*, theory, or the social scientists' accounts, will be generated from everyday accounts and theories. Within the *abductive* research strategy, theory is the end product of the research, not the starting-point.

An important feature of the use of quantitative methods is their highly structured nature. They are located within a research design that includes a set of predetermined stages, and the data gathering will be accomplished by the use of predetermined procedures and pre-tested instruments. In using such methods, the researcher is aiming to have maximum control over the data gathering and to achieve uniformity in the application of the techniques. Usually, it is only after the data are collected that the analysis will begin. The main justification for the uniformity, control and rigid stages is to achieve some notion of objectivity and replicability. In my experience, quantitative methods tend to be used by researchers who prefer order, predictability and security, and who have a low level of tolerance for uncertainty and ambiguity.

This contrasts with the use of qualitative methods in which the procedures are much more open and flexible. Frequently, qualitative researchers have a very limited idea of where they should start, how they should proceed, and where they expect to end up. They have to accept opportunities when they open up and they will want to follow leads as they occur. They see research as a learning process and themselves as the measuring (data-absorbing) instrument. They will want to allow concepts, ideas and theories to evolve and they will resist imposing both preconceived ideas on everyday reality and closure on the emerging understanding. Qualitative data gathering is messy and unpredictable and seems to require researchers who can tolerate ambiguity, complexity, uncertainty and lack of control.

Researchers who are wedded to quantitative methods may also use qualitative methods. However, the role that is given to qualitative methods is usually different to that adopted by researchers who regard them as their primary or only methods. A common use of qualitative methods by quantitative researchers is in an exploratory stage that is used to suggest hypotheses or to facilitate the development of research instruments. Qualitative methods are viewed as being only supplementary to quantitative methods and, perhaps, as inferior. The range of qualitative methods used is likely to be limited to those that come closest to quantitative methods, for example semi-structured interviews or observation. I have come across some quantitative researchers who regard open-ended questions in a mainly structured questionnaire as constituting qualitative data gathering. The fact that the questions are in the researcher's language, and that the method used to code the responses is devised by the researcher, makes it a very different kind of data collection to the more traditional use of qualitative methods.

Quantitative versus Qualitative Research

There has been considerable debate about the relative merits of quantitative and qualitative methods, with the protagonists invariably adopting tactics to bolster their own position and denigrate that of the 'opposition'. For decades, quantitative researchers have adopted the methodological high ground; quantitative research has been regarded as the orthodoxy and qualitative researchers the troublesome but largely irrelevant sect. Qualitative researchers have tended to struggle under the shadow of this dominant orthodoxy and have had to be content with much lower levels of funding for their research.[2] These debates have been conducted in terms of various contrasts in purpose and style and have produced a slate of pejorative terms used to defend preferred methods, and to abuse other methods. Table 7.1, based on Halfpenny (1979), provides some examples of such contrasting labels.

Almost all data used by social researchers begins in a qualitative form. It is only after work has been done on it, to transpose words into numbers, that quantitative data come into being.

Table 7.1 Contrasting qualitative and quantitative labels

Qualitative	Quantitative
relativistic	universalistic
holistic	atomistic
inductive	deductive
ideographic	nomothetic
descriptive/exploratory	explanatory
speculative/illustrative	hypothesis-testing
grounded	abstract
subjective	objective
exposes actors' meanings	imposes theory
flexible/fluid	fixed
case-study	survey
political	value-free
non-rigorous	rigorous
soft	hard
dry	wet
good	bad
bad	good
story-telling	number-crunching
feminine	masculine

The last two pairs of labels were not part of Halfpenny's (1979) list.

[2] The dominance of quantitative methods has been most evident in decision-making associated with research grant allocations. You only have to ask any qualitative researcher how difficult it is to compete for research funds, and examine the statistics on the distribution of grant allocations within the broad range of the social and behavioural sciences. For example, economics and psychology consistently fare much better than sociology, anthropology and history in the grants allocated by the Australian Research Council.

> We can regard all of the information which we acquire about the world as qualitative, and then see that under some circumstances we can use this information to create a particular kind of data, quantitative data, to which the properties of number can be applied. (Turner 1994: 195)

Halfpenny (1996) has argued that in spite of the surface differences between words and numbers, quantitative and qualitative data are not fundamentally different.

> Quantitative data is usually produced by coding some other data, which is reduced to a number by stripping off the context and removing content from it. Later, after manipulating the numbers, they are interpreted, that is, expanded by adding content and context which enable one to see through the numerical tokens back to the social world. (Halfpenny 1996: 5)

It is the order and power offered by numerical analysis that have made quantified information so attractive and led qualitative information to be treated with suspicion. However, for quantitative data to achieve these apparent advantages, it is necessary to assume that the properties of a number system correspond to some features of the original data.

> The power offered by numerical systems of analysis can only be developed and used if we can find a sufficiently close correspondence, a sufficient degree of isomorphism, between the properties of the portion of the world under investigation and the properties of the mathematical or number system which we might use. A moment's reflection will reveal to us that, even where the use of numerical analysis seems most self-evident, to use it we need to make certain working assumptions. We may regularly count apples or sheep or pounds sterling. But every apple, every animal, is unique. When we count, we merely agree, tacitly, that for this everyday purpose, we are willing to apply rules which disregard the differences between individual apples or individual sheep, and which stress their similarities for numbering purposes. (Turner 1994: 195)

While studies are frequently classified as being either quantitative or qualitative, some use both kinds of data. Quantitative studies may collect some data in words (e.g. they use open-ended questions in a survey, or use text on which content analysis is to be undertaken). By means of some coding process, these data will be transformed into a numerical form. Similarly, some qualitative studies may produce simple tables of frequencies and percentages to summarize some features of non-numerical data. In recent years, British sociology has experienced a wholesale disposal of counting, along with the positivistic bath water. In response, Silverman (1985, 1993) has argued that 'simple counting techniques can offer a means to survey the whole corpus of data ordinarily lost in intensive, qualitative research' (Silverman 1985: 140). Such counting in qualitative research can provide some support for the representativeness of certain features within a social group or category. However, Silverman went on to argue that it is important to count the countable, preferably by using the categories of the social actors rather than those of the researcher.

As indicated in table 7.1, the quantitative/qualitative comparison is often equated with the objective/subjective distinction. This practice is very misleading. While it is not possible to enter into all the complexities of the debates around 'objectivity' and 'subjectivity', I need to make a brief comment here. Just as all data begin in the qualitative form, all attempts at measuring or recording aspects of the social world are fundamentally subjective. The only defensible meaning of 'objectivity' in the context of social research arises in the situation where two or more researchers compare their 'subjective' experiences of measuring or recording and can establish that they have produced the same or very similar results. In other words, so-called 'objectivity' is achieved through corroboration, replication and consensus, not by the selection of particular research methods. If researchers use the same data-collection techniques or measuring instruments, and their results are the same, then it is simply a convention to regard their methods and their data as being 'objective'.

It just so happens that corroboration and replication are easier to achieve with quantitative rather than qualitative methods. If you say there are ten people in a particular room, and I and others agree with you, we may reach a consensus about our results. Our methods and data would then be regarded as 'objective'. Of course, we have to work with the same theory of numbers to achieve this (how we count, what we mean by 10, that 10 is greater than 9 and less than 11, etc.). This is one sense in which it can be said that observations are theory-dependent.

The character of qualitative data makes corroboration and replication more difficult, some would say impossible. In qualitative research, the researcher is usually the measuring instrument and no two instruments are the same. If you conduct in-depth interviews with twenty people about their working life, you may discover three different types of work orientations. Clearly, it would be difficult for me and others to then interview these same people. However, we could interview samples of people from the same population. Even if we have agreed ahead of time to discuss the same topics, my conversations with my sample may be different from those you had with your sample, and similarly for other interviewers. We may end up with a variety of typologies, or, if we happened to agree on the types, there may be differences in the details of our descriptions of each type. However, this is not to suggest that one of us has produced the correct account and the others are wrong. Each of our accounts may be *authentic*, i.e. they may correctly report what *we* learnt from *our* sample of people.

Quantitative and qualitative researchers have different methods for achieving rigour in their research. Traditionally, the former have focused on establishing the 'validity' and 'reliability' of their measurements, that their instruments measure what they claim to measure and that they do so consistently. If you examine the methods by which validity and reliability are established, you will find that they involve corroboration and replication. There are no ultimate standards against which a measuring instrument can be compared; there are only well-used instruments in which communities of researchers have a high degree of confidence. Objectivity is always relative.

Qualitative researchers are rather divided on the need to establish the authenticity of their findings. Some would argue that researchers produce their unique accounts and that corroboration or replication is impossible. They would claim that if they have acted professionally, and have explained how they went about their research, their accounts should be trusted. Other qualitative researchers have argued that the social actors concerned must corroborate any account that a researcher gives of social life. In other words, the researcher's account must correspond closely to social actors' accounts. Schütz (1963b) proposed a 'postulate of adequacy' which requires that social actors must be able to recognize themselves in sociologists' accounts. Similarly, Douglas (1971) insisted on researchers 'retaining the integrity of the phenomenon', and ethnomethodologists have referred to 'member validation'. Like all forms of validation, this one has its particular difficulties. However, it is an attempt to keep sociological constructions close to social constructions of reality. (See Blaikie 1993a for a discussion of this issue.)

Preoccupations of Quantitative and Qualitative Researchers

As a way of exploring the major concerns and assumptions that accompany the use of quantitative and qualitative methods, let us examine the common preoccupations of researchers who use these methods. Of necessity, this discussion presents two ideal-typical descriptions of common assumptions and practices, an abstracted account of these differences. We have encountered some of these differences in assumptions in the elaboration and discussion of the research strategies in chapter 4. In this discussion, however, I do not wish to imply that there is a one-to-one relationship between research strategies and methods. As we shall see later in the chapter, some methods can serve a variety of ontological assumptions and can be used within a number of research strategies.

Quantitative Researchers

Researchers who use quantitative methods have a number of preoccupations (Bryman 1988).[3]

Measuring concepts

Firstly, there is a primary concern with concepts and their measurement. The problem is deciding what to measure, and how to measure it, i.e. how to operationalize a concept to turn it into a variable. Part of the process of measuring a concept is to establish whether the procedure is reliable and valid: whether the measure is internally consistent (such as a scale being unidimensional); whether it operates consistently over time (reliability); and whether there is a good fit between the concept and the variable, that is, the measurement procedure measures

---

[3] Bryman has provided a clear and balanced review and discussion of quantitative and qualitative methods. This section makes extensive use of his work.

what it claims to measure (validity). Concern about reliability and validity is typical of quantitative researchers because of the belief that they are dealing with an 'external' reality. For discussions of these concepts in qualitative research, see, for example, Kirk and Miller (1986), Hammersley (1990, 1992) and Silverman (1993).

Concepts that are to be measured can be derived from a variety of sources. They may come from theory in the process of deducing hypotheses, they may be drawn from a theoretical perspective or conceptual scheme without entailing any tentative explanation, or they may just be considered to be relevant labels for an aspect of the phenomenon under consideration. These differences in the source of concepts may reflect differences in research objectives, between *description* and *explanation*. For example, two researchers may be interested in social deviance. One may be content to measure the frequency with which a particular kind of deviant behaviour occurs, or how frequently a particular individual engages in various kinds of deviant behaviour. The other may want to explain a particular kind of deviance. The first needs appropriate concepts to measure, while the latter needs to measure concepts contained in relevant theoretical propositions or hypotheses.

Establishing causality

The second preoccupation of quantitative researchers is the establishment of causality. Within the *inductive* research strategy, the concern is with establishing patterns as a basis for explanation. The notion of one variable causing another is considered to be irrelevant. Within the *deductive* strategy, however, simply correlating variables is considered to be inadequate; propositions should be derived from theory and then tested.

It is generally accepted that three conditions have to be met in order to establish causation.

- It has to be demonstrated that there is a relationship between two or more variables.
- This relationship is not the result of the presence of a third variable that produces changes in the two variables.
- There is a temporal order between the variables such that one has the possibility of causing the other.

These criteria can usually be met in research that uses experimental and control groups, as the temporal sequence is controlled by the researcher and the effects of other variables are either eliminated or randomized. It is in cross-sectional studies, for example in social surveys, that the second two conditions can be difficult to achieve.

Variables may be classified as 'independent' and 'dependent' being, respectively, variables that are assumed to do the causing and those that are assumed to be the effects. However, the time sequence has to be contrived through the use of such techniques as path analysis and multiple regression. Nevertheless, even if the

assumptions that are adopted are correct, these techniques cannot handle interactive or reciprocal causality between variables. For example, analysis may be
constructed to demonstrate that 'juvenile delinquents come from broken homes',
i.e. that a particular kind of family background causes juvenile delinquency. In
this case it would be claimed that family background is the 'independent' variable
and juvenile delinquency the 'dependent' variable. This involves the assumption
that the family situation precedes the juvenile behaviour. While it is possible that
a child may be born to parents whose marriage is unsatisfactory, and that this
may have a detrimental effect on the child's personal and social development, the
relationship between the family situation and the child's behaviour is likely to
be complex. It is possible that the experience of coping with a delinquent
child could lead a precarious marriage to break up. Of course, it is possible to
establish a sequence of events, such as when a marriage broke up and when
delinquent behaviour began to occur. However, simple causal models do not
readily allow for possible interactive effects between the behaviour of both
parents and child over time. Longitudinal designs may offer some assistance,
but they are more useful for establishing changes, rather than causal sequences
or interactive effects.

Generalizing

Generalization is the third preoccupation among quantitative researchers. There
is a desire to make descriptive statements, or to establish theoretical propositions,
that are universal. This is particularly the case in the *inductive* research strategy in
which the search is for universal regularities or laws. This search is also evident in
the *deductive* research strategy, although the theories that are developed and
tested will usually include conditional propositions that specify limits to the
application of the general propositions in the theory. For example, a theory
might contain the general proposition that 'juvenile delinquents come from broken homes', but this might be qualified with a condition that the relationship
applies only to those broken homes in which children have been socialized
inadequately and do not know which behavioural rules apply under which
circumstances.

In quantitative studies, there is usually a desire for research results to be
applicable beyond the population that is studied. While the *inductive* and *deductive* strategies have their own ways of trying to achieve this (by providing further
support for an established generalization, or by using universal propositions in the
theory from which the hypothesis is deduced), quantitative researchers appear not
to be content to accept the time and space limitations of all social research.
Regardless of how extensive the populations are that are studied, statements can
only be made beyond that population by means of argument that is based on
additional evidence, such as establishing similarities with the characteristics of
other populations. However, most attention is focused on the more technical issue
of how to generalize from a sample to a population. Here the focus is on the
representativeness of the sample, on achieving a high response rate, and on
selecting the appropriate statistical test (see chapter 6).

Replicating

The fourth preoccupation is with the possibility of being able to replicate the findings of any research project in the same or similar contexts. This is assumed to provide some kind of check on the extent to which a particular researcher might have allowed personal biases to enter into the research. It is assumed that if another (unbiased) researcher cannot produce the same results, there must be something wrong with the original research. Of course, there is always the possibility that two researchers, or the methods they used, may be similarly biased! Hence, replication does not guarantee 'true' conclusions.

The way that the concept of 'bias' is used here implies that there are ultimate truths to be discovered about an objective reality, that the truth status of specific pieces of data can be established, and that it is possible for researchers to set aside or control for their own values, prejudices and preconceptions. These are certainly central assumptions in survey research. Why else is so much attention paid to the validity and reliability of measurement procedures, to question-wording and to standardizing interviewing techniques? One of the major criticisms of qualitative methods is that they do not lend themselves to replication; that there is too much of the researcher in the data. However, what is curious about this concern with replication is that very little of it is actually done by quantitative researchers.

> Replication is often regarded as a somewhat unimaginative, low status activity among researchers. Why, then, is it so often regarded as an important facet of the quantitative research tradition? In all probability, it is not replication that is important so much as replic*ability*. (Bryman 1988: 38)

Focusing on individuals

The final preoccupation in the use of quantitative methods to be discussed here is the tendency for this type of research to focus on individuals. This may be due, in part, to the predominance of the use of survey methods that are administered to individuals, but there appears to be something more fundamental involved. In spite of Durkheim's inductivist injunction that social researchers should not give any credence to the way individuals perceive social reality, quantitative researchers proceed to measure 'individual' variables and then reify these into a reality that consists of nothing more than a network of relationships between these variables. The methods never get very close to the *social* world that respondents inhabit, and the process of analysis shakes people out of this conceptual and statistically reconstructed reality. At best, individuals exist in categories, such as 'female' or 'male', 'old' or 'young', 'rich' or 'poor', 'high education' or 'low education', or as holding favourable or unfavourable attitudes. It is highly likely that people in any one of these categories do not participate in any form of social activity together. Hence, users of quantitative methods should be very aware of the ontological assumptions that they are adopting, and that they are likely to be working with a *demographic* rather than a *social* reality.

Qualitative Researchers

The preoccupations of researchers involved in the collection of qualitative data contrast with those of quantitative researchers (Bryman 1988).

Using the social actors' point of view

The chief characteristic is a commitment to viewing the social world – social action and events – from the viewpoint(s) of the people being studied. This commitment involves discovering *their* socially constructed reality and penetrating the frames of meaning within which they conduct their activities. To do this, it is necessary to master the everyday language that social actors use in dealing with the phenomenon under investigation, in short, to discover their 'mutual knowledge', the concepts, and the meanings associated with these concepts. The investigation of this reality, and the language in which it is embedded, requires extended periods of involvement in the lives of the people, by means of participant observation and/or through extensive in-depth interviewing.

This position contrasts with that adopted by quantitative researchers who conduct research from *their* view of what constitutes social reality. This difference has been typified as being between an 'insider' and an 'outsider' stance, as a 'bottom-up' versus a 'top-down' approach, or, as I would prefer, as between *high* and *low* stances.

An associated difference concerns the existence of a single or of multiple social realities. Quantitative researchers tend to work with the idea that there is only one social reality, while qualitative researchers accept the possibility of, and search for, multiple realities or worldviews. The former work with *their* 'outside', expert construction of reality, while the latter accept that in any social context it is possible that people may inhabit different socially constructed realities, or variations on one, and may therefore have different ways of interpreting their actions and the actions of others.

Describing thickly

The second characteristic of qualitative research is the importance that is given to producing detailed or 'thick' descriptions of the social settings being investigated. As we have seen, some qualitative researchers hold the view that description is all that is possible or necessary to provide an understanding of any aspect of social life. They give a great deal of attention to describing what might appear to be minute and trivial details of social activity. It is argued that this is necessary to provide a backdrop within which actions and interactions can be understood. This is a long way from the kind of causal explanations attempted by some quantitative researchers, but it can facilitate the production of satisfying accounts of some aspects of social life.

> Thus an important contribution of descriptive detail for the ethnographer is to the mapping out of a context for understanding the subjects' interpretations of what is

going on and for the researcher to produce analyses and explanations which do justice to the milieu in which his or her observations and interviews are conducted. (Bryman 1988: 64)

However, as was noted earlier, some qualitative researchers wish to go beyond description to explanations of a causal kind. Weber (1964) and Schütz (1963a), for example, both argued that it is possible and desirable to seek explanations based on meanings through a process of hypothesis testing.

As we saw in chapter 4, an issue that divides researchers is whose language is to be used for description. This brings us back to the first preoccupation. Should description be in the language of the social actors, should it be in the language of the social scientist, or should it be in some synthesis of both languages? From a qualitative researcher's point of view, something more is required than simply publishing transcripts of in-depth interviews. In other words, it is very difficult to report the results of research purely from the point of view of the social actors; even elementary analysis will introduce something of the researcher's point of view. On the other hand, it is possible, and perhaps easier, for the researcher to reconstruct what social actors have said within a technical language of a discipline or a theoretical perspective. There are a number of ways in which this reconstruction can be done, and there is a range of possibilities in how far from the social actors' point of view the researcher wants to move. Schütz's notion of the need to derive the researcher's account from the social actors' everyday accounts, and the need to 'retain the integrity of the phenomenon', provides a defensible (*abductive*) strategy for linking the two languages.

Focusing on social processes

As a general rule, qualitative researchers view the social world as processual rather than static, as being about the dynamics of social relationships between social actors rather than the characteristics of individuals and the relationships between abstract concepts. They argue that, as the participants are engaged in social process, social researchers who wish to adopt the participants' view of social reality, and provide an insider's point of view, should also view social reality in the same way.

Adopting a flexible approach

The use of qualitative methods is often associated with the adoption of an unstructured and flexible approach to the conduct of research. There is an unwillingness to impose concepts and their relationships on any part of the social world in advance of an open investigation of it. Some qualitative researchers may even enter the field without a clearly formulated topic or without research questions, preferring to allow these to emerge as the fieldwork proceeds. To some extent, this is driven by the desire to see the world through the eyes of the social actors. However, it is also based on the view that the researcher is unlikely to have an adequate grasp of the situation, and that the unexpected is likely to arise through the process of participant observation or related methods.

> Irrespective of whether the research problem is closely defined, qualitative research-ers tend to the view that the predominantly open approach which they adopt in the examination of social phenomena allows them access to unexpectedly important topics which may not have been visible to them had they foreclosed the domain of study by a structured, and hence potentially rigid, strategy. (Bryman 1988: 67)

Developing concepts and theory

The final preoccupation of qualitative researchers discussed by Bryman (1988) brings us back to the issue of adopting the social actors' point of view. It involves the issue of whether or not research should begin with predetermined theory and concepts. Such a procedure is a vital feature of the *deductive* research strategy, and, certainly, concepts are needed in the *inductive* strategy. However, qualitative researchers who work with the *abductive* research strategy consider that adopting a theory in advance will not only put limits on the researcher but will also prevent them from taking the participants' point of view. Instead, the latter researchers are more interested in developing both concepts and theory in conjunction with data collection. If technical concepts are used early in the research, they play a sensitiz-ing role, a point of reference and a guide rather than predetermining the phenom-enon under investigation.

> This approach to the connection of concepts and data means that a concept provides a set of general signposts for the researcher in his or her contact with a field of study. While the concept may become increasingly refined, it does not become reified such that it loses contact with the real world. One concomitant of this approach is that the qualitative researcher is attuned to the variety of forms that the concept may subsume. As such, a sensitizing concept retains close contact with the complexity of social reality, rather than trying to bolt it on to fixed, preformulated images. (Bryman 1988: 68)

Generalizing in Qualitative Research

Many of the issues raised in the previous chapter about generalizing and theoriz-ing from case studies are echoed in discussions about the possibility of general-izing from studies that use qualitative methods. As indicated earlier, case studies can use any kind of method for data collection and analysis; they are not restricted to qualitative methods. However, the use of qualitative methods in any kind of research poses a similar set of problems; combine case studies and qualitative methods and the problems are exacerbated.

There are two aspects to the problem of generalizing in qualitative research. First, probability sampling is uncommon and, in any case, is inappropriate in many instances. Second, qualitative data do not lend themselves to the kind of generalization commonly used in quantitative research, such as using statistical techniques that are based on probability theory.

In the past, many qualitative researchers have given generalization low priority, and some researchers have explicitly rejected any form of context-free generalization as a goal (e.g. Guba and Lincoln 1981, 1982; Denzin 1983). In addition, the idea of replicating previous studies, a requirement of the *inductive* research strategy, and a goal of much experimental and survey research, is usually regarded as being inappropriate in qualitative research. The reflexive character of qualitative research means that individual researchers inevitably inject something of themselves into the research process and, hence, into the outcomes. In addition, social situations are never sufficiently similar, across space and time, to make replication possible. Hence, it is argued, replication is inappropriate. Studies conducted by different researchers, in different locations, and at different times, will be unique because of the particular characteristics of the researcher and the researched, their effects on each other, and the hermeneutic processes involved in the production of the researcher's account (see Blaikie 1993a). In contrast, quantitative researchers generally believe that their methods, and the application of them, can control for any possible researcher influence; they also ignore or try to eliminate the hermeneutic processes; and they tend to assume that time and space do not pose insurmountable limitations.

In discussing the possibilities for generalizing from qualitative research, Schofield has argued that

> at the heart of the qualitative approach is the assumption that a piece of qualitative research is very much influenced by the researcher's individual attributes and perspectives. The goal is *not* to produce a standardized set of results that any other careful researcher in the same situation or studying the same issues would have produced. Rather it is to produce a coherent and illuminating description of and perspective on a situation that is based on and consistent with detailed study of that situation....In fact, I would argue that, except perhaps in multisite qualitative studies...it is impractical to make precise replication a criterion of generalizability in qualitative work. (Schofield 1993: 202)

In spite of such claims, there has been a marked increase in interest in the issue of generalizability among qualitative researchers, particularly in educational research where qualitative methods are now used extensively in evaluation studies. Agencies that fund this type of research are usually interested in its relevance beyond the site in which it was conducted. Even researchers engaged in ethnographic studies in education are also likely to want their research to have wider relevance.

While qualitative researchers usually accept space and time limitations in their enquiries, various attempts have been made to achieve some kind of wider relevance for their findings. Even though ethnographic description, for example, may be interesting and illuminating, the desire to make connections and comparisons between such studies, and to theorize about them, can be very compelling for curious social scientists.

How can generalization be achieved in qualitative research? Answers to this question are mainly confined to generalizing from one research site to some other site or population. The aim is to make statements about this other location on the basis of the research results. One answer to this question is to use 'fittingness'

(Guba and Lincoln 1981, 1982), 'comparability' (Goetz and LeCompte 1984) or 'naturalistic generalisation' (Stake 1978). This requires detailed or 'thick' descriptions of both the site in which a study is conducted and the sites about which generalizations are to be made. Similarities and differences can then be taken into account in any judgement about the relevance of findings obtained from one site for some other sites (Schofield 1993: 207). The aim in such comparisons is generally to establish whether the research site is typical of other sites.

Attempts are also made to generalize across time as well as across research sites. Hence, a researcher may wish to make a judgement about whether the findings from a particular site will also hold in the future at the same site as well as at the same or other times at other sites (Hammersley 1992: 87).

Schofield (1993) has added a further dimension to this issue by suggesting that, in educational research in particular, it is important to be able to generalize to 'what is', 'what may be' and 'what could be'. Studying 'what is' means studying the typical, the common or the ordinary. She has argued that in selecting research sites, it is much more useful to look for typical situations rather than choose on the basis of convenience.

> However, even if one chooses on the basis of typicality, one is in no way relieved of the necessity for thick description, for it is foolhardy to think that a typical example will be typical in all important regards. Thus thick description is necessary to allow individuals to ask about the degree of fit between the case studied and the case to which they want to generalize, even when the fit on some of the basic dimensions looks fairly close. (Schofield 1993: 210–11)

Generalizability can be enhanced by studying the same issue in a number of research sites, using similar methods of data collection and analysis. A decision would need to be made about whether the multiple sites should be homogeneous or heterogeneous. Similar results from heterogeneous sites may be more useful than those from homogeneous ones. However, the risk in choosing heterogeneous sites is that results may be very different. While this might not contribute to generalizability, it will certainly raise further research questions and stimulate theory generation. The main disadvantage of multisite research is the cost and the time involved, particularly if ethnographic methods are used.

If the aim of a study is to anticipate 'what may be', i.e. what is likely to happen, then other factors enter site selection. The aim is to generalize from the present to the future.[4] Rather than focusing on what is typical, or searching for heterogeneous sites, Schofield has proposed both selecting sites that are more developed in the aspects being considered (e.g. computer usage in schools) and trying to assess how the future will differ from the present. In addition, given the longitudinal nature of ethnographic studies, it is possible to trace trends, particularly in phenomena that involve a life cycle.

---

[4] Philosophers such as Popper have argued that predicting the future is not a scientific activity. All theories require the specification of conditions in order to hypothesize outcomes. Even if we have well-tested theories available, we can never know the conditions in the future and can therefore not predict future outcomes. However, decision-makers need to anticipate likely futures. The method being proposed here is designed to produce intelligent guesses based on sound evidence.

Paying attention to where a phenomenon is in its life cycle does not guarantee that one can confidently predict how it will evolve. However, at a minimum, sensitivity to this issue makes it less likely that conclusions formed on the basis of a study conducted at one point in time will be unthinkingly and perhaps mistakenly generalized to other later points in time to which they may not apply. (Schofield 1993: 216)

Schofield's third aim in generalizing to 'what could be' involves establishing whether some goal or ideal can be achieved. Again, typicality and heterogeneity are not appropriate criteria for site selection. One possibility is to use a particular theory to suggest selection criteria with the result that an unusual site with special characteristics might be selected. In studies concerned with 'what may be' and 'what could be', comparison with typical sites may provide useful insights.

These issues around site selection are also pertinent to grounded theory, as adding sites or cases is central to the process of theory generation. However, the criteria of selection may be different from those required to generalize from one site to another. In this case, the purpose of the selection is different; it is used for comparative purposes to test emerging theoretical ideas.

Now let us turn this discussion on its head and tie it back to sampling issues discussed in the previous chapter. It is a mistaken belief that problems of generalizing are confined to case-study research and the use of qualitative methods. Rather, statistical generalization is only possible when probability sampling is used, and then only to the population from which the sample was drawn. While some populations may be large, for example in national studies, they can also be very limited in size, for example a class of students. Once sample results are statistically generalized to the population, the problem still remains as to whether the findings about this population can be generalized to other populations or to other social contexts, such as other countries or other classes of students. Therefore, if a researcher wishes to generalize beyond a population, whether or not sampling is used, issues concerning the selection of the population are similar to those in the selection of case studies and of research sites in ethnographic research. There are only limited advantages in using samples and quantitative methods when it comes to generalizing, as the scope of statistical generalization is limited to the population selected. Beyond that population, the problems and their solutions are the same, regardless of whether quantitative or qualitative methods are used.

A Parable of Four Paradigms: Part 2

In chapter 4 we left the JJans with each team having undertaken research using its particular research strategy. The teams returned to JJ immediately after the *abductive* team had completed its work. Then the debates began about which was the superior research strategy.

The Post-mortem

Despite the fact that all the teams began their research on the basis of the exploratory study, with the general objective of trying to understand something of social life on

Earth, the strategies they adopted inevitably led them to give a rather different emphasis to the research questions, or even to use rather different questions. More particularly, they searched in different places for the answers. Hence, their findings looked rather different and were not strictly comparable.

Many debates ensued in the debriefing sessions that followed the expedition. The Inductivists claimed that their research strategy, and their careful attention to the elimination of subjectivity and bias, ensured that their results were a true record. The Deductivists were not so confident about having arrived at the truth. They argued that, given time and the testing of a wide variety of possible theories, their research strategy would allow them to find the best theory and to get as close to the truth as possible. It was a case of trial and error, of eliminating false theories. The Retroductivists acknowledged that the process of constructing models of structures and mechanisms, and the subsequent establishment of their existence, was very time-consuming and was not always successful. However, they believed in the superiority of their research strategy in arriving at explanations based on the real tendencies in the way things behave, and not just on approximate theories. The Abductivists argued for the superiority of their research strategy because only it had the potential to grasp the nature of the socially constructed reality of the participants. They considered this vital for arriving at a meaningful and useful account of social life anywhere.

The experience of this journey to Earth had a surprising outcome. In spite of each team's insistence that their research strategy was the best, there emerged a view that some benefits might be gained from combining strategies. What they had in mind was combining the results that each team had produced in the hope that this would produce a more detailed and complex picture of social life on Earth. However, they were not quite sure how to do this. It turned out that the advocates of this idea were mainly interested in subsuming the findings of other teams within the assumptions with which their own team worked. This did nothing to reduce the suspicion of and criticism by each team of the other teams' approaches and findings.

The Sequel

Five years later, a second social science expedition from JJ visited another university campus on Earth. This visit was motivated by the discussion of the earlier findings and the disputes that had arisen between the research communities about which team had produced the best understanding of life on Earth. The initial interest in comparative research continued, but now the focus was on university teaching and learning rather than on social problems on Earth. The same four research communities were represented, including some members of the previous expedition. However, this time they included two additional mixed teams.

Regardless of the confidence with which the research communities continued to defend their research strategies, each held private reservations about some aspects of what they had managed to achieve on the first expedition to Earth. Of course, they did not share these reservations with the other communities. For their own reasons, each research community supported the suggestion that the second expedition should visit another similar location on Earth. The Inductivists wanted to collect more data to provide further support for the generalizations that they wanted to be able to claim as universal. The Deductivists wanted to replicate and refine the theories they had begun to test on the first expedition, in the belief that this would get them nearer the truth. The Retroductivists wanted more time to find evidence for the existence of the structures that they had hypothesized, and, if necessary, to modify them in the light of further research. The Abductivists wanted to establish whether their emerging typologies of people, activities and social situations could also be found on another university campus. While the Abductivists recognized that any understanding of social life is specific to a particular time and place, they were also curious about how extensive the culture of campus life was on Earth.

This second visit revealed important divisions among the Abductivists: one group argued that further research required only the development of more detailed descriptions; a second group was adamant that the process of collecting data could not be separated from its analysis; a third group wanted to test aspects of the rich theoretical ideas contained in the typologies, using the Deductivist research strategy; and a fourth group argued that, while abstracting from participants' accounts of their social world is very important, there was more to social reality than the participants' understanding of it. This latter group believed that the social researcher was in a position to have greater knowledge than the participants about the wider circumstances and conditions within which social activity occurs. Therefore, it was legitimate to critique the participants' accounts, possibly from within some theoretical perspective.

Despite the heated debates that followed the first expedition, the need for dialogue between the research communities had led to an awareness among some members that there were possibilities for co-operation. These minorities in each community decided that the staunchly defended boundaries between the four paradigms, and their accompanying research strategies, were largely the result of the rigid adherence to certain philosophical principles. For practical purposes, they believed that it was useful to combine elements of different strategies. As a result, two mixed teams had been included in the second expedition. As might be expected, they were both regarded suspiciously by the dogmatic defenders of each community from which they had come.

One of the mixed teams, known as the 'IDs', advocated that the research strategies of the Inductivists and Deductivists should be combined. They believed that the Inductivist logic of enquiry should be used to generate descriptions of regularities, and, hence, possible explanations, and that Deductivist logic should then be used to test the explanations arrived at in this way. In short, social research could be seen as consisting of an ongoing cycle of generating theories and then testing them. Therefore, the IDs attached themselves to the Inductivists for the first stage of their research, and to the Deductivists for the second stage. Given time, they would continue the cycle of generating, testing and modifying theories, until they were satisfied that they had arrived at the best theory available. The IDs claimed many advantages over the two teams to which they were related. For example, they did not stop at the description of regularities like the Inductivists, and they had a superior way of arriving at relevant and testable theories to the Deductivists.

The second mixed team consisted of a branch of the Retroductivist research community. It became known as the Constructivist Retroductivists in contrast to the original Retroductivists who were referred to as the Structuralists. The Constructivist Retroductivists shared with the Structuralist Retroductivists the belief that explanations are achieved by the discovery of largely hidden structures and mechanisms, although they were more concerned with mechanisms than structures. However, their views of research differed from those of the Structuralist Retroductivists in two important ways. For a start, they regarded mechanisms as being part of the socially constructed reality of the participants and the cognitive resources that participants bring to any social situation. Therefore, they looked for mechanisms in the rules and sanctions that guide social action, rather than in some independent 'external' reality. The other way in which they differed was in their assumptions about the nature of social reality. They were known as 'constructivists' because they shared the same ideas about social reality as the Abductivists. Therefore, they were happy to work with the Abductivists to explore the concepts and meanings used by the participants. However, they differed from them in their views of the later stages of research; they looked for evidence of the rules and sanctions rather than listening to the participants' explanations of their conduct. They argued that these rules took on a hidden character because the participants were not always aware of them and might therefore not be able to give an adequate account of them. This might involve the researcher in constructing a model of such mechanisms and then, as for the structures used by the Structuralist Retroductivists, searching for evidence of their existence. The Constructivist Retroductivists, like the Abductivists, claimed the superiority of their research strategy over the Inductivists and Deductivists because of their ability to grasp the everyday reality of participants in any social world. In turn, they claimed superiority over the ability of most of the Abductivists to provide explanations, rather than just 'thick' descriptions of social activities or episodes.

New Beginnings

A major purpose of both visits to Earth was to settle, once and for all, which of the paradigms and accompanying research strategies provided the best approach to social research. However, one of the consequences that followed from the discussion of the experiences and findings of the first visit to Earth, and the subsequent experiences of the second visit, was that the four research communities became less dogmatic about the superiority of their own approach to social research.

These visits to Earth had stimulated much greater dialogue between the adherents of the competing paradigms than had occurred previously on JJ. Perhaps this was stimulated by the fact that they had lived together on their spacecraft during their visits to Earth. Nevertheless, the outcome was unexpected. JJans were aware that each research community could continue to argue for the superiority of its paradigm in the hope that weight of argument or numbers, or better access to the political processes involved in decision-making regarding research funding, might win the day. What they now acknowledged was that none of these processes could settle the matter in any kind of generally accepted objective or scientific way. In fact, they had come to the conclusion that there was no way to settle the disputes between paradigms to everyone's satisfaction; each research community had its own criteria regarding what constitutes a truly scientific paradigm.

The existence of the two new mixed groups, and the fact that they had operated successfully during the second visit, suggested that further co-operation between the research communities might be possible. However, the issue that kept nagging at them was the incompatibilities in their ontological and epistemological assumptions. Right up to the beginning of the second expedition, each community had publicly maintained the purity of its own set of assumptions and insisted that at least some of the assumptions of the other paradigm communities were incompatible with theirs. However, the experience of having to address the same research topic in the same social context, far removed from their own familiar surroundings, had forced them to re-examine their dogmatic positions. In spite of their disagreements about the appropriate logic of enquiry, the Inductivists and the Deductivists began to recognize that they worked with the same ontological assumptions. Similarly, the Constructivist Retroductivists and the Abductivists became very comfortable with the elements of their shared ontology.

Running alongside the paradigmatic disputes was another controversy concerning the superiority of quantitative or qualitative methods of data collection and analysis. However, on these visits to Earth, they had made an important discovery that different research communities frequently used the same methods. For example, questionnaires and interviews can serve different purposes depending on the ontological assumptions within which their use happened to be located.

One of the most important discoveries from the two expeditions was that, in spite of ontological differences, any of the teams could use the results of the research done by the other teams. This introduced the idea that research can be done in stages, with the findings of one team helping another team to design its first or later stages. Some research strategies might be more suited than others to answering particular types of research questions. For example, during the exploratory stage of the research, the methods used were based mainly on the assumptions of the Inductivists. What is more, practitioners from all six teams used these methods. In the end, all the teams made use of these preliminary descriptions of regularities in Earthling behaviour as a basis for their own attempts to understand or explain the behaviour in question. Hence, the research strategies could not only be used in sequence, but they could also use the same methods, albeit for different purposes, without any disastrous consequences.

The outcome of the experience of conducting social research on Earth, and the discussion and reflection that followed, led the JJans to leave aside the issue about which was the best paradigm and research strategy for producing new knowledge. Instead, they tried to discover ways in which the research communities could usefully co-operate and contribute towards the others' attempt to answer their particular research questions. This was not necessarily achieved by trying to combine various methods of data collection and analysis to answer a particular research question, but by exploring ways of using different research strategies for the different stages of a research project. The most difficult aspect of this discovery was to recognize the need, at least in some cases, to shift ontological assumptions between the different stages of the research, and not to fall into the trap of trying to force the followers of the other research strategies to adopt their own ontological assumptions.

While still maintaining their assumptions about the nature of social reality, there developed among JJan social scientists a greater willingness than was previously the case to take other research strategies more seriously. More importantly, there was a greater acceptance of the idea that the research communities should co-operate in trying to find answers to research questions. The outcome of this practice was to produce richer and more complex insights into social life.

Thus emerged a new era of tolerance and co-operation between the research communities, each recognizing the strengths and limitations of its own research strategy while at the same time being willing, when appropriate, to use the findings from research based on other strategies. None of the communities advocated a synthesis of research strategies as they all recognized this to be methodologically impossible. What they learnt to do was to moderate their dogmatism and appreciate what the other paradigms have to offer in the task of generating new social scientific knowledge.

This became known as the era of sophisticated pragmatism. And they all researched happily together forever after.

Now it is possible to draw some morals from this parable.

- Never try to combine research strategies with different ontological assumptions.
- While methods for collecting and analysing data can be used in the service of different research strategies, they can only be combined when they are used with the same ontological assumptions. Alternatively, if a variety of methods are used with different ontological assumptions, they can be used in sequence, with careful attention being given to the shifts in ontological assumptions that are involved.
- As there is no ultimate way to settle which of the research strategies is the best one, and as they have their particular uses as well as advantages and disadvantages, co-operation between paradigm communities is more productive than sectarian wars.

Just like all fairy tales, this parable has a happy ending. It points to what is possible. However, unbeknown to the JJans, the same paradigmatic disputes were raging among social scientists on Earth. One of the main features of these disputes is the difficulty that adherents of the different approaches to social enquiry and research strategies have in recognizing that their attempts to produce new knowledge are dependent on the assumptions adopted and the logic used to produce it. *Inductivists* and *deductivists* tend to believe either that they are producing universal truths about social life, or that they are trying to get as close as possible to such truths. *Retroductivists* believe that they are establishing the existence of real structures and mechanisms. However, the *abductivists* have the potential to be reflexive about their strategy and the status of the knowledge that it produces. Their ontological assumptions require them to recognize time and space limitations. In addition, they are aware of their role in the hermeneutic process of generating knowledge, in mediating between everyday language and social scientific language.

In practice, it is difficult for adherents of the different paradigms and research strategies to overcome the tendency to adopt an absolutist position with regard to assumptions, logic, methods and the status of their knowledge. Theoretical perspectives and research paradigms have a tendency to be treated like religions and to be the major source of practitioners' sense of professional identity. To profess adherence to a paradigm, and then to go against its assumptions and practices, is to invite powerful sanctions and to risk one's career prospects.

An important implication of the pragmatic position that the JJans were moving towards was to view paradigms and research strategies as heuristic devices to answer research questions. A particular research strategy can then be selected because it is judged as being the most appropriate for answering a particular research question. Given the differences between 'what' and 'why' questions in particular, it may be necessary to adopt different research strategies to answer different research questions. For example, a 'what' question may be answered using either the *inductive* or *abductive* research strategies, and a 'why' question by using either the *deductive*, *retroductive* or *abductive* strategies. While *abductivists* can handle both types of research questions, *deductivists* and *retroductivists* need the *inductive* or *abductive* strategies to produce descriptions of the patterns that they wish to explain. Hence, practitioners of one research strategy need to rely on practitioners of one or more other research strategies, or they must use more than one research strategy themselves. To be limited to the use of only one research strategy is to place unnecessary restrictions on the conduct of social research. Similarly, researchers may need to use both quantitative and qualitative methods in the one project.

Combining Methods

An outgrowth of the debates about the relative merits of qualitative and quantitative methods has been the expanding chorus of support for the idea of combining different types of methods. This has been variously described as 'multiple operationism' (Webb et al. 1966), 'combined operations' (Stacey 1969), 'mixed strategies' (Douglas 1976), 'linking data' (Fielding and Fielding 1986), 'combining quantitative and qualitative research' (Bryman 1988, 1992), 'multimethod research' (Brewer and Hunter 1989), 'mixing methods' (Brannen 1992) and 'mixed methodology' (Tashakkori and Teddlie 1998).

I will not attempt to review this literature here. Rather, I shall present a point of view that I believe provides a practical and useful approach to combining quantitative and qualitative methods in a research project. First, I shall offer a critique of the use of *triangulation* in social research, an idea that now has an accepted place in discourses on research methods. The advocates of triangulation see it as providing a framework within which methods can be combined. I shall argue that many of these combinations are not legitimate for ontological reasons, while others are appropriate when used with ontological sensitivity.

Triangulation

Building on the ideas of Campbell and Fiske (1959), the concept of triangulation was introduced into the social sciences by Webb et al. in 1966, and was taken up and elaborated soon after by Denzin (1970). Webb et al. were concerned to overcome the complacent dependence on single operational definitions of theoretical concepts, and to supplement the use of the interview or questionnaire with unobtrusive, non-reactive measures 'that do not require the cooperation of the

respondent and that do not themselves contaminate the response' (1966: 2). In
short, they wished to improve the validity of the measurement of theoretical
concepts by the use of independent measures, including some for which there
could be no reactivity from respondents. In claiming that all research methods are
biased, they argued for the use of a collection of methods, or multiple operationalism, which, they believed, would reduce the effect of the peculiar biases of each
one. Thus Webb et al. advocated the triangulation of *measurement* processes in
the search for the validity of theoretical propositions: 'When a hypothesis can
survive the confrontation of a series of complementary methods of testing, it
contains a degree of validity unattainable by one tested within the more con-
stricted framework of a single method' (Webb et al. 1966: 174). It is important to
note here that what they advocated was not the combination of different methods
to produce more reliable results, but the testing of a hypothesis using different
measures of the same concept.

In taking up this concern, Denzin (1970: 13) argued that 'sociologists must
learn to employ multiple methods in the analysis of the same empirical event', on
the assumption that each method will reveal different aspects of empirical reality.
He used the work of Campbell and Fiske, and Webb et al., as his starting-point
and shared their concern about bias and validity. However, he advocated the use
of multiple triangulation that involves the use of a variety of data sources,
investigators, theories and methodologies.[5] Denzin allowed for both *within-
method* triangulation – using various measures within one method, such as a
survey questionnaire with different scales measuring the same 'empirical unit'[6] –
and *between-method* triangulation which combines dissimilar methods to measure the same unit or concept. Denzin preferred the latter because 'the flaws of
one method are often the strengths of another, and by combining methods,
observers can achieve the best of each, while overcoming their unique deficiencies'
(Denzin 1970: 308). Thus, the effectiveness of triangulation rests on the assumption that the methods or measurements used will not share the same biases. It is
claimed that their assets will be exploited and their liabilities neutralized (Jick
1983: 138). For Brewer and Hunter, the multi-method approach is a 'strategy to
*attack a research problem with an arsenal of methods that have non-overlapping
weaknesses in addition to their complementary strengths*' (Brewer and Hunter
1989: 17).

Neither Denzin nor his mentors acknowledged the source of the triangulation
metaphor. However, later supporters of his position have referred to its origin in
navigation, military strategy and surveying (Jick 1983: 136; Smith 1981: 357;
Hammersley and Atkinson 1995: 231). Berg (1995) has implied this source in his
definition of triangulation, which, like Denzin's, uses a symbolic interactionist
perspective, but assumes an objectivist ontology. He has suggested that when they
observe events,

---

[5] Denzin has used the concepts of 'method', 'methodology' and 'methodological' interchangeably. My
discussion of triangulation will concentrate on methods and data and will not include investigators and
theories. Combining investigators can be useful, but combining theories is difficult to put into practice,
unless by theories are meant perspectives or paradigms.

[6] This concept of Denzin's seems to imply a concern with variables rather than social processes.

researchers assume reality is deeply affected by the actions of all participants including their own. Each method thus reveals slightly different facets of the same
symbolic reality. Every method is a different line of sight directed toward the same
point, observing social and symbolic reality. By combining several lines of sight,
researchers obtain a better, more substantial picture of reality; a richer, more
complete array of symbols and theoretical concepts; and a means of verifying
many of these elements. The use of multiple lines of sight is frequently called
triangulation. (Berg 1995: 4–5)

An explicit statement of how the metaphor is supposed to apply to social
research comes from Hammersley and Atkinson.

> For someone wanting to locate their position on a map, a single landmark can only
> provide the information that they are situated somewhere along a line in a particular
> direction from the landmark. With two landmarks, however, their exact position can
> be pin-pointed by taking bearings on both landmarks; they are at the point where the
> two lines cross. In social research, if one relies on a single piece of data there is the
> danger that undetected error in the data-production process may render the analysis
> incorrect. If, on the other hand, diverse kinds of data lead to the same conclusion,
> one can be a little more confident in that conclusion. This confidence is well founded
> to the degree that the different kinds of data have different types of error built into
> them. (Hammersley and Atkinson 1995: 231)

However, I want to argue that the triangulation metaphor in social science grossly
misrepresents its use in surveying (see Blaikie 1991). As we have seen, the view of
triangulation commonly adopted by social scientists is that it refers to the measurement of some concepts by the use of two or more measurements or methods.
The equivalent in surveying is the 'fixing' of a position on the surface of the earth
by the 'observation' of two known positions from it. However, this is a special
case of what is technically known as resection. To elaborate, resection is used to fix
an unknown position by measuring from it, the angles subtended between at least
three known positions, or, less commonly, the true bearings to two known positions. Triangulation is used for something rather different. In geodetic surveying,[7]
it is the method for locating

> a point from two others of known distance apart, given the angles of the triangle
> formed by the three points. By repeated application of the principle, if a series of
> points form the apices of a chain or network of connected triangles of which the
> angles are measured, the lengths of all the unknown sides and the relative positions of
> the points may be computed when the length of one of the sides is known. (Clark
> 1951: 145)

This technique is used to accurately fix the position of reference points on the
surface of the earth.[8] It is an economical method of fixing such positions, as it

---

[7] Geodetic surveying is concerned with the precise location on the earth's surface of a system of widely
separated positions. The relative relationships of these positions, in terms of length and direction, and
their absolute position in terms of latitude, longitude and elevation above mean sea level, provide a
framework of controls in which more localized forms of surveying and engineering can take place.
[8] In some countries, these positions are marked with permanent signals called 'trig' stations.

requires the very accurate measurement of only one side of one of the triangles in the network;[9] the rest of the measurement is done by simply observing the angles of all the triangles in the network. The process provides a robust fixing of positions.

The purpose of this digression is to indicate that in its original form, triangulation was not used as a process for checking the reliability of single measurements, but for producing sufficient measurements to locate points on the earth's surface economically. Normally, any position requires only the minimum number of measurements to fix it. In so far as triangulation may incorporate an excess of measurements to fix a position, for example through an extended network of triangles, it simply allows for a more precise adjustment of 'errors' due to the limitations of the instruments and the observers, and the vagaries of the conditions under which the measurements are made. However, while such gains are considered to be important, they are usually small and have nothing to do with the adjustment of the so-called bias of a number of different methods of measurements. Apart from the measurement of one side of a triangle in a network, all other measurements (of the angles) are of the same kind using the same type of instrument.

Therefore, the use of the triangulation analogy in sociology is misleading. It has usually been concerned with reducing error or bias rather than simply establishing the existence of some phenomenon, or the value of some variable. As we have seen, in the original social science version it was intended to confirm a proposition by operationalizing theoretical concepts in a variety of ways, for example measuring social status by level of education, occupational prestige and level of income. However, each of these measures is different in character and entails different assumptions.

The triangulation metaphor makes some sense if it is applied to the common procedure used in questionnaires where a number of questions designed to elicit the same information are scattered throughout. Similarly, in attitude scaling, a number of items are used to measure an attitude, or a dimension of an attitude. In both cases, the multiple measures can improve validity, but, more particularly, precision. This was part of the original conception of triangulation and what Denzin (1970) has referred to as *within-method* triangulation.

In claiming for social science triangulation the possibility of more valid measurement, the advocates need to be able to interpret both convergence and divergence of results produced by the use of different methods or data sources. Brewer and Hunter have presented a confident view on this issue.

> The multimethod strategy is simple, but powerful. For if our various methods have weaknesses that are truly different, then their convergent findings may be accepted with far greater confidence than any single method's findings would warrant. Each new set of data increases our confidence that the research results reflect reality rather than methodological error. And divergent findings are equally important, but for another reason. They signal the need to analyze a research problem further and to be cautious in interpreting the significance of any one set of data. (Brewer and Hunter 1989: 17)

---

[9] These triangles commonly have sides of a few kilometres in length. Today, with electronic rather than just steel tape methods of linear measurement, sides of the triangles can also be measured. And even this advance has been supplemented by the use of satellites, known as the Global Positioning System.

While this is a useful caution in the case of divergent results, unfortunately, convergent results can also be achieved with methods that share the same weaknesses. To suggest that methods must be selected with complementary weaknesses is to assume that the weaknesses or biases are known. In addition, the idea of convergence assumes a single 'objective', external reality. Brewer and Hunter are so confident about the benefits of the use of multi-methods that they see it as providing a solution to the 'deep methodological divisions in the social sciences' (1989: 22).

There is a danger in adopting a simple-minded view of triangulation, i.e. that a combination of different methods and data will provide a more complete picture of some phenomenon, like taking photographs of an object from different points of view. 'One should not, therefore, adopt a naively "optimistic" view that the aggregation of data from different sources will unproblematically add up to produce a more complete picture' (Hammersley and Atkinson 1995: 232).

When researchers use the *inductive* or *deductive* strategies, convergence can be interpreted either as each measure being relatively unbiased, or both being similarly biased. However, lack of convergence leaves open the question of which of the measures might be biased. When researchers use the *abductive* strategy, with data from different social actors or groups, convergence may mean a consensus exists on how reality has been socially constructed; a lack of convergence may reflect legitimate and different constructions of reality and cannot be used to attribute bias to any method. When researchers use the *retroductive* strategy, there is no way that the validity of any 'empirical' data can be established; all measurement has to be directed and interpreted using the constructed hypothetical model. In the end, the degree to which any model is a valid representation of reality will be a matter of judgement. This is an inherent problem for the *retroductive* research strategy, regardless of issues associated with triangulation.

With an emphasis on the comparison of results from different quantitative and qualitative studies on the same issue, Firestone has supported Brewer and Hunter's position that such qualitative and quantitative studies can either corroborate each other, if they produce consistent results, or can suggest that more research is needed if their findings diverge. Comparing the results may suggest further lines of enquiry. In other words, different research projects can be triangulated.

> Each method type uses different techniques of presentation to project divergent assumptions about the world and different means to persuade the reader of its conclusions. Yet, they are not antithetical. They present the reader with different kinds of information and can be used to triangulate to gain greater confidence in one's conclusions. (Firestone 1987: 16)

However, Jick (1983) has acknowledged that it is difficult to decide whether or not results have converged. 'In practice ... there are few guide-lines for systematically ordering eclectic data in order to determine congruence or validity .... there are no formal tests to discriminate between methods to judge their applicability' (Jick 1983: 142). He went on to argue that

> the process of compiling research material based on multi-methods is useful whether there is convergence or not. ... Overall, the triangulating investigator is left to search

for a logical pattern in mixed-method results. His or her claim to validity rests on judgment.... One begins to view the researcher as builder and creator, piecing together many pieces of a complex puzzle into a coherent whole. (Jick 1983: 144)

The introduction of judgement to settle the matter of convergence or divergence makes the test of validity far more tenuous than the originators of triangulation had intended.

A number of more recent writers have moved beyond the naive view of triangulation and have argued that it can perform a variety of functions. For example, Rossman and Wilson (1985) have used combinations of quantitative and qualitative data for three purposes: *corroboration*, *elaboration* and *initiation*. At least they have recognized that data produced by different methods will invariably not converge. *Corroboration* is the classic use of triangulation to establish validity, *elaboration* occurs when the variety of data expands understanding of the phenomenon, perhaps by providing different perspectives, and *initiation* refers to the use of non-convergent data in a provocative way to produce new interpretations and conclusions, to suggest further areas of research, or to reformulate research questions. They have illustrated these uses in their own research.

Another approach to the problems of convergence, divergence and even contradiction has been proposed by Mathison (1988). She has been critical of two major assumptions used in triangulation: that bias inherent in any particular method, data source or investigator will be cancelled out if multiples of these are used, and that triangulation will result in convergence on the truth about some social phenomenon. She rightly points out that while different methods may produce different results because of the 'bias' in each measure, 'different methods may tap different ways of knowing' (1988: 14). We might add, different ways of knowing different realities.

In practice, triangulation as a strategy provides a rich and complex picture of some social phenomenon being studied, but rarely does it provide a clear path to a singular view of what is the case. I suggest that triangulation as a strategy provides evidence for the *researcher* to make sense of social phenomenon, but that the triangulation *strategy* does not, in and of itself, do this.... The value of triangulation is not a technical solution to a data collection and analysis problem, it is a technique which provides more and better evidence from which researchers can *construct meaningful propositions* about the social world.... So whether the data converge, are inconsistent, or are contradictory the researcher must attempt to construct explanations for the data and about the data. (Mathison 1988: 15)

Mathison has argued that constructing explanations requires locating the data at hand within an understanding of the wider situation in which they are located and against background knowledge of this type of phenomenon. In the process, the view of triangulation shifts from a technical solution to problems of validity, to placing the responsibility on the researcher to construct plausible explanations for whatever the various sources of data reveal.

This discussion of the uses of triangulation takes us back to the issue of the relationship between research strategies and research methods. While there may not be a tight relationship, it is possible that a researcher may adopt particular ontological assumptions when using a particular method. For example, a researcher may use a questionnaire within the *deductive* strategy, and then in-depth interviewing within the *abductive* strategy. To then attempt to combine the data produced by these two methods is to fail to recognize the differences in ontological assumptions within which each is used. What is more common is for a researcher to use a combination of qualitative and quantitative methods within one research strategy, say the *inductive* or *deductive* strategies. The ontological problems of combining different methods, particularly quantitative and qualitative methods, is not an issue in these two research strategies; all methods are interpreted within a consistent ontology. In this case, qualitative data are likely to be viewed as uncoded quantitative data that the researcher has to translate into variables rather than, say, evidence of the social actors' meanings or constructed reality. Where meanings are recognized, they will be conceived differently than they would in the *abductive* research strategy.

> From the perspective provided by the positivist approach,[10] data that are qualitative in the sense of describing actors' meanings are data about mental states or events that cause the people under study to behave the way they do. The problem that data thus conceived presents for positivists is that of obtaining reliable measures of these states or events, and the solution frequently offered is triangulation.... [However,] meanings of actions are not the same as the mental states of the actors. (Halfpenny 1979: 815–16)

Genuine users of the *abductive* research strategy will not find triangulation, as expounded, for example, by Denzin, an attractive proposition; issues of bias and validity have different meanings from those used in the *inductive* and *deductive* research strategies. With an ontology that allows for multiple realities (Schütz 1945), and an epistemology that recognizes that accounts of any social world are relative in time and space, and to the observer, the use of multiple data sources and multiple observers do not do for the *abductive* strategy what it is claimed they do for the *inductive* and *deductive* strategies. This is because Interpretivists do not share the same ontological assumptions, and, therefore, the same kind of anxiety about bias and validity. Triangulation, as originally conceived, is irrelevant to the *abductive* strategy.

In his critique of Denzin's style of symbolic interactionism, Silverman (1985) has noted Denzin's use of 'method triangulation' to overcome partial views and to present something like a complete picture.

> Underlying this suggestion is, ironically... elements of a positivist frame of reference which assumes a single (undefined) reality and treats accounts as multiple mappings of this reality. Interestingly, Denzin talks about 'measuring the same unit' and quotes from a text which supports multiple methods within a logic of hypothesis testing. Conversely, from an interactionist position, one would not expect a defence of hypothesis-testing nor, more importantly, of social 'units' which exist in a single form despite their multiple definitions....

---

[10] The *inductive* and *deductive* research strategies adopt the same ontological assumptions that Halfpenny attributed to 'the positivist approach'.

> For an interactionist...without bias there would be no phenomenon. Conse-
> quently...actions and accounts are 'situated'. The sociologist's role is not to adju-
> dicate between participants' competing versions but to understand the situated work
> that they do.
>   Of course, this does not imply that the sociologist should avoid generating data in
> multiple ways....The 'mistake' only arises in using data to adjudicate between
> accounts. (Silverman 1985: 105–6)

Cicourel (1973) advocated a specific use of triangulation in ethnomethodology
that is internally consistent and very different from its traditional use. He used
what he called 'indefinite triangulation' to 'reveal the irreparable but practical
nature of accounts used by subjects and researchers' (1973: 124). In essence, this
use of triangulation involves social actors, the researcher and typists, using audio
recordings and transcripts of conversations to produce a variety of versions of the
original interaction.

> I use the expression 'indefinite triangulation' to suggest that every procedure that
> seems to 'lock in' evidence, thus to claim a level of adequacy, can itself be subjected
> to the same sort of analysis that will in turn produce yet another indefinite arrange-
> ment of new particulars or a rearrangement of previously established particulars in
> 'authoritative', 'final', 'formal' accounts. The indefinite triangulation notion
> attempts to make visible the practicality and inherent reflexivity of everyday
> accounts. The elaboration of circumstances and particulars of an occasion can be
> subjected to an indefinite re-elaboration of the 'same' or 'new' circumstances and
> particulars. (Cicourel 1973: 124)

Cicourel illustrated this procedure from a study that gathered information on the
language acquisition of young children in the home setting. Mother and child were
tape-recorded for one hour during lunch. The tape was transcribed verbatim and
the transcript read by the mother while listening to the tape; her comments were
recorded to produce another version. The typist listened to the tape again and
described what she thought was going on; she corrected her original transcript
where she felt this was necessary. Phonetic transcription produced another version.

> With a number of different versions of an interaction scene, the problem is deciding
> which version captures the child's language, the child's referencing ability, the par-
> ent's constructions, and so on.
>   The reader could now say that we should simply combine the different versions to
> produce the 'best' one possible, but the point is that different versions could have
> been produced indefinitely by simply hiring different typists and providing the
> mother with different transcripts. (Cicourel, 1973: 124)

This use of triangulation is consistent with the ontological and epistemological
assumptions of at least some versions of the *abductive* research strategy. Nevertheless, the question arises as to why it should be called triangulation.
  Richardson (1994) has provided a postmodern critique of triangulation that
rejects the assumptions on which its validating role is based. She has argued
provocatively that in using mixed-genre texts, postmodernists do not triangulate;
they *crystallize*.

We recognize that there are far more than 'three sides' from which to approach the world.

I propose that the central image for 'validity' for postmodernist texts is not the triangle – a rigid, fixed, two-dimensional object. Rather, the central image is the crystal, which combines symmetry and substance with an infinite variety of shapes, substances, transmutations, multidimensionalities, and angles of approach. Crystals grow, change, alter, but are not amorphous.

Crystals are prisms that reflect externalities and refract within themselves, creating different colors, patterns, arrays, casting off in different directions. What we see depends upon our angle of repose. Not triangulation, crystallization. In postmodernist mixed-genre texts, we have moved from plane geometry to light theory, where light can be both waves and particles.

Crystallization, without losing structure, deconstructs the traditional idea of 'validity'... and crystallization provides us with a deepened, complex, thoroughly partial, understanding of the topic. (Richardson 1994: 522)

Triangulation has become an icon towards which researchers are supposed to genuflect. However, as we have seen, closer examination reveals some serious difficulties in its implementation. The distortion in its adaptation from surveying and navigation, the vagueness in the manner in which it has been formulated, the naivety with respect to differences in ontological assumptions, the tendency to impose a single, absolutist ontology on multiple socially constructed realities, and the problems of interpreting convergent and divergent results, make the triangulation of methods and data a very doubtful activity.

Perhaps it is time to stop using the concept of triangulation in social science (see Blaikie 1991). Some of the reasons for this are that:

- lip-service is paid to it but few researchers use it in its original conception as a validity check (mainly because convergence is very rare);
- it means so many things to so many people; and
- it encourages a naive view of ontology and epistemology.

What is needed is a more systematic understanding of how different research strategies, methods and data can be used creatively within a research project, for example, as a developmental process, or as a way of stimulating theory construction. Neither of these uses is remotely related to multiple 'fixes' on social reality. We need different metaphors to identify these activities (see Miles and Huberman 1984, 1994; Mathison 1988).

Legitimate Combinations

Recognition of the problems associated with the use of triangulation in the social sciences should not be interpreted as suggesting that methods cannot be combined. Many of the examples that are offered in the name of triangulation are actually examples of something else, namely, the use of different methods in sequence rather than different pictures of some reality. A great deal of research involves, or should involve, a series of stages in which methods produce data of a particular kind which is then used to make decisions about how to proceed with the data collection at the next stage. While it is necessary to use the same ontological assumptions at each stage, researchers can switch from one set of assumptions to another between stages.

A common example of such stages occurs in 'good' survey research when an exploratory phase, that might include observation or even participant observation, and, perhaps, in-depth interviewing, is used to assess respondents' level of knowledge about or awareness of the issue being investigated, the meanings associated with it, the language that they use to talk about it, and the range of possible responses that they might give if asked a particular question about it. All of this might be achieved using qualitative methods within an *abductive* research strategy. The results of this investigation can then be used to develop, say, a structured interview schedule that approaches the phenomenon from the point of view of the researcher's construction of reality. A further phase might follow in which a few carefully selected case studies from the sample are investigated in depth by one or more qualitative methods. This is but one way in which different methods can be used in sequence. What is important about this example is that the methods are not triangulated or even combined. Each is used in the service of a particular research strategy in order to develop an understanding of the phenomenon and to assist the researcher in presenting a case for a particular answer to a research question.

This idea of methods of different types being used sequentially is certainly not new. Some time ago, Sieber (1973) provided a very clear statement of how 'fieldwork' and 'survey methods' can be integrated in this way. It is still a useful statement. He has identified the following contributions that each method can make to the other.

1 *Survey design*   Fieldwork can contribute to the development of a meaningful survey design; a period of exploratory interviews and observations can assist in the formulation of the research problem (and research questions), the development of hypotheses, and the identification of suitable respondents.
2 *Survey data collection*   Exploratory interviews and observation can yield valuable information about the receptivity, frames of reference and span of attention of respondents; it can also help in the development of quantitative instruments (question wording, response categories, and items for scale development) and in gaining on-site support for the project.
3 *Survey analysis*   Fieldwork can assist in the analysis and interpretation of survey data by: providing a theoretical structure; validating or providing plausibility for the survey findings; clarifying puzzling responses; assisting in the interpretation of the results; and providing illustrative case studies.
4 *Design of fieldwork*   Surveys can provide statistical profiles of the populations within which the study is to be conducted. (Although they are not mentioned by Sieber, we could add that statistical patterns established by a survey can provide the source of the problem to be investigated or an answer to a 'what' question.)
5 *Fieldwork data collection*   A survey of a population's characteristics can help to ensure that the selection of informants in fieldwork is not biased in favour of

elites, and that information is available about categories of people who were not included as informants. A survey can also provide leads on the topics to be covered in interviews and can cover basic background data.

6 *Analysis of qualitative field materials*   Surveys can correct the holistic fallacy, the tendency of field observers to see all aspects of a social situation as congruent; they can demonstrate the generality of a single observation; they can verify fieldwork observations; and they can cast a new light on field observations.

Sieber's examples are confined to the mutual contributions of surveys and more informal methods such as observation and unstructured interviewing. Other combinations of methods could also be considered in the same way.

To repeat an earlier point, this practice of combining methods usually involves a time sequence in which the use of one method provides data that can inform the subsequent use of other methods. It matters not whether qualitative methods precede quantitative methods, or the reverse; a range of pragmatic considerations will determine that decision. It is possible that two methods of a different type might be used concurrently, but their role will still be to provide some assistance to the use of other methods, not to provide a more complete unbiased picture of social reality.

Research Strategies and Methods

The primary purpose of this chapter has been to examine the implications of the choice of research strategy for selection of methods of data collection and analysis, in particular, whether there is any relationship between research strategies and methods. There has been considerable discussion in the literature on the relationship between paradigms, or approaches to social enquiry, and research methods. However, as the literature on research methods has been largely silent on the topic of the logic of enquiry, or research strategies, and as I regard the choice of research strategy as central in the design of social research, we shall now review this relationship. I will do this in the context of summarizing the main issues covered in this chapter.

Qualitative and Quantitative Methods and Data

I hope I have shown elsewhere (Blaikie 1993a) that the qualitative/quantitative dichotomy does not do justice to different combinations of ontology and epistemology that can be identified in the major traditions in the social sciences. I consider the quantitative/qualitative distinction to be appropriate for classifying *methods* and *data*, for *researchers* who use these methods and data, and for *research* in which they are used. Beyond these uses, such as referring to qualitative and quantitative paradigms, the dichotomy just leads to confusion.

While it may be useful to classify methods as quantitative and qualitative, what needs to be identified is the type of data that is ultimately generated for analysis.

As we have seen, data can be presented either in numbers or in words at different stages in the research process. For example, we expect questionnaires and structured interviews to produce numerical data, even if some questions might initially have been open-ended. On the other hand, we expect in-depth interviews to produce mainly non-numerical data, even though some elementary counting might be used. Some methods, such as content analysis, can produce either numerical or non-numerical data, depending on the choice of the researcher. What can be distinguished clearly is the method of data analysis; some use numbers and some use words. However, when the results are written up, the outcomes of quantitative analysis will need to be presented in both numbers and words. The critical issue is what the words are based on. Words used to present the results of quantitative analysis simply express numerically based relationships, whereas in results from qualitative analysis, the words may be describing abstractions, such as ideal types, which have been derived from lay accounts and/or researchers' descriptions of observations and other encounters with social actors.

What is important to recognize is that when applied to data, the quantitative/ qualitative distinction is a matter of degree. Most data in the social sciences, certainly primary data, begin in a qualitative form; they are produced by either social actors or researchers about some aspect of social life. They are then processed or coded to some extent, either to remain in words or to be transformed into numbers. These processes distance the data from social life to varying degrees; some qualitative data 'retain the integrity of the phenomenon' while, at the other extreme, quantitative data can become very remote from their origins.

The researcher is largely responsible for determining how much processing they require social actors to do. This can range from asking them to provide accounts of some aspect of their world or experiences in their own language, to requiring them to transform their 'knowledge', or their awareness of their actions, into the researcher's language and categories. It is then up to the researcher to decide what to do with the various forms in which social actors 'respond'. Some data, of course, are produced directly by the activities of the researcher, for example by observation, thus requiring no processing on the part of social actors.

Secondary data introduce further steps in the processing, by social actors whom the researcher has not encountered directly (e.g. a diarist from the past), by intermediaries (e.g. journalists or record-keepers) and by other researchers. The final form of the data will determine the kind of analysis that can be undertaken and the options available for reporting it.

Paradigms and Methods

There is no necessary connection between approaches to social enquiry (paradigms), research strategies and methods of data collection and analysis. While some methods may be more commonly associated with a particular approach or research strategy, this is largely a matter of convention rather than a methodological requirement. However, this does not mean that methods can be used without ontological and epistemological assumptions. Rather, if a particular method (e.g. unstructured interviewing) is associated with the *inductive* research strategy, in that context it will be serving that strategy's assumptions. Similarly, if the same method is associated with the *abductive* research strategy, the data that it produces will need to be interpreted within that strategy's assumptions. In other words, methods can serve a number of masters, but they need to change their 'colours' to do so, and the data they produce will need to be interpreted within the particular ontological and epistemological assumptions that are adopted.

Many researchers appear to use particular methods with little or no awareness of the ontological and epistemological assumptions that they have adopted. In my experience, this is common among quantitative researchers who have been socialized in, or have confined themselves to, a narrow research tradition; their assumptions are taken for granted and are unlikely to be seen to involve choices. On the other hand, other researchers have the capacity, and find the need, to move between paradigms, either for different research projects, or even within a single project. This requires a sophisticated awareness of both the assumptions and the logics of enquiry that are being used at any time.

Combining Methods

There are two main ways in which different research methods can be combined in a single project: within a common approach or paradigm; or in a sequence, possibly with switches between approaches/paradigms. The first of these alternatives allows for the use of qualitative and quantitative methods together, provided both types are used with the same ontological assumptions. It is only under these circumstances that most of what has been written about triangulation is relevant. Different methods *can* be used to explore aspects of the same (assumed) 'objective' reality, regardless of whether they use words or numbers. They might also be used to explore (assumed) single or multiple socially constructed realities, although some methods (qualitative) might be more suitable for this than others. Data from different sources can be translated from one form to another (although usually from qualitative to quantitative) with impunity. However, what cannot be done is to combine data that are produced by methods that each deal with different (assumed) realities. It is not possible to use data related to a single 'absolute' reality to test the validity of data related to multiple 'constructed' realities, regardless of what methods are used in each case.

If different types of methods are used with the same ontological assumptions, the implications of achieving convergence or divergence of results can be handled, either in terms of providing reciprocal support, in the case of convergence, or as an explanatory challenge, in the case of divergence. When different methods are used with different assumptions, convergence and divergence take on different meanings; the results may relate to different realities. While converging results cannot be used as any kind of test of validity, or for mutual support, comparison *can* be used to stimulate theory development or further research.

The second alternative is to use different methods, possibly with different assumptions, for different stages of a research project. It is not necessary for each stage to adopt a consistent set of ontological and epistemological assumptions; the researcher can switch back and forth between research strategies during the course of the research. However, data from each stage cannot be readily translated, but can be *interpreted* in the light of data gathered at another stage. For example, statistical results from a survey could be interpreted, i.e. be better understood in terms of the meanings and motives that have produced the statistical patterns, using some in-depth interviews with a carefully selected subsample of respondents. Switching between paradigms requires considerable awareness of the various sets of assumptions that are being used and the capacity to keep the various (assumed) realities separate.

Conclusion

From the complexities of this review of the views on the relationships between qualitative and quantitative paradigms, methods and data, the following can be concluded.

1 At least five levels of decision in the research enterprise need to be distinguished: approaches to social enquiry (paradigms or perspectives); research strategies (logics of enquiry); methods of data collection; the form of the data (involving methods of data reduction); and methods of data analysis.
2 It is *not* appropriate to apply the 'qualitative' and 'quantitative' labels to approaches (paradigms) and strategies.
3 It *is* appropriate to apply these labels to methods and data, and to research and researchers who use the particular methods. However, the distinction between data that are labelled in these two ways is not only a matter of degree, but is also the result of the application of particular kinds of data reduction techniques.
4 Making these distinctions between levels allows for various combinations between them, depending on the research objectives, the social context and practical contingencies. Common combinations reveal conventions rather than logical connections.
5 However, there *are* fundamental differences in the research strategies. The extent to which researchers follow a particular strategy consistently, or combine them successfully, is an empirical question.
6 The extent to which approaches, strategies, methods and data can be combined needs careful consideration. There are legitimate combinations (particularly in sequence) and illegitimate combinations (methods of any type used in the service of different ontological and epistemological assumptions).
7 Convergent or divergent results of any kind can be used to stimulate theoretical development and to suggest new directions for research. Only in the special case when methods are used in the service of the same set of ontological assumptions can confirmation or a test of validity be entertained.
8 The aim of this analysis has been to help researchers become more aware of what they are assuming and doing when they make decisions about the various components of a research design.

Finally, I offer some specific comments on the relationship between research strategies and methods. When the *inductive* research strategy is being used, any kind of data is appropriate; generalizations can be produced from data in either words or numbers. While numbers may allow for more precise propositions, the relevance, or the possibility of achieving such precision, will be a matter of judgement or circumstances; sometimes using words alone may be all that is possible or necessary. In any case, propositions in words are still necessary in quantitative studies. The issue is how such propositions were arrived at, and that is a matter of choice or opportunity.

The *deductive* research strategy is more commonly used in association with quantitative methods and data, but this need not be so. Qualitative researchers may also construct theories in the deductive form, particularly as a conclusion to a study, but users of the *abductive* research strategy are unlikely to set out with a fully developed deductive theory. The more important issue is whether researchers are engaged in theory construction (*induction* or *abduction*) or theory testing (*deduction*) rather than the type of methods or data they are using.

Because the *retroductive* strategy is still relatively undeveloped in the social sciences, these comments must be tentative. However, it is clear from research inspired by Harré's constructivist version that a combination of methods can be used. Pawson (1995) and Pawson and Tilley (1997) have certainly advocated the use of both quantitative and qualitative methods, very much as a sequence, in terms of establishing and exploring observed patterns, contexts and mechanisms. Both these versions of Realism rely on cognitive mechanisms for their explanations and they incorporate constructivist (interpretive) elements. The question of the ontological status of cognitive mechanisms (in contrast to the structures and mechanisms in Bhaskar's version), that are dependent on the socially constructed reality social actors inhabit, needs further consideration.

In the *abductive* strategy, and other versions of Interpretivism, qualitative methods predominate because of the nature of the subject-matter (social actors' meanings, motives, and interpretations) at its core. However, the patterns for which understanding or explanation is sought may have been, or may need to be, established using quantitative data.

It should now be clear that the choice of research strategy does not determine the method or methods that should be used in social research. However, careful consideration needs to be given to what a method is supposed to do for a particular research strategy and the ontological and epistemological assumptions that lie behind its use at a particular time and in a particular place.

8

Sample Research Designs

Introduction

Now that the core elements and the choices involved in preparing a research design have been explored, I shall conclude with some examples of what research designs might look like, were you to follow the scheme laid out in the previous chapters. These four examples cover a range of research objectives as well as illustrating how each of the four research strategies can be used. They are intentionally simple designs of the kind that are common in postgraduate research, and they are presented in outline only. More complex designs, using more sophisticated methods, can easily be developed from these designs by researchers who wish to use them. My aim is to provide basic starting-points.

The four designs follow a research programme in the sociology of the environment. As I have been working in this field off and on in recent years, I am reasonably familiar with the literature and have had experience in doing this kind of research. Some publications on this research programme can be found in Blaikie (1992, 1993b), Blaikie and Ward (1992) and Blaikie and Drysdale (1994). However, I have made modifications to the actual research projects to simplify them.

The designs also follow a progression. The first is a descriptive study that establishes some patterns using the *inductive* research strategy. The next two designs take up some of these and other patterns and try to explain them using the *deductive* and *retroductive* research strategies. The fourth returns to description, but also tries to understand differences in behaviour using the *abductive* research strategy.

For pragmatic reasons, this research programme is assumed to have started with the first design in the early 1990s. As the other three designs build on the results from this project, they are set in the early and middle 1990s. Again for pragmatic reasons, I have not attempted to connect with all the relevant literature. The reviews of the literature are illustrative only.

Finally, I would not like these research designs to be used as exemplars. Their major purpose is to give some idea of what has to go into a research design, how it might be structured, and, depending on the topic, the kinds of research questions and the research strategies that might be adopted, and how these decisions relate to the context, the units to be studied, and the research methods. However, they are also written in such a way that they review what has been covered in the preceding chapters. Therefore, any slavish following of how I have presented them may not produce the most appropriate designs. In any case, there is rather more commentary in these examples than might be necessary in an actual design. Every research design has to be based on choices that are appropriate to the investigation of a topic and set of research questions, at a particular time, in a particular place, and taking into account the motives and goals of the researcher.

Research Design 1   Environmental Worldviews and Behaviour among Students and Residents

Statement of the topic/problem

The project will investigate the environmental worldviews and behaviour of people from different backgrounds in Melbourne, Australia.

Environmental issues have received considerable attention in the Australian media in recent years. Global problems, such as the greenhouse effect and the depletion of the ozone layer over the south polar region, have dominated, and have been the subject of discussion in public forums. At the same time, environmental issues have featured prominently in both federal and state politics, and in debates about the logging of native forests and mining in national parks.

While concern about the environment goes back many decades, with the 1970s seeing the most recent wave of interest, the level of public awareness, and the degree to which politicians have been willing to include it in their agendas, appears to be at a higher level now than at previous times. Many events around the world, not the least being the Chernobyl disaster, have brought into stark relief the global nature of environmental problems and the urgency with which they need to be addressed.

For anyone interested in raising environmental awareness and changing behaviour towards the environment, it is necessary to know the current status of environmental worldviews and behaviour. This project aims to provide such knowledge.

Motives and goals

The primary motivation for this study is the desire to fill a gap in knowledge about the nature of environmental worldviews and the level of environmentalism in Australia. Extensive research has been conducted in this field in the United States, and in some other parts of the world, but systematic data on Australia are largely absent. Hence, there is no basis for examining differences in environmental worldviews and behaviour in the Australian population. A related minor motivation is a curiosity about how the situation in Australia compares with that in the United States.

A second major motivation is to give students doing a degree in socio-environmental studies at the Royal Melbourne Institute of Technology some practical experience, not only in the use of social research methods, but on a topic of relevance to their programme.

Research questions and objectives

The study will be mainly descriptive, although an attempt will be made to establish socio-demographic correlates of environmental worldviews and behaviour. Hence patterns in certain relationships will be explored.

The following research questions provide the focus and direction for the research.

1 To what extent do students and residents hold different environmental worldviews?
2 To what extent is environmentally responsible behaviour practised?
3 What is the level and type of involvement in environmental movements?
4 To what extent, and in what ways, is environmental behaviour related to environmental worldviews?
5 To what extent and in what ways will environmental worldviews and behaviour change over the next five years?

Review the literature

This research will build on a tradition of environmental sociology that goes back to the 1970s in the United States. Various attempts have been made to conceptualize the changes in beliefs and values that appeared to be occurring then, and to measure changes in environmental concern, attitudes and behaviour. One tradition of this activity, centring on the work of Catton and Dunlap and their associates, has developed notions of various worldviews and paradigms (Catton and Dunlap 1978, 1980; Dunlap and van Liere 1978; Dunlap and Catton 1979; van Liere and Dunlap 1980). They argued that the worldview that had dominated American society was being challenged by the 'new environmental paradigm' (NEP).

Dunlap and van Liere (1978) developed a scale of twelve items to measure the NEP. This was constructed as a single dimension, but later replications have suggested that it consists of three dimensions: 'balance of nature', 'limits of growth' and 'man [*sic*] over nature' (Albrecht et al. 1982; Geller and Lasley 1985).

While the socio-demographic basis of the NEP appears to have received little or no attention, the basis of 'environmental concern' has been explored. Van Liere and Dunlap (1980) reviewed twenty-one studies, conducted between 1968 and 1978, in which some or all of the following variables were used: age, social class (income, education and occupation), place of residence, political partisanship, political ideology and gender. They concluded that 'younger, well-educated, and politically liberal persons tend to be more concerned about environmental quality than their older, less educated, and politically conservative counterparts' (van Liere and Dunlap 1980). The other variables were not systematically correlated with environmental concern, although a few studies had examined gender.

Age was found consistently to have the strongest association with environmental concern. This has been supported in subsequent studies by Buttel (1979), Lowe et al. (1980), Honnold (1981, 1984), Lowe and Pinhey (1982), Mohai and Twight (1987) and Arcury and Christianson (1990). Studies of the relationship between environmental concern and gender have produced conflicting results (McStay and Dunlap 1983; Blocker and Eckberg 1989; Samdahl and Robertson 1989; Acury and Christianson 1990).

Therefore, the associations of both age and gender with environmental worldviews and environmentally responsible behaviour will be explored. Five other variables will also be examined: marital status, number and ages of children, religious affiliation, religiosity, and political party preference. Apart from being standard variables, the first two may be associated with a concern for future generations, the second two may be a source of related beliefs and values, and last one may reflect such values.[1]

Research strategies

The study will adopt the *inductive* research strategy. It will collect data related to certain concepts, it will produce limited generalizations, and it will search for patterns in the data. Given the nature of the research questions, the choice must be made between the *inductive* or *abductive* research strategies. As the previous studies with which the findings of this research will be compared have all used the *inductive* strategy and quantitative methods, it is appropriate to use the same.

Concepts

The concepts to be investigated are defined as follows.

> *Environmental worldview*: attitudes towards issues such as the preservation of wilderness environments and natural flora and fauna, the conservation of natural resources, environmental degradation, environmental impacts of economic growth, and the use of science and technology to solve environmental problems.

> *Environmentally responsible behaviour*: individual actions that preserve nature and conserve resources, and involvement in communal actions that confront environmental problems and seek solutions.

---

[1] The standard practice of including such variables is usually based on some implicit theories about their explanatory relevance to particular types of attitude and behaviour. Because these theories are not spelt out, it is difficult to judge whether these variables should be used. Not too much harm is done including them in exploratory and descriptive research, but it is bad practice to expect that a selection of such variables will be any use in explanatory research, without first articulating the theory to which they might be related.

The following standard concepts are also included for possible later use. They are not required to answer the research questions.

Age: number of years since birth.

Gender: socially defined categories of male and female based on human biological differences.

Marital status: the legal or *de facto* relationship between couples.

Number and ages of children: the number of children of all ages for which the respondent is socially regarded as the parent or is the legal guardian. This definition would exclude unrecognized illegitimate children and any that have been given up for adoption.[2]

Religious affiliation: identification with a particular religion or religious denomination.

Religiosity: the degree to which an individual adopts religious beliefs and engages in religious practices.

Political party preference: support of a particular political party through voting at elections.

These concepts will be operationalized as follows:

Environmental worldview: by means of responses to a set of attitude items concerned with the range of environmental issues. The items will be drawn from existing scales: six from the NEP scale, six from the 'dominant social paradigm' scale (Dunlap and van Liere 1984), and eight from the Richmond and Baumgart (1981) scales, two with modifications to their wording. Another four have been added. Five Likert-type response categories will be used: 'strongly agree', 'agree', 'neither agree nor disagree', 'disagree' and 'strongly disagree'. These categories will be assigned values from 1 to 5 in the direction that gives the highest value to responses that are pro-environment. The scale will be pre-tested on a diverse sample of thirty and subjected to item analysis to establish the degree to which responses to each item are consistent with the total score. It will also be post-tested using factor analysis to establish its degree of unidimensionality and the possible presence of sub-scales.

Environmentally responsible behaviour: by three measures. First is the degree to which the use of environmentally dangerous products is avoided. Respondents will be asked how frequently they avoid such products ('regularly', 'occasionally' and 'never'), and then to list them. Second, the extent to which products made of paper, glass (e.g. bottles), metal (e.g. food and drink cans) and plastic are regularly recycled. For each type of product, responses will be made in the categories of 'do not use', 'regularly',

---

[2] The 'number of children' is another example of a superficially simple but in fact complex concept to define, particularly in this era of step-families.

'occasionally' and 'never'. These categories will be scored from 3 to 0 respectively. The responses to each type of product, as well as the total scores for all four types, will be analysed. Third, support given to environmental groups will be measured by two questions: the degree of support ('regularly', 'occasionally' and 'never'); and an open-ended question on the forms of this support (responses to be coded for analysis).

Age: by asking respondents how old they are in years.

Gender: by asking respondents whether they are male or female.

Marital status: by asking respondents to identify with one of the following categories: 'now married', '*de facto* stable relationship', 'never married and not in a stable relationship', 'widowed and not remarried', 'separated and not in a stable relationship', 'divorced and neither remarried nor in a stable relationship'.[3]

Number and ages of children: respondent's reporting of the number and ages of their biological and other children for whom they are responsible and/or regard as theirs.

Religious affiliation: by asking respondents with which religion or religious denomination, if any, they identify. Only the most frequently referred to religions and denominations will be given separate codes.

Religiosity: by asking respondents to what extent they regard themselves as being religious. Four response categories will be used: 'very religious', 'moderately religious', 'somewhat religious' and 'not religious'.[4]

Political party preference: by asking respondents what political party they would vote for if an election were held today. Categories for the major parties, and 'other' will be provided.

As this is a descriptive study, it will not test any theory. In any case, the *inductive* research strategy prohibits the use of hypotheses. However, it will examine the patterns of the relationships between environmental worldview and the various measures of environmentally responsible behaviour. These findings will be compared with previous research.

Data sources, types and forms

Data will be obtained from individuals in semi-natural settings. They will be asked to report on their attitudes and behaviour.

---

[3] Due to the changing forms of different-sex and same-sex relationships, and the relatively limited duration of many such relationships in most contemporary societies, this variable is no longer easy to operationalize.

[4] A more elaborate and perhaps more meaningful way to measure this variable would be to ask questions about attendance at public services of worship, type and frequency of private devotional practices, and participation in religious organizations.

Only primary data will be used. With a few exceptions, responses will be recorded in pre-coded categories. After the few open-ended questions have been coded, all the data will be quantitative. The levels of measurement for each of the variables will be as follows:

Environmental worldview: an interval scale of total scores, and sub-scale scores (if they are established), as well as four approximately equal (ordinal) categories ('very high', 'high', 'moderate' and 'low') based on divisions in the distribution of the total scores.

Environmentally responsible behaviour
(a) Avoiding environmentally dangerous products: an ordinal measure of the frequency of avoidance, a post-coded (nominal) list of 'types of products', and a ratio scale of the 'number of products avoided'.
(b) Recycling: ordinal 'frequency of recycling' categories for each of the four products, scores for each product, and a total 'recycling score' for the four products, based on an assumption of equal intervals between the 'frequency of recycling' categories.
(c) Support for environmental groups: ordinal categories for 'level of support', scores based on the 'level of support' categories, nominal categories for the 'forms of support' and scores for the 'number of types of support'.

Age: ratio scale in years and five (ordinal) age categories to produce a rectangular distribution.

Gender: dichotomous nominal categories.

Religious affiliation: nominal categories.

Religiosity: ordinal categories and scores based on the assumption of equal intervals between categories.

Political party preference: nominal categories and a 'conservative'–'liberal' dichotomy.

Some variables will be measured at more than one level to facilitate different forms of analysis.

Selection of data sources

As this is a low-budget study, and as it is designed to give students a variety of social research experiences, data will be collected from two main sources. The first will be from students in the university in which the study is being conducted. The second will come from residents in the Melbourne Metropolitan Area (MMA), Australia's second-largest and most ethnically diverse urban area with a population of about 3 million. It consists of independently administered city councils.

The student component will not only provide a significant proportion of young people, but will also include respondents who are likely to be environmentally aware because of their education and exposure to related student activities and movements. The study will work with two populations: first, university students from the Royal Melbourne Institute of Technology (RMIT); and, second, residents in the City of Box Hill[5] which is located in the eastern part of the MMA. This city has been selected as its socio-demographic characteristics closely match those of the MMA. It is important to note that both of these populations have been selected from larger populations on the basis of both judgement and convenience. This constitutes a prior stage in the sampling designs.

The student population is defined as 'students taking undergraduate degree courses at the RMIT city campus in the second half of the 1990 academic year'. The sample to be drawn from this population will be based on classes in the university-wide general education curriculum.[6] In the semester in which the sample will be drawn, 160 classes will be offered with an average of twenty-five students per class. Therefore, a population of about 4,000 will be taking these courses at this time; this is about half of all undergraduate students at the RMIT. A sample of one in eight of the classes (= 20) will be selected randomly. Assuming an average attendance of twenty students per class, the sample size should be about 400. This is regarded as adequate for the kinds of analysis to be conducted.

The resident population is defined as 'householders who occupy all types of residences in the City of Box Hill in October 1990'. A sample will be selected in three stages. The first stage will be a one in five random sample from the sixty census collectors' districts, i.e. reasonably small areas allocated to a person responsible for distributing and collecting the forms at the time of the census. Within the twelve collectors' districts, interviewers will select one in four residences using systematic sampling. They will select a starting-point at a corner of the district and proceed along the side of each street until the residences in the district have been covered. The address of each selected residence will be recorded and a letter explaining the study left in the mailbox. A week later, the interviewer will return and seek an interview with a person of at least 18 years of age who has responsibility for the household. Should more than one person present meet this criterion (e.g. a married couple or two or more adults), a selection – the third sampling stage – will be made giving preference to females in residences with even numbers and males in the case of odd numbers. Interviewers will need to stagger the distribution of the explanatory letters to correspond with the pace at which they can conduct the interviews.

While there is some variation in the size of the collectors' districts, they average about 200 residences. Allowing for a non-response rate of 30 per cent, this procedure should produce a second sample of about 400.

The sampling procedure will allow for statistical inferences to be made from the sample statistics to the population of residents in Box Hill. The extent to which these statistics can be generalized further, to the population of residents in the MMA or other urban areas in Australia, will be a matter of judgement

---

[5] The City of Box Hill no longer exists due to an amalgamation with an adjoining city and a name change. It still exists as a suburb and regional shopping centre.

[6] All undergraduate students are required to take four of the twenty general education courses offered in this programme. These courses are designed to expose students to a range of intellectual discourses and to address issues of relevance to a student's future role as a responsible citizen.

based on a careful comparison of demographic characteristics. It will be possible to apply inferential statistics to generalize the results from the student sample to the population of students taking classes in the general education programme at the RMIT in that particular semester. Judgement will be required to generalize to the whole student population at RMIT and to Australian university students.

A second study will be conducted in 1995 using similar samples, thus eventually creating a longitudinal study.

Data collection and timing

For the present, this will be a cross-sectional study. A week will be required to collect the data from the student sample, and, immediately after, the sampling of the residents will begin. The latter will take three weeks to complete. The actual timing of the data collection is still to be decided.

A self-administered structured questionnaire will be used with the student sample and a structured interview schedule with the sample of residents. The former is appropriate for administration to 'captive' groups and will ensure a good response rate. The latter will allow the sampling to be combined with the interviewing and will facilitate a better response rate than would be possible with a questionnaire. The two instruments will use identical questions but will be structured slightly differently. The questionnaire will be pre-tested with two classes, not included in the sample, a month before its administration, and the interview schedule will be pre-tested with thirty residents in an adjoining part of the MMA.

For the student sample, arrangements will be made with the lecturer responsible for the selected classes to have the students complete the questionnaire in class. This should take twenty-five to thirty minutes. The administration of the questionnaire will be organized and supervised by the students from the Research Methods class, operating in pairs. With forty students in the Research Methods class, each pair will be responsible for one class. A brief explanation of the purpose of the study will be given and ethical issues (e.g. anonymity, confidentiality and voluntary participation) will be explained. Responses will be recorded by ticking in boxes alongside the appropriate category.

Data from the residents' sample will be collected by structured face-to-face interview. The interviewers will be the same students from the Research Methods class. Forty students will each conduct ten interviews. Public transport is available to (train) and through (bus) the research site. Interviews will be conducted in the late afternoon and early evening during the week, and at weekends. Interviewers will be required to make up to two return visits if they fail to find someone at home on the first visit. Again, a brief explanation of the purpose of the study will be given and ethical issues explained. Respondents will be encouraged to participate to ensure the success of the study. They will be asked if they would like a copy of a summary of the report of the study. If the time is unsuitable, arrangements will be made for a return visit. Interviewers will make every effort to conduct the interview in private and in a relaxed atmosphere.

Responses will be recorded by circling the coding numbers alongside the appropriate category.

The interviewers will receive thorough training in interview techniques and the use of this particular interview schedule. In the week before the interviewing commences, an article will appear in the local suburban newspaper giving some background to the study. Interviewers will wear identification tags and carry a letter of authority from the university.

Data reduction and analysis

Very limited post-coding will be required. A codebook will be prepared for use with the questionnaire and for the open-ended questions in the interview schedule. An SPSS (PC version) data matrix will be prepared for each sample and the responses entered. This will be done directly from the questionnaires, using the codebook, and from the interview schedules. Following an initial frequency count, it may be necessary to re-code some variables, either reordering or collapsing some of the categories. The students in the Research Methods class will be involved in the coding, data entry and data analysis.

Data from the two samples will be analysed separately as well as combined. Comparisons will be made between the two samples and inferential statistics will be used to estimate the population parameters from the sample statistics.

To answer the research questions, the following methods of analysis will be undertaken with each sample and the combined sample.

RQ1 Means and standard deviations for the scores from the 'environmental worldview scale' and sub-scales; medians and inter-quartile range for the ordinal category version of the scale.

RQ2 Frequency counts and percentages for the categories in the list of 'products avoided'; frequency counts, percentages, means and standard deviations for the 'number of products avoided'; frequency counts and percentages for the 'frequency of recycling' categories for each product; mean and standard deviation for the 'recycling score'.

RQ3 Frequency counts and percentages for the 'level of support' and 'form of support' categories; frequency counts, percentages and means for the number of 'types of support'.

RQ4 Cross-tabulation and non-parametric tests of significance for environmental worldview scale (ordinal categories) with 'types of products', 'frequency of recycling' for each product, 'level of support' (ordinal categories) and 'forms of support' for environmental groups. Product moment correlation coefficients and a parametric test of significance will be used to correlate 'environmental worldview scale' and the sub-scales with 'number of products avoided', 'recycling score', 'level of support' (scores) and 'number of types of support'.

RQ5 A comparison of the results of all the analyses undertaken for Research Questions 1–4 across the two points in time. This can only be undertaken when a follow-up study is conducted.

Problems and limitations

A major strength of the study is that it will explore environmental issues systematically in this way for the first time in Australia. It will also develop a new environmental worldview scale and test it in local conditions. And it will provide students with valuable experience in developing and using research instruments, and in data analysis.

The major limitation derives from the exploratory and descriptive nature of the study. This has made it difficult to attract research funds; only a small seeding grant is available. The participation of the forty students from the Research Methods class will partially compensate, although the need to limit the extent of their involvement to only those experiences necessary for their course places another set of limitations.

As a consequence, sampling methods will have to be devised to produce a substantial size, with appropriate diversity, but with the available resources. While the student sample, in combination with residents, ensures a good age spread, university students may not be typical of young people in this age range. In addition, there are some weaknesses in the assumption that students taking the general education classes in a particular semester are typical of all students at RMIT, and of all university students in Australia. However, such claims will not be made, although readers of the research report may want to make judgements about these matters.

The selection of only one suburb in one city to represent urban Australia clearly has severe limitations. Again, readers of the research report will have to judge for themselves how typical this sample might be. What will be possible with these two samples is to undertake a separate analysis of the attitudes and behaviour of a sample of young educated people and to compare them with a reasonably typical sample of urban residents.

The major advantage in concentrating the study in one area, and using this particular sampling method, is that interviewing can be done efficiently, as little travelling is required. An alternative would have been to select samples from a diverse range of socio-demographic areas in the MMA. This would have involved a great deal of extra travelling for limited gains. A random sample of residents in the MMA would have been impossible with the available resources.

A technical point concerns the use of questionnaires with the student sample and structured interviews with the residents' sample. While the question wording will be the same in each instrument, differences in the methods of administration could produce differences in responses. Conducting interviews with a second sample of, say, 100 students could test this. If time and resources permit, this will be carried out.[7]

[7] In the original study (Blaikie 1992), two student samples were used. One of about 200 used the method described here, and another quota sample of the same size (with selection criteria of field of degree and gender) was interviewed. In spite of the radically different sampling methods, and the different method of administration, the distributions on the main variables were almost identical. Hence, the two samples were combined.

Research Design 2   Age and Environmentalism:
A Test of Competing Hypotheses

Statement of the topic/problem

Research over many decades in the United States has shown that there is a consistently stronger association between age and environmental attitudes and concern than with any other socio-demographic variable; younger people have more positive attitudes and greater concern than older people. However, just why age is associated with environmentalism is not clear.

Motives and goals

The main motive is to advance our knowledge of why some people have more favourable environmental attitudes and engage in higher levels of environmentally friendly behaviour than others. This may have some practical benefits for environmental education programmes and for groups and organizations that are committed to improving the quality of the natural and built environments.

Research questions and objectives

The research has two objectives: to establish the form of the relationship between age and environmentalism in Australia; and to develop and test a theory to explain it. Three research questions will be explored.

1 To what extent is age related to environmental worldviews and environmental behaviour?
2 If there are significant relationships, what are the forms of these relationships?
3 Why do these relationships exist?

Review the literature

Research in the United States has explored three hypotheses for the association between age and environmental concern. One suggests that it is due to the socio-biological ageing process (the 'ageing' hypothesis). The second suggests that important historical events have a differential influence on birth cohorts (the 'cohort' hypothesis). The third claims that there are period effects due to changes in social, cultural and economic conditions (the 'period' hypothesis) (Buttel 1979; Honnold 1984; Mohai and Twight 1987). The 'ageing' hypothesis is based on the view that young people have a lower level of commitment to dominant social values and institutions, the 'cohort' hypothesis relates to Mann-heim's (1952) theory of generations, or to C. Wright Mills's (1959) notion of the intersection of biography and history, while the 'period' hypothesis requires that both of these processes can be overridden by adaptations to changing circumstances.

There has been some support for the 'cohort' hypothesis (Mohai and Twight 1987; Samdahl and Robertson 1989) and the 'period' hypothesis (Honnold 1984). However, it is possible that all three processes can have an influence. The advocates of the 'cohort' hypothesis point to the events of the late 1960s and early 1970s in American society.

An examination of these three hypotheses suggests that the relationship need not be linear, i.e. that the level of environmentalism need not decrease with age. It is possible that a particular birth cohort of young people has been differentially influenced by a particular wave of interest in environmental issues. They may pass through a period of history as a ripple of environmental concern. This can be expressed as the following theoretical argument.

1 In the late 1960s and early 1970s, young people in Australia were influenced by a period of student radicalism and the concern for environmental issues that followed.
2 These experiences have had a lasting impact on this age cohort, even though the intensity may have subsided.
3 Until very recently, no events of similar historical significance have occurred in the past twenty years to influence the environmental attitudes of subsequent cohorts of young people.
4 Other 'period' changes, such as economic fluctuations, have influenced all contemporary generations more or less equally.
5 The youth cohort of the late 1960s and the 1970s, who are now in middle age, will be the most receptive present generation to the new wave of environmental concern.
6 Therefore, the present middle-aged cohort will have the most favourable environmental worldviews and the highest level of environmental concern.

The 'ageing' hypothesis would suggest that the present youth cohort would be the most susceptible to the current wave of environmental issues. The question is whether their one exposure matches the two exposures of the middle-aged generation.

The conclusion of this theory will be tested, i.e. that *the present middle-aged cohort has the most favourable environmental worldviews and the highest level of environmentally responsible behaviour.*

Research strategies

The *deductive* research strategy will be used. A theory has been proposed, based on some existing hypotheses, and a new hypothesis has been deduced for testing. According to the deductive research strategy, testing the conclusion of the theory tests the theory.

Concepts

The following concepts will be measured.

> *Environmental worldview*: attitudes towards issues such as the preservation of wilderness environments and natural flora and fauna, the conservation of natural resources, environmental degradation, environmental impacts of economic growth, and the use of science and technology to solve environmental problems.

> *Environmentally responsible behaviour*: individual actions that preserve nature and conserve resources, and involvement in communal actions that confront environmental problems and seek solutions.

> *Age*: number of years since birth.

(See Research Design 1 for the formal and operational definitions of these concepts.)

Data sources, types and forms

Data will come from the study on 'Environmental Worldviews and Behaviour among Students and Residents' (see Research Design 1).

These data were originally obtained from individuals in semi-natural settings. Therefore, this study will use secondary quantitative data. (See Research Design 1 for details of the levels of measurement for each variable.)

Selection of data sources

Samples will be taken from two populations, university students at the RMIT and householders in the City of Box Hill. (See Research Design 1 for the details of the sampling methods used.)

Data collection and timing

The data come from a cross-sectional study conducted in 1990. A self-administered questionnaire was used with the student sample and a structured interview with the sample of residents. (See Research Design 1 for the details of the timing and methods of data collection.)

Data reduction and analysis

The responses to all questions were coded in the previous study; the categories will be interpreted from the codebook supplied with the database. If necessary, some further re-coding will be undertaken. The original database is available on disk, and the same software package will be used. The following analyses will be undertaken to answer the two research questions and test the hypothesis.

RQ1   Cross-tabulation and non-parametric tests of significance for 'environmental worldview' (ordinal categories) with 'age' (ordinal categories). Product moment correlation coefficient and a parametric test of significance will be used for 'environmental worldview' (scores) with 'age' (in years). The same analysis will be undertaken between the 'environmental worldview' sub-scales and 'age'.

Similarly, the associations between 'age' and the ordinal and interval/ratio versions of the three 'environmentally responsible behaviour' variables will be analysed, where appropriate, using the same methods of analysis.

RQ2,RQ3 The 'age' distribution will be tabulated and plotted against the 'environmental worldview' scores and the sub-scale scores, and these will be presented in tables and graphs. Similar tables and graphs will be produced for 'age' against the measures of 'environmentally responsible behaviour'. The distribution of scores and ordinal categories against age, and the shape of the distributions and the curves in these graphs, will determine whether the hypothesis about 'age' and 'environmental worldview' is corroborated or needs to be rejected.

Problems and limitations

As secondary data will be used, the strengths and limitations of the previous study will also apply to this one. However, there is a further limitation in that this study has to accept the form and scope of the data provided. Some desirable data, such as respondents' reports of their involvement in the student movement of the 1960s and 1970s, and their level of environmental concern at that time, are just not available. Therefore, the theory can only be tested in a limited way.

Research Design 3   Gender Differences in Environmentalism: Towards an Explanation

Statement of the topic/problem

Gender differences in environmentalism have received much less attention than other socio-economic variables in the many studies on environmental attitudes, concern and behaviour over the past forty years. When gender has been included, the findings have been inconsistent and often of limited magnitude. More recently, eco-feminists have presented arguments that are based on fundamental differences in environmentalism between males and females. Hence, it is clear that further research is required to help clarify these issues.

This study will examine the gender differences in environmental worldviews and behaviour in an Australian context, and will attempt to explain the differences that are found to exist.

Motives and goals

The major motivation is to extend the understanding of environmental worldviews and behaviour. While gender differences in environmentalism appear to be rather elusive, it may be possible to learn important lessons from gender socialization, experiences and responsibilities. If women are more committed to an environmental worldview and are more likely to practise environmentally responsible behaviour than men, then discovering why this is so may help to understand how men's attitudes and behaviour could be changed.

Research questions and objectives

The project will address three research questions.

1 To what extent do women hold more favourable environmental worldviews than men?
2 To what extent are women more willing then men to engage in environmentally responsible behaviour?
3 Why do these gender differences in environmentalism exist?

Review the literature

Eco-feminists have argued that environmental problems are the result of male domination, and, that if women had had equality or super-ordination over men, there would be many fewer environmental problems (for reviews, see Salleh 1984, 1988/9, and Hallebone 1989). Nevertheless, research has provided only limited support for the existence of gender differences in environmental concern. In fact, the van Liere and Dunlap review (1980) provided no support, and Acury and Christianson (1990) found males to be more inclined to be environmentally aware than females. However, McStay and Dunlap (1983) found modest support for gender differences, even when controls for age, education, income and residence were introduced, but they argued that women, in contrast to men, are more likely to engage in behaviour concerned with environmental quality that is personal rather than public. Blocker and Eckberg (1989) found that women were no more concerned than men about general environmental issues, but were significantly more concerned about local environmental issues.

Blaikie (1992) found that while gender differences in environmental worldview were consistent, with females holding more caring attitudes towards the environment than males, the magnitude of these differences was relatively small. However, the gender differences were greatest on the issue of confidence in the capacity of science and technology to solve environmental problems: women were much less confident than men.

In terms of environmental behaviour, Blaikie and Ward (1992) found that females were more likely than males to avoid environmentally damaging products, but there were no significant differences in recycling behaviour or in the level of support for environmental groups. While these differences in environmental worldviews and behaviour are consistent with a feminist explanation, the relationship between environmentalism and gender is clearly a complex one. It is only in particular areas that females show stronger pro-environmental attitudes and behaviour, and then the differences are generally limited.

Research strategies

The first two research questions will be explored using the *inductive* research strategy. The third research question will use the *retroductive* strategy as expounded by Pawson and Tilley (1997). It is assumed that if there are gender differences in environmental worldviews and behaviour they are the result of the operation of different cognitive mechanisms in different social contexts.

Concepts and model

The central concepts for the first two research questions are defined as follows.

Environmentalism: the holding of a positive environmental worldview and the practice of environmentally responsible behaviour.

Environmental worldview: attitudes towards issues such as the preservation of wilderness environments and natural flora and fauna, the conservation of natural resources, environmental degradation, environmental impacts of economic growth, and the use of science and technology to solve environmental problems.

Environmentally responsible behaviour: individual actions that preserve nature and conserve resources, and involvement in communal actions that confront environmental problems and seek solutions.

Gender: socially defined categories of male and female based on human biological differences.

In order to establish why there are gender differences in environmentalism, the following model of the connection between cognitive mechanisms and social contexts has been constructed.

1 Attitudes towards the environment, and decisions to engage in environmentally responsible behaviour, are produced by a combination of the social contexts within which an individual is located and the particular roles performed in those contexts.
2 The child-bearing and child-rearing roles entail a concern for the welfare of succeeding generations.

3 The particular social contexts in which everyday activities occur produce differences in the scope and range of awareness and concern about human issues. These social contexts range from private (domestic/local community) to public (work/wider community).
4 Persons whose lives are predominantly in the public sphere will have a broad range of (global) concerns while persons whose lives are predominantly in the private sphere will have a narrower (local) range of concerns.
5 Persons who have primary responsibility for child-bearing and/or child-rearing will be concerned about the health and future of the next and succeeding generations.

Therefore, the following can be concluded from this model.

• Women who have been primarily involved in home-making and child-rearing will have a higher level of environmentalism and a greater concern with local environmental issues than men who have been primarily breadwinners and have pursued careers in the public sphere. In other words, differences in environmentalism between men and women will be greatest when both are involved in traditional segregated roles and social contexts.
• Women who have had a significant involvement in the public sphere will be more like 'traditional' men in their level of environmentalism and locus of concern about environmental issues.
• Men who have had and continue to have a significant involvement in the private sphere will be more like 'traditional' women in their level of environmentalism and locus of concern about environmental issues.
• Women who have never had child-rearing responsibilities will have a lower level of environmentalism than women with these responsibilities and who are involved in similar social contexts.

These conclusions will be examined to assess the relevance of the contexts and cognitive mechanisms postulated in the model.

Data sources, types and forms

Data to answer the first two research questions will come from previous research (see Research Design 1) and will entail secondary analysis. The third research question will require qualitative, primary data from individuals in semi-natural settings.

Selection of data sources

Two contrasting populations will be used, both defined as 'men and women who are married or living in a stable *de facto* relationship, aged between 25 and 50, and with dependent children'. The first population will include men and women who have 'traditional' marriages or *de facto* relationships, and the second will have 'modern' marriages or stable relationships. In order to achieve some matching in the social contexts, couples will be included.

Quota sampling will be used with the following criteria: couples who meet the definition of a 'traditional' or 'modern' relationship (two categories), who come from a variety of socio-economic backgrounds (three categories – 'high status', 'middle status' and 'low status', based on occupation and education), who live in both urban and rural areas (three categories – city, country town and rural), and who have a range of environmental behaviour (two categories). These criteria produce a matrix of thirty-six cells. Socio-economic background and urban and rural areas have been included as criteria only to ensure a diverse sample; they will not be discussed as contexts in the model.

Initially, thirty-six couples will be selected for intensive case-study research. If necessary, further cases will be added as the study proceeds.

Data collection and timing

Data will be collected by a combination of in-depth and 'realist' interviews, the latter using the method of interviewing advocated by Pawson (1995, 1996) and Pawson and Tilley (1997).

'Realist' interviewing is used to involve the research participants in the process of testing the model of their cognitive mechanisms and how these operate in particular social contexts. This process is different from that in which respondents are required to provide answers to the researcher's predetermined questions (as in the use of questionnaires or structured interview schedules), or where the researcher tries to faithfully report social actors' accounts of their worldviews and activities (as in some in-depth interviews). Rather, it

> requires a teacher-learner relationship to be developed between researcher and informant in which the medium of exchange is the CMO [context, mechanism, outcome] theory and the function of that relationship is to refine CMO theories. The research act thus involves 'learning' the stakeholder's theories, forma-lizing them, 'teaching' them back to the informant, who is then in a position to comment upon, clarify and further refine the key ideas. (Pawson and Tilley 1997: 218)

In short, the researcher has to learn about the research participant's cognitive mechanisms and contexts from them, construct a model of the mechanisms and the context, teach the informant about this model, and then seek feedback in order to either confirm or refine it.

The in-depth interviews will be conducted first. They will focus on the

- contexts in which everyday life now occurs, and has occurred in the past;
- roles undertaken in these contexts;
- involvement in child-rearing activities, past and present; and
- perceptions of threats to the welfare of the next and future generations.

Each interview is expected to take up to one and a half hours. Subject to the agreement of the respondent, all interviews will be recorded on audio cassette.

The 'realist' interviews will follow the in-depth interviews on a later occasion. Each interview will take about forty-five minutes, will be recorded, and will be conducted by the researcher.

The in-depth interviews will be used to refine the hypothesized model and to fill out the details of the contexts and mechanisms. The 'realist' interviews will then be used to present the model to the informants for confirmation or further refinement.

Data reduction and analysis

The secondary data to be used to answer the first two research questions have already been reduced. Some further re-coding may be undertaken as the analysis proceeds. The data generated to answer the third research question will come from the recorded conversations in the in-depth and 'realist' interviews.

The following analyses will be undertaken to answer the research questions.

RQ1 Cross-tabulation and non-parametric tests of significance for 'environmental worldview' (ordinal categories) with 'gender' (nominal categories). Product moment correlation coefficient and a parametric test of significance for 'environmental worldview' (scores) with 'gender' (as a dichotomous variable). The same analysis will be undertaken between the 'environmental worldview' sub-scales and 'gender'.

RQ2 The associations between 'gender' and the ordinal and interval/ratio versions of the three 'environmentally responsible behaviour' variables will be analysed, where appropriate, using the same methods of analysis.

RQ3 All interviews will be transcribed and formatted for entry into a NUD*IST database. The NUD*IST software will be used to create categories and index the data to assist with the elaboration of the model.

Problems and limitations

While the method of sampling will provide a diversity of respondents, it will not be possible to generalize statistically from it. However, as the aim is to understand how certain cognitive mechanisms operate in particular social contexts, this sample will allow for an exploration in a limited range of contexts.

Subject to what the study reveals, further cognitive processes (e.g. associated with different types of education, or different exposure to information in the media) and social contexts could be explored in further studies to expand our knowledge of gender differences in environmentalism. Similar models could be developed to understand differences in environmentalism associated with factors such as regional, ethnic, and religious differences, should they be found to exist.

Research Design 4   Motivation for Environmentally Responsible Behaviour: The Case of Environmental Activists

Statement of the topic/problem

This project addresses the issue of what motivates and sustains environmentally responsible behaviour. As solutions to many local and global environmental problems are dependent on changes in everyday behaviour, it is necessary to understand what motivates this behaviour in order to be able to develop programmes to try to increase it. Most research in this field has been quantitative and essentially descriptive; it has established levels of attitudes, knowledge, concern and behaviour, and the relationship between these variables and with standard socio-demographic variables. Some studies have begun to suggest that various forms of environmental behaviour, such as recycling, avoidance of environmentally damaging products, and energy conservation, are motivated by a range of factors. However, motivation has still to be studied intensively. What is therefore required is the development and testing of theories that will explain these forms of behaviour.

Motives and goals

The main motive is to provide a better basis for programmes designed to increase the practice of environmentally responsible behaviour. The continuation of social life as we know it, and survival of many species, including the human race, is at risk if dramatic change in human behaviour does not occur quickly.

Research questions and objectives

The research will address four questions.

1 In what range and types of behaviour do environmentally responsible individuals engage?
2 Why do these people act responsibly towards the environment?
3 Why do some of these people manage to sustain this behaviour?
4 How can the incidence of this type of behaviour be increased?

While the study will have a descriptive foundation, its main emphasis will be on understanding this behaviour. It is hoped that recommendations can be made concerning the fourth research question. However, the development and evaluation of programmes for this must await another project.

Review the literature

Beginning with the wave of environmentalism in the 1970s, and continuing into the middle of the 1980s, traditions of research have focused on attitudes towards the environment and environmental issues and problems, and levels of environmental concern and knowledge. More recently, these topics have been supplemented with research on everyday behaviour that either exacerbates environmental problems (e.g. pollution, global warming, depletion of the ozone layer, energy consumption, and the use of non-renewable resources) or contributes to their amelioration, i.e. on the extent to which people practise environmentally responsible behaviour.

Recently, various research projects have established patterns in environmental attitudes and the types and levels of environmentally responsible behaviour in the Australian population (e.g. Blaikie 1992, 1993b; Blaikie and Ward 1992; Castles 1993; Blaikie and Drysdale 1994; Environment Protection Authority of New South Wales 1994). It is now possible to compare the Australian situation with that in twenty-two other countries, using the study conducted by Dunlap et al. (1992).

Since the 1970s, environmental attitudes and behaviour in Western societies has been subject to considerable fluctuations. According to opinion polls in Australia, the most recent wave of concern, which began in the late 1980s, has exhibited considerable changes in environmental attitude. Some of these have been attributed to the effects of an economic recession on the capacity of governments and businesses to cope with the costs involved in acting responsibly towards the environment, and the more immediate pressures on the population in dealing with unemployment and economic insecurity.

The search for ways to motivate and facilitate pro-environment behaviour has engaged researchers in the United States for at least twenty years. Particular attention has been given to recycling (e.g. Reid et al. 1976; Witmer and Geller 1976; Humphrey et al. 1977; Luyben and Bailey 1979; Pardini and Katzev 1983/4; De Young 1986, 1988/9). Extrinsic incentives, such as the purchase of recycled materials or the provision of rewards for carrying out recycling, have had mixed success; they tend to produce only short-term results (e.g., Cook and Berrenberg 1981; Pardini and Katzev 1983/4) but not enduring behaviour change (Witmer and Geller 1976). This may be related to the finding that 'non-recyclers' need financial incentives and convenient recycling systems much more than regular 'recyclers' (Vining and Ebreo 1990). In many cases, the cost of the incentives exceeded the revenue from the collections (Jacobs et al. 1984). Similar problems in the balance of cost and benefit have been found with energy conservation (Newsom and Makranczy 1978; McClelland and Canter 1981).

Since the 1970s, psychologists, mainly in the United States, have applied behavioural (reward and punishment) techniques to environmental problems, beginning with the problem of littering (Burgess et al. 1971; Tuso and Geller 1976; Casey and Lloyd 1977; Cone and Hayes 1984; Lahart and Bailey 1984; Levit and Leventhall 1986). Some researchers have argued that the use of behavioural techniques to discourage littering is superior to methods of persuasion and education, and may be more cost-effective than traditional clean-up methods. While it has been argued that the same behavioural techniques can be applied to other problems, such as energy conservation and recycling, this approach has been criticized for providing only short-term solutions. As soon as the rewards are withdrawn the behaviour tends to return to previous levels (Gudgion and Thomas 1991).

The relationship between attitudes and behaviour, and the ability of attitudes to predict behaviour, has concerned social psychologists for at least sixty years (for reviews see Ajzen and Fishbein 1980; McGuire 1968; Fazio 1986; Chaiken and Stangor 1987). Theory and research on this relationship have gone through a number of stages (Zanna and Fazio 1982). Until the mid-1960s, the predominant assumption was that a one-to-one correspondence must exist between attitudes and behaviour. This was followed by a period of questioning of whether there is a relationship and whether it is worth pursuing. By the 1970s the question became: 'When do attitudes guide behaviour?' There was a shift in concern to the conditions under which attitudes might predict behaviour, with the result that many situational and personality variables were identified as moderators of the relationship. In the 1980s the question became: 'How do attitudes guide behaviour?' This has involved recognizing the effects of attitudes on perception, the role of interpretation (definition) of situations, and the intervention of norms (Fazio 1986). However, this extensive tradition has tended to neglect the relationship between agency and structure; it has ignored the alternative tradition that views attitudes as an epiphenomenon of a person's location in the social structure, and has virtually overlooked the effects of social context on behaviour.

The relationship between attitudes and behaviour has also been a central topic of research in environmental sociology and social psychology (e.g. Ehrlich 1969; Vicker 1969; Geller et al. 1982; Dunlap et al. 1983; Dunlap and van Liere 1984; Heberlein 1989; Gigliotti 1992). The predominant assumption has been that changing people's environmental attitudes will change their environmentally related behaviour. However, as pro-environmental attitudes have become more socially acceptable, and concern for the environment has become better established, the gap in this relationship has become a focus of attention. In some cases, environmental knowledge has been added to produce a two-stage model with causal implications: knowledge is related to attitude and attitude is related to behaviour (e.g. Pettus 1976; Ramsey and Rickson 1976; Borden and Schettino 1979; Hausbeck et al. 1990).

There has been a long tradition of research on environmental attitudes and behaviour in the Netherlands (see e.g. Scheepers and Nelissen 1989; Nelissen and Scheepers 1992). Using a variety of measures of environmental behaviour (recycling, consumption of ecological products, energy consumption, and means of transport) with a national sample in 1990, Nelissen and Scheepers (1992) identified patterns of consistency and non-consistency in a typology that related environmental attitudes (ecological consciousness) and behaviour: 'consistent non-ecologists' (low ecological consciousness and no ecological behaviour); 'inconsistent consciousness-ecologists' (moderate ecological consciousness and moderate ecological behaviour); and 'consistent ecologists' (strong ecological consciousness and consistent ecological behaviour). They found that one form of ecological behaviour, buying ecologically sound products and refraining from buying non-ecological products, had the weakest association with both ecological consciousness and other forms of ecological behaviour.

More recently, the role of social context has been given explicit recognition in the link between environmental attitudes and behaviour (Derksen and Gartrell, 1993). These researchers compared two Canadian cities (Edmonton and Calgary) and the remaining small towns and rural areas in the province of Alberta. Only one of the cities, Edmonton, had a well-developed and user-friendly recycling programme. They found a very high level of concern for the environment across the province, with a result that socio-demographic variables, such as age, gender, education and income, showed weak associations. Predictably, the Edmonton residents had a much higher level of recycling than in the rest of the province, particularly in the rural areas.

Changes in environmental attitudes and behaviour in Australia have been investigated between 1989 and 1994 (Blaikie 1992, 1993b; Blaikie and Ward 1992; Blaikie and Drysdale 1994) using samples of residents in the Melbourne Metropolitan Area and university students. These studies found that the strongest commitment to an environmental worldview is to be found in the middle-aged cohort; younger cohorts hold a middle position and older cohorts have the lowest levels of commitment. Compared with people generally, on average, university students did not rate higher on environmental worldview, were no more active in or supportive of environmental groups, and did not exhibit a higher level of environmentally responsible behaviour. This raises some questions about the extent to which a university education produces higher levels of environmental commitment and action.

American research has produced conflicting results on the relationship between environmental concern and gender (van Liere and Dunlap 1980; McStay and Dunlap 1983; Blocker and Eckberg 1989; Samdhal and Robertson 1989; Acury and Christianson 1990). Australian data indicate that women of all ages are only marginally more committed to an environmental worldview than men (Blaikie 1992).

Each type of environmental behaviour appears to have its own form of motivation (Blaikie and Drysdale 1994). While the level of 'avoidance of environmentally dangerous products' is associated as strongly as any other variable with 'environmental worldview', which products are avoided appears to have been influenced by the attention received in the media. In spite of the small increase in the level of 'support for environmental groups', this form of environmental behaviour has remained low; it is very much an activity of those with favourable 'environmental worldviews'. Dramatic increases in recycling have occurred, but this form of environmental behaviour shows little or no association with environmental attitudes; it is dependent on the availability of convenient, regular and publicly supported collection systems. However, it also appears to be motivated by attitudes, values and practices that have arisen from periods when conservation (i.e. making things last by taking good care of them and maintaining them well) and reuse were a necessity. People who lived through the depression of the 1930s and World War II can be keen recyclers without having favourable environmental worldviews.

It is clear from the literature that the relationship between environmental worldviews and behaviour is complex and that such worldviews are not good predictors of behaviour. The explanation for environmentally responsible behaviour must be sought elsewhere. Some useful ideas have emerged about how this type of behaviour can be changed. The following conclusions about changing environmental behaviour have been drawn from the literature.

1 Various forms of environmental behaviour have different types of motivation, thus requiring different strategies for changing environmental behaviour.
2 Changing environmental attitudes, certainly on their own, is not an effective way to change environmental behaviour.
3 Improving environmental knowledge, through education and the media, may change attitudes. Improving knowledge is a necessary condition for change in some forms of behaviour. However, this knowledge needs to be accompanied by both opportunity and meaningful motivation for behaviour to be sustained.
4 Some forms of behaviour can be dramatically changed, and, perhaps, can only be changed, with the establishment of effective, convenient and socially acceptable systems.
5 Generating social acceptance and support for different behaviour is an underrated, and, perhaps, a necessary condition for some forms of behaviour change.

While this project will not test these possible hypotheses by the more conventional *deductive* strategy, they will provide some ideas about the direction in which to look in the process of theory generation.

Research strategies

It is clear from the literature review that a different research strategy than the ones that have been used so far is required to understand environmental behaviour. As there are no clear theoretical leads from the literature, theory generation is required. Therefore, the *abductive* research strategy will be adopted in order to explore this understanding in depth.

Concepts

Some concepts will be used in a sensitizing mode to provide initial direction for the study. The aim will be to explore the meaning given to them by the people studied, and to discover other concepts they use that are roughly equivalent, or are different. The main concepts are:

- environment
- nature
- environmental problems
- environmental protection
- conservation

- recycling
- economic growth

No theories or hypotheses are proposed. Models in the form of ideal types will be developed to grasp the variety of motives and behaviour.

Data sources, types and forms

Primary data will be obtained from individuals in semi-natural settings. Apart from a few simple frequency counts and percentages, the data will be qualitative at all stages of the research.

Selection of data sources

The population will include individuals who engage in a range of environmentally responsible behaviour, such as:

- active involvement in environmental groups and movements;
- involvement in local protests on environmental issues;
- minimizing the use of non-renewable resources;
- avoiding the use of environmentally damaging products; and
- recycling 'waste' products.

The intention is to include both public and private activities.

Given the nature of the population, non-probability sampling will be used with a combination of quota sampling, as well as snowball and opportunistic sampling. Interviewers will collectively maintain a gender balance and an age and social class distribution in the selection of respondents. The aim will be to include as diverse a range of people as possible. Some respondents will be contacted through environmental organizations and the interviewers will recruit others, using their own friends and acquaintances. Persons contacted will be asked to suggest other possible respondents. It is expected that a sample of about 100 will be used.

Data collection and timing

Data will be collected by in-depth interviews over a period of four months. Each interview is expected to take about two hours. In addition to the researcher, five experienced interviewers will be employed. Subject to the agreement of the respondent, all interviews will be recorded on audio cassette. Each respondent will complete a one-page bio-data sheet.

Initially, the following themes will be used:

- meaning of 'environment', 'environmental problems', 'nature', etc.;
- knowledge and awareness of environmental problems;

- understanding of the causes and effects of these problems;
- views on who is responsible for dealing with them and whether individual actions can make a difference;
- actions taken by the respondent;
- motivation for these actions;
- influences of significant others; and
- experience with natural environments and animals as a child and youth.

After fifty interviews have been completed, the transcripts will be analysed. This may lead to some changes in the interview themes. After a further fifty interviews, further analysis will be undertaken. The first fifty respondents will be re-interviewed, using what has been learnt to increase the focus of the interview. Further analysis of these interviews will occur before the second fifty respondents are re-interviewed. Following the analysis of these transcripts, a few respondents may be selected for a third interview if it is felt that theoretical saturation has not been reached. In this way, the data collection and analysis will involve a spiral learning process in which each wave of interviews builds on the understanding gained up to that point. Re-interviewing will allow an in-depth understanding of all respondents.

As it is impossible to anticipate when theoretical saturation will be reached, the size of the sample must remain approximate at this stage. However, for budget purposes, it is assumed that a total of 225 interviews will be required.

Data reduction and analysis

All interviews will be transcribed and formatted for entry into a NUD*IST database. The basic information on the bio-data sheets will be included in the file for each respondent. The NUD*IST software will be used to create categories and index the data. The methods of open and axial coding (grounded theory) will be used to generate typologies and, hopefully, theory.

Alongside this method of analysis, interviewers will be asked to write a brief summary of their impressions of each interview, and, from time to time, their impressions of what they see developing from the interviews. The researcher will listen to all the cassettes and also record impressions and ideas from the recordings. Interviewers' impressions of each interview will be added to the transcript of the relevant interview. Overall impressions will be entered into separate interviewer files and will constitute additional data.

Problems and limitations

The major problem of a study of this kind is the uncertainty about how it will develop. A balance must be struck between the order of a planned programme and the flexibility required to allow the learning process to evolve. Another problem is the time required to collect and analyse the data. Given limited resources, and the developmental nature of the research strategy, the sample size must be limited.

The sample will not allow for generalization to a population. However, this is not the intention of this project. Its aim is to generate a theoretical understanding that can be used as the basis for an intervention programme. Any theory that emerges can be tested in other contexts to establish its range of application, as will the evaluation of any intervention programmes based on it.

Postscript

I hope that these sample research designs will provide not only some guidance as to what is required, but also encouragement to spend the time attending to the many decisions that must be made. In many ways, designing a research project is more difficult than doing it. If a project is well designed, the steps involved in carrying it out should follow reasonably smoothly. Of course, the ability to collect and analyse data successfully requires a great deal of knowledge, skill, persistence and ingenuity. It is also fraught with difficulties and barriers that have to be overcome, before and during the research process.

Even in the most carefully planned research projects, there is always the possibility that something will go wrong. We may have overlooked something, or factors outside our control may upset our plans; things do go wrong. Published reports of research rarely mention these. They present us with a 'reconstructed logic'. I have been guilty of this myself, and would therefore like to give an example of a problem and how it was overcome.

In the late 1960s I directed a class in social research methods to undertake a study of values and occupational choice among university students (Blaikie 1971). The research design included a combined stratified and systematic sampling method with students from three different degree programmes, arts (including most of the social sciences), law and science at Monash University in Melbourne. These three categories, as well as year at university (1, 2 and 3+), were used as strata. Systematic sampling, with different sampling ratios, was to be used to produce roughly the same number in each stratum. Lists of students in these programmes, and their addresses, were available from the university's administration and data were to be collected by a mailed questionnaire.

Precisely at the time that we were about to draw the sample, the university put an embargo on access to such student records. It was the time of the Vietnam War, and young Australians were being conscripted by ballot to go to fight. Some university students were trying to dodge the draft. Being the most radical campus in the country at the time, the very powerful student body had persuaded the university authorities not to release any information about students to anyone, without the individual student's written permission. Therefore, we were unable to get the anticipated access to the information required to draw the sample.

Clearly, there were some options. Abandon the study, get the students' permission, or modify the design. We couldn't really exercise the first option because the completion of the study was an integral part of the course. We considered the second, but it was impractical. How do you contact members of a sample without first drawing the sample? The university was not prepared to do this for us, and, in any case, as we had no research funds, this, and the cost incurred by the university in writing to all the students, could not be covered. In addition, this process would have taken some time, and we were operating within the limits of one semester. Time had already been lost in dealing with the problem. We had no alternative but to modify the research design.

Instead of the rather complex two-stage sampling plan, and collecting the data using mailed questionnaires, we used a quota sample with structured interviewing. Because this method of data collecting was more labour-intensive, and time was limited, we decided to restrict the sample to arts students. These changes clearly limited our ability to deal with some of the original research questions and to test the theoretical model (see the section on 'Theoretical Models' in chapter 5). Nevertheless, some useful and publishable results were obtained (see Blaikie 1971).

The core theme of this book has been that all social research needs to be planned thoroughly in order to ensure a successful outcome, and that inevitable setbacks will not be fatal. At the same time, it is recognized that research design is always a compromise between the ideal way of answering research questions and what is practical in the light of financial, time and other constraints. In short, good research designs are creative and professionally acceptable solutions to the problems and limitations that are encountered at the beginning and during the course of the research.

The time and care taken to prepare a detailed and comprehensive research design is bound to be worth the effort. It only remains for me to wish you well in your research activities and to hope that meticulous and creative planning will lead to successful and fruitful outcomes.

Appendix

Examples of Research Topics and Research Questions

Research Topics

Topic 1 'Absenteeism in the Public Sector: A Case Study of Hospital-based Nurses'

Topic 2 'Job Satisfaction among Administrative Staff at the University of Stewart Island'

Topic 3 'Student Plagiarism at the University of Alice Springs'

Topic 4 'Industrialization, Urbanization and Juvenile Delinquency in Malaysia'

Topic 5 'Changing Religious Practices and Orientations to the World of New Religious Movements: The Case of the New Light Sect'

Most topics can be stated at various levels of precision. To illustrate this, let us examine Topic 4. This could have been stated as 'Juvenile Delinquency in Malaysia', but this would be too general. It could be stated precisely in terms of both the key concepts to be investigated, and the location of the study, as 'Juvenile Delinquency and the Breakdown of Family and Religious Values in the Context of Industrialization and Urbanization in Penang, Malaysia'. This version has the advantage of being very informative, and it also illustrates how the scope of a research project can be focused and narrowed. However, it is rather long; too long for the spine of a thesis! Hence, it is useful to use a double-barrelled title. The general and long versions could be combined as 'Juvenile Delinquency in Malaysia: The Breakdown of Family and Religious Values in the Context of Industrialization and Urbanization in Penang, Malaysia'. Alternatively, the title above is a reasonable compromise.

The first four topics deal with social problems, and the last one with a sociological problem. The topic on 'absenteeism' no doubt stems from someone's concern about hospital management and patient care. Similarly, the topic on 'job satisfaction' would have been prompted by a perceived lack of efficiency in administration, or by the overt behaviour of the staff, such as complaints to supervisors or disruptive action. The topic on 'student plagiarism' could have emerged from anecdotal evidence reported by lecturers about the incidence of this practice in students' essays and papers, and a concern that this is a serious academic offence. The fourth topic, 'juvenile delinquency', may have arisen from evidence of rising rates of juvenile crime that seem to accompany the industrialization and urbanization associated with economic development. The specific problem is how to prevent young people becoming involved in such activities. The final topic is probably based on curiosity about new religious movements in general, and about the beliefs and practices of a particular religious sect. Just why a researcher has this interest is another matter.

Research Questions

Topic 1: Absenteeism

Absenteeism here refers to absences from work on other than approved leave.

1 What is the rate of absenteeism among nurses?
2 What kinds of nurses are most frequently absent from work unofficially?
3 What effects does absenteeism have on patient care and hospital management?
4 Why does absenteeism occur?
5 How can absenteeism be reduced?

The first two questions are seeking *descriptions* of the frequency and the types of nurses involved in absenteeism. Question 4 seeks an *explanation* for these, and Question 5 an *intervention* strategy. Question 3 is about the consequences of this behaviour for the organization; it could be regarded as being concerned with *impact assessment*, and it expresses this by asking a 'what' question. This example clearly illustrates a sequence of 'what', 'why' and 'how' questions.

Topic 2: Job Satisfaction

This topic has a rather more complex set of research questions.

1 What is the level and range of job satisfaction among the administrative staff?
2 To what extent can the level and range of job satisfaction be regarded as satisfactory?
3 Under what circumstances do staff experience job satisfaction and dissatisfaction?
4 Why do some staff experience job satisfaction and others dissatisfaction in these circumstances?
5 What consequences does level of job satisfaction have for work performance?
6 How can the level of job satisfaction be improved?

Again, the first three questions require *descriptions*, Question 4 an *explanation*, Question 5 refers to the *impact* of job satisfaction on relevant behaviour, and Question 6 seeks strategies for *change*. It is worth noting that Question 3, a 'what' question, verges on a 'why' question. This illustrates the point that answers to some 'why' questions can be achieved by asking a number of 'what' questions.

Topic 3: Student Plagiarism

This project has a similar sequence of questions.

1 What has been the extent of detected student plagiarism over the past five years?
2 In what types of plagiarism have students engaged?
3 What types of students have been caught plagiarizing?
4 What attitudes do lecturers and university administrators have towards plagiarism?
5 What consequences does plagiarism have for students' intellectual development?
6 Why do students plagiarize?
7 How can student plagiarism be eliminated?

Again, most of the research questions are 'what' questions (Questions 1 to 4), including one (Question 5) which is about *impact assessment*. This would be a very large, complex and difficult project as it would require a number of separate studies to complete it: secondary sources (Question 1–3); attitude surveys of both lecturers and administrators (Question 4); a longitudinal comparative study of plagiarizers and non-plagiarizers (Question 5); an in-depth study of the plagiarizers (Question 6); and a policy development study (Question 7). Question 5 would be the most challenging in this set of research questions.

Topic 4: Juvenile Delinquency

1 What is the incidence of the main types of juvenile delinquency in Malaysia?
2 Why do young people engage in these types of criminal activities?
3 To what extent has the incidence changed in the past ten years?
4 (If the incidence has increased): Why has there been an increase?
5 What is the role of industrialization and urbanization in this increase?
6 How can the incidence of juvenile delinquency be reduced?

This is a more complex set of questions. Questions 1 and 2 are concerned with the *description* and *explanation* of the present situation, while Questions 3 and 4 are concerned with the *description* and *explanation* of change. Question 4 has a subsidiary question which is proposing a possible answer, a broad hypothesis, that 'the increase in juvenile delinquency is a result of industrialization and urbanization'. However, this doesn't explain very much. What is needed is an understanding of how these social and economic changes affect family, community and religious life. This would require the development of a theory from which hypotheses could be deduced for testing. Finally, the study seeks solutions to what is regarded as a social problem. It may be difficult to answer such a 'how' question within this study. Further policy-oriented research to develop intervention programmes, and then evaluation studies of these programmes, would be required.

Topic 5: New Religious Movements

This study provides an example of how a research project might address only one research question.

> What internal and external changes are related to changes in the religious practices and orientation to the world adopted by new religious movements?

The question is also an example of how the descriptive answer to a 'what' question constitutes a possible answer to a 'why' question. For example, changes in membership or leadership, and social and economic changes in the wider society that result in the emergence of different individual needs, might be related to changes in beliefs and practices. Such a description could be an answer to the question, 'Why do new religious movements change their orientations to the world?' Both the internal and external changes may be regarded as a set of necessary and sufficient conditions, or as causal mechanisms operating in a particular context. (See Blaikie and Kelsen (1979) and Kelsen (1981) for an example of research on this topic.)

References

Aberle, D. 1966. *The Peyote Religion among the Navaho*. Chicago, Ill.: Aldine Press.

Abraham, J. H. 1973. *The Origins and Growth of Sociology*. Harmondsworth: Penguin.

Achen, C. H. 1982. *Interpreting and Using Regression*. Beverly Hills, CA: Sage.

Achinstein, P. 1968. *Concepts of Science*. Baltimore, MD: Johns Hopkins Press.

Ackoff, R. 1953. *The Design of Social Research*. Chicago, Ill.: University of Chicago Press.

Acury, T. A. and E. H. Christianson 1990. 'Environmental worldview in response to environmental problems: Kentucky 1984 and 1988 compared.' *Environment and Behavior* 22: 387–407.

Adelman, C., D. Jenkins and S. Kemmis 1977. 'Rethinking case study: notes from the second Cambridge conference.' *Cambridge Journal of Education* 6: 139–50.

Ajzen, I. and M. Fishbein 1980. *Understanding Attitudes and Predicting Social Behavior*. Englewood Cliffs, NJ: Prentice-Hall.

Albrecht, D., G. Bultena, E. Hoiberg and P. Novak 1982. 'The new environmental scale.' *Journal of Environmental Education* 13: 39–43.

Alexander, J. C. 1982. *Theoretical Logic in Sociology*, vol. 1: *Positivism, Presuppositions, and Current Controversies*. London: Routledge & Kegan Paul.

Anderson, R. E. 1992. 'Computer applications in the social sciences.' In E. F. Borgatta and M. L. Borgatta (eds), *Encyclopedia of Sociology*, vol 1. New York: Macmillan. Pp. 282–8.

Arber, S. 1993. 'The research process.' In N. Gilbert (ed.), *Researching Social Life*. London: Sage. Pp. 32–50.

Aron, R. 1965. *Main Currents in Sociological Thought 1*. London: Weidenfeld & Nicolson.

—— 1968. *Main Currents in Sociological Thought 1*. London: Penguin.

—— 1970. *Main Currents in Sociological Thought 2*. London: Penguin.

Aronson, E. and J. M. Carlsmith 1968. 'Experimentation in social psychology.' In G. Lindzey and E. Aronson (eds), *The Handbook of Social Psychology*, vol. 2: *Research Methods*. Reading, MA: Addison-Wesley. Pp. 1–78.

Asher, H. B. 1976. *Causal Modeling*. Beverly Hills, CA: Sage.

Atkinson, P. 1990. *The Ethnographic Imagination: Textual Constructions of Reality*. London: Routledge.

Axelrod, R. 1984. *The Evolution of Cooperation*. New York: Basic Books.

Babbie, E. R. 1975. *The Practice of Social Research*. Belmont, CA: Wadsworth.

—— 1990. *Survey Research Methods* (2nd edn). Belmont, CA: Wadsworth.

—— 1992. *The Practice of Social Research* (6th edn). Belmont, CA: Wadsworth.

Bacon, F. 1889. *Novum Organon*. Trans. G. W. Kitchin. Oxford: Clarendon Press.

Bailey, K. D. 1994. *Methods of Social Research* (4th edn). New York: Free Press.

Balnaves, M. 1990. Communication and Information: An Analysis of Concepts. Ph.D. thesis, Royal Melbourne Institute of Technology.

Barnes, H. E. 1948. *An Introduction to the History of Sociology.* Chicago, Ill.: University of Chicago Press.

Bassey, M. 1981. 'Pedagogic research: on the relative merits of search for generalization and study of single events.' *Oxford Review of Education* 7(1): 73–93.

Baxter, G. W. 1973. 'Prejudiced liberals? Race and information effects on a two-person game.' *Journal of Conflict Resolution* 12: 131–61.

Becker, H. A. 1997. *Social Impact Assessment: Method and Experience in Europe, North America and the Developing World.* London: UCL Press.

Becker, H. and H. E. Barnes 1938. *Social Thought: From Lore to Science.* London: Constable.

Becker, H. S. 1940. 'Constructive typology in the social sciences.' *American Sociological Review* 5(1): 40–55.

—— 1950. *Through Values to Sociological Interpretation.* Durham, NC: Duke University Press.

Behr, R. L. 1981. 'Nice guys finish last – sometimes.' *Journal of Conflict Resolution* 25: 289–300.

Beilharz, P. (ed.) 1991. *Social Theory: A Guide to Central Thinkers.* St Leonards, NSW: Allen & Unwin.

Bell, J. 1993. *Doing Your Research Project: A Guide for First-time Researchers in Education and Social Science* (2nd edn). Buckingham: Open University Press.

Bendor, J., R. M. Kramer and S. Stout 1991. 'When in doubt...Cooperation in a noisy Prisoners' Dilemma.' *Journal of Conflict Resolution* 35: 691–719.

Benton, T. 1981. 'Realism and social science: some comments on Roy Bhaskar's "The Possibility of Naturalism".' *Radical Philosophy* 27: 13–21.

Berg, B. L. 1995. *Qualitative Research Methods for the Social Sciences* (2nd edn). Boston, MA: Allyn & Bacon.

Bertaux, D. (ed.) 1981. *Biography and Society: The Life History Approach in the Social Sciences.* Beverly Hills, CA: Sage.

Bhaskar, R. 1979. *The Possibility of Naturalism: A Philosophical Critique of the Contemporary Human Sciences.* Brighton: Harvester.

—— 1986. *Scientific Realism and Human Emancipation.* London: Verso.

Biddle, B. J. 1979. *Role Theory: Expectations, Identities, and Behaviors.* New York: Academic Press.

Black, M. 1962. *Models and Metaphors: Studies in Language and Philosophy.* Ithaca, NY: Cornell University Press.

Blaikie, N. W. H. 1968. An Analysis of Religious Affiliation, Activity and Attitudes in St Albans, Christchurch. MA thesis, University of Canterbury, New Zealand.

—— 1969. 'Religion, social status, and community involvement: a study in Christchurch.' *The Australian and New Zealand Journal of Sociology* 5(1): 14–31.

—— 1971. 'Towards a theoretical model for the study of occupational choice.' *Sociology* 5(3): 313–33.

—— 1972. 'What motivates church participation? Review, replication, and theoretical reorientation in New Zealand.' *The Sociological Review* 20(1): 39–58.

—— 1974. 'The dialectics of social research, or where should I begin? In J. S. Williams and W. C. West (eds), *Sociological Research Symposium IV.* Richmond, VA: Virginia Commonwealth University.

—— 1977. 'The meaning and measurement of occupational prestige.' *The Australian and New Zealand Journal of Sociology* 13(2): 102–15.

—— 1978. 'Towards an alternative methodology for the study of occupational prestige: a reply to my reviewers.' *The Australian and New Zealand Journal of Sociology* 14(1): 87–95.

—— 1991. 'A critique of the use of triangulation in social research.' *Quality and Quantity* 25: 115–36.

—— 1992. 'The nature and origins of ecological world views: an Australian study.' *Social Science Quarterly* 73: 144–65.

—— 1993a. *Approaches to Social Enquiry*. Cambridge: Polity Press.

—— 1993b. 'Education and environmentalism: ecological world views and environmentally responsible behaviour.' *Australian Journal of Environmental Education* 9: 1–20.

—— 1994. 'Models and ideal types: the relationship between Harré's realism and Weber's interpretivism.' Paper presented at the XIII World Congress of Sociology, Bielefeld, Germany, July.

—— 1996. 'The use of scientific realism in the social sciences.' Paper presented at the Fourth International Social Science Methodology Conference, University of Essex, UK, July.

Blaikie, N. W. H. and M. Drysdale 1994. 'Changes in ecological world views and environmentally responsible behaviour between 1989 and 1994: an Australian study.' Paper presented at the XIII World Congress of Sociology, Bielefeld, Germany, July.

Blaikie, N. W. H. and G. P. Kelsen 1979. 'Locating self and giving meaning to existence: a typology of paths to spiritual well-being based on new religious movements in Australia.' In D. O. Moberg (ed.), *Spiritual Well-being: Sociological Perspectives*. Washington, DC: University Press of America. Pp. 133–51

Blaikie, N. W. H. and S. J. G. Stacy 1982. 'The dialogical generation of typologies in the study of the care of the aged.' Paper presented at the X World Congress of Sociology, Mexico City, August.

—— —— 1984. 'The generation of grounded concepts: a critical appraisal of the literature and a case study.' Paper presented at the European Symposium on Concept and Theory Formation, Rome.

Blaikie, N. W. H. and R. Ward 1992. 'Ecological world views and environmentally responsible behaviour.' *Sociale Wetenschappen* 25: 40–63.

Blalock, A. B. and H. M. Blalock 1982. *Introduction to Social Research* (2nd edn). Englewood Cliffs, NJ: Prentice-Hall.

Blalock, H. M. 1968a. 'The measurement problem: a gap between the languages of theory and research.' In H. M. Blalock and A. B. Blalock (eds), *Methodology in Social Research*. New York: McGraw-Hill. Pp. 5–27.

—— 1968b. 'Theory building and causal inference.' In H. M. Blalock and A. B. Blalock (eds), *Methodology in Social Research*. New York: McGraw-Hill. Pp. 155–98.

—— 1969. *Theory Construction: From Verbal to Mathematical Formulations*. Englewood Cliffs, NJ: Prentice-Hall.

—— 1979. 'Measurement and conceptualization problems: the major obstacle to integrating theory and research.' *American Sociological Review* 44: 881–94.

—— 1982. *Conceptualization and Measurement in the Social Sciences*. Beverly Hills, CA: Sage.

—— (ed.) 1985. *Causal Models in the Social Sciences* (2nd edn). New York: Aldine.

Blaxter, L., C. Hughes and M. Tight 1996. *How to Research*. Buckingham: Open University Press.

Blocker, T. J. and D. L. Eckberg 1989. 'Environmental issues and women's issues: general concern and local hazards.' *Social Science Quarterly* 70: 586–93.

Blumer, H. 1969. *Symbolic Interactionism: Perspective and Method*. Englewood Cliffs, NJ: Prentice-Hall.

Bogardus, E. S. 1933. 'A social distance scale.' *Sociology and Social Research* 17: 265–71.

—— 1940. *The Development of Social Thought*. New York: David McKay.

Borden, R. J. and A. P. Schettino 1979. 'Determinants of environmentally responsible behavior.' *Journal of Environmental Education* 10: 35–9.

Bourdieu, P. and L. J. D. Wacquant 1992. 'The purpose of reflexive sociology.' In P. Bourdieu and L. J. D. Wacquant (eds), *An Invitation to Reflexive Sociology*. Cambridge: Polity Press. Pp. 61–215.

Braithwaite, R. B. 1953. *Scientific Explanation*. Cambridge: Cambridge University Press.

Brannen, J. (ed.) 1992. *Mixing Methods: Qualitative and Quantitative Research*. Aldershot: Avebury.

Brent, E. and R. E. Anderson 1990. *Computer Applications in the Social Sciences*. New York: McGraw-Hill.

Brewer, J. and A. Hunter 1989. *Multimethod Research: A Synthesis of Styles*. Newbury Park, CA: Sage.

Brodbeck, M. 1968. *Readings in the Philosophy of the Social Sciences*. New York: Macmillan.

Brown, S. R. and S. Melamed 1990. *Experimental Design and Analysis*. Newbury Park, CA: Sage.

Bryant, C. G. A. and D. Jary (eds) 1991. *Giddens' Theory of Structuration: A Critical Appreciation*. London: Routledge.

Bryman, A. 1984. 'The debate about quantitative and qualitative research: a question of method or epistemology.' *British Journal of Sociology* 35(1): 75–92.

—— 1988. *Quality and Quantity in Social Research*. London: Unwin Hyman.

—— 1992. 'Quantitative and qualitative research: further reflections on their integration.' In J. Brannen (ed.), *Mixing Methods: Qualitative and Quantitative Research*. Aldershot: Avebury.

Bryman, A. and R. G. Burgess (eds) 1994. *Analyzing Qualitative Data*. London: Routledge.

Bulmer, M. 1982. *The Uses of Social Research*. London: Allen & Unwin.

—— 1986. *Social Science and Social Policy*. London: Allen & Unwin.

Burdge, R. J. and F. Vanclay 1995. 'Social impact assessment.' In F. Vanclay and D. A. Bronstein (eds), *Environmental and Social Impact Assessment*. New York: Wiley. Pp. 31–65.

Burgess, E. W. 1927. 'Statistics and case studies as methods of sociological research.' *Sociology and Social Research* 12: 103–20.

Burgess, R. G. (ed.) 1982a. *Field Research: A Sourcebook and Field Manual*. London: Allen & Unwin.

—— 1982b. 'Elements of sampling in field research.' In R. G. Burgess (ed.), *Field Research: A Sourcebook and Field Manual*. London: Allen & Unwin. Pp. 75–8.

—— 1984. *In the Field*. London: Allen & Unwin.

Burgess, R. L., R. N. Clark and J. L. Hender 1971. 'An experimental analysis of anti-litter procedures.' *Journal of Applied Behavior Analysis* 4: 71–5.

Buttel, F. H. 1979. 'Age and environmental concern: a multivariate analysis.' *Youth and Society* 10: 237–56.

Campbell, D. T. and D. W. Fiske 1959. 'Convergent and discriminant validation by the multitrait-multimethod matrix.' *Psychological Bulletin* 56: 81–105.

Campbell, D. T. and J. C. Stanley 1963a. *Experimental and Quasi-Experimental Evaluations in Social Research*. Chicago, Ill.: Rand McNally.

—— —— 1963b. 'Experimental and quasi-experimental designs for research in teaching.' In N. L. Gage (ed.), *Handbook of Research on Teaching*. Chicago, Ill.: Rand McNally. Pp. 171–246.

Campbell, J. P., R. L. Daft and C. L. Hulin 1982. *What to Study: Generating and Developing Research Questions*. Beverly Hills, CA: Sage.

Carment, D. W. and J. E. Alcock 1984. 'Indian and Canadian behaviors in two-person power games.' *Journal of Conflict Resolution* 28: 507–21.

Casey, L. and M. Lloyd 1977. 'Cost effectiveness of litter removal procedures in an amusement park.' *Environment and Behavior* 9: 535–46.

Cass, B. and H. Resler 1978. 'Some thoughts on reading Norman Blaikie's – "The meaning and measurement of occupational prestige".' *The Australian and New Zealand Journal of Sociology* 14(1): 78–81.

Castles, I. 1993. *Environmental Issues: People's Views and Practices*. Canberra: Australian Bureau of Statistics.

Catton, W. R. and R. E. Dunlap 1978. 'Paradigms, theories, and the primacy of the HEP–NEP distinction.' *American Sociologist* 13: 256–9.

—— 1980. 'A new ecological paradigm for post-exuberant sociology.' *American Behavioral Scientist* 24: 15–47.

Chadwick, B. A., H. M. Bahr and S. L. Albrecht 1984. *Social Science Research Methods*. Englewood Cliffs, NJ: Prentice-Hall.

Chafetz, J. S. 1978. *A Primer on the Construction and Testing of Theories in Sociology*. Itasca, Ill.: Peacock.

Chaiken, S. and C. Stangor 1987. 'Attitudes and attitude change.' *Annual Review of Psychology*, 575–630.

Chalmers, A. F. 1982. *What Is This Thing Called Science?* St Lucia, QLD: University of Queensland Press.

Christensen, L. B. 1988. *Experimental Methodology* (4th edn). Boston, MA: Allyn & Bacon.

Churchland, P. and C. Hooker (eds) 1985. *Images of Science*. Chicago, Ill.: Chicago University Press.

Cicourel, A. V. 1973. *Cognitive Sociology*. Harmondsworth: Penguin.

Clark, D. 1951. *Plane and Geodetic Surveying for Engineers*, vol. 2 (4th edn, revised and enlarged by J. Glendenning). London: Constable.

Coffey, A. and P. Atkinson 1996. *Making Sense of Qualitative Data: Complementary Strategies*. London: Sage.

Cohen, I. J. 1989. *Structuration Theory: Anthony Giddens and the Constitution of Social Life*. London: Macmillan.

Collins, L. (ed.) 1976. *The Use of Models in the Social Sciences*. London: Tavistock.

Cone, J. and S. Hayes 1984. *Environmental Problems/Behavioral Solutions*. Cambridge: Cambridge University Press.

Cook, S. W. and J. L. Berrenberg 1981. 'Approaches to encouraging conservation behavior: a review and conceptual framework.' *Journal of Social Issues* 37: 73–107.

Cook, T. D. 1998. 'The generalization of causal connections.' Paper presented at the XIV World Congress of Sociology, Montreal, August.

Cook, T. D. and D. T. Campbell 1979. *Quasi-Experimentation: Design and Analysis Issues in Field Settings*. Chicago, Ill.: Rand McNally.

Cook, T. D. and C. S. Reichardt 1979. *Qualitative and Quantitative Methods in Evaluation Research*. Beverly Hills, CA: Sage.

Coombs, C. H. 1964. *A Theory of Data*. New York: Wiley.

Coser, L. A. 1971. *Masters of Sociological Thought: Ideas in Historical and Social Context*. New York: Harcourt Brace Jovanovich.

—— 1975. 'Presidential address: two methods in search of a substance.' *American Sociological Review* 40(6): 691–701.

Cosley, D. J. and D. A. Lury 1987. *Data Collection in Developing Countries* (2nd edn). Oxford: Clarendon Press.

Craib, I. 1992. *Modern Social Theory* (2nd edn). New York: Harvester Wheatsheaf.

—— 1997. *Classical Social Theory: An Introduction to the Thought of Marx, Weber, Durkheim and Simmel*. Oxford: Oxford University Press.

Creswell, J. W. 1994. *Research Design: Qualitative and Quantitative Approaches*. Thousand Oaks, CA: Sage.

—— 1998. *Qualitative Inquiry and Research Design: Choosing Among Five Traditions*. Thousand Oaks, CA: Sage.

Cronbach, L. 1963. 'Course improvement through evaluation.' *Teachers College Record* 64: 672–83.

—— 1982. *Designing Evaluations of Educational and Social Programs*. San Francisco, CA: Jossey-Bass.

—— 1990. *Essentials of Psychological Testing* (5th edn). New York: Harper & Row.

Cuff, E. C. and G. C. F. Payne (eds) 1979. *Perspectives in Sociology*. London: Allen & Unwin.

Cuff, E. C., W. W. Sharrock and D. W. Francis 1998. *Perspectives in Sociology* (4th edn). London: Routledge.

Daniel, A. 1978. 'A researcher's reflections on the Blaikie contribution.' *The Australian and New Zealand Journal of Sociology* 14(1): 81–7.

Davis, A. 1995. 'The experimental method in psychology.' In G. M. Breakwell, S. Hammond and C. Fife-Schaw (eds), *Research Methods in Psychology*. London: Sage. Pp. 50–68.

de Vaus, D. A. 1995. *Surveys in Social Research* (4th edn). Sydney: Allen & Unwin.

De Young, R. 1986. 'Some psychological aspects of recycling: the structure of conservation satisfactions.' *Environment and Behavior* 18: 435–49.

—— 1988/9. 'Exploring the difference between recyclers and non-recyclers: the role of information.' *Journal of Environmental Systems* 18: 341–51.

Denzin, N. K. 1970. *The Research Act in Sociology*. London: Butterworth.

—— 1971. 'The logic of naturalistic inquiry.' *Social Forces* 50: 166–82.

—— 1978. *The Research Act in Sociology* (2nd edn). New York: McGraw-Hill.

—— 1983. 'Interpretive interactionism.' In G. Morgan (ed.), *Beyond Method: Strategies for Social Research*. Beverly Hills, CA: Sage. Pp. 129–46.

Denzin, N. K. and Y. S. Lincoln 1994. 'Introduction: entering the field of qualitative research.' In N. K. Denzin and Y. S. Lincoln (eds), *Handbook of Qualitative Research*. Thousand Oaks, CA: Sage. Pp. 1–17.

Derksen, L. and J. Gartrell 1993. 'The social context of recycling.' *American Sociological Review* 58: 434–42.

Deutscher, I. 1973. *What We Say/What We Do: Sentiments and Acts*. Glenview, Ill.: Scott Forsman.

Dey, I. 1993. *Qualitative Data Analysis: A User Friendly Guide for Social Scientists*. London: Routledge.

Diekmann, A. 1985. 'Volunteers' dilemma.' *Journal of Conflict Resolution* 29: 605–10.

Diesing, P. 1972. *Patterns of Discovery in the Social Sciences*. London: Routledge & Kegan Paul.

Douglas, J. D. 1971. *Understanding Everyday Life*. London: Routledge & Kegan Paul.

—— 1976. *Investigative Social Research*. Beverly Hills, CA: Sage.

Douglas, L., A. Roberts and R. Thompson 1988. *Oral History Handbook*. Sydney: Allen & Unwin.

Drysdale, M. 1985. Beliefs and Behaviours of the Community with Regard to Social Justice: An Application of Dialogical Method. MA thesis, Royal Melbourne Institute of Technology.

Dubin, R. 1969. *Theory Building: A Practical Guide to the Construction and Testing of Theoretical Models*. New York: Free Press.

—— 1978. *Theory Building: A Practical Guide to the Construction and Testing of Theoretical Models* (2nd edn). New York: Free Press.

Dunlap, R. E. and W. R. Catton 1979. 'Environmental sociology.' *Annual Review of Sociology* 5: 243–73.

Dunlap, R. E., G. H. Gallup and A. M. Gallup 1992. 'Health of the planet survey.' Paper presented at the International Conference on Current Developments in Environmental Sociology, Woudschoten, The Netherlands, June.

Dunlap, R. E., J. K. Grienecks and M. Rokeach 1983. 'Human values and pro-environmental behavior.' In W. D. Conn (ed.), *Energy and Material Resources: Attitudes, Values and Public Policy*. Boulder, CO: Westview Press.

Dunlap, R. E. and K. D. van Liere 1978. 'The "New Environmental Paradigm": a proposed measuring instrument and preliminary results.' *Journal of Environmental Education* 9: 10–19.

—— —— 1984. 'Commitment to the dominant social paradigm and concern for environmental quality.' *Social Science Quarterly* 65: 1013–28.

Durkheim, E. 1951. *Suicide*. New York: Free Press.

—— 1962. *The Rules of Sociological Method*. New York: Free Press.

Eckett, J. 1988. 'Ethnographic research on ageing.' In S. Reinharz and G. Rowles (eds), *Qualitative Gerontology*. New York: Springer.

Eckstein, H. 1975. 'Case study and theory in political science.' In F. E. Greenstein and N. W. Polsby (eds), *Handbook of Political Science*, vol. 7: *Strategies of Inquiry*. Reading, MA: Addison-Wesley. Pp. 79–137.

Edwards, A. L. 1957. *Techniques of Attitude Scale Construction*. New York: Appleton-Century-Crofts.

Ehrlich, H. J. 1969. 'Attitudes, behavior, and the intervening variables.' *American Sociologist* 4: 29–34.

Ellis, L. 1994. *Research Methods in the Social Sciences*. Madison, Wis.: Brown & Benchmark.

Environment Protection Authority of New South Wales 1994. *Benchmark Study on Environmental Knowledge, Attitudes, Skills and Behaviour in New South Wales*. Chatswood, NSW: Environment Protection Authority.

Eysenck, H. J. 1954. *The Psychology of Politics*. London: Routledge & Kegan Paul.

Fay, B. 1975. *Social Theory and Political Practice*. London: Allen & Unwin.

—— 1987. *Critical Social Science: Liberation and its Limits*. Ithaca, NY: Cornell University Press.

Fazio, R. H. 1986. 'How do attitudes guide behavior?' In R. M. Sorrentino and E. T. Higgins (eds), *Handbook of Motivation and Cognition*. New York: Guilford Press. Pp 204–43.

Featherman, D. L. 1976. 'Coser's ... "In search of substance".' *The American Sociologist* 11: 21–7.

Fetterman, D. M. 1989. *Ethnography: Step by Step*. Newbury Park, CA: Sage.

Fielding, N. G. and J. L. Fielding 1986. *Linking Data*. London: Sage.

Fielding, N. G. and R. M. Lee. (eds) 1991. *Using Computers in Qualitative Research*. London: Sage.

Fink, A. 1998. *Conducting Research Literature Reviews: From Paper to the Internet*. Thousand Oaks, CA: Sage.

Finsterbusch, K. 1983. *Social Impact Assessment Methods*. Beverly Hills, CA: Sage.

—— 1985. 'State of the art in social impact assessment.' *Environment and Behavior* 17(2): 193–221.

Firestone, W. A. 1987. 'Meaning in method: the rhetoric and quantitative and qualitative research.' *Educational Researcher* 16(7): 16–21.

—— 1993. 'Alternative arguments for generalizing from data as applied to qualitative research.' *Educational Researcher* 22(4): 16–23.

Flick, U. 1992. 'Triangulation revisited: strategy of validation or alternative.' *Journal for the Theory of Social Behaviour* 22: 175–98.

—— 1998. *An Introduction to Qualitative Research*. London: Sage.

Foddy, W. H. 1988. *Elementary Applied Statistics for Social Sciences*. Sydney: Harper & Row.

—— 1993. *Constructing Questions for Interviews and Questionnaires: Theory and Practice in Social Research*. Cambridge: Cambridge University Press.

Fontana, A. 1994. 'Ethnographic trends in the postmodern era.' In D. R. Dickens and A. Fontana (eds), *Postmodernism and Social Enquiry*. London: UCL Press. Pp. 203–23.

Fowler, F. J. 1993. *Survey Research Methods* (2nd edn). Beverly Hills, CA: Sage.

Fraenkel, J. R. and N. E. Wallen 1993. *How to Design and Evaluate Research in Education*. New York: McGraw-Hill.

Freeman, H. E. and P. H. Rossi 1984. 'Furthering the applied side of sociology.' *American Sociological Review* 49: 571–80.

Freese, L. 1980. 'Formal theorizing.' *Annual Review of Sociology* 6: 187–212.

Freire, P. 1970. *Pedagogy of the Oppressed*. New York: Seabury Press.

Friedrichs, R. W. 1970. *A Sociology of Sociology*. New York: Free Press.

Gadamer, H.-G. 1989. *Truth and Method* (2nd edn). New York: Crossroad.

Gans, H. J. 1967. *The Levittowners: Ways of Life and Politics in a New Suburban Community*. London: Allen Lane.

Garson, D. D. 1990. 'Expert systems: an overview for social scientists.' *Social Science Computer Review* 8: 387–410.

Geertz, C. 1973. 'Thick description: toward an interpretive theory of culture.' In C. Geertz (ed.), *The Interpretation of Cultures: Selected Essays*. New York: Basic Books. Pp. 1–32.

—— 1988. *Works and Lives: The Anthropologist as Author*. Stanford, CA: Stanford University Press.

Geller, E. S., R. A. Winett and P. B. Everett 1982. *Preserving the Environment: New Strategies for Behavior Change*. New York: Pergamon Press.

Geller, J. M. and P. Lasley 1985. 'The new environmental paradigm scale: a reexamination.' *Journal of Environmental Education* 17: 9–12.

Giddens, A. 1971. *Capitalism and Modern Social Theory*. Cambridge: Cambridge University Press.

—— 1976. *New Rules of Sociological Method*. London: Hutchinson.

—— 1979. *Central Problems in Social Theory: Action, Structure and Contradiction in Social Analysis*. London: Macmillan.

—— 1984. *The Constitution of Society: Outline of the Theory of Structuration*. Cambridge: Polity Press.

—— 1997. *Sociology* (3rd edn). Cambridge: Polity Press.

Giddens, A. and J. Turner (eds) 1987. *Social Theory Today*. Cambridge: Polity Press.

Gigliotti, L. M. 1992. 'Environmental attitudes: 20 years of change?' *Journal of Environmental Education* 24: 15–26.

Gilbert, G. H. and J. Doran (eds) 1993. *Simulating Societies: The Computer Simulation of Social Processes*. London: UCL Press.

Gilbert, N. 1993. 'Research, theory and method.' In N. Gilbert (ed.), *Researching Social Life*. London: Sage. Pp. 18–31.

—— 1995. 'Using computer simulation to study social phenomena.' *Bulletin de Méthodologie Sociologique* 47 (June): 99–111.

Glaser, B. G. and A. L. Strauss 1967. *The Discovery of Grounded Theory*. Chicago, Ill.: Aldine.

Gluckman, M. 1961. 'Ethnographic data in British social anthropology.' *Sociological Review* 9: 5–17.

Goetz, J. P. and M. D. LeCompte 1984. *Ethnography and Qualitative Design in Educational Research*. Orlando, Fla.: Academic Press.

Goffman, E. 1963. *Stigma*. Englewood Cliffs, NJ: Prentice-Hall.

Goode, E. 1992. *Collective Behavior*. Fort Worth: Harcourt Brace Jovanovich.

Goode, W. J. and P. K. Hatt 1952. *Methods in Social Research*. New York: McGraw-Hill.

Groves, R. M. and R. L. Kahn 1979. *Surveys by Telephone: A National Comparison with Personal Interviews*. New York: Academic Press.

Guba, E. G. 1978. *Toward a Methodology of Naturalistic Inquiry in Educational Evaluation*. Los Angeles, CA: Centre for the Study of Education, UCLA Graduate School of Education.

—— 1990. 'The alternative paradigm dialogue.' In E. G. Guba (ed.), *The Paradigm Dialogue*. Newbury Park, CA: Sage. Pp. 17–27.

Guba, E. G. and Y. S. Lincoln 1981. *Effective Evaluation: Improving the Usefulness of Evaluation Results through Responsive and Naturalistic Approaches*. San Francisco. CA: Jossey-Bass.

—— —— 1982. 'Epistemological and methodological bases of naturalistic inquiry.' *Educational Communication and Technology Journal* 30: 233–52.

—— —— 1988. 'Do inquiry paradigms imply inquiry methodologies?' In D. M. Fetterman (ed.), *Qualitative Approaches to Evaluation in Education*. New York: Praeger. Pp. 89–115.

—— —— 1989. *Fourth Generation Evaluation*. Newbury Park, CA: Sage.

—— —— 1994. 'Competing paradigms in qualitative research.' In N. K. Denzin and Y. S. Lincoln (eds), *Handbook of Qualitative Research*. Thousand Oaks, CA: Sage. Pp. 105–17.

Gudgion, T. J. and M. P. Thomas 1991. 'Changing environmentally relevant behaviour.' *International Journal of Environmental Education and Information* 10: 101–12.

Gullahorn, J. T. and J. E. Gullahorn 1963. 'A computer model of elementary social behavior.' *Behavioral Science* 8(4): 354–92.

Gummesson, E. 1991. *Qualitative Methods in Management Research*. Newbury Park, CA: Sage.

Habermas, J. 1970. 'Knowledge and interest.' In D. Emmet and A. MacIntyre (eds), *Sociological Theory and Philosophical Analysis*. London: Macmillan. Pp. 36–54.

—— 1971. *Towards a Rational Society*. London: Heinemann.

—— 1972. *Knowledge and Human Interests*. London: Heinemann.

—— 1987. *The Theory of Communicative Action*, vol. 2: *Lifeworld and System: The Critique of Functionalist Reason*. Cambridge: Polity Press.

Hage, J. 1972. *Techniques and Problems of Theory Construction in Sociology*. New York: Wiley.

Hakim, C. 1987. *Research Design: Strategies and Choices in the Design of Social Research*. London: Allen & Unwin.

Halfpenny, P. 1979. 'The analysis of qualitative data.' *Sociological Review* 27(4): 799–825.

—— 1996. 'The relation between social theory and the practice of quantitative and qualitative social research.' Paper presented at the Fourth International Social Science Methodology Conference, University of Essex, UK, July.

Hallebone, E. 1989. 'Environmental attitudes and gender.' Paper presented at the conference of the Australian and New Zealand Sociological Association, Melbourne.

Hammersley, M. 1985. 'From ethnography to theory: a programme and paradigm in the sociology of education.' *Sociology* 19(2): 244–59.

—— 1989. *The Dilemma of Qualitative Method: Herbert Blumer and the Chicago Tradition*. London: Routledge.

—— 1990. *Reading Ethnographic Research: A Critical Guide*. London: Longman

—— 1992. *What's Wrong with Ethnography?* London: Routledge.

—— 1996. 'The relationship between qualitative and quantitative research: paradigm loyalty versus methodological eclecticism.' In J. E. T. Richardson (ed.), *Handbook of Qualitative Research Methods for Psychology and the Social Sciences*. Leicester: British Psychological Society. Pp. 159–72.

Hammersley, M. and P. Atkinson 1995. *Ethnography: Principles in Practice* (2nd edn). London: Routledge.

Hanneman, R. A. 1988. *Computer-Assisted Theory Building: Modeling Dynamic Social Systems*. Newbury Park, CA: Sage.

Hanson, N. R. 1958. *Patterns of Discovery*. Cambridge: Cambridge University Press.

Haralambos, M. and M. Holborn 1980. *Sociology: Themes and Perspectives*. London: Unwin Hyman.

Harré, R. 1961. *Theories and Things*. London: Sheed & Ward.

—— 1970. *The Principles of Scientific Thinking*. London: Macmillan.

—— 1972. *The Philosophy of Science: An Introductory Survey*. London: Oxford University Press.

—— 1976. 'The constructive role of models.' In L. Collins (ed.), *The Use of Models in the Social Sciences*. London: Tavistock. Pp. 16–43.

—— 1977. 'The ethogenic approach: theory and practice.' *Advances in Experimental Social Psychology* 10: 283–314.

Harré, R. and P. F. Secord 1972. *The Explanation of Social Behaviour*. Oxford: Blackwell.

Hart, C. 1998. *Doing a Literature Review: Releasing the Social Science Research Imagination*. London: Sage.

Hausbeck, K. W., L. W. Milbrath and S. M. Enright 1990. 'Environmental knowledge, awareness and concern among 11th grade students: New York State.' *Journal of Environmental Education* 24: 27–34.

Heberlein, T. A. 1989. 'Attitudes and environmental management.' *Journal of Social Issues* 45: 37–57.

Hedrick, T. E., L. Bickman and D. J. Rog 1993. *Applied Research Design*. Newbury Park, CA: Sage.

Heise, D. R. 1969. 'Problems in path analysis and causal inference.' In E. F. Borgatta (ed.), *Sociological Methodology*. San Francisco, CA: Jossey-Bass. Pp. 38–73.

Hempel, C. E. 1966. *Philosophy of Natural Science*. Englewood Cliffs, NJ: Prentice-Hall.

Henry, G. T. 1990. *Practical Sampling*. Newbury Park, CA: Sage.

Hesse, M. B. 1963. *Models and Analogies in Science*. London: Sheed & Ward.

—— 1974. *The Structure of Scientific Inference*. London: Macmillan.

Hindess, B. 1977. *Philosophy and Methodology in the Social Sciences*. Hassocks: Harvester.

Hoinville, G. and R. Jowell 1977. *Survey Research Practice*. London: Heinemann.

Homans, G. C. 1964. 'Contemporary theory in sociology.' In R. E. L. Faris (ed.), *Handbook of Modern Sociology*. Chicago, Ill.: Rand McNally. Pp. 951–77.

Honigmann, J. J. 1982. 'Sampling in ethnographic fieldwork.' In R. G. Burgess (ed.), *Field Research: A Sourcebook and Field Manual*. London: Allen & Unwin. Pp. 79–90.

Honnold, J. A. 1981. 'Predictors of public environmental concern in the 1990s.' In D. Mann (ed.), *Environmental Policy Formation*, vol. 1. Lexington, MA: Lexington Books. Pp. 63–75.

—— 1984. 'Age and environmental concern: some specification of effects.' *Journal of Environmental Education* 16: 4–9.

Huberman, A. M. and M. B. Miles 1994. 'Data management and analysis methods.' In N. K. Denzin and Y. S. Lincoln (eds), *Handbook of Qualitative Research*. Thousand Oaks, CA: Sage. Pp. 428–44.

Hughes, J. A. 1990. *The Philosophy of Social Research* (2nd edn). Harlow: Longman.

Humphrey, C. R., R. J. Bord, M. M. Hammond and S. H. Mann 1977. 'Attitudes and conditions for cooperation in a paper recycling program.' *Environment and Behavior* 9: 107–23.

Hutheesing, O. K. 1990. *Emerging Sexual Inequality among the Lisu of Northern Thailand*. Leiden: E. J. Brill.

Inbar, M. and C. S. Stoll 1972. *Simulation and Gaming in Social Science*. New York: Free Press.

Inkeles, A. 1964. *What is Sociology?* Englewood Cliffs, NJ: Prentice-Hall.

Inter-organizational Committee on Guidelines and Principles 1994. *Guidelines and Principles for Social Impact Assessment*. Washington, DC: Department of Commerce.

Jacobs, H. E., J. S. Bailey and J. I. Crews 1984. 'Development and analysis of a community-based resource recovery program.' *Journal of Applied Behavior Analysis* 17(2): 127–45.

Jick, J. D. 1983. 'Mixing qualitative and quantitative methods: triangulation in action.' In J. van Maanen (ed.), *Qualitative Methodology*. Beverly Hills, CA: Sage. Pp. 135–48.

Jocher, K. 1928. 'The case study method in social research.' *Social Forces* 7: 512–15.

Johnson, T., C. Dandecker and C. Ashworth 1984. *The Structure of Social Theory: Dilemmas and Strategies*. London: Macmillan.

Jones, F. L., P. McDonnell and P. Duncan-Jones 1978. 'On bubble-gum and Blaikie.' *The Australian and New Zealand Journal of Sociology* 14(1): 76–8.

Jones, P. 1985. *Theory and Method in Sociology: A Guide for the Beginner*. London: Bell & Hyman.

Jorgensen, D. L. 1989. *Participant Observation: A Methodology for Human Studies*. Newbury Park, CA: Sage.

Kalton, G. 1983. *Introduction to Survey Sampling*. Beverly Hills, CA: Sage.

Kaplan, A. 1964. *The Conduct of Inquiry: Methodology for Behavioral Science*. San Francisco, CA: Chandler.

Keat, R. and J. Urry 1975. *Social Theory as Science*. London: Routledge & Kegan Paul.

Kelsen, G. P. 1981. The Process of Radical Self-Change or Conversion: A Study in World View and the Maintenance of Reality, with Particular Regard to Minority Religious Sects. Ph.D. thesis, Monash University.

Kennedy, J. T. 1985. *An Introduction to the Design and Analysis of Experiments in Behavioral Research*. Lanham, MD: University Press of America.

Keppel, G. and J. R. Saufley 1980. *Introduction to Design and Analysis: A Student's Handbook*. San Francisco, CA: Freeman.

Kerlinger, F. N. and E. J. Pedhazur 1973. *Multiple Regression in Behavioral Research*. New York: Holt, Rinehart & Winston.

Kidder, L. H. and C. M. Judd 1986. *Research Methods in Social Relations* (5th edn). New York: CBS Publishing.

Kirk, J. and M. Miller 1986. *Reliability and Validity in Qualitative Research*. London: Sage.

Kish, L. 1965. *Survey Sampling*. New York: Wiley.

Krausz, E. and S. Miller 1974. *Social Research Design*. London: Longman.

Krueger, R. A. 1988. *Focus Groups: A Practical Guide for Applied Research*. Newbury Park, CA: Sage.

Kuhn, T. S. 1970. *The Structure of Scientific Revolutions* (2nd edn). Chicago, Ill.: Chicago University Press.

Kumar, R. 1996. *Research Methodology: A Step-by-Step Guide for Beginners*. Melbourne: Longman.

Labovitz, S. and R. Hagedorn 1976. *Introduction to Social Research*. New York: McGraw-Hill.

Lahart, D. E. and J. S. Bailey 1984. 'The analysis and reduction of children's littering on a nature trail.' In J. Cone and S. Hayes (eds), *Environmental Problems/Behavioral Solutions*. Cambridge: Cambridge University Press.

Lakatos, I. 1970. 'Falsification and the methodology of scientific research programmes.' In I. Lakatos and A. Musgrave (eds), *Criticism and the Growth of Knowledge*. Cambridge: Cambridge University Press. Pp. 91–195.

Lancy, D. F. 1993. *Qualitative Research in Education: An Introduction to the Major Traditions*. New York: Longman.

Land, K. C. 1971. 'Formal theory.' In H. L. Costner (ed.), *Sociological Methodology 1971*. San Francisco, CA: Jossey-Bass. Pp. 175–220.

Lave, C. A. and J. G. March 1975. *An Introduction to Models in the Social Sciences*. New York: Harper & Row.

Layder, D. 1993. *New Strategies in Social Research*. Cambridge: Polity Press.

—— 1994. *Understanding Social Theory*. London: Sage.

Lazarsfeld, P. F. and N. W. Henry 1966. *Readings in Mathematical Social Science*. Cambridge, MA: MIT Press.

Lazarsfeld, P. F. and M. Rosenberg (eds) 1955. *The Language of Social Research*. Glencoe, Ill.: Free Press.

Lee, R. M. (ed.) 1995. *Information Technology for the Socialist Scientist*. London: UCL Press.

Leik, R. K. and B. F. Meeker 1975. *Mathematical Sociology*. Englewood Cliffs, NJ: Prentice-Hall.

Lenski, G. E. 1961. *The Religious Factor*. Garden City, NY: Doubleday.

Levine, R. A. 1987. 'Program evaluation and policy analysis in Western nations: an overview.' In R. A. Levine et al. (eds), *Evaluation Research and Practice: Comparative and International Perspectives*. Beverly Hills, CA: Sage. Pp. 27–66.

Levit, L. and G. Leventhall 1986. 'Litter reduction: how effective is the New York State Bottle Bill?' *Environment and Behavior* 18: 467–79.

Levy, M. C. 1985. 'Mediation of Prisoners' Dilemma conflicts and the importance of the cooperation threshold: the case of the Manibia.' *Journal of Conflict Resolution* 29: 581–603.

Lewis-Beck, M. S. (ed.) 1994. *Factor Analysis and Related Techniques*. Thousand Oaks, CA: Sage.

Lichbach, M. I. 1990. 'When is arms rivalry a Prisoners' Dilemma? Richardson's models and 2 × 2 games.' *Journal of Conflict Resolution* 34: 29–56.

Likert, R. 1970. 'A technique for the measurement of attitudes.' In G. Summers (ed.), *Attitude Measurement*. Chicago, Ill.: Rand McNally. Pp. 149–58.

Lin, N. 1976. *Foundations of Social Research*. New York: McGraw-Hill.

Lincoln, Y. S. and E. G. Guba 1985. *Naturalistic Inquiry*. Beverly Hills, CA: Sage.

Lindesmith, A. R. 1947. *Opiate Addiction*. Bloomington, Ind.: Principia Press.

—— 1952. 'Comments on W. S. Robinson's "The logical structure of analytic induction".' *American Sociological Review* 17: 492–3.

Lindskold, S., P. S. Walters and H. Koutsourais 1983. 'Cooperation, competitors and response to GRIT.' *Journal of Conflict Resolution* 27: 521–32.

Lofland, J. 1967. 'Notes on naturalism.' *Kansas Journal of Sociology* 3: 45–61.

—— 1971. *Analyzing Social Settings: A Guide to Qualitative Observation and Analysis*. Belmont, CA: Wadsworth.

Lorr, M. 1983. *Cluster Analysis for Social Scientists*. San Francisco, CA: Jossey-Bass.

Lowe, G. D. and T. K. Pinhey 1982. 'Rural–urban differences in support for environmental protection.' *Rural Sociology* 47: 114–28.

Lowe, G. D., T. K. Pinhey and M. D. Grimes 1980. 'Public support for environmental protection: new evidence from national surveys.' *Pacific Sociological Review* 23: 423–45.

Lundberg, G. A. 1929. *Social Research*. New York: Longman, Green.

—— 1942. *Social Research: A Study in Methods of Gathering Data* (2nd edn). New York: Longman, Green.

Luyben, P. D. and J. S. Bailey 1979. 'Newspaper recycling: the effects of rewards and proximity of containers.' *Environment and Behavior* 11: 539–57.

Majchrzak, A. 1984. *Methods for Policy Research*. Beverly Hills, CA: Sage.

Manly, B. F. J. 1992. *The Design and Analysis of Research Studies*. Cambridge: Cambridge University Press.

Mannheim, K. 1952. 'The problem of generations.' In *Essays on the Sociology of Knowledge*. New York: Oxford University Press. Pp. 276–320.

Marinoff, L. 1992. 'Maximizing expected utilities in the Prisoners' Dilemma.' *Journal of Conflict Resolution* 36: 183–216.

Markley, O. W. 1964. 'A simulation of the SIVA model of organizational behavior.' *American Journal of Sociology* 73: 339–47.

Marsh, C. 1982. *The Survey Method: The Contribution of Surveys to Sociological Explanation*. London: Allen & Unwin.

Marshall, C. and G. B. Rossman 1995. *Designing Qualitative Research* (2nd edn). Thousand Oaks, CA: Sage.

Martin, P. Y. and B. A. Turner 1986. 'Grounded theory and organizational research.' *Journal of Applied Behavioral Science* 22: 141–57.

Martindale, D. 1960. *The Nature and Types of Sociological Theory.* Boston, MA: Houghton Mifflin.

—— 1963. 'Limits to the uses of mathematics in the study of sociology.' In J. C. Charlesworth (ed.), *Mathematics and the Social Sciences.* Philadelphia, PA: American Academy of Political and Social Science. Pp. 95–121.

Marx, G. T. and D. McAdam 1994. *Collective Behavior and Social Movements.* Englewood Cliffs, NJ: Prentice-Hall.

Mason, J. 1996. *Qualititative Researching.* London: Sage.

Mathison, S. 1988. 'Why triangulate?' *Educational Researcher* 17(2): 13–17.

Matza, D. 1969. *Becoming Deviant.* Englewood Cliffs, NJ: Prentice-Hall.

Maynard, M. and J. Purvis (eds) 1994. *Researching Women's Lives from a Feminist Perspective.* London: Taylor & Francis.

McClelland, L. and R. J. Canter 1981. 'Psychological research on energy conservation: context, approaches, methods.' In A. Baum and J. E. Singer (eds), *Advances in Environmental Psychology*, vol. 3: *Energy Conservation: Psychological Perspectives.* Hillsdale, NJ: Lawrence Erlbaum.

McCracken, G. 1990. *The Long Interview.* Beverly Hills, CA: Sage.

McDaniel, W. C. and F. Sistrunk 1991. 'Management dilemmas and decisions: impact of framing and anticipated responses.' *Journal of Conflict Resolution* 35: 21–42.

McGuire, W. J. 1968. 'The nature of attitudes and attitude change.' In G. Lindzey and E. Aronson (eds), *The Handbook of Social Psychology*, vol. 3 (2nd edn). Reading MA: Addison-Wesley. Pp. 136–314.

McIver, J. P. and E. G. Carmines 1981. *Unidimensional Scaling.* Beverly Hills, CA: Sage.

McNeill, P. 1990. *Research Methods* (2nd edn). London: Routledge.

McNiff, J. 1988. *Action Research: Principles and Practice.* Basingstoke: Macmillan.

McStay, J. R. and R. E. Dunlap 1983. 'Male–female differences in concern for environmental quality.' *International Journal of Women's Studies* 6: 291–301.

Medawar, P. B. 1969. *Induction and Intuition in Scientific Thought.* London: Methuen.

Menzies, K. 1982. *Sociological Theory in Use.* London: Routledge & Kegan Paul.

Merton, R. K. 1959. 'Notes on problem-finding in sociology.' In R. K. Merton, L. Broom and L. S. Cottrell, *Sociology Today: Problems and Prospects.* New York: Basic Books. Pp. ix–xxxiv.

—— 1968. *Social Theory and Social Structure.* Glencoe, Ill.: Free Press.

Michener, H. A. 1992. 'Game theory and strategic interaction.' In E. F. Borgatta and M. L. Borgatta (eds), *Encyclopedia of Sociology*, vol. 2. New York: Macmillan. Pp. 737–48.

Michener, H. A., M. S. Salzer and G. D. Richardson 1989. 'Extension of value solutions in constant-sum non-sidepayment games.' *Journal of Conflict Resolution* 33: 530–3.

Michener, H. A. and K. Yuen 1983. 'A text of M bargaining sets in side-payment games.' *Journal of Conflict Resolution* 27:109–35.

Michener, H. A., K. Yuen and S. B. Geisheker 1980. 'N-person side-payment games.' *Journal of Conflict Resolution* 24: 495–523.

Mies, M. 1983. 'Towards a methodology for feminist research.' In G. Bowles and R. D. Klein (eds), *Theories of Women's Studies.* London: Routledge & Kegan Paul. Pp. 117–39.

Miles, M. B. and A. M. Huberman 1984. *Qualitative Data Analysis: A Sourcebook of New Methods.* Beverly Hills, CA: Sage.

—— 1994. *Qualitative Data Analysis: An Expanded Sourcebook* (2nd edn). Newbury Park, CA: Sage.

Mill, J. S. 1947 (1879). *A System of Logic.* London: Longman Green & Co.

Miller, D. C. (ed.) 1991. *Handbook of Research Design and Social Measurement* (5th edn). Newbury Park, CA: Sage.

Miller, G. 1992. 'Case studies.' In E. F. Borgatta and M. L. Borgatta (eds), *Encyclopedia of Sociology*, vol. 1. New York: Macmillan. pp. 167–72.

Mills, C. W. 1959. *The Sociological Imagination*. New York: Oxford University Press.

Millward, L. J. 1995. 'Focus groups.' In G. M. Breakwell, S. Hammond and C. Fife-Schaw (eds), *Research Methods in Psychology*. London: Sage. Pp. 274–92.

Minichiello, V., R. Aroni, E. Timewell and L. Alexander 1995. *In-Depth Interviewing: Researching People* (2nd edn). Melbourne: Longman Cheshire.

Mitchell, J. C. 1983. 'Case and situation analysis.' *Sociological Review* 31(2): 187–211.

Mitchell, M. and J. Jolley 1992. *Research Design Explained* (2nd Edn). New York: Harcourt Brace Jovanovich.

Mohai, P. and B. W. Twight 1987. 'Age and environmentalism: an elaboration of the Buttel model using national survey evidence.' *Social Science Quarterly* 68: 798–815.

Morgan, D. L. 1988. *Focus Groups as Qualitative Research*. Newbury Park, CA: Sage.

Morse, J. M. 1994. 'Designing funded qualitative research. In N. K. Denzin and Y. S. Lincoln (eds), *Handbook of Qualitative Research*. Thousand Oaks, CA: Sage. Pp. 220–35.

Moser, C. A. and G. Kalton 1971. *Survey Methods in Social Investigation* (2nd edn). London: Heinemann.

Moustakas, C. 1994. *Phenomenological Research Methods*. Thousand Oaks, CA: Sage.

Murnigham, J. K. and A. E. Roth 1983. 'Expecting continued play in Prisoner's Dilemma games: a test of several models.' *Journal of Conflict Resolution* 27: 279–300.

Nachmias, D. and C. Nachmias 1996. *Research Methods in Social Sciences*. New York: St Martins Press.

Nelissen, N. and P. Scheepers 1992. 'Ecological consciousness and behaviour examined: an empirical study in the Netherlands.' *Sociale Wetenschappen* 35(4): 64–81.

Neuman, W. L. 1997. *Social Research Methods: Qualitative and Quantitative Approaches* (3rd edn). Boston, MA: Allyn & Bacon.

Newsom, T. J. and U. J. Makranczy 1978. 'Reducing electricity consumption of residents living in mass metered dormitory complexes.' *Journal of Environmental Systems* 1: 215–36.

O'Hear, A. 1989. *An Introduction to the Philosophy of Science*. Oxford: Clarendon Press.

Oja, S. N. and L. Smulyan 1989. *Collaborative Action Research: A Developmental Approach*. London: Falmer.

Oliver, P. 1980. 'Selective incentives in an Apex game: an experiment in coalition formation.' *Journal of Conflict Resolution* 24: 113–41.

—— 1984. 'Rewards and punishments as selective incentives: an Apex game.' *Journal of Conflict Resolution* 28: 123–48.

Open University 1979. *Research Design*. Milton Keynes: Open University Press.

Oppenheim, A. N. 1992. *Questionnaire Design, Interviewing and Attitude Measurement*. London: Pinter.

Ortolano, L. and A. Shepherd 1995. 'Environmental impact assessment.' In F. Vanclay and D. A. Bronstein (eds), *Environmental and Social Impact Assessment*. New York: Wiley. Pp. 3–30.

Outhwaite, W. 1975. *Understanding Social Life: The Method Called Verstehen*. London: Allen & Unwin.

—— 1987. *New Philosophies of Social Science: Realism, Hermeneutics and Critical Theory*. London: Macmillan.

Pardini, A. U. and R. D. Katzev 1983/4. 'The effects of strength of commitment on newspaper recycling.' *Journal of Environmental Systems* 13: 245–54.

Parsons, T. and E. A. Shils 1951. 'Introduction' to Part 2, 'Values, motives, and systems of action.' In T. Parsons and A. E. Shils (eds), *Toward a General Theory of Action*. Cambridge, MA: Harvard University Press. Pp. 47–52.

Patton, M. Q. 1988. 'Paradigms and pragmatism.' In D. M. Fetterman (ed.), *Qualitative Approaches to Evaluation in Education*. New York: Praeger. Pp. 116–37.

—— 1990. *Qualitative Evaluation and Research Methods*. (2nd edn). Newbury Park, CA: Sage.

Pawson, R. 1989. *A Measure for Measures: A Manifesto for Empirical Sociology*. London: Routledge.

—— 1995. 'Quality and quantity, agency and structure, mechanism and context, dons and cons.' *Bulletin de Méthodologie Sociologique* 47(June): 5–48.

—— 1996. 'Theorizing the interview.' *British Journal of Sociology* 47(2): 295–314.

Pawson, R. and N. Tilley 1994. 'What works in evaluation research?' *British Journal of Criminology* 36: 291–306.

—— —— 1997. *Realistic Evaluation*. London: Sage.

Peirce, C. S. 1931a. *Collected Papers*, vol. 1, ed. C. Hartshorne and P. Weiss. Cambridge, MA: Harvard University Press.

—— 1931b. *Collected Papers*, vol. 2, ed. C. Hartshorne and P. Weiss. Cambridge, MA: Harvard University Press.

—— 1934a. *Collected Papers*, vol. 5, ed. C. Hartshorne and P. Weiss. Cambridge, MA: Harvard University Press.

—— 1934b. *Collected Papers*, vol. 6, ed. C. Hartshorne and P. Weiss. Cambridge, MA: Harvard University Press.

Pettus, A. 1976. 'Environmental education and environmental attitudes.' *Journal of Environmental Education* 8: 48–51.

Pfaffenberger, B. 1988. *Microcomputer Applications in Qualitative Research*. Beverly Hills, CA: Sage.

Phillips, D. C. 1990. 'Postpositivistic science: myths and realities.' In E. G. Guba (ed.), *The Paradigm Dialogue*. Newbury Park, CA: Sage. Pp. 31–45.

Platt, J. 1988. 'What can case studies do?' *Studies in Qualitative Methodology* 1: 1–23.

Plummer, K. 1983. *Documents of Life*. London: Allen & Unwin.

Popper, K. R. 1959. *The Logic of Scientific Discovery*. London: Hutchinson.

—— 1961. *The Poverty of Historicism*. London: Routledge & Kegan Paul.

—— 1972. *Conjectures and Refutations*. London: Routledge & Kegan Paul.

Preece, R. 1994. *Starting Research: An Introduction to Academic Research and Dissertation Writing*. London: Pinter.

Queen, S. 1928. 'Round table on the case study in sociological research.' *Publications of the American Sociological Society* 22.

Ragin, C. C. 1987. *The Comparative Method: Moving Beyond Qualitative and Quantitative Strategies*. Berkeley, CA: University of California Press.

Ragin, C. C. and H. S. Becker 1989. 'How the microcomputer is changing our analytic habits.' In E. Brent and J. L. McCartney (eds), *New Technology in Sociology*. New Brunswick, NJ: Transaction Press.

—— —— (eds) 1992. *What is a Case? Exploring the Foundations of Social Inquiry*. New York: Cambridge University Press.

Raison, T. (ed.) 1969. *The Founding Fathers of Social Science*. Harmondsworth: Penguin.

Ramsey, C. E. and R. E. Rickson 1976. 'Environmental knowledge and attitudes.' *Journal of Environmental Education* 8: 10–18.

Reid, D. H., P. D. Luyben, R. J. Rawers and J. S. Bailey 1976. 'Newspaper recycling behavior: the effects of prompting and proximity of containers.' *Environment and Behavior* 8: 471–81.

Rex, J. 1971. 'Typology and objectivity: a comment on Weber's four sociological methods.' In A. Sahay (ed.), *Max Weber and Modern Sociology*. London: Routledge & Kegan Paul. Pp. 17–36.

—— 1974. *Sociology and the Demystification of the Modern World*. London: Routledge & Kegan Paul.

Reynolds, P. D. 1971. *A Primer in Theory Construction*. Indianapolis, Ind.: Bobbs-Merrill.

Richards, L. and T. Richards 1987. 'Qualitative data analysis: can computers do it?' *The Australian and New Zealand Journal of Sociology* 23: 23–36.

——— 1991. 'The transformation of qualitative method: computational paradigms and research processes.' In N. Fielding and R. Lee (eds), *Using Computers in Qualitative Research*. London: Sage. Pp. 38–53.

——— 1994. 'From filing cabinet to computer.' In A. Bryman and R. G. Burgess (eds), *Analyzing Qualitative Data*. London: Routledge. Pp. 146–72.

Richards, T. and L. Richards 1994. 'Using computers in qualitative research.' In N. K. Denzin and Y. S. Lincoln (eds), *Handbook of Qualitative Research*. Thousand Oaks, CA: Sage. Pp. 445–62.

Richardson, L. 1994. 'Writing: a method of inquiry.' In N. K. Denzin and Y. S. Lincoln (eds), *Handbook of Qualitative Research*. Thousand Oaks, CA: Sage. Pp. 516–29.

Richmond, J. M. and N. Baumgart 1981. 'A hierarchical analysis of environmental attitudes.' *Journal of Environmental Education* 13: 31–7.

Riggs, P. L. 1992. *Whys and Ways of Science: Introducing Philosophical and Sociological Theories of Science*. Melbourne: University of Melbourne Press.

Ritzer, G. 1980. *Sociology: A Multiple Paradigm Science* (rev. edn). Boston, MA: Allyn & Bacon.

——— 1996a. *Modern Sociological Theory* (4th edn). New York: McGraw-Hill.

——— 1996b. *Classical Sociological Theory* (2nd edn). New York: McGraw-Hill.

Robinson, W. S. 1951. 'The logical structure of analytic induction.' *American Sociological Review* 16: 812–18.

Rosenberg, M. 1968. *The Logic of Survey Analysis*. New York: Basic Books.

Rossi, P. H. and H. E. Freeman 1985. *Evaluation: A Systematic Approach* (3rd edn). Beverly Hills, CA: Sage.

Rossman, G. B. and B. L. Wilson 1985. 'Numbers and words: combining quantitative and qualitative methods in a single large-scale evaluation study.' *Evaluation Research* 9(5): 627–43.

Salleh, A. K. 1984. 'From feminism to ecology.' *Social Alternatives* 4: 8–12.

——— 1988/9. 'Environmental consciousness and action: an Australian study.' *Journal of Environmental Education* 20: 26–31.

Salmon, W. C. 1988a. 'Introduction.' In A. Grünbaum and W. C. Salmon (eds), *The Limitations of Deductivism*. Berkeley, CA: University of California Press. Pp. 1–18.

——— 1988b. 'Rational prediction.' In A. Grünbaum and W. C. Salmon (eds), *The Limitations of Deductivism*. Berkeley, CA: University of California Press. Pp. 47–60.

——— 1988c. 'Deductivism visited and revisited.' In A. Grünbaum and W. C. Salmon (eds), *The Limitations of Deductivism*. Berkeley, CA: University of California Press. Pp. 95–127.

Samdahl, D. M. and R. Robertson 1989. 'Social determinants of environmental concern: specification and test of the model.' *Environment and Behavior* 21: 57–81.

Sarantakos, S. 1998. *Social Research* (2nd edn). London: Macmillan.

Sayer, A. 1984. *Method in Social Science: A Realist Approach*. London: Hutchinson.

——— 1992. *Method in Social Science: A Realist Approach* (2nd edn). London: Routledge.

Scheaffer, R. L., W. Mendenhall and L. Ott 1996. *Elementary Survey Sampling* (5th edn). Belmont, CA: Duxbury Press.

Scheepers, P. and N. Nelissen 1989. 'Environmental consciousness in The Netherlands.' *Netherlands Journal of Housing and Environmental Research* 4(3): 199–216.

Schofield, J. W. 1993. 'Increasing the generalizability of qualitative research.' In M. Hammersley (ed.), *Social Research: Philosophy, Politics and Practice*. London: Sage. Pp. 200–25.

Schroeder, L. D., D. L. Sjoquist and P. E. Stephan 1986. *Understanding Regression Analysis*. Beverly Hills, CA: Sage.

Schütz, A. 1945. 'On multiple realities.' *Philosophy and Phenomenological Research* 5: 533–76.

—— 1963a. 'Concept and theory formation in the social sciences.' In M. A. Natanson (ed.), *Philosophy of the Social Sciences*. New York: Random House. Pp. 231–49.

—— 1963b. 'Common-sense and scientific interpretation of human action.' In M. A. Natanson (ed.), *Philosophy of the Social Sciences*. New York: Random House. Pp. 302–46.

Schwandt, T. R. 1990. 'Paths to inquiry in the social disciplines: scientific, constructivist, and critical theory methodologies.' In E. G. Guba (ed.), *The Paradigm Dialog*. Newbury Park, CA: Sage. Pp. 258–76.

—— 1994. 'Constructivist, interpretivist approaches to human inquiry.' In N. K. Denzin and Y. S. Lincoln (eds), *Handbook of Qualitative Research*. Thousand Oaks, CA: Sage. Pp. 118–37.

Scott, J. 1995. *Sociological Theory: Contemporary Debates*. Aldershot: Edward Elgar.

Sedlak, R G. and J. Stanley 1992. *Social Research: Theory and Methods*. Boston, MA: Allyn & Bacon.

Seidel, J. 1984. 'The ethnograph.' *Qualitative Sociology* 7: 110–25.

Seltiz, C., L. S. Wrightsman and S. W. Cook 1976. *Research Methods in Social Relations* (3rd edn). New York: Holt, Rinehart & Winston.

Shaw, C. 1927. 'Case study method.' *Publications of the American Sociological Society* 21: 149–57.

Sieber, S. D. 1973. 'The integration of fieldwork and survey methods.' *American Sociological Review* 78(6): 1335–59.

Silverman, D. 1985. *Qualitative Methods in Sociology: Describing the Social World*. Aldershot: Gower.

—— 1993. *Interpreting Qualitative Data: Methods for Analysing Talk, Text and Interaction*. London: Sage.

Smaling, A. 1994. 'The pragmatic dimension: paradigmatic and pragmatic aspects of choosing a qualitative or quantitative method.' *Quality and Quantity* 28: 233–49.

Smith, H. M. 1981. *Strategies of Social Research: The Methodological Imagination* (2nd edn). Englewood Cliffs, NJ: Prentice-Hall.

Smith, J. K. 1983. 'Quantitative versus qualitative research: an attempt to clarify the issue.' *Educational Researcher* 12(3): 6–13.

Smith, J. K. and L. Heshusius 1986. 'Closing down the conversation: the end of the quantitative–qualitative debate among educational inquirers.' *Educational Researcher* 15(10): 4–12.

Smith, M. J. 1998. *Social Science in Question*. London: Sage.

Smith, P. 1995. Industry Transition and Sustainable Development: Management Perspectives in the Urban Water Industry. Ph.D. thesis, Royal Melbourne Institute of Technology.

Sorensen, A. B. 1978. 'Mathematical models in sociology.' *Annual Review of Sociology* 4: 345–71.

Spector, P. E. 1981. *Research Designs*. Beverly Hills, CA: Sage.

Spencer, H. 1891. *The Study of Sociology*. New York: Appleton.

Spradley, J. P. 1979. *The Ethnographic Interview*. New York: Holt, Rinehart & Winston.

—— 1980. *Participant Observation*. New York: Holt, Rinehart & Winston.

Stacey, M. 1969. *Methods of Social Research*. Oxford: Pergamon.

Stacy, S. J. G. 1983. Limitations of Ageing: Old People and Caring Professions. Ph.D. thesis, Monash University.

Stake, R. E. 1978. 'The case-study method in social inquiry.' *Educational Researcher* 7: 5–8.

—— 1994. 'Case studies'. In N. K. Denzin and Y. S. Lincoln (eds), *Handbook of Qualitative Research*. Thousand Oaks, CA: Sage. Pp. 236–47.

—— 1995. *The Art of Case Study Research*. Newbury Park, CA: Sage.

Stanley, L. and S. Wise 1993. *Breaking Out Again: Feminist Ontology and Epistemology* (new edn). London: Routledge.

Stewart, D. W. and M. A. Kamis 1984. *Secondary Research Information Sources and Methods*. Beverly Hills, CA: Sage.

Stewart, D. W. and P. N. Shamdasani 1990. *Focus Groups: Theory and Practice*. Newbury Park, CA: Sage.

Stinchcombe, A. 1968. *Construction of Social Theories*. New York: Harcourt Brace World.

Stockman, N. 1983. *Antipositivist Theories of the Sciences*. Dordrecht: Reidel.

Stouffer, S. A., L. Guttman, E. A. Suchman, P. F. Lazarsfeld, S. A. Star and J. A. Clausen 1950. *Measurement and Prediction*. Princeton, NJ: Princeton University Press.

Strauss, A. and J. Corbin 1990. *Basics of Qualitative Research: Grounded Theory Procedures and Techniques*. Newbury Park, CA: Sage.

—— 1999. *Basics of Qualitative Research: Grounded Theory Procedures and Techniques* (2nd edn). Thousand Oaks, CA: Sage.

Stringer, E. T. 1996. *Action Research*. London: Sage.

Stuart, A. 1984. *The Ideas of Sampling*. New York: Oxford University Press.

Sutherland, E. H. and D. R. Cressey 1966. *Principles of Criminology* (7th edn). New York: Lippincott.

Tashakkori, A. and C. Teddlie 1998. *Mixed Methodology: Combining Qualitative and Quantitative Approaches*. Thousand Oaks, CA: Sage.

Taylor, C. 1964. *The Explanation of Behaviour*. London; Routledge & Kegan Paul.

Tesch, R. 1990. *Qualitative Research: Analysis Types and Software Tools*. New York: Falmer.

Thomas, E. A. C. and T. W. Feldman 1988. 'Behavior-dependent contexts for repeated plays of the Prisoners' Dilemma.' *Journal of Conflict Resolution* 32: 699–726.

Thomas, W. I. and F. Znaniecki 1927. *The Polish Peasant in Europe and America*. New York: Alfred A. Knopf.

Thurstone, L. L. and E. J. Chave 1929. *The Measurement of Attitudes*. Chicago, Ill.: University of Chicago Press.

Trieman, D. J. 1976. 'A comment on Professor Lewis Coser's Presidential Address.' *The American Sociologist* 11: 27–33.

Trochim, W. M. K. 1984. *Research Design for Program Evaluation*. Beverly Hills, CA: Sage.

Turner, B. A. 1981. 'Some practical aspects of qualitative data analysis: one way of organising the cognitive processes associated with the generation of grounded theory.' *Quality and Quantity* 15: 225–47.

—— 1994. 'Patterns of crisis behaviour: a qualitative inquiry.' In A. Bryman and R. G. Burgess (eds), *Analyzing Qualitative Data*. London: Routledge. Pp. 195–215.

Turner, J. H. 1987. 'Analytical theorizing.' In A. Giddens and J. H. Turner (eds), *Social Theory Today*. Cambridge: Polity Press; Stanford, CA: Stanford University Press. Pp. 156–94.

—— 1988. *A Theory of Social Interaction*. Cambridge: Polity Press.

—— 1991. *The Structure of Sociological Theory* (5th edn). Belmont, CA: Wadsworth.

Turner, R. H. 1953. 'The quest for universals in sociological research.' *American Sociological Review* 18(6): 604–11.

Turner, R. H. and L. M. Killian 1972. *Collective Behavior* (2nd edn). Englewood Cliffs, NJ: Prentice-Hall.

Tuso, M. W. and E. S. Geller 1976. 'Behavior analysis applied to environmental/ecological problems: a review.' *Journal of Applied Behavior Analysis* 9: 526.

van Fraassen, B.C. 1980. *The Scientific Image*. Oxford: Clarendon Press.

—— 1985. 'Empiricism in the philosophy of science.' In P. Churchland and C.A. Hooker (eds), *Images of Science: Essays on Realism and Empiricism*. Chicago, Ill.: University of Chicago Press. Pp. 245–307.

van de Gronden, E. D. 1994. 'Use and effectiveness of environmental impact assessment in decision making.' Report of a pilot study by BCR Consultants. Rotterdam (25 May).

van Liere, K. D. and R. E. Dunlap 1980. 'Social bases of environmental concern: a review of hypotheses, explanations and empirical evidence.' *Public Opinion Quarterly* 44: 181–97.

Vanclay, F. and D. A. Bronstein (eds) 1995. *Environmental and Social Impact Assessment*. Chichester: John Wiley.

Vicker, A. W. 1969. 'Attitudes vs. action: the relationship of verbal and overt behavior responses to attitudinal objects.' *Journal of Social Issues* 25: 41–78.

Vining, J. and A. Ebreo 1990. 'What makes a recycler? A comparison of recyclers and non-recyclers.' *Environment and Behavior* 22: 55–73.

von Wright, G. H. 1971. *Explanation and Understanding*. London: Routledge & Kegan Paul.

Wallace, R. A. and A. Wolf 1999. *Contemporary Sociological Theory: Expanding the Classical Tradition* (5th edn). Upper Sadle River, NJ: Prentice-Hall.

Wallace, W. L. 1971. *The Logic of Science in Sociology*. Chicago, Ill.: Aldine-Atherton.

——1983. *Principles of Scientific Sociology*. Chicago, Ill.: Aldine.

Ward, H. 1990. 'Three men in a boat, two must row: an analysis of a three-person chicken pregame.' *Journal of Conflict Resolution* 34: 371–400.

Waters, M. 1994. *Modern Sociological Theory*. London: Sage.

Wathern, P. 1988. 'An introductory guide to EIA.' In P. Wathern (ed.), *Environmental Impact Assessment: Theory and Practice*. London: Unwin Hyman. Pp. 3–30.

Webb, E. J., D. T. Campbell, R. D. Schwartz and L. Sechrest 1966. *Unobtrusive Measures: Nonreactive Research in the Social Sciences*. Chicago Ill.: Rand McNally.

Weber, M. 1958. *The Protestant Ethic and the Spirit of Capitalism*. New York: Scribner.

——1964. *The Theory of Social and Economic Organization*, trans. A. M. Henderson and T. Parsons. New York: Free Press.

Weiss, C. H. 1972. *Evaluation Research: Methods for Assessing Program Effectiveness*. Englewood Cliffs, NJ: Prentice-Hall.

——1976. 'Using research in the policy process: potential and constraints.' *Policy Studies Journal* 4: 224–8.

Weiss, C. H. and M. Bucuvalas 1980. *Social Science Research and Decision-Making*. New York: Columbia University Press.

Whyte, W. F. 1943. *Street Corner Society*. Chicago, Ill.: University of Chicago Press.

——(ed.) 1991. *Participatory Action Research*. Newbury Park, CA: Sage.

Willer, D. 1967. *Scientific Method: Theory and Method*. Englewood Cliffs, NJ: Prentice-Hall.

Williams, M. and T. May 1996. *Introduction to the Philosophy of Social Research*. London: UCL Press.

Winch, P. 1958. *The Idea of Social Science*. London: Routledge & Kegan Paul.

Winter, R. 1987. *Action Research and the Nature of Social Inquiry*. Aldershot: Avebury.

——1989. *Learning from Experience: Principles and Practice in Action Research*. London: Falmer.

Witmer, J. F. and E. S. Geller 1976. 'Facilitating paper recycling: effects of prompts, raffles, and contexts.' *Journal of Applied Behavior Analysis* 9: 315–22.

Wolfe, A. B. 1924. 'Functional economics.' In R. G. Tingwell (ed.), *The Trend of Economics*. New York: Alfred A. Knopf.

Yin, R. K. 1989. *Case Study Research: Design and Method* (rev. edn). Newbury Park, CA: Sage.

——1993. *Applications of Case Study Research*. Newbury Park, CA: Sage.

Young, P. 1939. *Scientific Social Surveys and Research*. New York: Prentice-Hall.

Yow, V. R. 1994. *Recording Oral Histories: A Practical Guide for Social Scientists*. Newbury Park, CA: Sage.

Zanna, M. P. and R. H. Fazio. 1982. 'The attitude–behavior relation: moving toward a third generation of research.' In M. P. Zanna, E. T. Higgins and C. P. Herman (eds),

   Consistency in Social Behavior: The Ontario Symposium, vol. 2. Hillsdale, NJ: Erlbaum.
   Pp. 283–301.
Znaniecki, F. 1934. *The Method of Sociology*. New York: Farrar & Rinehart.
Zuber-Skerrit, O. (ed.) 1996. *New Directions in Action Research*. London: Falmer.

Index